PRAXIS II

Service-Learning Resources for University Students, Staff and Faculty

By Joseph Galura, Rachel Meiland, Randy Ross, Mary Jo Callan and Rick Smith (Editors)

Series Editors: Joseph Galura and Jeffrey Howard

University of Michigan
Office of Community Service Learning
2205 Michigan Union
Ann Arbor, Michigan 48109
(313) 763-3548

1993

The OCSL Press
2205 Michigan Union
Ann Arbor, Michigan 48109
(313) 763-3548

First Printing

Printed in the United States of America

ISBN 0-9638136-0-9 (the series)

0-9638136-1-7 (Praxis I)

0-938136-1-5 (Praxis II)

Table of Contents

Acknowledgments

We are grateful for the confidence communicated by the Michigan Campus Compact in granting us the funds to publish these two volumes on service-learning. We wish to express our thanks to the Commission on National and Community Service for providing the funding to the Michigan Campus Compact that enabled us to proceed with this project. And, perhaps most importantly, we acknowledge our indebtedness to the Kellogg Foundation, for the credibility that comes with funding from this Foundation, and under whose auspices we have proceeded with these publications.

We would be remiss not to express our deep gratitude to Mark Chesler, who has never flinched from his commitment to service-learning and to our office. He is our primary stimulus for our reflection on the issues of service-learning pedagogy.

We wish to thank Frank Cianciola, E. Royster Harper, and Maureen Hartford for their continuing confidence in our efforts to make the campus "safe for service learning."

We would also like to thank the Praxis II contributors for their actions and reflections on the field.

This series would not have been possible without the secretarial support of Venus Sage and Tamara Agnew. We particularly appreciated Tammy's long hours of data entry, word processing—and formatting the Bibliography.

Thanks also to Cris Zerkel-Shankleton for her work on the series' graphic design. It looks great, Cris!

Finally, we want to acknowledge the specific work of the Praxis II Editorial Board. Rachel Meiland was this volume's primary editor, Randy Ross and Mary Jo Callan compiled and revised material for Part Three throughout the Winter '93 term, and Rick Smith volunteered more global suggestions and insight. Thanks again.

—Joe Galura & Jeff Howard

PART ONE

The Meaning of Praxis

The Meaning of Praxis

By Joe Galura, Rachel Meiland, Randy Ross, Mary Jo Callan and Rick Smith

(The publication of this series was made possible by a grant from the Michigan Campus Compact. Praxis I: A Faculty Casebook on Community Service Learning was written by 18 University of Michigan faculty in 14 academic disciplines. Praxis II: Service-Learning Resources for University Students, Staff and Faculty features the work of selected UM students and staff.

The Editorial Board met on July 9 and 21 to review the contents of Praxis II. Our hope is that the following transcript of our conversations will serve as the reader's introduction to this volume.)

Joe: In Project Community, we tend to draw heavily from Freire (1970): praxis is action and reflection upon the world in order to change the world. One of the best coordinator papers I have read recently made he following analogies: in praxis, action is to reflection as practice is to theory as service is to learning—and as site is to seminar.

For me, praxis continues to be the course's most interesting challenge, specifically, coordinating student's site work with all the seminar-related opportunities for reflection: relevant readings, discussion questions and activities, journal assignments and meaningful, integrative papers. The combination of service in the community with an intentional, varied and well-coordinated series of opportunities for reflection has the potential to be interesting, enlightening, instructive and in some cases, even life-changing for those who participate...Any other remarks?

Rick: I remember a conversation I had six years ago with someone in high school. He said he didn't really learn much. He only went to school because it was one big social gathering. I think that says a lot about our educational system: the classroom isn't for learning so much as socializing.

In Project Community, on the other hand, students often feel they learn. I think this has a lot to do with praxis. Students have the opportunity to apply what they learn and reflect on the service activities in which they participate. This combination of observing and learning is something that happens in the world instead of in some enclosed space apart from the world.

I tend to get angry when people say, "Oh, you've graduated, now you're a part of the real world." I get angry because I happen to think I've been in the real world for the past 22 years, and haven't ever left it. Through praxis, Project Community helps break down the paradigm of "learning happening only inside classroom walls and what is learned there has no relationship on the outside world."

Randy: One person during the "Reflectors Anonymous" chapter said that many of her classes had become a blur on a transcript and PC was one of those classes that hadn't. Partly because of the experience, and partly because of the opportunity to reflect, partly because it had become part of a life-changing event—an ongoing changing event, too. And that's something that says a lot for PC. I don't think it has to be just someone that's recovering. I think that happens for a lot of people. It is something you can learn from, really appreciate and look upon fondly.

Rachel: I've done a lot of work on the material written by recovering students and I think that the service-learning experience is different for those in recovery.

Randy: I think it's almost more intense.

Rachel: It's like they're more self-reflective.

Randy: There are still a lot of those components for other people, too.

Rachel: No, I agree with that, I just think that it's clear to read through the quality of the writing, the way stuff is written for recovering people. It's a lot easier for them to reflect on themselves, or a lot more. It just happens. I think that it's something that's difficult for people who aren't in recovery because they don't necessarily do that in other parts of their lives. So, it's not a value judgement, it's just that the writing is very, very different.

Joe: I think that we can tie this to the different parts of the PC pedagogy. People that are in recovery need to deal with their connectedness, particularly around that issue of how drug use impacts the rest of their lives.Almost all of those recovering people were in chemical dependency sites, so it's always before them.

Mary Jo: I think you're right though, about Chemical Dependency sections at least. I think that students who are recovering seem to feel more connected to the projects of which they are a part. They definitely seem to get more out of the experience.

Rick: I think that is a good example of how historicity is an important issue for those involved in PC. Most people I've met don't seem to think that they have a history. I'm not surprised, considering the way history is taught as if it's something disconnected from the world we live in today. In PC we're trying to see how each person's history, both personal and communal, affects the way they view the world and find their place in it. This relates to praxis because while reflecting on your actions, you can see the inertia that your history gives you and how it influences those beliefs and actions.

Rachel: Actually I was just thinking about the Migrant Labor Camp material: and maybe it isn't just recovery that causes writing to be self-reflective, maybe it's being closer to the service-learning experience because of one's own experience.

Rick: Like the one woman whose grandparents were migrant camps workers in Adrian. That was very close to her situation.

On Part Two—"Service-Learning at the University Level: Some Guiding Principles"

Joe: First, I want to thank Mark Chesler for expanding my thinking with regard to the scope of this project. When I asked him for a letter of support, he challenged my focus in this part of the series as serving to benefit only my program areas, Criminal Justice and Chemical Dependency. I now believe that this volume is helpful for both campuses with an already established service-learning program and also for those interested in initiating programs "from the ground up". Also, I want to acknowledge the work of Jeff Howard in helping me to gather what I see as the best work of the University of Michigan service-learning community.

Rick: I thought "Promoting Service-Learning on Campus" was very straight forward.

Randy: That piece sounded more like a plea to this office or this University to include a position like that rather than a suggestion to other universities to do something like that. Maybe it's because I know Jeanne and talked with her a lot about that during the course of the year.

Joe: I still think the ideas are helpful. Rachel and I have talked before about how applicable some of this stuff is to other campuses. I think it's important when you think about establishing a service-learning office or a service-learning course that you also think about "How am I going to promote it?"

Rachel: And whether it really works on other campuses is a different issue. I don't think we can really get into that. Because I know if they don't have programs like Growing Tree somewhere else then people are going to be working with Growing Tree and obviously programs like that in the first five years aren't going to have the kinks worked out. So it's an issue of how well it transfers but that's not an issue we can deal with here.

Joe: To quote the recovery chapter again, you know "all we can do is share our experience, strength and hope."

Rachel: I think her point that it's hard work is important, too. I think people often get involved in work that is hard, such as being involved in PC, or work or any number of things that people do, and forget to process how hard it is sometimes and it gets really frustrating.

Randy: I think sometimes people think that doing community service work to get credit is easy and I think promotion could clear that up. That it's not just as easy as people think it is but it is something that could be rewarding, actually better than most classes.

Rick: I used to respond to questions like, "We have a coursepack?" or "You mean, we have to write a paper?" by saying, "Guess what, this is not a fluff class."

As far as Jeanne Gray's article is concerned, I think she's right about promotion: word of mouth works best. She mentions students being overwhelmed with classes and extra-curricular activities, but one of the things service-learning could attempt is to network through courses and student organizations. The SERVE chapter mentions work with Greek and other campus organizations. I know Anita Bohn works with religious campus groups in recruiting for Project SERVE. That's only one example of how groups can be pre-organized and ready for service. In this way, I think networking is more important than marketing.

Randy: She talks a lot about numbers and accountability. That's something we've been able to provide that the University has recognized and is actually now using to gain more credibility for our office.

Joe: There is sort of a general principle here, certainly: if people have heard of you, then you are more credible and it's easier to promote.

Rick: For example, if you've been on ABC News.[1]

Joe: We haven't commented yet on the first three chapters in Part Two —Elias' "Establishing a Service-Learning Course," Howard's "Advocating for Service-Learning" and Scott's Journal Workshop. I almost think of the Elias and Howard chapters as bookends. On the one hand, we have the nuts-and-bolts details of how to get a service-learning course "up and running": on the other, some campus-wide attempts at systemic change.

An interesting sub-theme came up for me when I was reviewing the final chapter in this book, "An Insider's Round Table." Jeff indicates that the series' primary audience is faculty—and I don't challenge that statement. For Jeff, yes, faculty, particularly faculty on other campuses, comprise his primary audience. His chapter makes that focus clear.

As I conceived of the grant, however, I thought of this faculty audience as secondary and external to our work here on campus. My primary goal has always been to equip and empower coordinators in their work with other students in the community, to give these student leaders a tool kit, a bag of tricks that have been proven effective over time. I think that my commitment to this internal and primary audience, the students to whom I will actually give copies of this text to assist them in their service-learning experiences, shines through in the majority of the chapters we've edited together.

Having said that, I also think that, taken together, the five chapters in this section really do encapsulate many of the necessary guiding principles for campuses interested in starting service-learning programs "from the ground up." Still, when I reflect on this primary and internal audience, I foresee immediate benefit in having them read Wylie and Scott. Randy once said that it takes a while before student leaders realize that they're part of "a service-learning machine"—I think that the other three chapters are helpful in illuminating the different aspects of "a service-learning machine" and how they could be organized on campus.

Randy: I had an interesting read of Margaret's chapter about the Trained Volunteer Corps. because I sat in for Margaret for a term while she was on her maternity leave[2] and, yes, that's how it runs. The chapter is about not just starting it but also continuing it. I went through and reviewed some of the site contracts that Margaret mentions. It's not just a one time thing. Those are the keys to getting started.

Joe: Rick and I talked about that article briefly in my office this afternoon.

Rick: It's so much like Project Community that you get credit in Sociology 389.

Joe: For me, the important part of our conversation was that many of the chapters, once you move outside of Part Two, assume the Project Community/Sociology 389 structure. This chapter clearly tells you what the structure is and how it works and that's important to establish a context for the rest of the book.

Randy: I liked the one point where she talks about offering sites with varying degrees to fit the needs of the students. I thought that was very important. I thought that was an interesting piece and I think other campuses should look to that when they decide to start a program like this.

Joe: Let's talk about the other piece that goes with that: Jeff's.

Rick: It certainly underlined that the faculty was his audience. I like the way he assessed what sort of institution he was dealing with. One of the things that's peculiar, well it's not necessarily peculiar about the University of Michigan, is the decentralization that influenced his choices in building a coalition among faculty. You have to do a lot of repetitive work because the University doesn't tend to communicate as well horizontally as it does vertically.

Randy: I thought of three words to describe this piece: This makes sense. It's a quote that Jeff says when he's talking about Praxis and doing the work that we're doing for the grant. But even this piece, it's important as far as getting things started and actually trying to make some type of institutional change. You have to consider these factors when you do that. It does makes sense.

Rick: It's nice to know that there are faculty you have been doing service-learning, and didn't even know that there was an Office of Community Service Learning!

Joe: Joan's article on journal writing...

Rachel: I thought the same thing about this as I thought about one of Jeanne's articles. I understood the importance of teaching students how to read other student's journals and why it's important.

Randy: There are some nuts and bolts things about responding to journals that are important.

Joe: And which things would you point out?

Randy: Where it starts, "An Approach to Reading and Commenting on Journals." It talks about support and challenge and process. Those are things you have to keep in mind when you're reading and responding to journals.

Rick: My seminars didn't tend to focus on journals as much as they could have and this presented a way in which they could have.

Rachel: I think it's really easy to criticize and not so easy to support or to do it in a way. When I read other people's writing or my own writing, I find it's really easy to rip on it. I'm really good at journal writing, and it's hard to remember that it doesn't come naturally to other people. I can't do math, but I can write journals very well. So I was thinking that it's very important to be aware that it doesn't come all that easily to some people.

Randy: It seemed like at the beginning she was talking more to an administrator, and then it switches it's focus audience to coordinators or students who were actually going to be reading and responding. I think it's important to note that change in focus.

Rachel: I wanted to say that Janet Wylie's piece was really interesting. And it seemed deliberate to me, just like the journal writing piece. Having worked with kids, it makes a lot of sense to do it that way. I 've worked with kids in a different setting, but it does make a lot of sense to lay it out there like that for potential coordinators.

Randy: In my first experience as an elementary school tutor, one of the things that I liked about PC from the beginning was that we did a lot of trust games, like the group juggle, but I just couldn't remember what they were. This article brought back a lot of good memories about that seminar and why I continued on in PC.

Rachel: I was also thinking that we do a lot of this stuff in treatment with kids who are supposedly a different population. You wouldn't think that kids would get this stuff but they really do, like the trust falls and that's very interesting I don't know what the relationship is there, but I think there is one.

Rick: I wish I had this article for my two seminars, because my first one really needed something and this would have been just the right remedy. We did things like this in Youth Group in high school. I loved them, but I don't think anyone else did.

Rick: Yeah, people will say they won't like it, but they'll get a lot out of it.

Mary Jo: I think that Wylie's piece is very useful, since initiative activities lend themselves perfectly to a format like PC where a primary goal is to build a safe community for learning. I've seen these activities be effective in helping groups to achieve high levels of trust and cooperation in very short time periods.

Randy: Like you've always said with the activities in the Wizard, the success of the activity depends on how much the presenter believes in it.

On Part Three—Off To See The Wizard

Joe: When I accepted my program director position in 1988, Criminal Justice was run very differently from the current program. Most notable to me was the fact that each site had a different course pack—Court Watching, Juvenile Justice, Jails, Prisons and Women in Prison. This necessitated the program director and teaching assistant to meet individually with each coordinator, however I noticed that many of the topics and key readings on each syllabus were the same. Because of this, one of my first acts as program director was to create a "Core Curriculum" which required all the students and coordinators to be reading about the same issues at the same time. This also allowed Matt Kinney, the Sociology teaching assistant at that time, and I too schedule and require coordinators' attendance at a weekly staff meeting.

I wanted to make staff meetings an event coordinators would not want to miss. During the first year, I created a series of handouts especially for that staff meeting and only distributed them at staffing. These were discussion questions and activities that Matt and I developed. We had two criteria for these handouts. First, the questions and activities needed to be based on the readings: as we prepared the handouts, Matt would often ask, "how can we summarize the Sociology that we want communicated in one simple sentence?" Second, the activities and questions needed to be exercises that coordinators—usually undergraduates and often with little background in Sociology and in facilitating groups—could replicate with some success in their seminars later that week.

Thus, these early staff meetings would consist of Matt or I leading a discussion activity with coordinators and then concluding the meeting with questions such as: do you think this exercise would work in your seminar and what changes would you propose to make the activity more relevant to your site?

Following up these staffings was very important. Often, "process time" was allotted at the beginning of each meeting so that coordinators could report and reflect on how the previous week went at their site and in their seminar. I required weekly journals from coordinators, outlining their agendas for each week and describing the week just past. Additionally, I promised written feedback to any journal within 24 hours so that coordinators could incorporate my comments on their agendas, if they decided to do so.

Finally, recognizing that I was new on the job, that most of my coordinators were undergraduates and relatively inexperienced in performing some of the tasks the job required and that the residents at our sites may at times be difficult to work with, I invited my coordinators to take advantage of my office hours. I let them know that anytime between 8 AM and 5 PM, Monday through Friday, was fine —no appointment needed. Furthermore, I told them that if I did have other things to do, it was my responsibility to tell them.

During the '89/'90 academic year, I added the Chemical Dependency program and finalized the syllabus outline for both CD and CJ. Basically, in addition to a Core Curriculum existing for each content area, key articles on the Project Community pedagogy would also appear at the beginning, middle and end of each term. This presents an opportunity for each coordinator and each seminar to study both content and also to reflect on their own process of teaching and learning.

At the end of this academic year, I had enough discussion activities and coordinator comments to publish the first edition of Off to See the Wizard. At that time, I simply thought that distributing all the activities at once would be an improvement over passing them out each week during the staff meeting. I was quite surprised by the positive affirmation from Mark Chesler and from the coordinators themselves.

Perhaps the most significant addition since Joe's beginning (to work in PC) in 1988 is his book. Off to See the Wizard is partly a guide to each week of our training, and partly feedback from previous coordinators. It's a way for coordinators to see which activities are available and which activities have been successful. We use the book as an educator and as a reference point.

—Jennifer Rabiah and Korey Miller

Korey and Jennifer make an important point about coordinator training that I would like to emphasize. My sense is that in CJ before 1988, coordinator training tended to be about broad and mostly theoretical principles in discussion facilitation because seminars where not reading the same articles at the same time. By specifying a reading list, I was then able to build training on specific techniques into how a particular article could be discussed. For example, the first of Three Rounds with Howard and Kahn requires students to use an "I Statement". This technique not only follows from the text but once introduced into the seminar, can become the way in which group members communicate with one another.

This is not to say that there is not a benefit in having a large group coordinator training at the beginning of the semester, only that the emphasis needs to be on what coordinators can specifically apply to their most pressing needs. I can still recall one coordinator's criticism of the '88 large group meetings:

This theoretical stuff about pedagogy may be fine but each week, I don't face theoretical dilemmas in a theoretical seminar with theoretical students: to me these issues are flesh and blood, not some intellectual theory.

'90/'91 was the first year I used Off to See the Wizard as the CD/CJ coordinator handbook and was also important for another reason. My coordinator staff tends to consist mostly of first-term Soc. 395 students in the Fall and mostly second-term Soc. 395 students in the Winter but never was this more pronounced than during the Winter '91 term. 20 of my 21 coordinators had previously coordinated for me before. This led me to think about coordinator training in a new light.

Since Fall tended to be when mostly new coordinators were coming onto my staff, the focus of the staff meetings needed to mostly address their fears, sometimes spoken, sometimes unspoken, about their ability to actually perform all the difference aspects of the coordinator job. Thus, Off to See the Wizard provides some reassurance —coordinators, often people that they know, have done this work before and encountered similar dilemmas and successes.

However, in the Winter term, the question is no longer "can I do this job?" but rather "how can I improve on the bench marks that I set in the first term?" In the Winter '91 term, I intentionally framed the semester as "Your Project Community Legacy". Using Off to See the Wizard as an example of how a staff could build on what previous coordinators have learned and experienced, I challenged coordinators to think about how future terms could benefit from what they were doing now in their section.

Although I didn't know it then, Off to See the Wizard serves as a testament to our accumulated wisdom in running CD/CJ seminars and my challenge had more to do with how site knowledge could be identified, codified and passed on.

A partial answer came from Julie Mathews, a coordinator who was also an officer in her sorority. Her idea was that as sorority officers kept "successor notebooks" throughout their terms, coordinators, too, could keep notebooks to pass on to their successors. I could incorporate this as part of a monthly coordinator journal assignment and I even published Julie's Successor Notebook in later editions of Off to See the Wizard as an example to current staff.

In a sense, all the chapters in Part Four spring from Julie's idea.

Rick: I had the pleasure of seeing Edition I of Off to See the Wizard and I was amazed that anyone could make sense of it. I guess that shows the evolution of the Wizard, moving from handouts to something that's accessible to people who aren't going to a staffing every week and having Joe gloss the handouts so they make sense.

Joe: You looked through the book and said,"This is a coursepack!"

Rick: Right, it's very coursepacky. It was a relief to flip through Wiz III after a frustrating seminar and read comments from past coordinators who were feeling the same thing. I think that is the value of the evolving Wizard. Not only does one have handouts, but several layers of coordinator experience. By the time Wiz IV is finished, the glossing in the text will have become the text. It's almost like scripture in that way.

Joe: Jenny Kellman did comment once that the Wizard was like her PC Bible.

Mary Jo: I think that Part Four is basically a testimonial to successor notebooks and how they can serve to help others to carry on the PC mission. Stepping into the role of coordinator can be overwhelming, even if you've been a student in the section. I think that this section will make it possible for other universities to create a program.

Randy: I think that somebody from another university, in reading this section in particular, will realize that this is microcosm of CD/CJ. There's a lot more to it, but this captures a lot of the options that you have to run seminar—a lot of the fears, a lot of the dilemmas, a lot of the solutions and positive experiences that we've had over the last five years. This is basically as Joe has always said, "The best of". I don't think that anybody reading this for the first time trying to start a program or even improve a program would want to believe that this is real easy. We've said for a first time coordinator to go ahead and see that everybody's had these fears or similar experiences is very comforting, very helpful.

Randy: I think that a good support staff can do that

Joe: I think that a kind of interesting piece that we can put in here is that each of you has had kind of different experiences with the second and or third edition of Wizard...how it was helpful, how it was not helpful, how you see what we've done this term as benefiting other people. Do people want to talk about that now?

We've tried generally introducing this edition, but I think all of you have used it for at least a semester, or as in Randy's case four or five. Do you want to say anything specific, more personable about that experience?

Rick: I think that seminars that I prepared by reading the corresponding Wiz chapter went a lot better. Not that would ever happen.

Randy: To prepare for staffings, we're supposed to read the particular part of the Wiz before going to staffing. Sometimes I didn't always do that because I was a second term coordinator I had already done it; I already knew what the activities were. But even during my second term coordinating, if I had done the activities already and gone back over and reviewed them, it helped a lot to see some of the things you might have forgotten.

Rick: I think reading the Wiz helps orient you, clarifies your goals and introduces you to issues so that when you go to seminar or staffing you don't have the feeling that you're building the barn from ground up. The framework is already in place there, and you only have to put on the wood paneling.

Mary Jo: In addition to its benefits to seminar, the Wiz made staffings much more meaningful in that, many of the activities helped students focus on important sociological concepts contained in the readings. I have also been able to use some of the activities from the Wiz, the ice breakers for example, in areas outside of PC.

Randy: I remember several times where my coordinator Josee just came in with the Wiz and you could tell that she hadn't really prepared anything and read word for word right out of the Wiz. The activities went well but it gave her a little less credibility. She hadn't prepared anything or at least gone through it beforehand...So as a coordinator I think you want to be as prepared as you can be.

Rick: Another aspect of the Wiz relates to a choice that Joe made as program director of CJ/CD. He chose to have joint coursepacks for all the sections, rather than individual coursepacks for each sections. The two of us discussed the relative advantages of each last week. The joint one has the advantage of a staffing that can center on the same issues, the other one has the advantage of individual attention and focus. The coursepacks would be specialized so that each reading is more or less directly applicable to site. Oftentimes my students wondered why they were reading about juvenile justice, for example, when our site was an adult facility. Although this may be a disadvantage for some, on the other hand, it gives students the opportunity to make connections outside their direct experience. As a coordinator, I felt like I had the best of both worlds. I took advantage of Joe's office hours so much that it was like having my own individual coursepack. Except it wasn't in the obligatory polyethylene package.

Randy: There were two comments about the options available to coordinators. One is Pauline, in the If PC were activity, ("If PC were a food, it would be salad bar because you take what you want and leave the rest.") In "Oz Plus Five," there's a similar statement. There is a lot of information that's available. We have supplements that are more specific. So, in addition to core articles, there are more relevant articles for a specific site.

Rick: I found it helpful when Joe referred to the supplementary coursepack. I wouldn't have read it otherwise. It was just another big huge pile of paper.

Joe: I think that particular decision you talked about Rick represents my own bias in designing the program and how important it is in building a community of learning. My bias is that once you've built that community, you can make the adjustments so that people within it can get what they need. And I've always thought you can go the other way in trying to specify something for ten to twelve individual people without first trying to build that community but it's much more difficult.

Mary Jo: I think that it's useful to have a core group of articles about issues involving the CJ system, and CD issues. Our goals at PC need to include having our students leave here with the ability to apply some general knowledge about sociological issues.

Randy: You can then use your sociological imagination.

Rick: That might be another defect of our educational system. It forces people to specialize too early, too fast. It lulls people into thinking that the only person who can make a cogent analysis on any issue is someone who specializes in that issue. Whereas in everyday life we have to make everyday decisions using our everyday know how. We struggle, but somehow we make it. I think it should be noted that Joe is wearing his Van Gogh tie.

On Part Four—"Service-Learning Projects Affiliated with Sociology 389"

Joe: It would be an overstatement to say that all the chapters in this section are the direct descendants of Julie Mathews' Successor Notebook. Still, there is some connection and each of the Praxis Editors have an interesting perspective on that connection.

I heard this cliche when I had a summer job in direct sales: "you can have twenty years experience or you can have one year's experience repeated 20 times, over and over." The idea behind the chapters in this section is first to emphasize the service that students actually perform on-site but with an eye on how these experiences could be of immediate benefit to the students at the same site in the next term. Hopefully, these experiences can then be generalized to students with similar interests. Over the past few years, English Professor Buzz Alexander and I co-coordinated several students fieldwork between some new and some established prison projects. Near the end of our time together, Buzz remarked, "this meeting saved me at least 20 hours of work."

Mary Jo: You seem to have a theme of twenty there Joe.

Joe: Any introductory remarks on the "County Jail" chapter?

Randy: I can remember while I was at the jail hearing that, from the jail's standpoint they know that they can't change somebody in the short time that they have to deal with them. They hope they can do something to give the inmates an edge to avoid rearrest and reincarceration. The things like GED and AA and NA...those are the edges that they had in mind and that was something that we were able to let the inmates know about and I don't know how successful we were, but I know a lot of people were abler to take part in the activities because of our presence there. Hopefully, that gave them the edge that we were hoping for.

Rick: That's the underlying question. Do we really accomplish social change? I think this paper makes it clear that needs assessments connect inmates with services within bureaucratic constraints. I'm sure some individuals may be bumped from one particular underprivileged position to another, perhaps better position. Jenny once said, "Making a difference with one inmate was better than not making a difference at all." This maxim is central to all those involved in any sort of bleeding heart do-gooder social service culture. I've heard this at least once a week for the past ten years, and my reflection on that maxim is rather grim. First of all, the maxim focuses on the individual level. That's the first mistake. Social change occurs on a macro, and not personal level. To borrow from Freire's critique on traditional social work, by focusing on inmate, you end up being the safety valve that keeps the dysfunctional or oppressive system alive. You might not be doing something positive in the global sense at all.

Joe: Let's move on to Rick's piece...

Randy: As a bystander in staffings, that section has always been one of the most exciting ones to hear about. I can remember Bush Helzberg used to always read poems and various other things the inmates had written, Todd Berg did the same thing, I don't think Rick did that as much. Reading the account that Rick wrote sounds exactly like the week by week accounts that we got in staff meetings. We felt like we really knew what was going on there, even if you'd never been there you felt like you had because of the way the piece was written.

Rachel: My impression of it was more than other pieces it gave you a sense that the people you're working with at the prison are people—that they're not just this nameless faceless population who you're helping or condescending to. That's one of my problems with a lot of this writing is that I felt like they're an object and we're acting on them. Your piece of writing didn't do that because it included a lot of detail and how things went and what their experience was. I thought that was good.

Rick: To gloss my own piece, when I first conceived of it, I thought I'd write a step-by-step guide. When I started writing it, that became very tedious and boring. I instead decided to focus on issues that come up while participating in this particular service learning project. I touched on issues in facilitating a seminar and the issues of working in a correctional facility. I wrote about "incidents," to use correctional facility speak, that come up. I even included as an appendix, a list of activities to try at site. I think it's important for people doing this program to think of their own activities. Part of the challenge of experiential learning is to fell like you're taking a part in developing your own curriculum. For that reason, it's important to ask your clients at site what sorts of activities they'd like to do.

Joe: I wanted to mention also that your piece unlike all the others contains a lot of writing from the inmates which is also very powerful. Okay, Jeanne's "Growing Tree" piece...

Mary Jo: I think that she did a very good job also, describing the experience and the mission of the Growing Tree.

Joe: Jeanne has an interesting perspective on that because unlike a lot of these other pieces she and I co-initiated that particular section as opposed to inheriting it.

Rick: Jeanne mentions that she thought this program was really special because it just doesn't treat the individual who is chemically dependent but the whole family. She thought that was the way to go. I agree.

Randy: Systems theory!

Rick: The other thing I found fascinating was the activities that she conducted with small children around chemical dependency issues. It was powerful for me to read about the application of heavy theory with such intense emotional weight pedagogically to small children.

Joe: "Migrant Labor Camp"...

Rick: I like this piece because it makes me feel like I'm back home. I spent two months in Tijuana. It's nice to know that there's a little Tijuana less than forty minutes away. I guess it's not nice to know. It's more like a human tragedy, another offense. I identified with this piece as an Anglo-American trying to develop programs for Chicano youth who may or may not know English. It's exhausting.

Mary Jo: What I was first struck by, again in applying a community service learning program to other universities, is that anything, and any kind of program, is possible. If you make up your mind to attempt to create social change through service-learning, there are endless possibilities out there.

Rick: As I was reading this piece, I was getting angrier and angrier, because I was thinking about the whole issue of migrant workers in the US. I thought the genius of the piece was the way coordinator and contributor comments ended up giving me the insight into the issues that I needed to hear. I liked hearing UM students understand how the migrant labor system is one of the greatest human injustices in this country and no one does a thing about it with the exception of the United Farm Workers of America. I wondered if PC could work with UFWA and try to improve the conditions of migrant workers. One of my crazy ideas was to parade forty Chicano youth around John Engler's office at the Capitol with t-shirts that say, "I'm an exploited migrant worker." If only to make a symbolic ruckus.

Rachel: I didn't know that this happens until I read this piece and I'm from Ann Arbor. Adrian isn't very far away after all.

Rick: I know because migrant labor was common back home, although it has become significantly reduced in the past five years. I understand, although housing conditions are better than what these families are used to in Texas or Mexico, they are still sub-standard compared to what we're used to.

Mary Jo: More than any other, this piece really compelled me to think about social change, and the commitment necessary to achieve it.

Rick: This touches on the pedagogical power of Project Community. These students really learned about migrant labor and the relationship between Mexico and the US. I felt that none of them ever reached the point where they felt empowered to change the system, although I suspected some may work for social change in the future.

Randy: Was it Rebecca Story who actually went into legal aid after her involvement in Project Community? It's nice to see that people do that.

Rick: That's part of "Oz Plus Five," the follow up.

Joe: Rick was at the Fall '92 staffing which inspired Amy and Tracy's chapter. At that meeting, a first term coordinator, asked the group for help—suggestions in planning site activities at her placement with state wards. I was impressed how the group responded, both on an interpersonal level to that coordinator and also with the breadth and depth and insight they had into working creatively with institutionalized juveniles. I thought immediately that these suggestions needed to be gathered and passed on to future groups working with the same population.

Rick: I think the essence of the piece was the way they catalogue various activities for that specific audience. I think that's the value of the piece, it's for people who do work with juveniles to give them ideas for activities. They also noted potential problem areas with that particular group.

Randy: One of the challenges of working with juveniles, and we've seen it in staffing is that you can't just go there and lecture to them, "I'm a college student and I'm a positive role model." You have to do something with them and show them that you exert this type of positive energy and are justified in even trying to be a role model. That's something that's always been important to those sites.

Joe: SALSA was the first of this volume's transcribed conversations. When I first approached Joan Scott with the proposal of writing for Praxis, she was very concerned about the time constraints. When I suggested that she tape record a conversation with the key students who worked on the project, she was very receptive. After all, we both imagined Freire doing a similar thing after we attended a seminar he held here last July.

Rick: My favorite part was the different sorts of institutional difficulties they had in "South City" with the "South City" district school principal. It was interesting how this principal suspected that they were somehow organizing a Latino revolution to take over "South City" and they needed to talk to someone at UM for a half hour to get permission to do this. I liked the way it was student issued. The students had a need for their organization and they saw a need in their Latino community and then they poked around until they found a way to institutionalize this need so it could be taken care of in the future.

Rachel: I thought it was very good for all of those reasons. I thought it was interesting how resistant the administration was at the school and how paranoid, "Oh my God, they're going to try and organize some kind of uprising." I guess our reputation precedes us. So we can take heart if we're worrying that we're not social justice oriented enough. We knew about the administrators and it was really silly. They sounded like the caricature of somebody who's scared of change. I thought that SALSA does a really good job of being true to themselves and also getting done what they want to get done within whatever constraints there are. I thought that was impressive and I noticed that with all of the stuff that Christy Ochoa is affiliated with, and I haven't noticed that with other people. I know with a lot of groups I've worked with, it's "If you won't do it and look at it our way, then forget it, we're not going to do it" and these people haven't done this.

Joe: How do you know Christy?

Rachel: She was in my Spanish class and she was running for a bunch of student government stuff so I remember talking to her a lot.

Rick: I actually know Areli and her husband, she's from Texas. She was involved in the Chicano movement down there and she brought some of her enthusiasm to the UM campus and has really made a difference.

Joe: The Prison Literacy chapter?

Rick: Again we have a situation where a site institution is resistant to having TVC. It seems that Jeanne was very diplomatic and persistent in developing a site there or re-developing a site. I was always comparing the experience at Milan to my experience at Cotton. "Gosh, these state institutions must be so laid back in comparison. Our orientation was only two hours." What more can you say?

Randy: I think as we have this set up here, this is going to go after the piece by Jenny and myself about what we've done at the County Jail. They're going to go interestingly well, back to back. Then you'll see two different components. In the County Jail needs assessment pre-release, students are referring inmates to these programs and other PC students are making sure that these people get these services. It's a shame that they don't work in tandem, but it's worked well so far. They've been able to inform the inmates and also provide the services, and that's great.

Joe: Any comments on the After-School Tutoring chapter?

Rick: Part II was very task oriented. It gave us an agenda and it was exciting to see what happened and I felt like I could coordinate this. It didn't feel like and overwhelming task, after reading it: "Oh my God, ten kids for an hour and a half!" The history was interesting. The reflections of how staff and space constraints can lead to a very major change in the focus of a program and it's "locus of control" as Joan puts it. It gives us something to think about in developing sites.

Joe: It had an Off to See the Wizard kind of touch. Carmen actually does put the activities that they did right in the middle of it.

Joe: Mary Jo's chapter differs from the others in Part Four because her assignment last term was to, based on her site experience, completely revise the drug prevention program that her students presented in elementary classrooms. That means that her emphasis was different. All the chapters describe the authors' experiences, and to some extent contained some reflection and some advice/direction for the future. However, this advice was only meant to modify the existing program, not totally revise it.

Rick: I was actually very impressed with the vision of the piece. Having grown up in the "Just Say No" culture, I went through many years of the public school anti-drug indoctrination which always included policemen with their guns, bringing in the confiscated contraband and the shots of people with noses falling off. It was wonderful to read a piece that had a step towards developing a program that moved towards students actually talking about the issues, getting in touch with their values and building a realistic approach. I don't know if anyone has seen the trendy Ad Council commercials that have a Black young boy running through he streets and he's thinking, "My teacher is saying Just Say No, but she doesn't have to walk home through my neighborhood." It's really powerful and this gives students an opportunity to really examine the constraints they're under.

Mary Jo: Thanks for saying that. Hopefully it's a wonderfully flowing piece. I hope that it will serve as something to make people think about how we approach the whole idea of drug prevention and intervention and I don't have any delusions of grandeur that this program will stop kids from using drugs or getting into trouble with drugs and alcohol. I guess my intention was just to create a program that people can use as a starting point. It's just a starting point, just an idea about the way you look at programs like this.

Rachel: I was thinking, as I read this last night, that I was really impressed with it. I was sitting there working this midnight shift in this treatment center surrounded by all of these little fifteen year olds who haven't said no and have no self esteem. In high school, I saw Nancy Reagan give her "Just Say No" speech at this conference in Georgia. I got a mega dose at this conference of what that's all about and what the thinking has been about prevention. I have a hard time with prevention anyway unless it's with small kids, which seems to be whom you are addressing. It's just gotten into me to address it the way you're addressing it, in terms of underlying issues that people have about self-esteem and family. The one exercise that I thought was really powerful was the one where you were taking away from or adding to a kid's self-esteem in one kid's day. It just made a lot of sense the way you chalked it out. It makes a lot of sense to think about kids that way. The exercise was basic enough to get through to me.

Mary Jo: I'm glad I included it. It's not my exercise, it's taken from Quest from among other places. I do think that it serves as a real memorable, basic way to get kids to look at self-esteem. I agree with you. I don't know if there is such a thing as prevention. I think that there's early intervention because kids are going to experiment with drugs and alcohol, except for maybe in that 1% of cases. But I agree with you. I don't think anyone aiming at a drug prevention program is being realistic in their goal. Also, what I didn't address in this paper, but could be addressed and should be addressed is just the whole way we look at drugs in this country with Bush and Reagan: that we need to get the drug suppliers, arrest them, and destroy the crops then the problem will be all gone. I think that that's ridiculous. Unless we really look at the demand and why people are making millions of dollars selling drugs and killing people, then this problem will never be solved and never go away.

Rachel: It's the same kind of thinking that we can treat these symptoms. When I think about the disease concept, I think about it being about a lot of different kinds of things other than just drugs, and drugs being the top layer of it. The whole focus of everything I've ever seen in treatment programs is "treat the drugs and don't treat what's underneath." Like addicts are never going to relapse. I also think it's interesting, if I were to think about ten kids doing this exercise in 2nd grade and 3rd and 4th grade, even if those kids do end up using drugs, maybe a result will be some critical thinking about what using drugs means. I don't think everyone is using drugs in a destructive way. So maybe it's "healthier drug using."

Mary Jo: Drug use, not abuse.

Rachel: Right. There is a difference and most of the time people dealing with chemical dependency don't think that there's a difference between using and abusing. There are people who don't abuse but use. I thought that maybe this intervenes on the way kids may think about drug use in the future. Not just that they won't do it, because they will.

Rick: Before we end here, I should say something about the systemic constraints on drug use and the cycle of poverty and capitalism and workers and jobs.

On Part Five—"Service-Learning Projects Not Affiliated with Sociology 389"

Joe: I am indebted to Anita Bohn, the director of Project SERVE, for helping me think through this section. As I began to generate the list of course-based service-projects for Part Four, she reminded me that several UM non-credit initiatives enjoy strong state and national reputations. Furthermore, if this series is truly to feature service-learning here at UM, these opportunities needed to be spotlighted.

Our follow-up conversations clarified the contents in this section. We chose not to devote separate chapters on UM service-learning projects administered nationally, such as Into the Streets and Alternative Spring Break, and concentrated instead on student-run initiatives originating on this campus.

Randy: I think all three of these pieces are a real testament to student empowerment and student initiative. It's not somebody taking something just to get credit. They're realizing that they really can make a difference and realizing something's gone on in their life. It's different from the PC experience. But I think that's ultimately the goal of PC, for people to not need the idea of academic credit to get involved. To take a look around us and have a belief in social responsibility and to do something about it.

Rachel: I think what is interesting to me in the Bursley program is that there is a lot of difficulty getting institutional support for programs like this, stuff doesn't get funded, but these people have made it part of an institutional thing, a rule that people have to do this as RA's. I think that's really impressive, it's a systematic change within what they can do towards something that maybe the University could learn from. I thought that was interesting. When I was reading the stuff about SERVEwork and the Alternative Career Center that was in the Residential College for four years, it was clear that there hadn't been that much institutional support for that sort of thing and that was one thing that hindered it. I was impressed by the initiative they took in making it mandatory.

Randy: Specifically related to the SERVE piece, I can remember last term when Jeff Salinger asked me, "How do you go about getting a job?" similar to mine or if I knew of any other openings. I think at the time SERVEwork had not been opened and I told him to go down there and take advantage of the resources available. For somebody who is committed to service-learning like Jeff is, it's just a shame that he even had to ask a question like that. There should be more institutional support, actually more societal support, too.

Rick: I was very impressed with Project SERVE. I agree with Randy, all these students can accomplish so much because it doesn't cost money for them to volunteer their time. The University doesn't have to pay them. I'm still glad student's have the opportunity to develop leadership skills.

Rick: I didn't know the University hired a coordinator for BCV. That's amazing. BCV should be changed to Housing CV because it coordinates service projects for all the residence halls.

Randy: My freshman year I lived in Bursley. I can remember when I first started hearing about BCV. It sounded like something I really wanted to do, and at the time, I felt overwhelmed with starting at a large university. I felt that I didn't have the time to become involved but was still looking for something along those lines to get involved in. That's how I happened upon PC. It's nice to see the bringing together of both worlds.

On Part Six—"Reflections"

Joe: Last summer, I ran into Mary P., a former client. I asked her if she knew how members of her therapy group were doing over the past ten years. Rick A. died in prison, Mary told me: Mike T. has been in and out of prison repeatedly and Paul G. was dying of AIDS. She didn't talk much about herself but later I discovered that Mary was about to graduate from college with honors and a degree in Psychology and was preparing to work as a chemical dependency therapist. Mary's story is not uncommon.

I relate it here because often the negative consequences of Chemical Dependency are emphasized without celebrating the successes of recovery. In my work as a therapist, I've come to know hundreds of recovering UM students, faculty and staff: I've chosen the experiences of six students to highlight the unique perspective that people in recovery bring to service-learning. In "Reflectors Anonymous", the first four writings are excerpts from the journals of Rick D., Mack M., Whitney M. and Ron A. The two longer pieces are by Matt M. and Mary K.

Matt's story is written by a person newly sober who tutored one semester in a treatment center for adolescents. Mary's story is written by a person with a few year's sobriety who reflects on her involvement in Project Community over several terms.

Finally, I wanted to note that pseudonyms are used throughout this chapter in keeping with AA's Eleventh Tradition:

Our public relations policy is based on attraction rather than promotion; we need always maintain personal anonymity at the level of press, radio and films.

"Oz Plus Five" grew out of a conversation I had with Sociology teaching assistant Toni Caldwell during the Winter '92 term. She asked me, "how many former coordinators keep in touch with you?" I actually hadn't thought much about it until that point. I responded by saying that over the holidays, I had heard from all the coordinators on the Fall '89 Chemical Dependency staff. Toni wondered how many other college instructors could say the same thing. I chose to invite my Fall '88 staff to co-write this chapter with me because in our most recent correspondence with each other, we all could scarcely believe that we first met—five years ago!

Regarding the final chapter, I wanted to give credit where credit is due. In May, Jeff Howard showed me a copy of David Schoem's Multicultural Teaching in the University (1993). Schoem's Table of Contents helped me think through how to organize this volume: his Introduction and final chapters greatly influenced how this book begins and ends.

Randy: It was very compelling.

Mary Jo: I think that the question raised by Toni about the number of coordinators with whom you keep in contact, is an important one, as the answer tells so much about the effectiveness of the PC mission. Almost from the beginning of my involvement with PC, I thought of you (Joe) as more of a mentor and a friend than a teacher. While you "teach" as much or more than any other teacher ever could, you have always been the perfect model of a liberationist educator. For myself, and many other coordinators, it's incredible to have been a part of a university course that is so "un-university." PC gives its students a sense of purpose and belonging; more so than any other class.

Randy: I think it definitely is a great read. It is a pleasure to see that people have been able to enjoy the PC experience and to share some of that experience to help others grow. Those people should be commended. Also, related to "Oz Plus Five," I know that I've only been around for three-plus years, but I really owe it to Toni Caldwell for challenging me to become involved at a higher level in PC—the challenge and responsibility of becoming a coordinator. It has been wonderful. I do still keep in touch with her too.

Joe: Any other remarks? If not, then I think it's time to move into our business section.

Project Community's Historicity

Project Community began as a grass roots student organization to address needs in the community. One of its first projects was to initiate a breakfast program for elementary students (in 1962). Later, it evolved into a formal student organization called the "Tutorial and cultural Relations Project." Around 1968, a few students approached Professor Mark Chesler of the Sociology Department to see if they could get academic credit for their community service work. Having the authority to give credit for "Independent Study in Sociology," Mark complied with their request. By 1970, enough students were involved to justify establishing a separate course number ("Sociology 389:

Practicum in Sociology"), which was readily approved by the College Curriculum Committee. A few years later, the same committee conducted a formal review of the program—something not routinely done—and concluded that the course could be offered for "credit," but NOT for a letter grade. Hence, course credit was changed to Pass/Fail status. More recently, two additional programs have been appended to Project Community. Project SERVE was launched in 1988 with University funds to improve undergraduate education, and in 1990, the Trained Volunteer Corps (TVC) was established with a grant from the W.K. Kellogg Foundation. These three service-learning programs are currently combined under the auspices of "The Office of Community Service Learning" (OCSL) which reports to the Associate Vice President of Student Affairs.

—From a Winter '92 term paper

Since 1992, the Associate Vice President of Student Affairs has become the Dean of Students.

Project Community's Course Structure

(Project SERVE involves students in not-for-credit community service and is featured in another chapter in this text. TVC's course structure is identical to Project Community's and is also featured in another chapter.)

In Project Community, students are required to participate in a weekly 90 minute seminar on campus and two to six hours of service at a particular site in the community. The seminars are small group discussions, facilitated by other students designated as coordinators. These coordinators can be either undergraduate or graduate students who report to a particular program director and teaching assistant. Coordinators receive letter grades, based on the program director's assessment of their work at site and seminar and the faculty sponsor's evaluation of their term paper. Students in the seminars receive credit based on the coordinator's recommendation that they did competent work in the classroom and in the field and based on the teaching assistant's reading of their term paper.

There are numerous variations in the above paragraph. One is that students generally have a number of different program areas to choose their site placements from—current program areas include At-Risk Youth, Chemical Dependency, Criminal Justice, Education and Women's Issues. Second is that credit options are available in both Sociology and Education, depending on the site. Third, the number of credits is usually determined by the amount of time students spend in the community: for example, a student volunteering for six hours per week through this course would receive more credit hours than one volunteering at the same site for three hours per week. Fourth, it is possible for either students or coordinators to volunteer their services through the course: in either case, however, they must agree to meet all the requirements except for writing the term paper. Fifth, being a coordinator is a work-study position for students who are eligible.

NOTES

1. ABC News did a feature on OCSL which aired on the Morning News and Good Morning

America after the Los Angeles Riots in 1992. Jeff Howard was interviewed on campus, and Randy Ross and Anita Bohn were filmed providing service to the community.

2. Randy Ross, Jeff Howard and Jeanne Gray all assumed different aspects of Margaret Elias' job responsibilities during her Fall '92 maternity leave.

PART TWO

Service-Learning at the University Level: Some Guiding Principles

Chapter 1

ESTABLISHING A SERVICE-LEARNING COURSE
The Making of the Trained Volunteer Corps

By Margaret J. Elias

Introduction

Three years ago I joined the staff of the Office of Community Service Learning as the program director of the Trained Volunteer Corps (TVC). My charge was to develop service-learning programs in four areas: youth at risk, the elderly, homeless, and adult literacy. I brought with me a background in clinical social work and experience as both a service-learner and teacher. My teaching experience included teaching preschoolers, working as a teaching assistant in a psychology service-learning course, and supervising graduate social work interns in their field work. I came to the position with ideas and expectations about what the program should offer and with the notion that the startup could be expeditious. I found that developing a new program requires a great deal of flexibility and the capacity to quickly accommodate the unexpected. It took almost two years for the program to reach a point of stability. As we now celebrate our third year we hope to pass along some of what we have learned in the process.

I was given four months to prepare seminar materials, select sites, hire staff and create an evaluation process. The initial TVC staff team included five graduate students from the public health, social work and sociology departments and myself. TVC operated out of the Project Community office, a service-learning program which had existed at the University of Michigan for nearly 30 years. This sponsorship brought both opportunities and limitations. As an already well established program Project Community had a transportation system for students to get to and from sites; some traditional avenues for publicity and some familiarity among students through word of mouth. In addition, nearly 20 years ago Project Community became a sociology course through which students could earn ungraded course credit. While recognizing that these are critical elements to a campus service-learning program, we will not be addressing them in this chapter.[1]

The TVC organizational structure was also a given with our association with Project Community. The major staff roles were the coordinators, the sociology teaching assistant and the TVC program director. Coordinators were graduate or undergraduate students whose job it was to facilitate course seminars and act as liaison with host agencies. They were compensated for their work through the financial aid work study program or, in combination with an academic component, through an upper level sociology course. The teaching assistant brought the sociological prespective to the course and was responsible for the academic work students were required to do in order to earn credit. The teaching assistant occasionally visited the seminar sessions, but worked primarily through meetings with the coordinators and program director. The program director oversaw the program as a whole, supervised coordinators in their work with the seminar groups and acted as ongoing liaison with host agencies. The director of the Office of Community Service Learning and a professor from the sociology department provided overall supervision and consultation.

The student role in the TVC course consisted of weekly site work and an opportunity for reflection through weekly seminars, reading and writing assignments. Enrollment was not limited to any major or class level and no prerequisites were required. The course structure was designed to offer optimal service and learning opportunities to a diversity of students.

When developing the course, the TVC staff were aware that the content and structure had to satisfy the needs of several key players. It had to contain the rigorous academic material and evaluation process to meet standards for credit eligibility at the University. For students the course had to provide stimulatng community work and channels for personal and intellectual reflection. TVC had to provide agencies with qualified and responsible volunteers and a program structure that would fit with their own. Finally the course had to contain the vehicles for evaluation and accountability to students, sites and the grantor, the W.K. Kellogg Foundation.[2] In the following pages we offer some discussion of three key elements in the development process: the site, the seminar, and evaluation.

The Site

Our first step at the Trained Volunteer Corps was to identify the sites that would fit into our plan for the course. The site experience would be the foundation of the course. For students, it would be the action about which the thought and reflection would take place. We assumed that a challenging and invigorating work experience would be the top priority for students. This assumption was borne out in the give and take of the course startup, where we found students to be much more accomodating about bugs in the seminar process than bugs in the site experience.

We began to develop a network of local agency contacts by conducting informational interviews. Using the phone book, a United Way listing and ideas from colleagues we began calling agencies. We offered an explanation about our grant and what we hoped to accomplish. For each contact we filled out a form that we had developed to meet our information needs about the organization's client populations, location, hours of operation, potential need for volunteers, etc.

Using the information we had gathered we took the second step and scheduled site visits with those agencies that fit our program criteria. We were aware that although community needs are great and agencies are plentiful, our own and the agencys' logistical limmitations could make quality sites difficult to find. We used two elements to develop our site criteria: the quality of the work experience for volunteers and the realities of fitting a volunteer job into the prescripts of a semester timeframe which is set for another purpose entirely.

Our first criteria was that the service experience offer students an opportunity to interact in a meaningful way with individuals being served by the agency. This may sound simple. It wasn't. There was a good deal of debate among TVC staff about the definition of a quality experience. For some, it meant that a demonstrable change would take place for the individual being served. A homeless person might find a place to live or a child who has been skipping school might begin attending more regularly, thanks to the work of our students. For some of us, however, to expect this or make it a goal seemed unrealistic, given the limitations of time and responsibility of our volunteers.

Our focus came to rest instead on the relationship(s) we could build in the course of the term and the impact these might have on the people being served. We concluded that we might have to be content to mean a little something to someone for a little while. We hoped that along the way we might teach some skills or provide some needed support or help with a specific task, but the goal of our program and the quality we sought in the site experience was to be the quality of the relationship(s) students were able to form with clients.

More than we would have liked, the second criteria which influenced our choice of sites was the simple matter of logistics. Our semester was 14 weeks long and with course start up, exams and vacations, the volunteer committment shrunk down to about 11 weeks. For many agencies a committment of so few weeks was seen as detrimental to their clients and hardly worth the time it would take to incorporate the volunteers. According to the University guidelines for administering academic credit, the time required to earn the 2 to 3 credits offered had to be shared among the reading, writing and fieldwork tasks, leaving the fieldwork with only 2 to 6 hours per week. Another logistical factor was location and travel time.

We therefore were looking for sites that offered an opportunity for students to build meaningful relationships through work that could be broken into manageable blocks of time. Our preference was for agencies that offered the volunteer experience in a defined place and time such as an after-school program that ran each day from 2:00 to 5:00 or a homeless shelter that had resident meetings and chores each evening from 7:00 to 10:00.

When we offered sites that placed much of the responsibility for intiating the contact in the hands of the students, we were disappointed. We tried working with a well established youth mentor program in the community in which our students had to make all arrangements to see their mentees. We found that frequently the relationships never got started or were started but dwindled away during the term. This was in contrast to a mentor program we run in which mentor/mentee matches are set up by a school social worker and students meet their mentees at the same time each week at the child's school. This program has had excellent attendance and feedback from all involved.

Our third step was to develop contract agreements with the agencies we had chosen. This was a time consuming process and by no means foolproof. Each agency had its own way of working with volunteers. Agencies often had a high rate of staff turnover so that we were working with several representatives of the same agency. This meant that we sometimes received inaccurate or conflicting information which only became apparent after students had started to work at the site. Drastic changes in funding occasionally caused agencies to abruptly cancel programs we had agreed to serve with our volunteers.

Some agencies relied heavily on volunteers and had an institutionalized system for intake and training. If this fit into our semester schedule it was great. If it did not, for example because their interviews and orientation came too late in the term, we faced the dilemma of eliminating a good site or the extra effort of trying to make special arrangements with them.

In the contracts we were as specific as possible about hours students were expected to work, tasks they would perform, length of committment and supervision they would receive from agency staff. The contracts sometimes had to be altered during the course of the semester but were invaluable as a way of making sure that both TVC and the agencies understood what was expected of one another.

A potential concern raised by many of the agencies was the reliability of our students. This has proved to only occasionally be a problem, largely because our students are highly motivated to play a meaningful role in the community. A second reason is the fact that earning course credit depends on their fulfillment of all site responsibilities. This expectation is made very clear at the start of the term. Coordinators follow up on students' attendance and job performance at site throughout the term so that any problems can be quickly and effectively addressed. Knowing that such a system was in place allayed the fears of many agencies and was a deciding factor for some as to whether or not to participate.

In our first term we offered a total of 16 sites. The variety of these sites reflected the compromise and attempt at balance that took place throughout the course development process. In the youth at risk program, for example, we offered work as a mentor in a school district with a significant population of children in need. The work was intense, challenging and often troubling. In another school district we offered an after school recreational and tutoring program which allowed our students to become involved with the children on a less intense level. Similarly, in our program on homelessness, we offered a site at the overnight emergency shelter where students had some interaction with the homeless clients during social hours at the shelter, did no casework or advocacy, but did do laundry! Another site required 40 hours of training and a one year committment and allowed students to staff the crisis phone line, conduct intake interviews and provide counselling. We felt that by offering sites with varying levels of challenge and intensity we were meeting the often diverse needs of our students, some of whom had already acquired a vast repertoire of service experience while others had none.

The Seminar

We saw the site as the foundation of the course, much like the foundation of a house. We envisioned the seminars as the rooms of the house students would walk through together throughout the term. In the seminar group each student would begin by seeing the rooms in his or her own way, from the perspective of his or her individual biography. By the end of the term the student would be able to see how the rooms might look to others and to understand why that was so. A sense was gained of how those rooms fit together, with the foundation, to form a house.

The semester consisted of 12 seminar sessions. The seminar served two functions. The first was to create a small community for personal reflection; a safe place where people could take some risk and share some vulnerability. The second function was to enable students to synthesize the experience of site with the sociological and social policy materials to which they were introduced through the course. Once the semester got rolling each seminar ran for an hour and a half with a three part agenda—1) reporting in on site work; 2) a group activity related to group process or to course material; and 3) discussion.

A Safe Place

TVC staff felt it was imperative for students to have a supportive environment where they could talk openly about beliefs, feelings and experiences. Although we were clearly not seeking to create a therapy group, we drew on that model to some extent to incorporate the kind of trust building and acceptance it offers. We recognized that there would be times, because of the nature of the site work and the topics of the course syllabus, when seminar members would be asked to engage in difficult and challenging discussions. For example, each term the issues of race and gender were addressed as they related to the students and the client populations. A safe and accepting seminar group was essential for students to be able to discuss, in a constructive way, beliefs and feelings that might not be politically correct but may have been part of their personal biographies.

Part of the need to have the seminar be a safe place came out of the fact that it served as peer group supervision for processing the site experience. The agencies at which we placed our students frequently did not have the staff time to provide much on-site training or supervision. We therefore built into the weekly seminar an opportunity for each student to report on their experience at site that week. At times these were brief, updating reports - like one student's announcement that her mentee finally asked the girl he liked out on a date and she accepted! Often, however, they were a chance for a student in distress to gain the ideas and support of his/her group members. One of our student mentors at an elementary school was called to the principal's office and chastised for her handling of remarks the child had made which might have indicated abuse at home. While this also required the intervention of the TVC program director, the student got some ideas from her peers about how to handle the situation, some commiseration about the particular school in question and some affirmation that she had acted appropriately.

We set about the process of making seminars be safe learning communities in several ways. We attempted to keep our enrollment down to no more than 10 students per group. We found that 7 or 8 was ideal, allowing for the intimacy of a small group as well as enough people to insure some diversity of perspective. After the first meeting groups often decided not to meet in a classroom setting, but to find a space more conducive to the interactive learning climate they were seeking to create. At the first three or four seminars progressively more interactive icebreakers were used to enable group members to get to know one another and to begin a process of group development that would continue throughout the term. At the second seminar the group developed a list of norms or rules that they could refer to during the term as guidelines to ensure a safe place.

A critical element in our attempt to build a safe place was the decision to engage students—often undergraduates—to be our coordinators. Although this model had both advantages and disadvantages, it was our experience that the gains were worth the risks and any extra investment of time or training that had to be made. An underlying philosophy of the course was that we learn from one another. For example, students learn from clients at site as much as clients might learn from students. It followed that the seminar would not be structured with traditional student and teacher roles but rather would consist of peers—members of a group sharing an educational experience. While we did not believe that it would be impossible to create such a co-learning group with persons of varying levels of ascribed status in the university community, it was our sense that the process was significantly facilitated with undergraduate coordinators.

Problems can exist with such a model. While we professed to offer a seminar of co-learning peers, the reality was that in order to profer credit we had to be sure that a certain level of academic experience took place. The two were not necessarily mutually exclusive, but were often rather strange and contrary bedfellows. The burden then placed on the coordinator was that of being both peer and authority; both group participant and group leader. He or she had to struggle with conflicts between wanting to be liked and accepted by the group and his/her credibility as a representative of the TVC administration. The coordinator began the seminar session with a great discussion about Paulo Freire and the pedagogy of liberationist education, only to move on to the task of handing out the attendance and course requirements! (Freire, 1970) This contradiction required that throughout the term coordinators work to establish balance in their roles.

In our efforts to create a safe place we did not fail to recognize the need for clear rules and boundaries. We had some concerns, through experience, that the concept of the safe place might lead some to believe that the academic expectations and student responsibilities did not have to be taken seriously. We learned that the more clear we were at the outset about expectations and consequences, the more smoothly the semester went for all. Beginning in our second year, we made it a practice to distribute our site and seminar attendance policy at the very first seminar. Our policy included the specifics of the attendance expectations and the consequences for failure to comply. We found that this made the job of the coordinator much easier by clearly making the students responsible for their own attendance.

The Syllabus

The development of syllabi for the program areas has been an ongoing process. Because of the nature of the course it was especially important that issues be timely and reading materials be up to date. We brainstormed a list of issues that we felt were relevant in each program area. We asked our site contacts to contribute to this list, realizing that they were in the front lines of work with the problems on which we were to focus.

We reviewed our list of topic ideas and looked for the common threads that ran through them and could become the binding force of the course. For example, for both the youth at risk and the homeless programs what stood out was the impact of poverty on these populations and any attempts at problem solutions. In the program on the elderly we addressed some of the many issues the elderly face such as loss, health problems, and poverty with an eye toward our country's changing demographics and the the implications of the aging of our population. In the adult literacy syllabus the way literacy can maintain the status quo among a nation's citizens and the role it plays in the function of a democracy were our themes. Keeping these in mind we narrowed our list to 10 tentative seminar topics, leaving the first and last seminars open for introduction and closure.

Once we had our topics for the term we began searching for reading materials. In our first term we were rather overambitious and overtechnical in our selection of readings. The feedback from students led us to realize that less is sometimes more. We shifted our priorities a bit and instead of trying to present everything there was to know about a particular issue, we strove to find a balance that would provide some information, ask and sometimes answer relevant questions, and stimulate discussion. Because of the variety of perspectives and viewpoints we could represent, we used many articles and excerpts from books rather than a particular text. We made an effort to be balanced in our treatment of the issues addressed, recognizing that students would be coming in with a diversity of beliefs and opinions.

With our syllabus topics and most of the readings in hand we began to develop a leader's guide for each program area. We intended it as a shed of tools available to coordinators to use as needed. We encouraged coordinators to add their own ideas and imprint to the seminar plans and often included these in the next term's guide. The leader's guides contained the reading materials; group exercises; journal questions and discussion starters and points for each of the seminars. A sample plan for one seminar topic is presented at the end of the chapter.

Based on student feedback, one of the high points of the seminar session was the group activity. These were developed to illustrate one or more points of the topic that week or simply to stimulate discussion. Activities were also used to challenge viewpoints or sterotypes held by students, or to personalize a particular issue. The activities tended to foster a sense of cohesiveness among members and set a positive tone for the discussion to follow.

Coordinator Training and Supervision

The role of the coordinator was pivotal in the model we utilized. It was this person who handled much of the practical work of getting students started at site. The coordinator was then responsible for the challenging job of community building, personal and intellectual reflection that would take place in the seminar. He or she read and responded to student journals and facilitated the discussion that took place in class.

TVC provided coordinators with two training sessions before the semester began; weekly staff meetings; and individual meetings with the program director as needed. The initial training sessions focused on the semester startup including icebreakers and community building exercises; administrative tasks; and the process of having students choose and prepare for sites. These sessions were also used to address issues the coordinator might face such as role conflict;

having friends in the seminar; and ways to present attendance requirements while maintaining a peer learning environment.

A component of training which we found to be most effective was to invite former project coordinators to return and share their experiences. They were able to prepare new coordinators for what might happen and how they were best able to handle situations that arose. Often the group of coordinators for a given term consisted of both new and returning coordinators, allowing this sharing to continue at staff meetings throughout the term.

The weekly staff meeting, like the seminar, was intended to be a safe community in which coordinators could freely share their site and seminar experiences. The meeting was attended by coordinators, the sociology teaching assistant and the program director. We limited the size of this staff meeting as we did with student seminars in order to facilitate the formation of a cohesive group.

In our staff meetings we reviewed how the previous week's seminar had gone and planned for the next. We sometimes tried out the group exercise planned for the seminar that week so that coordinators could get a feel for how it worked. Time was devoted to any problems in seminar such as an individual who never talked or one who talked all the time, a group that did not seem to be forming, individuals not turning in assignments, etc. Although the program director and teaching assistant were there to offer supervision, the group generally operated with individuals working together to share ideas and solve problems.

Evaluation

One of the most valuable elements to the program development process has been our use of evaluation. As a condition of the TVC grant an organization was hired to conduct evaluation and provide progress reports to the grantor. For our own formative evaluation, however, we found it most helpful to ask for feedback frequently and from many sources.

Regular followup with agency representatives was critical. At times they expressed concerns that we would not have known about if we had not initiated the feedback process. Having an ongoing, open channel of communication made it easier to address any difficulties that did arise. Whenever possible we shared positive feedback with agencies so that communication was not only limited to problems. While it lacked an opportunity for confidentiality, we conducted our followup with agencies by phone several times throughout and at the end of the term. We found that their time was so limited that they preferred a brief phone call to a questionnaire.

Coordinators were an invaluable source of feedback both about the program and about their own experiences in the role of coordinator. Feedback from them came primarily through an informal process we built into the weekly staff meetings. Other program directors at the Office of Community Service Learning have used anonymous staffing evaluation forms to provide coordinators with a confidential means to offer feedback. Information from coordinators was particularly useful because, in the dual role of student and staff person, they were able to see many issues from a unique perspective.

Academic evaluation was based on two papers students were asked to write. The content of these was developed by the sociology teaching assistant with the input of the coordinators and the program director. Like the seminar, the papers functioned as an opportunity for students to reflect on the work they were doing at the site in conjunction with the materials they were reading and their discussions with other students.

From students we gathered feedback using brief questionnaires at several points during the term and informal discussions in seminar. The questionnaires were anonymous so that students could be completely candid. We included specific items about how they saw the program going and more open questions to encourage them to offer ideas about how they might design the program. From this feedback we were able to make many program corrections and add new ideas. While we could not always incorporate student suggestions (like ditch the coursepack and the papers), we made an effort to respond to all feedback. The feedback loop we incorporated gave us a wealth of useful information and gave students a valuable sense of ownership of their learning experience.

For our closing we offer one student's feedback about his/her experience with TVC:

> *When I first decided to enroll in TVC I was merely interested in finding time to do some volunteer work before I graduated. I figured that doing it for academic credit would ensure that. As a creative writing major, I was vaguely interested in adult literacy, so I enrolled into the section of the course. I never imagined how much I would gain from the experience—self-knowledge, knowledge about others, and a view into the educational process from the other side of the fence, as a tutor, not a student. But I was still a student, because I was constantly learning. I learned that I was capable of facing the challenges which remained.*
>
> *—Adult Literacy section*
> *April, 1991*

NOTES

1. Project Community's Historicity is discussed near the end of Part One.
2. The goals of the Kellogg grant are discussed in the next chapter's Introduction.

Sample Seminar Plan—Homeless
Week 3—Who are the homeless?

Reading assignment
(assigned the week before)

Chapter I, "Who are the homeless?", pp. 1 - 21, in Homelessness, health and human needs, Institute of Medicine (U.S.). Committee on Health Care for Homeless People., Washington, D.C.: National Academy Press, 1988.

Purpose:
—to inform about who actually are the homeless in this country.
—to begin to see the complexitity of the problem because of questions about how to define homelessness, how to accurately count the homeless, how to address the many problems of each subgroup, etc.

Journal question
(assigned the week before)

Write an entry entitled "how I became homeless".

Purpose:
—to personalize the homeless experience.
—to get a sense of the particular problems a subgroup of homeless persons may face.

Site followup reports

Group Activity

1. Ask the group to list all the different populations of homeless people. Record these on the board.
2. Next to each category make a list of the needs of that particular group.
3. Divide the group into pairs and have each develop a definition of homelessness, keeping in mind the lists on the board. Ask each pair to report their definition back to the group at large and begin the discussion.

Purpose:
— to increase awareness that there are many subgroups of homeless.
— to challenge stereotypes of the homeless that may arise from the media or from those homeless people who are most visible.
— to become aware of the breadth and intractability of the problem because of the diverse needs of the subgroups.

Discussion Points
—How do the populations and needs we have listed compare to the clients at your site?
—What difficulties did we have arriving at a definition of homeless? Why?
—Do we/society tend to view some of these populations more sympathetically than others? Do you see this at site?
—Do we categorize people in terms of deserving versus nondeserving poor? How does this affect our solutions?

Chapter 2

ADVOCATING FOR COMMUNITY SERVICE LEARNING AT THE UNIVERSITY OF MICHIGAN

By Jeffrey Howard

Introduction

A three-year grant from the W. K. Kellogg Foundation[1] provided funding for two primary inter-related objectives. The first, aimed at student and community impact, was to extend the level of student involvement in community service learning at the University of Michigan; a review of our efforts undertaken in the service of this goal appears in the preceding chapter. The second goal, more ambitious and more amorphous, was aimed at institutional impact: to strengthen the University's commitment to student community service learning in undergraduate education. In essence, we were seeking to enhance the University's valuing of undergraduate participation in community service, especially when those service experiences are integrated with academic learning.

In this chapter we will describe our experience with this second goal, in particular, reviewing our assessment of relevant institutional dynamics and factors, the set of activities we undertook over the last three years, highlights of the intended and unplanned outcomes, and learning outcomes that will inform our future advocacy efforts. The specificity of content in this chapter is guided by its anticipated value to readers who may wish to undertake a community service learning advocacy campaign on their own campus.

Campus Assessment

For the purposes of determining how to undertake an advocacy campaign to enhance the valuing of community service learning at the University of Michigan, we found the following factors significant about the University of Michigan:

1. it is a very large institution (about 1500 faculty)
2. it prides itself on being a leader in the higher education community
3. it places a premium on quantitative research
4. it takes great pride in its capacity to attract external funds
5. it values positive attention from the media
6. faculty value student learning more so than student community service
7. it is a de-centralized organization, with each unit, department, and

faculty member having a great deal of autonomy
8. there is formal and informal separation of the academic and student affairs divisions

These institutional factors, borne out by pre-grant interviews with selected faculty and administrators, led us to plan an advocacy campaign on behalf of community service learning that included the following measures:

1. integrally involve faculty
2. establish a credible research presence
3. advocate on both the institutional and individual faculty levels
4. utilize the University's publications to enhance credibility of our work and of our field

The Kellogg Faculty Committee on Service-Learning

Curriculum matters at the University of Michigan are largely in the hands of the faculty. To impact the number of service-learning courses at the University required that we involve faculty from the beginning. Therefore, we established a faculty committee to serve as both advisors to our advocacy campaign as well as links to other faculty. We called upon faculty who we knew, who we knew had leanings toward community service learning, and who (we surmised) had credibility with their colleagues. We approached a total of 13 individuals, receiving affirmative responses from 12. Though each faculty member had her/his own unique motivations for joining our committee, the intersection of their drives was 1) a concern for undergraduate education and 2) their own personal values toward service in the community. The resulting committee membership included 9 faculty (representing 8 disciplines), 1 academic dean, 1 student affairs dean, and myself.[2]

Not all the members were equally fluent in the issues surrounding community service learning. Therefore, the agenda for the initial meetings was to review the committee's purpose, to differentiate community service from service-learning, and to review institutional and individual faculty impediments to strengthening community service learning at the University.

Once the group was grounded, the next order of business was to determine a name, one that conveyed institutional and academic credibility, and of course, relevance to the task at hand. The committee agreed to be called "The Kellogg Faculty Committee on Service-Learning."

A core group of seven members was most involved in the Committee meetings, and decided that an effective advocacy plan would begin with two strategies. The first would be to find an intersection with the Committee charged to blueprint a vision for undergraduate education on behalf of the Literature, Science and Arts College. The second effort would be to write and distribute a position statement on community service learning for a faculty and administrative audience.

The thinking on the first intervention was that this L.S.A. Committee would have a great deal of influence in shaping the future of undergraduate education, and we wanted to insure that service-learning was represented in that reform movement. Though the L.S.A. Committee was very supportive, we quickly learned that they were focusing on more macro-level issues. However, we did have it confirmed for us that the real locus of power for change in undergraduate education would be at the departmental and individual faculty member levels.

The position statement by the Kellogg Faculty Committee (see Appendix I) was intended to educate about, and to promote, service-learning. The document introduced the Committee, defined service-learning, discussed the rationale for integrating community service into the curriculum, described the consequences and features of service-learning, and articulated three Committee recommendations:

1. enable greater faculty utilization of service experiences in academic courses
2. articulate social responsibility as a goal of undergraduate education
3. encourage further study of the impact of service-learning experiences on undergraduates

In our conversations around the position paper, Committee members struggled over two particular issues. One was boundaries, e.g. what were the precise criteria that distinguished a service-learning experience from an internship? The Committee's resolution was to identify the boundaries question in the section "questions still requiring attention."

The other issue that drew much attention from the Committee members had to do with how to help students utilize their service experiences as learning resources, and the faculty's role therewith. That discussion ended by agreeing to indicate in the paper that 1) students need intentional structured opportunities to help them glean the learning from their service experiences, and 2) the role of an instructor in a service-learning course takes on a co-learner aspect.

The paper concluded with a set of questions for further consideration. The thinking here was that asking questions can work to influence others as much or more so than merely taking a stand. Asking questions implicitly 1) demonstrated that we did not have all the answers, and 2) invited others to join us to find answers.

By the time the position statement was completed we were coming to realize that our greater hope for change would be accomplished via grass roots rather than institution-wide efforts; we kept hearing how difficult it is to rally the faculty around any single issue. Therefore, rather than a broad distribution we disseminated the paper only to key faculty and administrators involved with reforming undergraduate education.

Thereafter, for the remainder of the grant period, we consulted with individual members of the Kellogg Faculty Committee, most notably the Chairman, who was very familiar with community service learning and with the formal and informal workings of the University.

Research

Informed by the dominant role research plays at the University of Michigan, we established a research arm of our Office of Community Service Learning. Research projects on the outcomes of student involvement in community service learning, especially the academic ones, would be influential in strengthening the campus' valuing of community service learning. At the University of Michigan, the academic culture primarily endorses quantitative research, so we set our sights on initiating quantitative research projects on outcomes for community service learners.

We enlisted the consultation services of Wilbert McKeachie, Professor Emeritus at the University of Michigan, because of his credibility as a researcher and his broad name recognition. He had been Chairman of the Psychology Department when Project Outreach, a community service learning course, began in 1966, and he still had strong affections for that course and its experiential and service-learning orientation.

His suggestion was that we approach faculty members about conducting an experiment in their respective courses. A desirable course-based research design would include a randomly selected treatment group involved in community service, and a control group that would not be involved in the community. We would then compare each group's grades and course evaluations.

We approached a number of faculty who already involved their students in the community, or who taught courses in which a community service intervention would be applicable. We were successful in locating two faculty members interested in supporting a research project in their respective courses. However, low enrollment in one, and a research design defect in another, led us to abandon these efforts. It would have been counter-productive to broadcast the results of what would have been perceived as weak or sloppy research.

Those faculty who we approached that were unwilling to participate in such a study explained that it would involve too much additional work for them, or that they had an ethical problem with conducting experiments on their students (e.g. if they were convinced that community service would enhance academic learning, then they would not want just some of their students to be exposed to this learning intervention).

Finally, Gregory Markus, a faculty member in political science, and I, collaborated on a research design, and undertook what turned out to be a very clean study. The results, which were very flattering for community service learning, are contained in a research paper now under review by a journal (also see Gregory Markus' chapter in Praxis I).

Perseverance had paid off. Not only did we now have favorable results of a quantitative research study to lend credibility to our work, but we were able to broadcast these through a University press release; and, because of its timeliness with federal discussions about national service, it received a good deal of air time. We are now receiving requests to replicate the study, as well as searching for our own additional replication sites. We will continue to initiate research projects on academic outcomes for service-learners.

The other research area we investigated was the correlation between involvement in community service learning and consequences for students' level of social responsibility. We wanted to determine whether a semester-long service involvement would affect a student's level of social responsibility. To this end, Dr. McKeachie and I developed the Social Responsibility Inventory (see Appendix II). For the purposes of this Inventory we conceptualized social responsibility as having five components: community service, charitable giving, orientation toward others/away from self, social justice, and recognition that social responsibility is a citizen duty.

On this same Inventory, we also included items on four tangential outcomes of community service learning that we expected would be of interest to specific sub-groups of faculty and administrators at the University of Michigan: tolerance and appreciation for others, belief that one can make a difference in the world, sense of purpose or direction in life, and understanding the role of external forces as shapers of the individual.

We have utilized this Inventory, on a pre- and post-test basis, at three research sites, and are preparing an article that reviews the findings.

Faculty Networking

With regard to reaching out to the faculty, the arrival of the Kellogg grant gave us:

- incentive (we had made a commitment to Kellogg)
- credibility (we were acting under the auspices of a grant from Kellogg)
- psychological permission (to initiate collegial relationships with faculty)

At a large and decentralized University, networking is a slow and labor-intensive process. However, publicity can be a networker's best friend. Faculty who read in the University publications about our grant and our subsequent work contacted us; at the same time, we contacted faculty described in University publications who appeared to be doing work that was aligned with community service learning. In this way, many faculty contacts were made, in each case enabling us to co-assess what role, if any, the faculty member might play in our advocacy campaign.

Unplanned Efforts

In addition to the non-tangible factors of incentive, credibility, and psychological permission, the grant also released 20-30% of my time to work on this grant. This tangible release time was earmarked almost entirely to advocacy efforts. As I reflect back upon the grant period, the most significant factor that the grant contributed to our advocacy campaign, beyond the credibility factor, was the time I now had to initiate and collaborate on other projects. A number of unplanned efforts were instigated as a result of this time availability.

Faculty Award for Distinguished Student Community Service Learning

I was invited to talk with the Faculty Advisory Committee on University Relations, one of whose members had returned from a conference charged to replicate a scholarship program for students involved in community service. When it became apparent at the meeting that such a program, because of its cost, was unlikely to happen (this was a good benchmark that we still had a long way to go in our advocacy campaign), I proposed that we create a faculty award for student service-learning. It was supported by the Committee because it would still recognize student involvement in community service, and it did not cost much money.

Over the ensuing months the award became known as the Faculty Award for Distinguished Student Community Service Learning (see Appendix III), and it received good campus publicity. It is an award for a student who has excelled in community service learning, selected and given by the University faculty.

Praxis: Two Volumes on Community Service Learning

When the Michigan Campus Compact received funding from the Commission on National and Community Service, it, in turn, sent out a request for proposals that would advance service-learning at Michigan institutions of higher education. Joe Galura, a program director in our Office who has been publishing service-learning materials annually since 1990, suggested that we propose to publish some comprehensive materials on community service learning. This made sense. Not only do we have 20 year's experience in the service-learning business, but publications would provide another outlet for faculty involvement in our advocacy campaign.

The first of the two-volume set, PRAXIS: A Faculty Casebook on Community Service Learning, due out in late September, consists of about 18 chapters each written by a faculty member at the University of Michigan about how she/he incorporates community service into an academic course. When we submitted our proposal to Michigan Campus Compact in December we had enlisted 11 faculty authors. During the ensuing five months, we had contact with an additional seven faculty members, on our initiation or theirs, who agreed to write a paper for our publication.

This gives us pause. Two years ago, if we had been asked to estimate the number of UM faculty utilizing community service learning, we would have answered about five. To date we have discovered 25 additional faculty at the University of Michigan who involve their students in community service as a way to enhance academic learning. What we have learned is that there have been, for years, many faculty who have involved their students in the community. They may call it by another name, but all utilize community service experiences in the service of educating students. It is our suspicion that there are many other community service learning faculty on our campus, and on other campuses, who are involved in this kind of pedagogy.

At the time that we received the grant we realized that these volumes would serve us well in two ways. First, they would enable us to inform and encourage faculty around issues related to community service learning. Second, the publication of a set of two hardbound volumes would add local credibility to our work.[3]

What we didn't realize was that our advocacy campaign had taken a new direction—not only advocating on behalf of community service learning at the University of Michigan, but contributing to advancing the community service learning field. If this, in turn, reflects back positively upon the University, then it will also serve our advocacy plan.

Journal of Community Service Learning

Another unplanned effort, resulting from our time committed to advocacy, was a successful grant from the Michigan Campus Compact to publish an inaugural edition of a new journal that will fill the current void for a scholarly-oriented publication in the field of community service learning. The funding received from the Michigan Campus Compact will enable us to inform and encourage faculty around community service learning. This will serve our advocacy campaign in precisely the same ways as the Praxis series—inform and encourage new faculty, stimulate those already involved, and add credibility to our office, the University, and the field. This, in turn, may strengthen the University's valuing of community service learning.

Dinner and Mini-Symposium to Celebrate Community Service Learning

With all of these new endeavors, it became apparent that we ought to plan an event that would tie together and celebrate these disparate strategies. We held a dinner for the faculty who have been involved with our advocacy efforts. 35 faculty attended this dinner, a benchmark that our advocacy campaign was gaining steam.

Task Force on Community Service Learning

In March of this year, two of the University's executive officers established a Task Force on Community Service Learning. The members include faculty, staff, students, and community agency representatives. The noteworthy components of the task force's charge are to:

- Identify and deconstruct any institutional impediments or barriers to having community service learning be more prominent at the University
- Insure the University's national leadership in community service learning

This was a very strong message to those of us in the local community service learning field—that the University wants to become a leader in this field, sees the potential for that, and was prepared to recruit a host of individuals on campus and in the community to work on such a project.

The CSL Network

Through our projects, and the publicity generated by each, faculty continue to contact us to join forces with others so inclined. We now have a critical mass of faculty, staff, and student leaders to convene a University of Michigan Community Service Learning Network. To keep the network stimulated, we will create a message group on e-mail, plan a brown-bag lunch series for and by faculty, and will hold periodic get-togethers.

Public Relations Mileage

Not enough can be said about the importance of providing positive exposure for the University, especially in these times in which the higher education community is often on the defensive. Community service learning has great potential in this way. This was made vivid for us when we were asked to be one of four vignettes spotlighted in the University's multi-media billion dollar capital campaign kickoff. Being featured on ABC's Good Morning America was a good example of the kind of positive exposure our Office could offer to the University.

What We've Learned

There is an important distinction to be made between institutional change (e.g. the academic culture) and grass root change (e.g. individual faculty). The greatest success in expanding service-learning at the University of Michigan can be achieved at a grass roots level—with individual faculty members giving service-learning a try in their respective courses. Our role is to encourage and enable this.

With regard to receptivity to service-learning, faculty may be divided into four groups:

- those who would never consider service-learning; an advocacy campaign would have to be fairly well advanced to have a chance to convert those in this group.

- those who are curious about and might be willing to try service-learning; our role is to inform and encourage those who fall into this category.

- those who know they would like to utilize community service learning but lack the time and resources, or know- how; our role with this group is to provide resources and assistance, and serve as a networking broker.

- those who are already involved; our role here is to provide on-going stimulation and opportunities to network with similarly inclined faculty.

There are many faculty who fall into the latter three categories.

Determine a way to take advantage of publicity so that faculty, staff, and administrators know that your office is the place to contact regarding community service learning.

Non-tenured junior faculty have a much greater risk for becoming involved in the labor-intensive service-learning pedagogy than do senior faculty. Therefore, in the initial stages of an advocacy campaign, ally with those faculty who are tenured.

Change takes time. Even if an effort does not bear immediate fruit, it often plants a seed that may be harvested later.

Select Grant Evaluation Findings

The part of our grant evaluation that assessed our advocacy campaign involved interviews with a select group of faculty and administrators on a pre-grant and post-grant basis. Findings from the post-grant interviews include:

—promoting service-learning at the University of Michigan requires that we link this with learning more than with service, that we insure quality checks,

—the University should provide credited service-learning opportunities because they are an important type of learning experience and because they connect the practical with the intellectual

—the best way to positively change faculty skeptics' attitudes toward community service learning is to have an opportunity to have an exchange with faculty who are already involved; the next most common response was to change the University reward structure to encourage faculty involvement

Conclusion

Each campus is unique and therefore requires a unique set of strategies to impact the level of valuing of community service learning by faculty and administrators. The factors that were most influential in our campaign were the credibility communicated by receiving a grant from the Kellogg Foundation, the staff time that the grant provided to undertake intentional advocacy strategies, and capitalizing on the availability of campus publicity.

Though the grant has expired, the advocacy will continue.

NOTES

1. Jeffrey Howard's proposal received $156,000 from the Kellogg Foundation, beginning July, 1990.
2. Jeffrey Howard is the director of the Office of Community Service Learning, an administrative unit within student affairs. Four OCSL program directors (all with MSW's) place and coordinate the learning for 2,000 service-learners each academic year.
3. In the process of preparing to publish the two Praxis volumes, we have generated new material which we will publish as Praxis III.

Appendix I

SERVICE-LEARNING AND THE CURRICULUM
Kellogg Faculty Committee on Service-Learning
University of Michigan
December 1991

Introduction

"...we recommend that every student complete a service project... The goal is to help students see that they are not only autonomous individuals but also members of a larger community to which they are accountable."
(College: The Undergraduate Experience in America, Boyer, Ernest, 1987, p. 218)

"It is a misconception to imagine that outreach programs for students and faculty are merely an application of scholarly knowledge to the world beyond the academy. These programs are, in fact, learning tools, actively contributing to and transforming classroom and scholarly learning."
("A Michigan Education," P-CUE Report, L.S.A. College, 1990, p. 81)

These two references are amongst many in higher education reports endorsing student community service activities as important educational tools, both to enrich academic learning and encourage social responsibility.

Kellogg Faculty Committee on Service-Learning

The University of Michigan has received a grant from the W. K. Kellogg Foundation to further student participation in community service-learning activities. One objective is to strengthen the University's support for service activities when they are integrated with academic coursework.

Under the auspices of this grant the Kellogg Faculty Committee on Service-Learning is serving as a link to the broader faculty and to those responsible for undergraduate education. The 12 members on this committee represent four colleges at the University and four departments within the L.S.A. College; two additional members represent the Office of Student Affairs.

We offer this statement as an embarcation point for dialogue with our colleagues.

What is Service-Learning?

Service-learning is an approach to education in which relevant community service experiences are integrated with academic course learning.

Why Integrate Service into the Curriculum?

There are a host of good non-credit campus-based community service programs. However, we advocate for more academic courses that integrate service because:

1. service experiences are valuable sources of knowledge and valuable

resources for scholarship.
2. faculty can enable students to tap the learning potential of their service activities by structuring opportunities for reflection and discussion, and by offering relevant theoretical frameworks with which to analyze their service experiences

Academic Consequences

Imagine, if you would, students in a course on the socialization of the child who concurrently serve at a pre-school two hours each week. What would be the academic consequences of such an arrangement?

At a minimum, students' service experiences would raise questions, provoke reflection and discussion, and intellectually empower the students. Service-learners would come to class with questions they could not answer, with answers to questions previously asked or unasked, and with the motivation and enthusiasm to continue to want to learn.

At a maximum, per capita learning would increase, research possibilities would emerge (for students and faculty), students would become stronger critical thinkers, and a general student thirst for learning might spill over to other courses.

The teacher's role, of course, would be expanded to include not only conveying knowledge but to co-learning with students.

Features of Service-Learning

Service-learners:

1. **Apply Knowledge**—by testing and applying academic learning.
2. **Synthesize Knowledge**—by bringing together past and present learning, giving coherence to students' studies
3. **Critically Think and Analyze**—by learning to distinguish what is and isn't important in the unfiltered context of the real world.
4. **Learn About Cultural Diversity**—by learning with, from, and about people of other races, ages, economic means, and competencies.
5. **Develop Values**—through first hand interaction with community issues.
6. **Learn Inductive Reasoning**—by using the specific as an embarcation point for hypothesizing and theorizing.

Recommendations

The Committee recommends:

1. greater faculty utilization of service experiences in their courses
2. the articulation of social responsibility as a goal of undergraduate education
3. further study of the impacts on students of service-learning experiences

Study Questions

We continue to wrestle with the following questions:

1. What demarcates a service-learning experience from a practicum or internship?
2. What pedagogical models and resources could guide faculty on how to enable students to tap the learning potential from their service experiences?
3. What are the outcomes for service-learners?
4. How can we encourage faculty to utilize service placements as course learning enhancers?

Conclusion

The community is an untapped learning and research mecca. Students who serve in the community bring into the classroom a renewed and focused desire to learn. They bring new intellectual resources and challenges. And, they bring a thirst for knowledge to help them understand the world around them. Therefore, to vitalize classroom learning, to add coherence, relevance, and realism to the undergraduate experience, and to strengthen students' capacity for public responsibility, we ask our colleagues to join us in better understanding, valuing, and utilizing service-learning.

Loren Barritt (Education)
Mark Chesler (Sociology)
Hilary Cohen (English)
Michael Gordon (Business Admin)
Patricia Gurin (Psychology)
Royster Harper (Dean of Students)
Jeffrey Howard (OCSL)
Richard Lichtenstein (Pub Health)
Allen Menlo (Education)
Jerry Miller (Psychology)
David Schoem (LSA Dean)
Nicholas Steneck (History)

Appendix II

STUDENT SURVEY
University of Michigan

Please complete the following survey. Your answers will be treated confidentially. Answering the questionaire is voluntary, and it is your right not to answer any or all of the questions. However, your cooperation will be helpful both for this course and for other courses in which it is given.

Please return this form to the envelope that the instructor has been given. Thank you.

A. Student I.D. # ______________________________

B. Course ______________

C. Section ______________

D. Sex: 1. male 2. female

E. Race (optional):

1. African-American	2. Asian-American
3. Caucasian	4. Hispanic
5. Native American Indian	6. Other (specify)________________

F. Class Standing:

1. freshman	2. sophomore
3. junior	4. senior
5. graduate	

Part 1: using the scale below please indicate the <u>importance to you personally</u> of the following:

1 not important
2 somewhat important
3 very important
4 essential

__ G. working toward equal opportunity for all U.S. citizens

__ H. developing a meaningful philosophy of life

__ I. becoming involved in a program to improve my community

__ J. being very well off financially

__ K. volunteering my time helping people in need

__ L. giving 3% or more of my income to help those in need

__ M. finding a career that provides the opportunity to be helpful to others or useful to society

Part II: Using the scale below please indicate your response to the following items:

1 strongly disagree
2 disagree
3 undecided
4 agree
5 strongly agree

__ N. adults should give some time for the good of their community or country

__ O. having an impact on the world is within the reach of most individuals

__ P. most misfortunes that occur to people are frequently the result of circumstances beyond their control

__ Q. if I could change one thing about society it would be to achieve greater social justice

__ R. I can learn from prison inmates

__ S. I make quick judgments about homeless people

__ T. individuals should be ready to inhibit their own pleasures if these inconvenience others

__ U. people, regardless of whether they have been successful or not, ought to help those in need

__ V. people ought to help those in need as "payback" for their own opportunities, fortunes, and successes

__ W. if I had been born in poverty, chances are that I would not be attending the University of Michigan

__ X. I feel that I can make a difference in the world

(Part III is only on the post-test)

Part III: Using the scale below please indicate the degree to which participation in this course has increased or strengthened your:

1 not at all
2 somewhat
3 quite a bit
4 a great deal

__ Y. intention to serve others in need

__ Z. intention to give to charity to help those in need

__ AA. sense of purpose or direction in life

__ BB. orientation toward others and away from yourself

__ CC. intention to work on behalf of social justice

__ DD. belief that helping those in need is one's social responsibility

__ EE. belief that one can make a difference in the world

__ FF. understanding of the role of external forces as shapers of the individual

__ GG. tolerance and appreciation for others

Developed by Jeffrey Howard and Wilbert McKeachie, 1992
Permission for use required

Appendix III

Faculty Award for Distingished Student Community Service Learning

Introduction

In February, 1992, the faculty of the University of Michigan agreed to recognize at least one student per year for distinguished achievement in community service learning.

Goals

1. to recognize at least one student for distinguished community service learning
2. to communicate to students that the faculty of the University of Michigan support and value their involvement in community service
3. to communicate to the entire University community that student involvement in community service is important to undergraduate education
4. to inform faculty about exemplary student community service and its educational value for students
5. to contribute to the linking of academic and non-academic student life

Faculty Selection Committee

1. Advise on matters pertaining to the award
2. Help to solicit nominations from faculty colleagues
3. Review nominations (on paper and in person) and make selection
4. Attend award ceremony

Award Criteria

1. quantity and quality of meaningful outcomes for the community or individual(s) in the community
2. innovation and creativity
3. leadership
4. dedication and perseverance
5. articulation of educational value of service experience (via an interview)

Chapter 3

A JOURNAL WORKSHOP FOR COORDINATORS

By Joan Scott

Introduction

Journaling has long been considered a valued tool of experiential learning educators. In our quest for ways to evaluate students' participation and growth and in our commitment to reflection as a necessary component of the movement to new understanding, it seems a "natural." Yet, is it really so natural? When done haphazardly as part of course expectations it can simply be an exercise in busywork for the journal writer, and for the reader. At worst, with inappropriate commenting by the reader, I think it even can be harmful. The reality of getting students to be reflective in a way that "works" for them, and that goes beyond platitudes and superficiality, however, is not easy. An additional challenge is that of responding to the journal writing in a way that is helpful to the writer and "works" for the responder. When coordinators who are given the task of reading and responding to the journals are themselves students, balancing roles as paraprofessionals and service-learning peers as in our program, we as staff or faculty have a responsibility to provide them with tools or guidelines that will help them with the process. It is not fair to them or realistic to expect them to know how to do it instinctively.

In twenty-five years of asking students of varying ages from ten or twelve to adult to be reflective in writing I have seen a truth emphasized for me over and over again; that is that some folks process their experience (in writing) thoughtfully, carefully and with insight, and others just don't seem able to look inside and translate what they are thinking and feeling, and the personal connections they are making, to the written word. It doesn't come "naturally" to all students. Any of you who have read students' writing know what I mean. There's the student who produces, with minimal coaching, pages of the kind of reflection that makes you say "wow!," and request permission to share; there's the student who does a great job in the hands-on setting of the service and the immediacy of the discussion, but who forces a few lines of what happened onto the page and seems truly non-plussed when you ask her or him to tell you more, or explore what this meant or how she/he felt in the situation, or what questions this raised for her/him.

There are a number of issues here, and they are interrelated. One has to do with the journaler and the responder as individuals, and the recognition that there are various ways persons think and learn and know. Some of that is developmental; some may not be. Another has to do with the types of journal assignments and methods that can be useful in opening up the students' journaling. Another acknowledges what was expressed above—that if the journals are expected to be seen by someone other than the journaler in more than a cursory "check at the top" manner, how the reader responds is extremely important.

In the best of situations in the training of student coordinators, I would prefer to be able to spend several workshop hours on each of these important areas. In the reality of having to get our student coordinators prepared to deal with many things in a very limited number of hours at the beginning of the term, I have developed a workshop which at least provides an introduction to each of the above issues, and sends them away with some beginning tools. My intent for the purposes of this article is to share with the reader the components of that training. I acknowledge at the outset that much more could be done than is shared here.[1]

I have used this material in two ways, either in two parts at sequential sessions, or all together in a longer training session. The former method allows the students to get the "Learning and Knowing" background, then take and read on his or her own the handout, "An Approach to Reading and Commenting..." before coming back to do more work together. If used all at one session, I have sometimes given the students time to read the handout before proceeding, and sometimes have presented it on newsprint and verbally, backed-up with the handout as a "take-home" for reference. The last option makes for more "trainer talk" than I am comfortable with, however, if I have just been in the presenter mode with the "Learning and Knowing" section.

Part 1: Learning and Knowing

I. I begin by asking the coordinators to come up with as many responses as they can collectively generate in answer to a hypothetical student's question, "Why are we expected to write a journal in this course?" The responses are put on newsprint, and I encourage the mundane and cynical (i.e. "tradition", "the directors think it's important", "you need something to do in the five minutes before seminar") as well as the philosophically or educationally lofty. The task is actually useful on a second level, in that our coordinators usually do get asked the question at some point, and it also lets them know that we are not out on a cloud about this. Responses typically show a range of sophistication and understanding of the use of journaling, and personal experience with it as a student or as a previous coordinator. That can be helpful to me as further information about the support needs of my coordinators.

When the responses run out, I ask them to focus on the three or four responses that they think are most important for the goals of our course. In the brief discussion that occurs, I can expand or add as need be.

II. At this point I shift into a "presenter" mode, assuming that few if any of them are familiar with theories of student and adult cognitive development. My goal is not to present a crash or in-depth course, but rather to introduce them to some ideas that may be useful to them as seminar facilitators, problem-solvers with students about service concerns, and journal readers, and that "ring true" to their experience. At the outset I make it a point to say that it has only been recently that the work of women such as Mary Belenky, and Carol Gilligan on the development of girls and women's ways of knowing has had an impact on our ideas about development.

I choose to use Perry's categories (Perry, 1970) and Belenky's (Belenky, 1986), acknowledging that Perry's work was done on Harvard males. And that Perry describes a process that assumes a linear direction for growth, in which it is impossible for students at one stage to function and reason at a "higher" stage. I find it helpful to have on newsprint or as a handout a summary of Perry's theory of intellectual and ethical development, captured in four main categories or positions,[2] and Belenky's suggested ways in which women "know." (See Addendum I and II)

We talk about Perry's positions of "Dualism," "Multiplicity," "Relativism," and "Commitment in Relativism" as representing types or, modes of thinking. I ask the coordinators to think about their own cognitive development and whether they can at this time place themselves as operating primarily out of one or another mode. Usually an interesting conversation develops, as some recognize the dualistic thinking that they engaged in not too long ago in their adolescence, or as freshpersons, and others say, "You know, it seemed that, even when I was thirteen or fourteen I saw the world as more complex than most of my friends did," or "I remember hating it when there was "supposed to be" a "right answer," or a right way and a wrong way of thinking about problems and issues. It even got me in trouble because I always wanted to argue against whatever rigid position was being expressed." They are typically hesitant to place themselves as having "arrived" at "Commitment to Relativism" but like to think of themselves as operating out of "Relativism." They also typically question whether persons move in a strictly linear way from one position or mode to another, perhaps seeing in themselves and others a less consistent pattern, at least in some areas of their lives.

When I lay Belenky's "ways of knowing" alongside Perry, there are always nods of recognition. Women in particular appreciate, understand, and recognize something of their own and of women they know in the women interviewed. If any of the students are familiar with Woman's Ways of Knowing I invite their input. I tell them that I've noticed that Belenky's interviewees are social class and education stratified; for example, her interviewees whose "way of knowing" is "Procedural", or "Constructed" are college educated or beyond, while her interviewees whose mode is "Received Knowledge-Listening to the voices of others", or "Subjective Knowledge" are women who are less educated, with fewer options. Does that ring true to their experience? We talk about "separate" and "connected" knowing. To what extent might the more subjective ways of knowing be valuable to them? Is the implication that we should not rely on those ways of knowing as we become more educated? What does the university traditionally value? How do they feel about it?

An exercise that can be useful here is to ask the students to take a moment to identify a significant shift that has taken place in their own thinking—a point in their lives they can recognize in which an event, or interaction, or series of interactions, or intellectual prodding caused them to see the world and "knowledge" differently. I ask them to represent that however they wish on paper, and then each student shares their experience with two or three others. The important information here is the nature of the shift, and what they understand the precipitators to have been. It can be helpful to have the student coordinators do the individual part of this exercise as an assignment before the workshop, bringing the paper with them.

I ask them if they think all this relates to what we are doing in our seminars and in our responding to students' journals. They readily see that how they facilitate discussion and how they respond to journals is important—that people are in different places in their cognitive orientation developmentally or as women or men, or as socialized by our culture. Awareness is a first step. Work on sensitive discussion facilitation, and good question-asking comes at another time.

Part 2: Introduction to an Approach

What follows is the outline that I use in part two of the training, specifically geared to help coordinators respond appropriately and with confidence to the required journals. As stated earlier, it can be handed out ahead of time, so that the student coordinators come to the session having read it. That allows us to do a bit of practice work following an opportunity to raise questions, comments or observations about the suggested process. The form is that of the handout, and therefore the assumed reader in this portion is the coordinator.

I allude below to the variety of models for journal assignments or types of journals that are possible. In my own setting I do provide coordinators with suggestions that I believe can be appropriate models for our use.

An Approach to Reading and Commenting on Students' Journal Writing

A journal can be a powerful tool for growth. Keeping a journal (and there are a variety of kinds of journals) causes one, hopefully, to take the time to reflect, to ask oneself questions, to allow connections to be made, to examine thoughts and feelings, and to integrate parts of your life or learning with other parts. We teach people in our places of higher learning to take things apart, to analyze, but we do not do as good a job as we might in allowing students the opportunities to listen to their hearts and pay attention to feelings, to honor intuition, to integrate and construct and connect as a way of forming their own knowledge.

I am concerned here, of course, with a learning journal, and one which will be read by someone other than the writer. I do not mean to imply that learning and new knowledge cannot take place without the reader-commenter; it can and does, and that acknowledgment can lighten the sense of responsibility of student coordinators. The comments of the reader, however, can add to the learning possibilities. The fact of it not being a totally private of piece of writing means that a few guidelines need to established at the outset.

1. Anything that is very personal and does not relate in some way to the course should not be written in <u>this</u> journal.
2. Permission must be gotten from the writer before any part of the writing is shared with others.
3. The reader-commenter is not a therapist or counselor, and will not respond on that level. That does not mean that a good reader might not make a suggestion or referral about some personal concerns or issues that crop up that seem to warrant attention.

A Process...

One way to approach the task of responding is to consciously focus on three aspects of the student's journal writing:

1. **The cognitive aspect**—how does this student think?
2. **The social and emotional**—what is this student concerned about? What is impacting him or her? What is "going on" emotionally?
3. **The topic choice**—This is related to #2, unless a specific assignment to write on a certain topic has been given.

A good rule of thumb is to read each journal entry three times through. Leave the pencil down until after the first reading.

First time: Read for the student's perspective, the "big picture". How is she/he seeing the "world"? Try to understand where she/he is coming from, what intellectual assumptions and emotion seem to underlie the writing. Also, is this a reaction to a class discussion, or to a reading? Is it a response to a specific journal topic assignment? Is the student thinking about his/her own thinking or evaluating process? Is it a personal issue of concern? Is the student sharing a site issue and her/his questions or feelings? What is the <u>primary</u> focus and what might the student be looking for from you?

Second time: Add your comments. Decide what impact you want to have, and what seems most important to respond to. Make sure to support as well as challenge. Both are needed and appropriate for assurance, confidence-building, and growth. Try to be aware of Perry's categories, and of the importance of sensitivity to "the inner voice" and "connected knowing" as well. Don't overwhelm the student with <u>your</u> thoughts, however. And it is important to realize what commenting is within the limits of your capability.

Third time: After the third reading, write a brief "end-of-entry," summary comment. It can be an overall impression, encouragement, or question or challenge. Again, don't overwhelm. As student coordinators doing this perhaps for the first time, it perhaps is better to weight your response on the side of support.

Challenge is appropriate when...

a) there is a cognitive development goal. You want to nudge the student toward another mode of thinking, to have her/him make connections between issues or observations, or raise questions he/she might ask.

b) there is a "personal" social or skill growth goal. You believe the student can expand options, or take action beyond what he/she has tried or considered, and simply needs a "push" in that direction.

c) there is a question of appropriateness of behavior or intent for this project. Be careful...challenge here needs to be within the felt context of (overall) support. (I always ask coordinators to consult with me when they have a concern about appropriate behavior or intent.)

Support is appropriate when...

a) the student is in a transition between an "old" or comfortable way of thinking and knowing, and a "new" position or mode. "Old" ideas or processes with their assumptions are being left behind; "new" ones being "tried on". This can be uncomfortable, and reinforcement for the process may be needed.

b) the student is aware of what she/he needs to do or change, or would like to do (for example, in a site situation) and simply needs assurance and confidence.

c) the student is experiencing feelings and reactions to happenings or interactions in seminar or site, or to readings, that he/she risks expressing. Validation ("it's OK to express these feelings") may be needed, with encouragement to explore what the student might need to do about the reactions.

d) the student is doing a great job, making a significant contribution, says something insightful, and a "kudo" is in order!

I believe that you, the journal reader, can both support and challenge, in your role, but you need to approach the challenges with care. For one thing, it is somewhat presumptuous to think you can recognize where the student is developmentally. Keep the challenges humble, but don't be afraid to use them carefully, and combine them with support, and you will be OK!

Examples of "Challenge" Comments

Many younger students are still quite "dualistic" in their thinking. (Many older people are too, for that matter.) Examples of the type of comments that challenge students to move beyond that limited way of thinking, while still respecting their positions are:

"How can you really be so sure?"

"Have you thought about whether the situation (or issue) might be more complex than that?"

"I'm wondering what evidence you might have for this position. Would all the evidence, or all experience point to the same conclusion?"

"What would the perspective of X (another person or group involved in the interaction or system) be? Can you 'look through her eyes?' What might she say?"

"Have you considered any alternatives? (explanations, solutions, causes. etc.)?

"OK—you liked the reading so much. What can you critique about it?"

"Have you thought about <u>why</u> this might be so?

"OK—you have a very negative reaction to this. Is there anything positive about it that you could name?"

Often a student who has been accustomed to listening to others lay out the way to think and act, or who has been discounted, needs support and challenge together in order to trust her own ideas and feelings and to act on them. This is particularly so if they differ from those of "authority". The service-learning seminar and journal can be a safe place for this movement toward discovery of self and one's own knowledge. Examples of the type of comments that can be helpful in this situation are:

"It seems that this issue (or situation) is important to you. What does your own past experience, and your feelings say toyou that might add to or change the view expressed by X?"

"You have really thought about this a lot—and have some valuable ideas. I encourage you to find the right time to share them with (staff person) at the (site)."

"I wish you had said this during our discussion! Your experience would have been of interest to others. Take the risk. We don't have to agree..."

"Can you talk about this more in the next journal? It could be helpful to think about it from your own perspective, and from that of someone else in the situation—and see where the connections are."

"What a situation to have to deal with! It sounds like you did just the right thing. It seems to me your experience and intuition were "right on" about it.

"The author can be challenged! What critique would you offer of that position?"

In Conclusion...

You have a challenging job. You are commenting, in many cases, as a peer. One way to legitimize that is to share this process with the group. You may let them also read the handout, so that they know what you are doing. One idea is to plan with them for one or more times when they will trade journals and do commenting themselves. (It is essential to schedule this in advance so that group members know that someone other than you will be reading their writing that time. The change will affect how and what they write.) They each have the perceptiveness and sensitivity to add a new thought or awareness to a colleague's reflections!

Part 3: Practice Responding to Journals

Practice is always a helpful component of training. Following questions, feedback, clarifications about the material on the handout, comes the "hands-on" time. I like to use several different examples of anonymous student journal writing from my files, distributing them so that at least two student coordinators share the same example. There are advantages and disadvantages to having everyone deal with the same example at the same time. Time usually dictates my using more than one at once. I choose brief writing (one to two pages) that brings up different issues or concerns, and that hopefully illustrates some of the ways of thinking that we have talked about. I ask them to

1. Read the piece through individually
2. Talk with their partner(s) about "the big picture", the primary issue that they might want to respond to, the way in which this student is thinking, and feeling, etc. (I refer them to the "first time" questions in the Part 2 handout.)
3. Read the piece again, individually writing comments
4. Share with each other (partners) the comments written
5. Read the piece a third time, and decide together what "end-of-entry" comment would be appropriate.

The final part of the process is using the whole group as a sounding board. At this point I allow everyone a few minutes to quickly read the journal entries of the other partners. Partners then share with the group their responses to tasks 2, 3 and 5 (selectively, for task 3). Brief discussion is possible.

If time allows, a second set of journal entries is distributed, and the process is repeated.

We close with reflection on our own process. What did they learn that was helpful? What suggestions would they make for next time this is done? And very importantly, how do they feel, at this point in time, about reading and responding to students' journals? As a final word, I remind the coordinators that this is not something that they will be expected to do from a perspective of expertise, but rather, as a co-traveler, a co-learner with a particular responsibility. They will learn much in the process and in the practice.

NOTES

1. I am indebted for some of the content of this approach, specifically the use of Perry's categories as adapted by Stonewater and Stonewater, and portions of the outline for reading for challenge and support to Cynthia Straub, PhD., "Developmental Journal Workshop," student services staff in-service, University of Michigan, 1985. I have added to it and adapted it for use in service-learning settings with student coordinators.
2. The four major categories used here, drawn from Perry's nine positions or stages, are suggested by Barbara Stonewater and Jerry Stonewater, in "Developmental Cues: An Aid for the Practitioner," National Association of Student Personnel Administrators Journal, 1980.
3. Just this Spring I have read Carol Gilligan's Making Connections (1982), which examines the ways in which female adolescents at a private girl's school make ethical decisions and judgements. Though Gilligan and the other essayists using the study data acknowledge that more work needs to be done, they find that the girls, as they mature tend to value the "connections", the relationships between people, and the quality of those more than many of their teachers were aware. They learned to balance a "justice" orientation and a "care" orientation. The girls' approach to academic subject matter - the kinds of questions they were interested in—as well as their ethical decisions were impacted.

Appendix I

A brief summary of Perry's positions, in the four major categories suggested by Stonewater and Stonewater, NASPA Journal is given below. For a more thorough description, see Perry, (1970).

Dualism

Students see the world in terms of right and wrong, either—or. Authority has the "right" answers, or should have. The student is very frustrated by the idea of alternatives, and only two options, right and wrong, exist for him or her. Ambiguity is difficult to tolerate. This student expects and wants to be told what to do, and what the correct viewpoint is.

Multiplicity

The world is not seen in exclusively right and wrong, either-or terms. The student realizes that there can be more than one option, or "right" way of looking at some situations and issues. Solutions to problems can be more complex. Authority is understood as perhaps not having found the right answer yet-but the assumption is usually that the answer will be found at some time. The student is fairly tolerant of others' views. Perry describes later stages of "multiplicity" as a "do your own thing" approach. ("Since we don't know, then one idea or way is as good as another.") It is difficult for students in this "stage" to consider the weighed "relative merit" of perspectives and reach a conclusion of differential worth. This student may look at various perspectives as "the way they want us to think."

Relativism

This "stage" represents a major shift in thinking, as the student understands that in many areas there are no right answers, and that he or she needs to think in contextual and relative terms. A new realization is that authority has to reason this way also. This can be scary, because the guideposts need to be more of one's own making. As the student moves into Perry's later stage of relativism, she or he begins to weigh perspectives and make commitments on relative, contextual merit.

Commitment in Relativism

This category represents Perry's positions 7, 8, and 9. While the first three categories (six positions) represent cognitive development "structural" changes, this last category is one of qualitative change as the student makes and lives with a series of decisions and commitments. The implications of contextual decision-making become part of identity. The student accepts contradictions and questioning as life.

Appendix II

Mary Belenky's "modes" or "ways" of knowing are listed below and very briefly (and inadequately) identified. For a discussion of these the reader is urged to see Woman's Ways of Knowing, (1986).

1. Silence

The woman does not have a "voice" and does not understand herself as having knowledge. She is what she is described by others to be. She does not consider speaking from her own "self."

2. Received Knowledge - Listening to the Voices of Others

Knowledge is received from others—those in authority, and men. What she is, and what she thinks, has been taught to her. She does not consider challenging this received knowledge, even to herself.

3. Subjective Knowledge—The Inner Voice

The woman begins to listen to her "intuition", to what she knows because of who she is. She begins to trust her "inner voice" in decision-making.

4. Subjective Knowledge—The Quest for Self

A searching process takes place, what Belenky calls "a quest for self." The women interviewed questioned "received knowledge" for themselves.There is greater reliance on one's own experience, and on the experience of others who may not be "authority."

5. Procedural Knowledge - The Voice of Reason

6. Procedural Knowledge - Separate and Connected Knowing

In the two above "ways," analytical and critical thinking, the traditional mode of higher education are adopted. The women interviewed were able to use these ways of knowing and be successful doing so. However, there is a strand that persists and is strong in some interviewees, which recognizes the knowledge that is gained in relationship and connection. Knowledge is shared experience, both intellectual and personal, and contextual.

7. Constructed Knowledge - Integrating the Voices

The women in this mode comfortably use the "inner voice," "connected knowing" and the procedural mode to construct their own truths, to examine options and make decisions, and to live with the contexts and flow of their lives. Their knowledge honors feeling and relationship as well.

Chapter 4

USING INITIATIVE ACTIVITIES TO BUILD COMMUNITY WITHIN A SERVICE-LEARNING CLASS

By Janet Wylie

Introduction

For most university students, taking a service-learning course is a new educational experience. In contrast to more traditional classes where they take notes from a lecturer or discuss concepts in an abstract manner, these students have the opportunity to learn by doing. At the University of Michigan, students have many service-learning courses to choose from, offered through the Department of Sociology's Project Community program. They range from tutoring middle school students to working with senior citizens to volunteering in preschool programs. The general goals of Project Community courses are:

1. To positively impact the students' service ethic
2. To introduce the students to what sociology has to say about education, children, the environment, etc., and how sociological issues (i.e., race, class, gender, institutions) affect people.
3. To provide the students with an alternative learning experience.

In order to address these goals, the format of a Project Community course must encourage the students to share their experiences with others, and must challenge the paradigm that the "teaching" in the course will be done by the facilitator, and that the "learning" will be done by the students. Along with this it is important that the course allows the students to really take responsibility for their learning experience by giving them opportunities to make choices and to look at things from different perspectives.

Initiative activities, borrowed from the field of adventure education, are an excellent means for laying the groundwork for a successful service-learning experience. Project Adventure, the foremost authority on adventure education, describes initiatives in the following manner (Rohnke, 1984):

> *Initiative exercises offer a series of clearly and often fancifully defined problems. Each task is designed so that a group must employ cooperation and some physical effort to gain a solution. Some problems are more cerebral than physical and vice-versa. This problem-oriented approach to learning can be useful in developing each individual's awareness of decision-making, leadership, and the obligations and*

strengths of each member within a group. Participants engage the problem in groups to take advantage of the combined physical and mental strengths of a team. These initiative problems also can be employed to promote an individual's sense of his own competence, and they also serve to help break down some of the stereotypes which exist so comfortably in our social network. Finally, initiative problems are a nonpareil for building morale and a sense of camaraderie.

Because the group dynamics that result from working through initiative activities so closely parallel the ones we hope our Project Community students will adopt, I decided to incorporate a few carefully chosen initiatives into the first two weeks of class. I drew upon my own experiences and those of my colleagues at the University of Michigan's Challenge Program to design scenarios for these initiatives which would address the course-specific issues I had in mind. For example, I wanted my students to challenge the notion that I was their teacher and thus the sole source of information in our group. Instead, I wanted them to look to each other for ideas, and to be able to assimilate a variety of past experiences into a plan for the semester's field placement. An application of this might be learning from others who may have had similar experiences, and feeling comfortable sharing ideas and thoughts with one another, or asking questions. In the following pages, I will describe in detail how I implemented initiative activities into my course, and will give suggestions for other folks who are interested in doing so.

Initiative Activities and the Experiential Learning Cycle

Traditionally, initiative activities are employed within the framework of the experiential learning cycle. This consists of four steps: the briefing, the action, the debriefing, and the transfer.

Briefing

Briefing for these activities, usually done by the group's facilitator, includes describing the task at hand ("you must get everyone in your group balanced on this teeter totter at the same time"), discussing the restrictions ("everyone must enter and exit at the fulcrum of the teeter totter, you will have five minutes to plan and then you may not talk any more"), the resources ("for this activity, your only resources are yourselves; a person who is still on the ground may not touch or help balance a person who is up on the teeter totter"), and the consequences ("if either end of the teeter totter touches the ground, or if anyone speaks after the planning period is up, you must all get off and begin again").

Action

After the briefing, the action takes place. Basically, this is the time period during which the group members are actively attempting to accomplish the task at hand. It may include planning or discussion time, but typically it also involves physically working together.

Debriefing

The debrief is an opportunity for the group members to discuss what happened, what went well, what roles people assumed, the ideas generated, group processes they liked/disliked, and what they would like to take from this activity into the next one, or into their "real-life" situation. Often, the facilitator will initiate some of this discussion by asking questions, but ideally the group members will generate their own questions, and discuss things with one another rather than "answering" the facilitator.

Transfer

The transfer occurs after the debrief, when group members are given the opportunity to apply something they have learned or identified in a previous debrief. For example, if a group decides that they want to employ certain norms for working together, such as always appointing a group leader or coordinator for each activity, the transfer could occur by presenting them with a task that allows them to try that process. Whether or not they actually implement their process, this leads to great debriefing with that next activity, and also allows the group to assess and revise their ideas.

How to set up initiative activities for use in a service-learning course

Often, it is useful for the facilitator to set up the initiative exercises with a story line that relates to the group's "real life" situation. Although great debriefing and transfer can occur with a more straightforward set up, the storylines can help make the connections clearer for groups who may not yet be functioning well as a unit, or for groups who less familiar with the experiential learning cycle. Compare the following two methods of setting up the same initiative.

Activity: Teeter Totter
Set up: Straightforward

"Your task here is to get your entire group balanced on this teeter totter at the same time. Each person must enter and exit at the fulcrum, and a person who is on the ground may not touch anyone who is up on the teeter totter. You will have five minutes to plan, but after your planning time is up, you may no longer talk. If either end of the teeter totter touches the ground at any time that any group member is on it, the entire group must dismount and begin again. The same will occur if anyone talks once your planning period is over. You will be given one additional planning period of two minutes. As a group you must choose when to use it, and you must tell me when this will be before you begin the activity."

Set up: Service-learning course scenario

"Over the course of the next semester, you will have a unique opportunity to work together as a group. Although you may all have different tasks to accomplish in that time, and you will most certainly have different experiences, you are also all connected as members of this class. In this challenge, the teeter totter represents your field placement experiences. Because we really need everyone to fully invest in this course to have everyone's experience be as good as possible, you must get your entire group balanced on the teeter totter at the same time for a count of fourteen (there are 14 weeks in the semester). If either end touches at any time, it represents an unfortunate incident that could occur this semester that affects some or all of the group members. Should this happen, the entire group must start all over.

"As you know, we will have a limited amount of class time in which to discuss people's placement experiences, and we will have to make good use of this time. Much of this discussion will occur in class, away from your field placement sites. Thus, you may only talk while you are all touching this tree (away from the teeter totter). At any given time in this activity, you must all either be touching the tree and planning, or you must all be at the teeter totter and silent. You may not split the group and have some plan while others get on. Should anyone talk while the group is away from the planning tree, the entire group must begin again."

I set up the Teeter Totter using the latter description above with my class. Actually, I chose to use course-specific scenarios for each of the three initiatives I used. This was partly due to the fact that I had not yet spent much time with this group of students, and I did not know how readily they would make connections between the activities and our course. Had I used initiatives again later in the term, I might have chosen a more straightforward or even fanciful approach, as then I was certain that they were well aware of the dynamics occurring within the class.

Piloting initiative activities in a Project Community course

The course I facilitate is called "Environmental Education with Preschoolers." In this course, my students and I meet once a week for two hours to discuss how young children perceive and interact with their environment, and how to utilize environmental education (EE) to heighten their "sense of wonder" with the natural world. Because this course if offered through the Department of Sociology, we also look at how certain sociological issues (such as family, gender, race and class) affect how these children are relating to their environment. My students spend four hours each week for eight weeks in a preschool setting. During one hour of each week, they lead a variety of EE activities with the youngsters. Although my students are not required to develop their own activities for these sessions, they are responsible for choosing appropriate ones from a variety of resources, and they prepare themselves and all the materials they need for each week's activities.

Much of our discussion time focuses on the students' field placement experiences. They compare notes with one another on a variety of issues, ranging from how successful certain activities were, to how boys and girls seem to perceive or interact with things differently at that age, to the different environments at each preschool and how they are related to the socioeconomic background of the families whose kids go there.

Because so much of the learning in this course takes place during the field placement, the degree to which my students can communicate with one another and their ability to help each other creatively address challenging situations can greatly impact the success of the course. It is with this goal in mind that I decided to use initiative activities as a tool for building the sense of community within our class that would enable my students to have the best semester possible. Although there are countless initiatives and variations available which could be adapted for such a setting, I chose to use three. I feel that these were particularly successful for our situation. What follows is a description of each activity and the subsequent discussions which arose from them.

Activity #1—Group Juggle with a Random Factor

Materials needed:	several stuffed animals or other soft, non-sports related objects
Time frame:	10-15 minutes

I start this activity by asking the group to stand in a circle. I tell them, "The first part of this challenge is to set up a pattern for a group juggle. We'll use "Louise" the stuffed lobster to do so. The lobster will start with me, and I'll toss her to someone across the circle from me to begin the pattern. Then that person will toss to someone who has not had the lobster yet, and it continues in that manner until everyone has had the lobster once and only once. The last person then tosses Louise back to me. Remember who you toss her to, and who tosses to you."

Once that pattern is established, we might practice it once to make sure we do indeed remember the pattern. At that point, I will describe the next part of the challenge. I show the group that I have several stuffed animals. I ask them to think of the animals as "tasks" they each need to accomplish or manage during the course of this semester. Managing a task is represented by "juggling" it through the pattern we have set up without dropping it. I ask them how many tasks they think we as a group can manage at the same time. Usually, people have different ideas about how many the group can really handle. Thus they need to come to a consensus. Once our goal is set, we attempt to juggle that many tasks. Once I have tossed the first animal, I quickly feed the correct number of additional stuffed animals, or tasks, into the juggle pattern. I usually let the tasks go through the juggle pattern 3-4 times. When an animal returns to me the third or fourth time, I drop it to my feet.

After the first attempt, we talk about what happened. Were there any dropped tasks or any mid-air collisions? Unless the group has set a goal which is way too easy, there invariably will have been. We then talk about ways to improve our quality, ranging from changing the process (toss it gently, underhand, call people's names, etc.) to changing the product (increasing or decreasing the number of tasks as is necessary). When we are ready, we try again, implementing any changes we have agreed upon. This discussion and refinement process may continue for several rounds.

When we have finally had a juggle which was relatively flawless, I introduce the "Random Factor," a juggle item which looks very different from the rest. This Random Factor could represent anything unexpected that comes up in day-to-day life that demands immediate attention. The stipulations are that when the Random Factor is introduced, it must be dealt with immediately, but it cannot be fed into the regular juggle pattern. Because it has special needs, it must be dealt with differently, and it cannot be tossed out of the circle or put into a pocket. As with the other tasks, dropping it represents not managing it. I do not allow the group to plan a mechanism for dealing with the Random Factor, we just begin the juggle again. After all regular tasks are in motion, I toss the Random Factor to someone. Then the mayhem begins. Most people react to the Random Factor by trying to get rid of it at once, often not checking to see whether the person they toss it to is ready or not. Common results of the introduction of the Random Factor are that other tasks get dropped and people abandon all of their customary practices (calling names, tossing gently, or whatever they have adopted as a group).

Usually, I will stop the action at some point when some of the tasks are on the ground. We discuss what is happening to the normal process. People often describe the panic they feel when they get the random factor, and their desire to get rid of it as soon as possible. They also talk about how the random factor took precedence over their normal tasks. I like to ask people to give examples of random factors they might encounter within their groups' "real life" setting.

My students mentioned people getting sick at the last minute before field placements, coming to class unprepared, personal emergencies that arise and take focus or time away from school work, children not responding to an EE activity they are leading, etc. We talked about how we would like to handle these random factors that could come up over the course of the semester. My students agreed that being in communication with one another in between class sessions was crucial, and they agreed to do so via the university's electronic mail system which is accessible to all students. They also decided that having a back-up plan for each day's EE activities was essential. We discussed how people felt having unexpected responsibilities tossed at them when they weren't prepared, as occurred with our random factor. They mentioned feeling angry, startled, and that they needed to put self-preservation as a priority over group harmony. Most people did not like how the random factor seemed to cause the group to lose its feeling of unity, and we agreed to try to avoid those situations whenever possible by communicating and planning for the unforeseen.

Activity #2—Teeter Totter

Materials needed:	two 2" X 10" X 10' boards, held together with duct tape to make a 4" X 10" X 10' teeter totter; one cinder block
Time frame:	twenty minutes

I used this activity to begin our second class session. I used the scenario described above for service-learning courses. The discussion that followed focused mostly on how to get everyone to buy into and stay invested in the course. It was in this discussion that my students developed a method for ensuring that each person would come to class prepared to discuss the week's readings. They decided to have a student facilitate the readings discussion each week.

That way, the students were responsible to each other, not just to me, and they would be putting the discussion leader in an awkward position by showing up ill-prepared to talk about the week's readings. It followed sort of a "Do unto others..." theme. No student wanted to have to lead a discussion where no one else was prepared, and thus each one was less likely to put another student in that situation.

Activity #3—The Minefield

Preparation—Set up a boundary for the pathway through which you want your group to pass. This boundary can be on the floor or raised (i.e., rope wrapped around tree trunks). Throw a variety of objects into the pathway (things like old pop cans, tennis balls, yogurt containers and the like work great —try to choose a variety of shapes and sizes). Make sure that there are enough objects to make travel through the minefield challenging, but not so many that it is virtually impossible. Approximately one item per square foot of minefield is a good guideline, but you can vary the level of challenge by adding or subtracting from this number. Be sure to make the entrance and exit clear. The entrance might be an opening in the boundary, and the exit might be a Frisbee or piece of paper that the traveler must step onto (or touch with a finger or their nose...be creative!) at the far end of the minefield. Having a very specific place for people to step as an exit ensures that their direction-giver will give them their full attention to the very end, as opposed to someone saying "take two more steps and you'll be out" as they walk away. It is nice for the traveler to be able to greet their direction-giver at the end, and helps to make people feel safer as they take off their blindfolds. Another interesting component is to add something about midway that they must either step over or crawl under. A slack piece of rope works well for this, and you can vary the height to make it an obvious "step over," an obvious "crawl under" or something about midway that different people will need to approach differently due to their own abilities/ limitations/preferences.

Procedure—Tell your group that this mess they see before them is a treacherous minefield (or whatever you want to call it). Their challenge is to get the entire group through successfully. They must enter at the entrance and leave through the exit (point out where each is and any specifics they need to know - i.e., you are safely out when you rest your chin on the squeaky toy on the chair at the far end, or whatever). The trick is that people may only travel through the minefield blindfolded, and they may only get <u>verbal</u> assistance. No one on the outside of the minefield may touch anyone on the inside. There is no limit to how many people may travel through at the same time, but don't tell them that. (Most groups will start with only one at a time thinking that it will be too confusing otherwise. They usually soon abandon that plan for a more efficient method which sends several through at once.)

If a person traveling through the minefield touches any part of the minefield (boundaries, strewn objects, etc.) they are frozen. The only way to become unfrozen is to have another blindfolded traveler tag or touch them.

The time limit depends on the number of people. Three minutes per person in the group usually works well, although once you get above 10 people, only add 2 more minutes for each additional person (for example, give a group of eight 24-25 minutes, a group of ten 30 minutes, and a group of fifteen 40 minutes). I usually give the group 3-5 minutes to plan before starting the official time. Some groups use this well and others do not—a great part of the discussion after the activity.

For my Project Community course I used the following scenario:

—Travel through the minefield represents their travel through this course over the next semester.
—The boundaries represent parameters set by the university within which we all must work (i.e., assignments, hours at placement).
—The strewn objects represent a variety of obstacles that each person might come across within the course or at their placement site. Don't tell them specific examples of what they might be, because that will be a great part of the discussion.
—The time limit represents the fact that the course is only a semester long, and that they have a lot to accomplish within that time frame.
—Although they are all taking this class and facing this minefield as a group, each person's experience will be different in both situations, and that as a group they must decide how to help each person's experience be the best it possibly can be.
—Tell them that, much like they are largely responsible for directing their own learning in Project Community courses, as a group they will be responsible for quality control in the minefield. In other words, tell them that you are not going to referee the activity, and that it is up to them as a group to monitor when people have touched a part of the minefield and are frozen.

Potential topics for discussion after the activity that tie things back in with your class, based on the discussion that resulted in my class:

Start by asking them if they enjoyed the activity. Let this part of the discussion flow if it is necessary for people to share their feelings (i.e., if it wasn't enjoyable for one person because they did not feel cared for while in the minefield, or if someone was particularly uncomfortable being blindfolded, etc.).

The strewn objects in the minefield represented a variety of obstacles that they might encounter over the course of the semester. Ask people to identify what some of those obstacles might be. How did they help each other with obstacles in the minefield, and how would they like to help each other with obstacles in the class?

Was it easier to be a blindfolded person or a direction-giver? (In most groups you will have some folks who preferred one and some the other). Why? Discuss leadership and followership, and the responsibilities of each. How can we take this into account in situations that arise in this course?

How was their quality control in the activity?

Have them rate their performance as a group from 1 to 5 (with 5 highest). If not all 5's are given, ask what they would like to see happen differently to improve things to all 5's. If all 5's are given, ask them to identify specifically why they feel that way.

Conclusion

At the end of the semester, I got feedback from my students about the course in general. They consistently identified the initiative activities as a key to helping them form the sense of community that helped us through some challenging situations. Specifically, they noted that they felt more willing to ask questions, and looked to each other as well as to me for answers or ideas. They also described a feeling of camaraderie with their fellow classmates that helped each one stay on track at one time or another. Perhaps more importantly, most of my students said they felt that they had adopted a new way of looking at things, and found that they were more aware of the power of "learning by experience" in other areas of their lives as well. All in all, the students felt that it had been one of the most enjoyable courses they had ever taken, and many attributed this to the feeling that as a group they had responded very well to the challenge of taking more responsibility for their learning experiences.

After using the above three activities in my class, my students were well prepared to take on many other responsibilities they would have over the course of the semester as well. These responsibilities were not limited to the course requirements, but their need to invest in the class, to communicate with one another, to ask for assistance from others, and to be willing to contribute questions and ideas to class discussions. Because service-learning courses such as the ones we offer through Project Community are so different from the students' experiences in their other courses, I feel that it is necessary to lay some groundwork prior to jumping into such a setting. As evidenced by their success with my students, initiative activities are certainly one way to lay this groundwork. Not only are they fun, but they serve to bring the group together and get them to think about and look at things creatively. What better way to enable students to connect with and contribute to their community, than to introduce them to the processes by which communities are built and continue to grow?

Chapter 5

PROMOTING SERVICE-LEARNING ON CAMPUS

By Jeanne M. Gray

Introduction

According to the recent study conducted by Gregory B. Markus, Jeffrey P. Howard, and David King,[1] "good deeds in the community are linked to good grades in the classroom." The students that were co-jointly engaged with a Political Science class as well as performing community service did better academically. They also reported that their course work was "more up to their potential" and that they were challenged to apply the principles of the course to new situations. They developed a greater understanding of "societal problems," and felt that the academic material that was learned was more pertinent to every day living.

"Markus regards his study as a good example of President Clinton's idea that community service enriches education by helping students not only take the lessons they learn in the classroom out into the community, but bring the lessons they learn in the community back into the classroom." The interest in community service learning based classrooms continues to grow in popularity across the country. More and more professors are stressing the importance of both academic learning, and experiences in the community that can enrich a student's academic growth as well as personal growth.

The Need for Promotion

A question which accompanies the growing awareness of the need for this type of learning is how to educate students about the availability of these types of programs. When students arrive on a new campus, they are bombarded with different activities and programs that they can participate in. There are sororities and fraternities. There are intramural sports. There are dorm parties. There are professors assigning incredible amounts of reading materials. There are all the different and interesting co-eds. In the overall adjustment to college life, community service learning courses can be easily overlooked—if not forgotten. For this reason, it is valuable to discuss different ways to advertise and recruit students to participate in community service learning programs.

I have had the advantage of being at all stages of the community service learning process and hopefully some of the methods that I have employed can prove to be useful to others trying to broaden campus awareness to these programs. I also had the assistance of Stacia Fredericks, a senior in the marketing program at the University of Michigan, who looked in depth at some different models of recruitment already in place at the University of Michigan.

Present Marketing Techniques

Marketing, as it currently exists in the Project Community office, takes a variety of different forms. Flyers are sent out to incoming students delineating the programs that exist. Ads are put in the student newspaper. There are mass meetings held at the beginning of each semester that provide information and recruitment for different segments of Project Community. Whereas all these methods can be effective, I believe that Project Community's success in recruitment comes primarily from "word of mouth." The rate of return is huge in Project Community courses. In the sections that I either participated in or coordinated, more then fifty percent of the class either continued the following semester in the same class, or sought out another service-learning activity. Coordinators can serve to recruit in this fashion, or direct students to other service learning classes. Students can also be directive in recruiting their friends to do the section. A good experience in a Project Community class can be one of the most effective recruiting methods available.

This form of advertisement, while being extremely valuable, is also limiting. It only encompasses a small percentage of the University population, who otherwise might be interested in community service learning. Promotion reaches only a segment of the University population that already have some ties to Project Community.

Project SERVE

Project SERVE is a two-fold program that has extremely effective marketing strategies. Project SERVE places students at various volunteer assignments throughout the community. They also sponsor different events campus-wide throughout the year. For example, they organize an Alternative Spring Break program in which students go to various major urban areas to volunteer in impoverished communities. Because their marketing techniques reach such a large number of students, I thought it would be valuable to examine some of the strategies they use.

Anita Bohn, the director of Project SERVE met with us to discuss some of the ways that they recruit students. For starters, SERVE has a specific position created for the promotion of SERVE on campus. This person's job is to advertise and recruit students to be involved. One of the most effective methods that SERVE uses is communicating with the dorms. For example, Project SERVE contacts the building directors and asks them to relay information about their organization to resident advisors who in turn, inform their residents. This can happen simply by word of mouth, or at a dorm meeting. Attending a residence hall meeting and speaking on the various programs can be very helpful in educating students for two reasons. First, this is a good way to reach a large number of students in a short period of time. Secondly by actually being there, or having someone there to represent the programs, students with questions can have them answered on the spot. Information sheets with phone numbers and contact people can be handed out so that students who wish to follow up may do so.

In a similar fashion, sororities and fraternities can be contacted and presentations can be made to them. Obtaining a list of the organizations is easy, and since Greek organizations generally have weekly house meetings, this is a perfect time to target this population. By actually having a representative present, the members may be less likely to overlook the opportunities that are available for service. The information sheets should be posted when the students move in, so that when a representative of the community service learning program comes to speak, the students are already somewhat familiar with the programs.

This is effective for a variety of reasons. The first is the "safety in numbers" theory. Students are more likely to enroll in a program if their friends are doing it as well. This is especially true for sites that they are a bit apprehensive about. When I taught a prison literacy site, I had a number of roommates who were involved. They said they felt "safer" going out to a site if they were with someone that they knew. Going into the "unknown " was easier if they were doing it with someone that they were familiar with.

Another reason that this method is effective is because it makes it easy to follow up with students. They may see a flyer or information sheet, but forget about it in the hustle and bustle of daily classes. By actually having someone speaking in person about the program, it is reinforced in the minds of the students. Also, any questions that the students may have can be addressed at that specific meeting.

Although this may appear to be incredibly time consuming, the work can be split up and delegated. In Project Community's current system, student coordinators are hired at the beginning of each semester Almost always, these are returning students that are familiar with many of the different programs that Project Community has to offer. As seminars do not usually start until the third week of the term, this could be a good time for the coordinators to be recruiting on this level.

Another method of advertisement that SERVE uses is the MTS system. "MTS" is the university-wide computer message system and can be accessed by all students. Messages can be sent out in an "umbrella organization" method which is basically targeting all members of various organizations and sending them an across the board message about a mass meeting, or a general information memo. The key time to use MTS or a similar message system is right before registration when students are tying to figure out their schedules or looking for another class to pick up.

Some Other Methods of Recruiting

The mass meeting is an extremely effective way of recruiting students. The mass meeting is held at the beginning of each term, and offers a large amount of information in a short period of time. One of the most important components of this meeting is actually having other students or coordinators there to talk to potential students. The potential students probably have been exposed to the basic divisions of Project Community such as School, Hospitals, Prisons, Chemical Dependency, and Youth-at-Risk. But what they don't know is the actual happenings of the course. It is incredibly valuable to have coordinators there who have already done the site, to answer questions such as "where will I be working?" or "what will I be doing?" Having coordinators describe their experiences can also help to sway potential students that are uncertain of what they want to do or where they want to go.

Similar to this are the orientation meetings held for incoming students. Generally, there is a specific time or "information" fair delegated for students to be exposed to organizations such as this. Having a representative and information sheets at these events can serve to alert students about the program, as well as answer questions about the programs. Again, I believe that specificity is important in advertising community service learning. An incoming freshman may not have a clue about what service-learning means, but having someone there talking about their actual experiences tutoring at a federal prison is a very specific and compelling influence.

The publication organizations at a specific university can also be used as a source of advertisement. The daily paper can serve to advertise the actual programs as well as the mass meetings. It also can serve to help define what is meant by community service learning in the context of the university. The radio stations can be utilized to broadcast ads that talk about specific sites. I think that the daily paper can be used in much the same fashion. A weekly expose', for example, could be used to highlight one particular section.

I believe that all of these publication methods need to be very specific. For instance, rather than talking about the "community service learning classes" available, I think it would be more effective to target a specific area, such as education. The term "community service learning" is a bit vague, and can be confusing to someone leafing through a paper. However, if you talk about a specific site, such as "adult literacy" and explain what it is that you will be doing, students will be more likely to respond. Once they do, other sites can be introduced.

The method that proved to be most effective for my sites was going to related classes offered by the University and discussing the opportunities to serve. This was especially true with new sites. For example, last semester we opened an "elderly" site which was composed of working with elderly citizens in the community. Early in the semester, I contacted the professors of classes concerning aging and discussed the site with them. Most of them were receptive, and invited me into the class to talk to the students. One class in particular was doing a research project about that required the students to work with an elderly person during the semester. So, the site fit in perfectly with what the professor was trying to achieve.

I also targeted beginning Sociology courses. Although the classes were not directly related to "juvenile justice" or "prison literacy", most sociology classes touch upon these issues, and the experiences that students have in these sites can serve as a valuable tool along with the class. The Sociology professors that I dealt with were very supportive of this, and encouraged their classes to participate, again often times creating assignments to match the site that the particular students were involved in.

Creating and maintaining this type of relationship with professors can prove to be very valuable. I believe that there is a tension between disciplines that stems from ignorance Many professors are uncertain of what Project

Community is all about, and may regard community service learning as an easy way to get academic credit. By involving them in the process, and allowing them to see the personal growth experienced by students, professors can gain a better understanding of what is actually done in community service learning.

A Commitment to Promotion

Right now, Project Community does not have a specific ad campaign, each area of service is primarily in charge of recruiting their own students. Again, this method is effective and should not be ignored. However, I believe that as an organization, any service-learning program can benefit by having one specific division whose job is promotion on campus. There is a direct relationship between credibility and numbers. What I mean is that it is more difficult for a university to cut back on the budget of a class whose size continues to increase. Unfortunately, we are all victims of this system, and in order for community service learning to be valued, the numbers of students involved needs to be consistent.

All of the techniques that we have discussed are incredibly time consuming for the already over-burdened directors. I think that the coordinators can pick up some of the recruitment tasks, as I have pointed out, however, we should not rely primarily on them. I think that it would be valuable to have a position with that primary focus. This would bring together all the individual efforts for recruitment, and free up the directors to do other tasks. It would also prevent the "cross over" of recruitment efforts. I think another important aspect of this job would be the promotion of community service learning outside of the university setting.

Right now, I think that the community is uninformed about the services that are provided by students. A public relations person could educate and include the surrounding community in the service-learning activities performed in that specific community. After all, the community benefits from this as well as the student, and an integration of the two would be beneficial for both

These are just some of the ideas that we had about promotion. I think that the primary focus should be "getting the word out" to all students. The experiences provided by community service learning programs are invaluable. I can attribute much of my educational growth to these programs, as well as most of my personal growth throughout my college years. Community service learning programs provide an opportunity for students to experience situations that they would never be otherwise exposed to. It also creates an environment for students to actually practice what they are being taught. For these reason, I believe a commitment should be made on campuses to promote these programs on a large scale, to reach out to students campus-wide and provide them with this opportunity to learn and grow.

NOTES

1. Markus' version of this study appears in Praxis I.

PART THREE

Off to See the Wizard

Foreword

THE WIZARD WITHIN

As we are transported from the ordinary ways of learning and teaching that dominates the traditional university landscape, and as we enter the visionary world of Project Community, we need to find new and different pedagogies. Our best companions on this journey will be a compassionate understanding of our own and our students' feelings, the wisdom to know how to translate this understanding into teaching/learning strategies, and a stout heart full of courage to risk new approaches with our students. Our goal is to find and cherish the "wizard" within each of us...and within each of our students.

In this volume, this roadmap for the pedagogical traveler, Joseph Galura has gathered much useful wisdom about teaching and learning, and about facilitating others' learning. He also provides us with some very practical tools and many examples of how we may work with students in ways that help them collaborate with peers and take an active role in the learning process. Joe has not done this task alone: he has used lessons learned from generations of Project Community facilitators, thus empowering them and all of us with their insights, down-to-earth suggestions, and on-the-spot inventions. Readings and suggested seminar activities are tightly linked and feed off each other.

Off to See the Wizard is a wonderful resource, organized and presented in a caring and useful manner. Although it is written most explicitly for Project Community staff and students working with the Sociology Department, it would be useful and should be read by undergraduate facilitators, graduate teaching assistants and faculty throughout the University. It is a starting point, and each of us may use and build off this resource with our own ideas and practical experiences in mind.

Best,

Mark Chesler

Mark Chesler
Arthur F. Thurnau Professor of Sociology
Director of Undergraduate Studies
Department of Sociology
University of Michigan, Ann Arbor

Introduction

"WELCOME TO THE TWILIGHT ZONE!"

> *The most important part of the new edition, however, would be "Welcome to the Twilight Zone!" When I went to my first staff meeting[1], I came out dazed and confused. What is "Jeopardy!"[2]? Does it relate to Project Community? Am I supposed to talk during process time[3]? What do I say? Should I tell them the truth or tell them everything is fine? After our first meeting, I thought there was no way I was passing—let alone getting a good grade in this class! I was also mad at Marni Levine (my coordinator) for letting me come to this strange place! She said it was fun—well, don't worry: it is fun once you get into the groove!*
>
> *—Claudia Philips*

My goal in writing this edition of Off to See the Wizard was to make the content and format of the text more accessible to an audience beyond the Chemical Dependency and Criminal Justice coordinators who work with me each semester. With this in mind, the chapters, when applicable, now contain the following four features:

Focus Questions—Written by Sociology Teaching Assistants Pauline Gianoplus and Sabrina Tyuse, these questions appear at the beginning of Chapters 3 through 13. The questions are meant to help coordinators prepare for their seminar by focusing on the key points of that week's assigned reading. Each chapter in this text corresponds to one week on the syllabus

Discussion Activities—Small group exercises, based on the readings, are described in the text. These activities are the same for students in Chemical Dependency and Criminal Justice in Chapters 1, 2, 3, 4, 8, 13 and 14: in the remaining chapters, activities are separated according to Criminal Justice and Chemical Dependency.

Coordinator Comments—Italicized and usually following the Discussion Activities, these reflections on the course are taken from journals, term papers and course evaluations over the years. I have often been told that these remarks are the most helpful aspect of the text.

Suggested Journal Questions—Potentially, coordinators could assign these questions to their students to follow-up their discussion from seminar. Some students have found it helpful to write about how their site and seminar experiences connect with the course pack in their journals. Once a semester, I publish excerpts from students' journals in The Chronicle, the office newsletter.

I wanted to conclude with these comments from two former coordinators:

> *I've found it very helpful to discuss the various options for activities before using them. I guess most of all, it's been very reassuring to have the book as a sort of map to where to go with seminar. Initially, I had feared that designing a seminar would be completely up to me. While I am glad that I still have flexibility in where to take it, I'm relieved to have the book as a guide. I suppose that, in a way, it also enhances my sense of community with the other coordinators. That is, I can read a chapter and base a seminar on it and realize that everyone else is doing the same thing (not exactly, I realize). It helps me even more to know that "we're all in this together." Earlier, I compared the book to a map. To further the analogy, I might say that Wizard is a road map that takes you to "Project Communityville", while staffing is like the specific directions that guide you to "Seminar Street."*
>
> —*Ben Macrory*

> *I'd like my successor to relax. You'd be surprised at how forgiving your students are—and you'd be surprised at how fast you'll learn. Be open. Let students' concerns, ideas and thoughts guide your seminar. Once you address these problems, you can focus on the things you need to teach. You'll also be amazed at how much they teach themselves (and you) if you let them. Don't lose sight of your objective. Keep the big picture in mind and setbacks won't seem like failures. Remember, it's a process. Everyone will grow and learn together. Mistakes will be made, but use them as an opportunity to grow.*
>
> —*Rachel Story*

NOTES

1. "Staff meetings" or "staffings" are my terms for coordinators' weekly seminars with the teaching assistant and program director. One rule of thumb I use is to schedule them for 90 minutes for a group of ten or more and an hour for a group of less than ten.
2. "Jeopardy!"—Rick Smith once told me that my staffings resembled "a bad game show." One reason for this is my "Jeopardy!"-style format: I open, close and introduce each item on the agenda with trivia questions. The trivia has a common theme and some connection with the agenda item. For example, a "Jeopardy!" theme for the staffing on icebreakers could be "Famous First Lines."
3. "Process Time"—Usually, this is the middle third of the staffing. Coordinators are invited to reflect on this week's site, seminar or any related Project Community business. I usually

reference the norms generated in Chapter Three before Process Time begins: course evaluations usually rate Process Time as the one item most helpful in preparing students for their role as coordinators.

Chapter 1

THE MASS MEETING[1]
"But I'm Not Catholic!"

Hi, everybody! This is Chris, and I'm a junior at this University majoring in history. More specifically, I study Byzantine History and American Diplomacy, an odd mix, I know. It's a much-told story by now, but I can't help indulging in it again about how I got involved with Project Community. So here it is again. In mid-September of last year, I was enrolled in a Comparative Literature class here. The Teaching Assistant was an overly-pompous woman with oversized glasses and a terribly phony French accent. After two class meetings, we probably went at it a half-dozen times before I finally blew my top. We were reading the works of Walter Benjamin and discussing them when I got involved in the discussion, I referred to him as Walter BEN-JAH-MIN and was reprimanded because it was correctly pronounced BEN-HEE-MENE. I thought that sounded more like a cough medicine than a last name, so I continue to refer to him as BEN-JAH-MIN. Finally, she demanded to know whether I had the ability to pronounce his name the correct way. I just packed up my stuff, mumbled a couple of obscenities in her direction and never came back. The next day, I realized that I only had 11 credits so I went to Angell Hall to try to find another class that interested me. I was having a lot of trouble finding something good, so I decided to leave. Outside of the Fishbowl, I saw Aaron Romain walking toward something he called a "Mass Meeting." Aaron listened to my problem and invited me to the Mass Meeting. At first I declined, telling him, "I'm not Catholic," but then, all joking aside, I went upstairs, greeted Joe Galura with my sometimes brisk ignorance and decided that Project Community is for me! I hadn't seen Aaron for five months before that day, and needless to say, it was a very opportune time to run into him.

—Chris Wright[2]

The goal of the Mass Meeting is for my staff to recruit and orient 80-120 students to the Chemical Dependency and Criminal Justice sections of Project Community. The information disseminated to students in-

cludes: options for site placement, academic and administrative course requirements.

An Overview of the Course

The Mass Meetings are scheduled for 90 minutes during the first Monday evening of each semester, in a room large enough to hold approximately 100 students. As students enter the room, they are handed a copy of The Chronicle, the office newsletter based on journals and course evaluations from past students in the Chemical Dependency and Criminal Justice sections of Project Community.

I open the meeting formally by introducing myself and then reading the Office of Community Service Learning Mission Statement.

> *The Office of Community Service Learning is committed to student involvement in community service and social action, both to improve the lives of those in need as well as to enhance student learning and development. By engaging in service and complementary active scholarship, students grow in social responsibility, assess personal values, develop critical thinking skills and come to better understand themselves. Students serve individuals in the community who experience social inequalities, and learn with, from and about them.*

I then outline the course requirements. The specifics are outlined at the end of this chapter. This handout was developed at the suggestion of Claudia Philips and Amy Rotberg during the Fall '92 term.

Randy Ross suggested having all the coordinators sit at the front of the room, at a table, in the order in which they are to speak, once I am done outlining the course requirements. At this point in the meeting, coordinators usually describe their favorite aspects of their site experience. In response to the Winter '93 Mass Meeting[3], I have further suggested that, as a staff, (1) we pause only for questions after each coordinator has described her or his site and (2) that site and seminar times, section name and number, and the number of credits are posted on placards in front of each coordinator.

Excerpts From The Winter '93 Mass Meeting Confer[4]

> *As I left our staffing[5] last week, I felt adequately prepared for the Mass Meeting. I was wrong! I didn't realize that I would have to speak to the entire group (approximately 100 students) about my section. I'm sure, though, that I did a great job of concealing my fear and anxiety—right, Joe?*
>
> —*Mary Jo Callan*

> *I was really impressed with the attendance. There should be a more organized system of referring people to other sections. Rick Smith and I were at a loss when so many people came to us for overrides because we hadn't discussed how to handle that. We ended up turning some people away and getting some*

extra overrides. Afterwards, we realized that our section will be much more difficult with such a big group, and I wish we had encouraged people to talk with other coordinators at the Mass Meeting, because now it's too late.

—Stacey Brown

As I stood up after the formal part of the Mass Meeting, I figured that everybody would walk right past me to another section. I imagined myself like a carnival barker, shouting "section 36, get your section 36, right here, right now!" But then something happened. Somebody tapped me on the shoulder. Yes. Inspiration. "Is this section 35?" Oh, no! "No, sorry, this is 36." Frown. "Oh, can you direct me to the guy that's doing that South Seventh project?" "Yeah, that's me." Smile. And then I looked around. There had to be at least ten people with hands extended, looking for an override. I panicked. "Uh, hold on." O.K. What do I do? "Joe!!!" He's surrounded! "Hey, Randy." He's busy, too. A critical moment was this, as I watched one of my potential students walk away. My fundamental problem was how to determine who gets overrides.

—Chris Wright

Yes, I agree. Also, we should be more organized about knowing which sections are open when people stop by or call the office after the Mass Meeting. Yes, the prior staff meeting prepared me for the Mass Meeting, however...I talked to one coordinator who didn't even know that a staffing was scheduled. In the future, we should make every effort to contact everyone right when we get back from break.

—Stacey Brown

I think the idea of having placards or signs or something to indicate your section is a good idea. And if nobody does this, at least I'll do it when I coordinate next year, and I'll watch my section fill up quickly and painlessly (hopefully!).

—Chris Wright

Academic and Administrative Requirements

Because Sociology 389 is a course based on experiential learning, student participation is required in all aspects of the class. Academic credit is awarded on a credit/no credit basis. Students are expected to read and discuss the specified articles at seminar, respond to their coordinator's questions in weekly journals, attend site and seminar each week, and successfully complete two paper assignments.

One absence from either site or seminar will be excused during the term. Two absences require the student to arrange make-up work with her or his coordinator. Three absences place the student's credit in jeopardy and require a meeting with the program director and/or the teaching assistant. It is the student's responsibility to initiate meetings regarding her or his standing in the course: any uncompleted work is the basis for not receiving academic credit.

First and second papers are due in the Project Community office during the weeks of your sixth and twelfth seminars, respectively. Papers are graded on a mastery basis. That is to say that papers which the teaching assistant judges to insufficiently address the key sociological aspects of the course will be returned for students to re-write. At that point, it is the student's responsibility to contact the teaching assistant for further clarification. Incomplete paper assignments are the basis for not receiving credit in this course.

Syllabus for Sociology 389

Chemical Dependency and Criminal Justice Sections
(Complete references appear in the Bibliography)

First Seminar
Chemical Dependency
Napier and Whitaker, The Family Crucible (1988)
Criminal Justice
Bayse, Helping Hands (1993) and MCCD Executive Summary (1993)

Second Seminar
Introduction: What Is the PC Pedagogy? Howard (1990) and Kahn

Third Seminar
What Is the Sociological Imagination? Peck (1978) and Mills (1959)

Fourth Seminar
Chemical Dependency: What Is the Disease Concept?
Olhms (1981) and Wallace (1989)
Criminal Justice: What Are Some Liberal and Conservative Perspectives on Crime?
Walker (1985), Herrnstein and Wilson (1985), Kime and Wanger (1993), Ansley (1992)

Fifth Seminar
Chemical Dependency: Should Drugs Be Legalized?
Greve (1989), Beale (1989), Bush (1989), Forsgren (1989), Meadors (1989), Shine and Mauer (1993)
Criminal Justice: Drugs and Crime—Is There a Link?
Shine and Mauer (1993), Rosenblatt (1982)

Sixth Seminar
Chemical Dependency: 12 Step Programs—Cure Or Cover?
Herman, Bufe, Perrin and Colemann, Peele, Collett, Berenson, Schaef (all 1988)
Criminal Justice: Does the System Promote Racial Inequality?
Williams (1991), McIntosh (1989) and Collins (1983)

Seventh Seminar
The PC Pedagogy: What Is Our Midterm Evaluation? Freire (1970)

Eighth Seminar
Chemical Dependency: What Is Codependency?
Haaken (1993) and Black (1982)
Criminal Justice: How Do their Social Roles Influence Correctional Staff?
Haney and Zimbardo (1973), Roush (1990) and DeShaw (1992)

Ninth Seminar
Chemical Dependency: How Do Roles Develop In an Addict's Family?
Epstein and Epstein (1990), Black (1982)
Criminal Justice: Do the Poor Get Prison?
Reiman (1984), Deparle (1990), Flynn (1991), Gilbert (1993)

Tenth Seminar
Chemical Dependency: Codependency—Any Personal Implications For Me?
Lamb (1990) and Beattie (1987)
Criminal Justice: What Does Incarceration Accomplish?
Krajik and Gettinger (1982), Frelberg (1990), Salerno (1991) and Hengesh (1991)

Eleventh Seminar
Chemical Dependency: What Is Incremental Intervention?
Muldoon and Crowley (1986), NASW News (1990)
Criminal Justice: How Can the System Be Improved?
Schorr (1988), Martin (1982), Nidorf (1989), Barton/Streit/Schwartz (1991), Mauer (1992)

Twelfth Seminar
The PC Pedagogy: What Are Our Final Reflections? Palmer (1987)

Chemical Dependency Paper Assignment # 1

This paper will draw on your site experiences and the concept of systems theory as described in The Family Crucible (1988) and discussed in our paper meetings. It has two parts:1. In the first part of the paper describe any three systems **except the family system** which affect you, *and* how you are a part of them. Be sure to explain why you're defining your systems as systems. What makes each one its own system? In this section of the paper your understanding of systems theory should be clearly illustrated. 2. In the second part of the paper discuss how your position in each of these three systems affects your participation at your particular Project Community site. You might think about how life experience in those systems influences your approach to site and the people there. In doing so it may be helpful to compare and contrast your various positions in society's systems to other people's, especially the people's at site.

The paper should be 5-7 double-spaced, typed pages (1,250-1,750 words). No bibliography is necessary if your only source is The Family Crucible (1988).

Chemical Dependency Paper Assignment # 2

For your second paper you may select either one of the alternatives offered below. Your paper should be 4-5 double-spaced pages (1,000-1,250 words).

A. In the second paper I ask you to analyze and evaluate your Project Community experience this semester. Using Palmer's (1987) concepts of community and conflict ("Community, Conflict and Ways of Knowing: Ways to Deepen Our Educational Agenda"), evalulate Project Community. How does the Project Community structure facilitate the type of learning environment which Palmer advocates, and how doesn't it? If you feel that we haven't achieved Palmer's ideal, how would you change things? When considering these points, remember to talk about how the various components of Project Community—site, seminar and the readings—affect the overall learning community. Please draw on your concrete, real life experiences to illustrate points.

OR

B. In this paper you will analyze and evaluate your Project Community experience in light of Howard's four areas of experiential learning (see Jeffrey Howard "On Experiential Learning")[6]. That is, how did Project Community compare to Howard's ideals for 1. contextual learning, 2. academic learning, 3. socio-emotional learning, and 4. experiential learning? When considering these points, remember to think about how the various components of Project Community—site, seminar and the readings—affect each of Howard's learning areas. In writing this paper, please draw on the specifics of your site and seminar.

Criminal Justice Paper Assignment # 1

The requirements for this semester are to rewrite:

Daniel J. Bayse's Helping Hands: A Handbook for Volunteers in Prisons and Jails. Kirby Lithographic Company, Arlington, Va, 1993.

This will be done in two stages or rather two papers. The first paper should begin with a thorough reading of C. Wright Mills' "Promise" (1959). Next demonstrate your understanding of Mills by writing at least two or more paragraphs summarizing his work. Now how does this understanding of Mills drive your rewriting of Helping Hands? This paper can consist of an outline of the sections and chapters you intend to change or modify in some way. In this paper you should include examples of what, how, and why you are proposing to make these changes.

This paper should be approximately 2-5 pages (500-1,250 words) and should be typed or word processed.

Criminal Justice Paper Assignment # 2

Paper two (2) will consist of your final draft of the rewrite of Daniel J. Bayse's Helping Hands: A Handbook for Volunteers in Prisons and Jails. Kirby Lithographic Company, Arlington, VA, 1993.

This paper should draw on at least 3 relevant readings from the coursepack and can include outside reading as well but this is not a requirement. I suggest you use C. Wright Mills' "The Promise" (1959) and two additional articles from the following list:

1. Reiman, And the Poor Get Prison (1984)
2. Williams The Alchemy of Race and Rights (1991)
3. "Rehabilitation is effective if done well" (1990)
4. "A Blueprint for Youth Corrections" (1991)
5. Friere, Pedagogy of the Oppressed (1970)

Each student should draw on and include personal experiences from their particular site as well.

This final paper can only be accomplished successfully after a thorough reading of Helping Hands. Since Chapter 1 of Helping Hands includes information and facts that do not change over time, you may decide not to make any changes to that chapter.

This paper will require a significant amount of reading, writing, and typing on your part, and it is therefore necessary to begin work on this paper at the beginning of the semester. I can be reached during office hours, by phone, or e-mail to answer questions or to discuss the paper assignments further.

The final paper should be typed or word processed with necessary citations and bibliography page(s).

NOTES

1. "Mass Meeting"—Only the Criminal Justice and Chemical Dependency sections of Project Community hold Mass Meetings. The remaining sections enroll students during Early Registration of the previous term or during the current term's Drop/Add period, usually the first three weeks of the semester. Personally, I prefer having a Mass Meeting at which students are informed about the course and recruited into specific sections. The biggest advanatage of this is that the Mass Meetings set a definite starting point that lends a sense of urgency to planning first staff meetings, seminars and site visits.
2. Chris Wright is writing here as a student in Sociology 389: later in this chapter, he will be writing as a coordinator. Quotations in italics are generally from coordinators, unless otherwise noted.
3. I ran two or three Mass Meetings per term during the Fall '91, Winter '92 and Fall '92 semesters. Winter '93 was the first time I scheduled only one Mass Meeting.
4. "Confer" is an electronic mail computer program that allows a group of people to read and comment on a given item.
5. At UM, the semester generally starts on a Thursday. In preparation for the Mass Meeting on the first Monday in a term, I schedule the first staffing on the first day of class.
6. Kahn's "Some Thoughts About Seminars" and Howard's "On Experiential Learning" are unpublished articles, reproduced and distributed by this office.

Chapter 2

DON'T BREAK THE ICE

First Seminar

The goal of the first seminar is for the seminar to have a" meaningful group experience" by participating in one of the group activities outlined in the chapter. My hope is that this group experience will foreshadow what students will eventually read about regarding the process of teaching and learning in Palmer (1987), Freire (1970), and Kahn and Howard (1990).

It is suggested that coordinators read Palmer's "Community, Conflict and Ways of Knowing"(1987)[1]. When students read Palmer for the last seminar, the activity will call for them to reflect on their learning process throughout the semester.

It is easy for a coordinator to get caught up in the busy work during the first seminar—the paper blizzard and questions about site, among other things. Still, I believe that the most important objective at that first meeting is for the seminar to have "a meaningful small group experience."

To help coordinators arrive at a definition of this for themselves, in the past I've lectured on the Johari Window[2] and Stages of Group Development (at the end of Chapter Two)[3] during staffings. I've also suggested making a statement to your students during the first meeting like, "Most of your educational experience may have focused on individual competition: in our seminar, I would like our emphasis to be on group/community cooperation."

Specific icebreaker activities have varied from term to term, but the following are exercises that coordinators have used most frequently in their first seminar.

The Coat of Arms

During the Winter '89 Term, I introduced the Coat of Arms at our staff meetings. The categories (see chart on page 109) I set up are influenced by the Johari Window, but can be modified for your seminar. Coordinators can also decide whether to have their group draw pictures or write in their answers for each category. My preference is to encourage people to draw, which requires group members to relate to each other in an offbeat way.

I thought the second staffing went amazingly well. For a group that was complaining that 8:30 a.m. was too early, everyone seemed up for the dialogue during the Coat of Arms activity. I had never done the exercise in my many years with PC and was pleasantly surprised at the openness. It is true that you may not see any of the works in the Detroit Institute of Arts, or any other museum, for that matter, but that was not the point of the activity.

—Randy Ross

I love the Coat of Arms because every time I've done it, I've been the only one with a strong drawing background.

—Rick Smith

The Johari Window

During the '89/'90 academic year, I introduced two different versions of the Partner Interview at our staffings. In Partner Interviewing, the group is split into dyads. Each student in the pair takes a turn interviewing his/her partner. The activity concludes with each student introducing his/her partner to the whole group. This activity allows each group member to get to know one other person reasonably well, but later brings the seminar together as a whole.

During Fall '89 staffings, I lectured on the Johari Window. Basically, the Johari Window is a theoretical construct that represents a person's interaction within a group. The "window" has four quadrants that form a 2 x 2 matrix. Along the horizontal or x-axis are "things that other people know about me." Along the vertical or y-axis are "things that I know about myself." Thus, the intersection of the axes creates the following four quadrants:

1) Open/Public—Things that other people know about me that I also know about myself.
2) Secret/Hidden—Things that other people do not know about me that I know about myself.
3) Blind Spots—Things that other people know about me that I don't know about myself.
4) Unconscious—Things that other people don't know about me that I don't know about myself.

After explaining each quadrant, I had coordinators write out questions appropriate for that quadrant—for example, name? project? major? hometown? etc. are questions in the public quadrant. These coordinator-generated questions would then form the basis for the Partner Interview.

Whereas this may be a good way to help people understand the Johari Window, and even though the activity did seem to work in staffings, one problem with the activity in a seminar setting was that some of the questions the exercise generated could make some people uncomfortable.

On the Fall '89 Staffing Evaluations, coordinators commented:

The Johari Window was a useful introduction into the

semester...The Johari Window...really helped to get us started.

The Time Line

During Winter '90, I introduced the Time Line variation of the Partner Interview to coordinators at the staffings. The Time Line is actually three parallel lines that cover the last four months in a person's life. Basically, each person charts the significant events in his or her partner's life in the following areas:

World Events

School Events

Personal Notes

"World/School events" is meant to help students connect with Mills (1959) when that reading comes up later in the term. "Personal" is a catch-all category for anything that doesn't fit in the first two categories. Instruct the interviewer to chart a minimum of one or two events in each category.

> *This was the best icebreaker that [I] had ever seen.*
> —*Dora Brantley*

Joan Scott thought this could also be a good closure activity, with the first category being changed to Project Community.

> *This is just my opinion, and you can take it or leave it. But I really hate Partner Interviewing. I think that it is worse than introducing yourself. I'll agree it does have advantages, but I personally have a dislike for it...At least at times, when I've experienced Partner Interviewing, it still seemed that the tension did not really dissolve. It was mostly mechanical.*
> —*Kathy Garcia*

Empty Your Wallets

Kathy Russell, Laurance Polatsch and Marc Zeplin had their seminars "empty their wallets" as an icebreaker. The idea is that each person takes three items out of their wallet (or purse or book bag) and explains to the group the personal significance of each item. One advantage of having people introduce themselves to the group this way is that it allows them to "come into the group" at their own comfort level.

Marc and Laurence's successors, Andrew Kramer, Julie Mathews, Elaine Murphy and David Oppenheim, were very enthusiastic about this icebreaker. It was used in most seminars during the '90/'91 academic year with almost universal success.

A Vast Wasteland

This icebreaker was inspired by Andrew Kramer and David Oppenheim's activity—"what are your three favorite cartoons?" My version calls for people to list three to five of their favorite television shows or events, and then talk about their personal connection to these events or shows. I concluded by giving coordinators a list of TV's Single Most Memorable Programs[3], from the Sienna Research Institute's Survey, "The Best of the First Fifty Years of Television" (1939-1989)—the list is reprinted below. My hope was that people could relate their lists to the broader social context, thus preparing them for Mills (1959).

1. The Assassination of JFK
2. Moon Walk
3. "Roots"
4. Challenger Disaster
5. "See It Now"
6. "The Day After"
7. Final Episode of MASH
8. "The Prisoner"
9. "Harvest of Shame"

> *The activity, Favorite TV Shows, is great. I believe using it the first seminar and Empty Your Wallets the second seminar is a good idea. Using Favorite TV Shows first allows you to learn something about the person, but the person doesn't have to be too personal. The Empty Your Wallets game allows you to learn more about people and you can be as personal as your want.*
>
> *—Korey Miller*

Building A Whatsis

This activity gives the group a specific time to build a Whatsis—some type of object like a collage, or a sculpture or whatever the imagination can come up with—using newspapers, masking tape, scissors and markers. At the end of that time, people are asked to reflect on the meaning of the Whatsis for the group. The activity's goal is to have seminar members discover their group's unique pattern of interaction.

Jennifer Rabiah usually left the room after assigning the Whatsis to her seminar. Liz Rosenberg divided her seminar into two groups and told them each to build a house of cards.

> *The exercises themselves were generally helpful—the Whatsis was particularly good at inspiring togetherness and cooperation.*
>
> *—Ben Macrory*

Julie Zelman's "Whom To Leave Behind?"

During the Fall '91 and Winter '92 semesters, Julie Zelman led this activity in her Court Watching seminars. First, Julie passed out the following information to her group members.

"The eight persons listed below have been selected for a flight to another planet because tomorrow the planet Earth is doomed for destruction. Due to changes in space limitations, it has now been determined that only five persons may go. Any five persons qualify...You are to select the three people to be left behind on your own. Then, together with your group, come up with another list of people to be left behind...If your list was in disagreement with the group's list, you may be called on to explain why your choice(s) were different."

—An accountant
—A biochemist
—A liberal arts coed
—An armed policeman
—A Black medical student
—A pro basketball player
—An accountant's pregnant wife
—An intelligent female movie star

Julie Zelman's Whom to Leave Behind? provided immediate discussion and good group interaction.

—Greg Richards

I did this activity at my second seminar because I felt it was a great way for people to communicate and work in groups. Instead of having them decide which people were to be left behind, I assigned each student to act as that specific person (on the list). Therefore, three people would actually be sacrificing their own lives for the group.

I split the class into two groups and assigned one person in each group to be one of the characters. At the end of class they explained to each other who they chose to leave behind and why.

—Julie Zelman

The Dream Celebrity Softball Match

This icebreaker was inspired by a "Guindon" cartoon with the following caption: "The Dream Celebrity Softball Match—Socrates, Plato, DaVinci, Bach, Shakespeare, Galileo, Aristotle, Nietzsche and Jane Austen play the jocks from WLLZ."

In this activity, group members first individually create their own "Dream Teams" and then attempt to come to a single, consensus all-star team. I presented the following initial choice to my group at the CJ Winter '92 staffing:

Pitcher	Paulo Freire
Catcher	Anne Wilson Schaef
First Base	Cecil Fielder
Second Base	Joe Galura
Third Base	Moses
Shortstop	Jesus
Left Field	Jane Addams
Right Field	Elton John
Center Field	George Lucas
Manager	Pericles

Jane Klaes wanted Geronimo (and his horse) to play Center Field, Courtney Loveman nominated Jason Priestly to be our team mascot and Tom Cook thought that having both Nietzsche and God on our team would "keep things from getting dull." Jenny Kellman did this icebreaker in her section. Jeff Salinger, then a student in Jenny's section, liked the exercise, noting:

> *...it got people to reveal a lot about themselves without really having to talk about themselves.*

First Seminar Coordinator Reflections

> *Seminar: friendship, sympathy, support, unity, community, etc. That's my goal for the seminar. I want us to become a team that likes and enjoys working together. I want people to feel what it's like to be part of a healthy, functioning group. And I want us to feel the power of our love and commitment to each other and at site. In a word, I want our seminar to be empowering!*
>
> *—Rebecca Story*

> *I am looking forward to my first seminar this upcoming Tuesday, I cannot wait to introduce others to such a unique and profound experience by participation in Project Community. Excitement, however, is usually accompanied by some form of apprehension. My apprehension relates to my first encounters with a group. Sometimes I feel a little self-conscious—like all eyes are on me! In this instance, however, I do not feel as apprehensive as usual because I feel like I know the ropes and that adds to my security. My own feeling of self-consciousness is something I have to deal with myself, within myself. And, what I have realized through experience is that just because I may feel a certain way does not mean I have to act on it. This may be a secret part of me, in terms of the Johari Window, maybe something I might want to share later in the semester or perhaps on the first day of seminar! The Johari Window was certainly a beneficial experience and I plan to use that as my icebreaker activity for seminar.*
>
> *—Wendy Lassen*

> *Actually, I am rather anxious, as well as excited, about our first seminar. I think back at our first seminar with Prentice and smile. Sure, it was a little tense, like all first meetings tend to be, but I left there with a good feeling. The reason I left there with a good feeling was primarily due to knowing Prentice really cared about our Project, and that he cared about us—as individuals and as a group. If Rebecca and I can convey this sincerity and enthusiasm, then I will feel that our seminar and leadership were successful, as well as feel confident that we are*

off to a good, healthy start .

—Amanda Carlson

I really enjoyed my first seminar. Going into it, I had lots of ideas—things to do, say, etc..., and most of them were based on the thought that COMMUNITY BUILDING IS IMPORTANT. So that although we got to the essential administrative things, we focused mostly on "who am I?" and "who are you?." I liked that, and upon reading their journals, they liked, appreciated and respected it, too. They all said that it is not what they expected "seminar" to be like. They figured it was a "lecture and notes" kind of thing. I was glad to erase that notion. I must admit that when I heard about having a football player in my group, I was a bit nervous. For a split second (I timed it...), I thought about not doing some of my planned activities, because of him—stupid thought. I'm glad I didn't change a thing. I'm so much more conscious of others in my seminar now—I mean we all listen to each other. We also seem to be supportive of each other—good sign.

—Kathleen Doherty

Below is a list of Questions and Answers compiled by Susan Webster and Elissa Zelman to address concerns frequently expressed by coordinators during their first term.

1. *What do I do at my first seminar?* At your first seminar, it's a good idea to introduce yourself and your position in Project Community. It's also a good idea to play some kind of icebreaker game with your students. Chances are your seminar group will be relatively small, so it's better if everyone is pretty comfortable with each other. Also, your first seminar is a time to go over the whole concept of Project Community, your role as coordinator, the roles your students play, the attendance policy, the journals, the papers, etc. The main idea is to go through all of the common, first day, administrative things you have been doing in your classes since you began school. So just do what feels natural and don't worry about having to fill up the whole 1 1/2 hours at your first meeting.

2. *Will my students listen to me?* As long as you set the ground rules during your first seminar, your students will listen to you as well as they listen to any other teacher.

3. *Can I be entertaining for 1 1/2 hours?* Not always—everything always looks better on paper. Sometimes the agenda you prepared appears as if it will keep the seminar busy for the entire time, and then you get to class and boom—it has all been said in thirty minutes. A former coordinator, Prentice Zinn, once said, "Students are more interested than they appear and learn twice as much as you think they do. " So just have confidence in yourself and your students will have

confidence in you too.

4. *What do I do about attendance/absences?* It is important to stress to your students that attendance is imperative in this class because so much of Project Community is based on group experience and class participation. This should be heavily stressed at the first seminar.

5. *How do I assert my authority without being condescending and without losing the respect of my students?* It's important to tell your students that we are all in a learning environment and it's important that we all learn from each other. But at the same time, there must be a group leader to keep things organized and coherent for everyone.

6. *How do I enforce journal assignments?* Project Community is so activity-based that it's necessary for the coordinator to have personal responses from each student in order to improve his/her personal progress. Journals tend to vary with each coordinator, but as coordinators, we feel that journals tend to help us as an enforcing agent in keeping up with readings and class time. Journals are also important because coordinators are not always with their students at site, so it keeps coordinators informed about how students are doing there. If students fail to turn in all of their journal assignments, they will receive an incomplete until they succeed in doing so.

7. *How do I respond to journal assignments?* Openly and honestly. Many times students elaborately summarize an article, but they never tell how they feel. Our job in responding to the journals is to help students think critically about what they are writing.

8. *What do I know that my students do not know? In other words, what are my qualifications?* Part of the idea of Project Community is that everyone has something to offer to each other—we can all learn from each other. Coordinators have often been in Project Community before and can share their experiences with their students. We also have weekly staffings in which we learn new ideas for seminars and for reading discussions. Also, we do not do the final grading on their paper assignments, which may help you to feel more comfortable with your position.

9. *How do I approach and deal with the staff and residents at site?* It's a good idea to go out to site by yourself first and introduce yourself to the residents and staff, then bring your students later. This will make everyone involved feel more comfortable.

10. *Is there any physical danger at site?* There is an element of physical danger in everything we do, so just use common sense and everything should be fine. Often the residents at site have committed serious crimes. Because of this, people often have reservations concerning what the residents are capable of. Also, the agencies that run the

community services follow many precautions with the residents' visitors.

11. *What conversation is appropriate for our seminar group to use with the residents and staff at site?* It's not appropriate to discuss any personal issues with the residents at site. It's not appropriate for the residents to have your phone number or address, as they are in a confined situation and many may not be stable enough to deal with outside situations.

12. *How do I react to questionable behavior from the site residents?* (Such as when they ask you for your address or phone number, or they ask you out on a date.) When there is inappropriate behavior, it's important to reinforce to the residents that you are a student volunteer and you are here to help them—not to take verbal abuse. Should the problem continue, seek assistance from your site contact.

13. *How do I deal appropriately when I have friends in seminar?* Talk to your friends before they take your seminar and explain that you are happy they are in your class, but you cannot treat them any differently from any other student. This will help to avoid possible later conflicts.

14. *When students act irresponsibly, how do I enforce my authority?* (For example, missing class or not turning in journals.) Explain to them that you both have responsibilities and that you will live up to yours, but they must also live up to theirs. If they fail to do so, then that is no longer your responsibility—you should not feel responsible for their actions.

15. *What do I do if I have to miss a seminar?* Most of us have had to miss a seminar at one time or another. If you are co-coordinating, then your co-coordinator can hold seminar alone. If you are coordinating alone, then it's a good idea to reschedule seminar at a time convenient for your seminar members.

16. *Who pays for the extra expenses at site?* Most likely you do. So, if you are going to do a group project with your seminar, you may all want to pitch in. If not, try writing a letter to one of the major grocery stores on PC stationery. They usually give supplies to volunteers.

Suggested Journal Questions

What are your expectations for the course? Do you have any past experiences that may be relevant to site? What prompted you to enroll in this particular site?

*** These questions are extremely important. You will note that throughout the course, and especially over the first three seminars, students are asked about expectations and past experiences. One reason for re-asking the same questions is that at the end of past terms, the students most frustrated by Project Community's non-traditional learning usually said, "The class did not live up to my expectations."

NOTES

1. The readings by Bayse (1993), Napier and Whitaker (1988) that appear on this syllabus for this week are so that students can begin the reading for their paper assignment. It might be helpful for coordinators to conclude the first seminar by asking the group, "did the reading generate any questions that you would like to ask at our site orientation?"
2. A more complete explanation of the Johari Window can be found in Luft (1984).
3. My thanks to the Student Organizational Development Center at UM for permission to reprint this handout. I've included it here to give coordinators a brief summary of group process. Throughout the semester, I often lecture on and assign excerpts from Peck (1987) to illustrate aspects of community building. Cris Zerkel's reflection on Peck and her experience as a coordinator appears in Chapter Thirteen.
4. This list is quoted from the October 9, 1990 Ann Arbor News.

The Coat of Arms

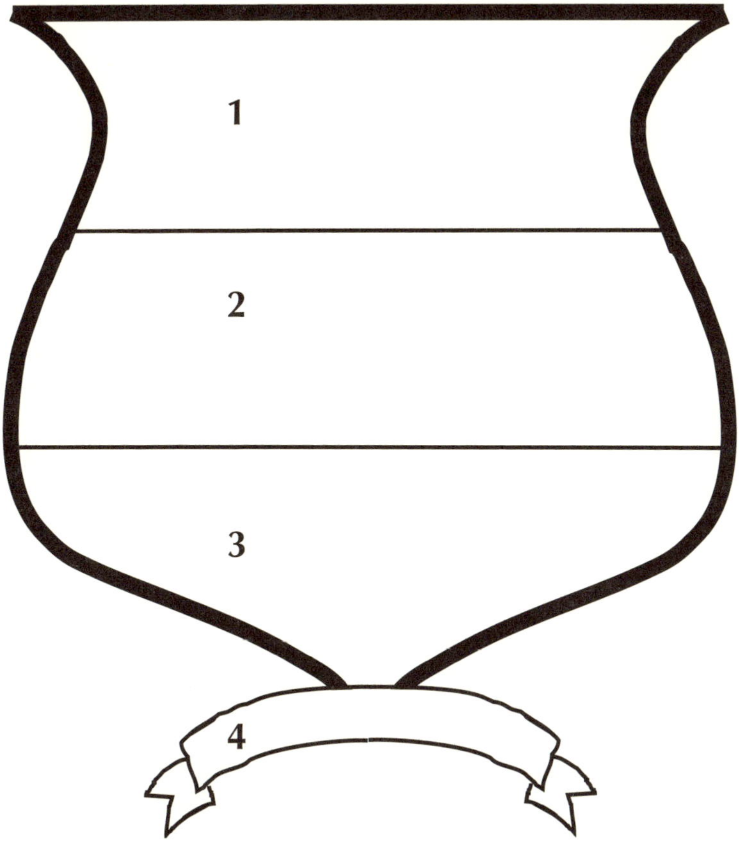

Key

In the spaces provided draw...

1. Something I'm good at
2. An image that describes my learning style
3. Something about me that I learned from another person
4. Write three words or a phrase that apply to me

The Johari Window

Things that I know about myself

Things others know about me

Open/Public (1)	**Secret (2)**
Blind Spots (3)	**Unconscious (4)**

Notes

1. Let people come into the group at their own comfort level; however, your own honesty, openness and willingness to disclose helps to set the tone.
2. This exercise focuses on three aspects of group process—the group being made up of individual members, the relationships between members and the group as a whole.
3. Discussion in a group generally begins in Quadrant 1 and hopefully moves into Quadrants 2 and 3.

STAGES OF GROUP DEVELOPMENT

Student Organization Development Center **2202 Michigan Union**
The Michigan Union **763-5900**

As a group or organization forms, it goes through certain predictable stages, progressing from a loose collection of individuals to a cohesive group working together more or less effectively for a common cause. Two dimensions are present in any group and influence its development. These are task functions and personal relations.

FOUR STAGES OF GROUP DEVELOPMENT

Stage I

1. Personal relations are characterized by dependency on the leader to provide structure.
2. Major task functions concern the orientation of group members to the work they are being asked to do. The issues have to be specified.
3. Common behavior at this point is questioning why we are here, what we are supposed to do, how are we going to get it done, and what are our goals?

Stage II

1. Personal relations: Conflict and confrontation among group members; who is responsible for what; what are going to be the work rules; what are going to be the limits; what is going to be the reward system; what are going to be the criteria?
2. The variety of organizational concerns that emerge reflect conflict over leadership structure, power, and authority.
3. It is important that strategies are implemented to help members move constructively from conflict toward renewed commitment to the group. If this does not happen, members may isolate or even remove themselves from the group during this phase.

Stage III

1. Personal relations are marked by cohesion; people begin to experience a feeling of groupness.
2. They begin sharing ideas, feelings, giving feedback to eachother, soliciting feedback, exploring actions related to the task and sharing information related the task.
3. This becomes a period during which people feel good about being part of a group, and there is a brief abandonment of the task and a period of play—the enjoyment of the cohesion that is being experienced.

Stage IV

1. Interdependence is achieved by group members; members can work singly, in any sub-groupings, or as a total unit. They are highly task and people oriented.
2. Group's tasks are well defined, there is a high commitment to common activity and support for experimentation with solving problems.
3. A collective, interdependent organism is the final outcome of the process of group development.

POSSIBLE COURSES OF ACTION

Stage I

— Leader should provide as much structure as possible; team building is important here.

Stage II

— Leader may need to provide clarification or justification to group members; leader may also spend time with individual members to help them clarify their feelings about group involvement.

Stage III

— Leader should identify the transition and capitalize on it; members are ready to work hard, so the leader must provide opportunities for this to occur.

Stage IV

— Leader can take a less active role and allow the group considerable autonomy. Member's interdependence, flexible approaches to task accomplishment, commitment to self-assessment and appropriate adjustment or adaptation readily occurs.

Reference: Sara Boatman, Group Development; Pfeiffer/Jones

Chapter 3

THREE ROUNDS WITH HOWARD AND KAHN

Second Seminar: What is the PC Pedagogy?

The goal of this seminar is to engage students in a structured activity where they will use key elements of the PC pedagogy—I-messages, identifying feelings, defining personal learning objectives, acknowledging the importance of the group for feedback and support.

Focus Questions: Do you think and feel that the Kahn and Howard (1990) ideals are attainable in the context of Project Community? Why or why not?

In designing this activity, I attempted to operationalize what Kahn and Howard (1990) write about. Round One is taken directly from Kahn's "Some Thoughts About Seminars"—"we found that a very good beginning for a seminar (even before sharing the cosmic question) is for everyone to go around and say how they're feeling right here and now." Round Two asks students to verbalize their CASE learning objectives (from Howard's "On Experiential Learning"). Round Three rephrases Howard's question from "Using Experiential Learning in the Classroom"(1990)—"What norms do we want to establish for this learning group?"

To prepare coordinators for their seminars, I lecture on basic communication skills in the staffing. Generally, I emphasize three points in my lecture. First, in Stage II Recovery, (1985) Larson states that people's behavior is related to both their thoughts and feelings and that people often confuse feelings and thoughts. Second, I introduce six basic feeling words—sad, mad, glad, hurt, ashamed, afraid, and encourage their use in staffings and in journals. Third, I note that one way to use feeling words in communication is the I-message. A typical format for an I-statement is:

I feel ______________________________ (feeling)
about ______________________________ (specific behavior or event)
because ____________________________ (reason).

Three Rounds with Howard and Kahn

Round One

The exercise is pretty straight forward. The leader explains the activity and begins by modeling an I-message. Then everyone has an opportunity to introduce themselves to the group, along with how they are feeling.

> *One woman, when we were doing the I-feel exercise, said 'I'm scared about site because I have no idea what to expect.' That seemed to be the general consensus of the group, so we spent the remainder of the time answering questions about the kind of stuff we'll be confronted with at Growing Tree.*
>
> —*Jeanne Gray*

In one of Sabrina Booth's seminars, a student stated, "I feel hungry." Other students in the seminar shared their candy with her. It was the beginning of a very close-knit group.

John Fohrman started all of his seminars by having his group make "I feel" statements, a legacy that was carried on by his successors, Ashley Andreae and Cris Zerkel.

Round Two

The second round calls for people to state their goals and expectations regarding the course. As in the first round, everyone is invited to share. In my experience, people tend to take their "turn" in the circle in order, generally without feedback.

Sometimes people find it helpful to reflect on their learning objectives before sharing them in seminar. If seminar members hadn't thought about them while reading through Howard's "On Experiential Learning," then include them in this week's journal.

Round Three

In the third round, the leader asks the group, "What do you need from this group/seminar/learning community in order for you to accomplish your goals?" The seminar members can address their needs to the group as a whole, or to individual group members. The leader can also state his or her needs during this round. I have found it useful to record the group's expressed needs on newsprint: the activities based on Freire (1970) and Palmer (1987) later in this term both refer back to this list.

After the third round, leave a few minutes to process the activity. Asking about people's thoughts and feelings about the list and about being a member of the group will help move in the direction of accepting this list of needs as the group's norms.

Fall '91 Staffing Norms

- *support from other coordinators*
- *what's not working*
- *suggestions*
- *receptive, open-mindedness*
- *share your mistakes*
- *confidentiality*

- *information about students*
- *sharing ideas*
- *humor*
- *a big group*
- *honesty*
- *enthusiasm*
- *be there*

The CD/CJ staff generated this list together at a Fall '91 meeting. It was referenced through the Fall and Winter '92 terms. At the end of the Winter term, Julie Zelman wrote:

> *I do think, however, that the support system that we currently have is amazing. In the beginning of the semester, Joe asked us to express our goals and expectations for norms in the staff meetings. He wrote them on poster sized paper and now he hangs them on the wall at each meeting. The list includes such things as support, listening to others, confidentiality, trust, etc. Every week we look at our list and we are reminded that we are all there for each other. At staff meetings we close the door just before we talk about our sites and seminars. We all understand that what is said in the room does not leave the room. We have learned to express our feelings to each other, ask for help and suggestions from each other, and to give everyone the opportunity to voice our own opinions and ideas. The support is incredible and I would not change a thing that occurs within the classroom setting.*
>
> *One activity I thought was particularly good was 'Feelings/ Goals/Needs' because it gives everyone the chance to reveal their concerns/fears/needs. I think it was one of the most constructive things we did.*
>
> *—Anne Hardy*

At the end of the term, the Winter '90 CD staff concluded that writing norms out on a piece of newsprint, posting them at each meeting, and then actually sticking to them were all key ingredients in the staffing's community building.

Howard's Bag O' Norms

Prentice Zinn created an interesting variation on this activity in his seminar. On a paper bag, he wrote:

HOWARD'S BAG O' NORMS
Traditional Flavor
Contents: oppressive and dysfunctional
classroom norms that inhibit learning, critical
thinking, community building and
overall human development.
May cause allergic reaction in
enlightened individuals.
WARNING: HAZARDOUS TO YOUR EDUCATION

In this variation, students were given several blank sheets of paper and told to write out traditional classroom norms that they have some feelings about. After writing out their norms, students presented them to the group one at a time. Following each norm, the student crumpled up the sheet of paper it was written on and threw it into the "Howard's Bag O'Norms."

Below are the norms from Prentice's seminar:

- *one person talks too much, and is stupid*
- *roboprof*
- *hierarchy between prof and student*
- *prof thinks their class is most important*
- *grade*
- *hate that you can never get a 'A' on the first paper*
- *learning is memorization, which is nothing*
- *one-ups-personship*
- *prof always lectures*
- *when the prof wears distracting clothes*
- *too theoretical*
- *non-discussion*
- *don't like when profs and especially TA's just lecture/no fun*
- *feeling stupid when the teacher calls on you*
- *profhogs*
- *the "right" answers*
- *don't like classes that have just three hourlies and a final*
- *the teacher is GOD and better and smarter than the students*
- *mostly men profs*
- *no real evaluation of prof*
- *early departures*
- *no say on readings, no control*
- *chit chat during class*
- *profs assume you know more than you know*
- *large lectures*
- *late arrivals*
- *profs having favorite students then always call on them*
- *competition*
- *not very participatory*
- *few visual aids*
- *prof won't stop for questions, ignores them or discourages them*

Kati Hanna called the exercise "infamous" and ran it successfully during both the Fall '90 and Winter '91 terms. Jennifer Rabiah borrowed Prentice's Bag to facilitate the activity in her seminar. She wrote:

> *So far, I've used many of the suggested activities, but the one that stands out in my mind was Howard's Bag O' Norms. I think it is going to be a great revolving point in my seminar this term.*

To help all coordinators, Prentice Zinn compiled the following:

If only someone had told me about....
Omar's Golden Laws of Seminaring

1. *At least one person will have not done the reading.*
2. *At least one person will be absent on any given day.*
3. *At least one person will be late.*
4. *Your group activities are only as good as you think they are.*
5. *All readings will be boring regardless of content and style.*
6. *Students are more interested than they appear and learn twice as much as you think they do.*
7. *The more topics and concepts you try to deal with the less people will learn.*
8. *You always do a better job at facilitating a seminar than you think.*
9. *No group meetings will live up to your expectations.*
10. *Rome wasn't built in a day.*
11. *Kathleen Doherty always has better group activities than you do.*

Suggested Journal Question

Describe three past experiences in groups that were important or significant to you. How would you compare these experiences with a "learning community?"

Chapter 4

JUST MY IMAGINATION

Third Seminar: What is the Sociological Imagination?

The goal of this seminar is for students to contrast a view of people based on our own outdated personal experiences (Peck, 1978) with the Sociological Imagination (Mills, 1959), which takes into account the person's race, social class, gender and place in history.

Focus Questions: Discuss one system with which you are associated. Explain why it is a system, how the system has impacted/continues to impact your life, and how easy or difficult it would be to change your position in relation to this particular system.[1]

The readings this week are Peck's "Transference—The Outdated Map", from The Road Less Traveled (1978) and Mills' "The Promise," from The Sociological Imagination (1959). Paper Dolls and The Wheel of Fortune are based on Peck; A Visit to Archie Bunker's Place and The Sociological Confrontation are based on Mills. In her lesson plan on these readings, Dora Brantley noted that it made a lot of sense to start with Peck and end with Mills, allowing seminar members the opportunity to compare and contrast psychological and sociological perspectives. This sequence, summarized below, is consistent with Professor Chesler's presentations at the Fall '90 and Winter '91 Saturday Coordinator Trainings.[2]

Cheslectures

The PC learning process generally attempts to move from the personal (I/Me) experience to the collective (We/They) experience, promoting insight and understanding of one's own and other's realities, experiences and life situations. It also attempts to move from reaction and experience in a unique and singular here and now setting to more generalized insights and perspectives on other (there and then) settings. Both dialectics or conversations—one between me and we and the other between here/now and there/then—involve processes of comparison and contrast.

The PC Learning Process

	Feel & Sense/ Here & Now	Reflect & Reasoning/ There & Then
I/Me	**1**	**2**
We/They	**3**	**4**

1. Student has a new experience at site and notes or reflects on it, perhaps in a journal.
2. Student reflects further on the similarities or differences between this experience in this setting and other experiences in other like or different settings (e.g. How is this prison(er) like other prison(ers)? How is the courtroom experience like a classroom experience? How is it unlike?). This can occur through self-reflection, through visits or through reading about other settings.
3. Student compares and contrasts his/her personal experience with others' experiences—either other students at site or in class or others who are not students, perhaps some who are institutional residents. This can occur through dialogue in seminar, through conversations with site participants, through readings about site, etc.
4. Student compares and contrasts his/her own and others' personal experiences in this site or situation with the experiences of other people (some like oneself and some unlike oneself) in other settings. In this step, both comparisons can occur simultaneously—comparing myself and my experience/reactions/view to others' and comparing one

setting to others. This, too, can be accomplished through classroom dialogue, site conversation, journal exchange, or readings.

If there is dialogue and exchange we may ask:

Do you care about hearing another's experience?
Do they care about yours?
How do they and you show such caring?
Are you able to be supportive of difference, of discovering and appreciating instead of denying or criticizing them?
Did you learn anything from this dialogue?

Paper Dolls

In the CJ staffings, I separated coordinators into groups based on whether or not the clients at site were adults or juveniles. Each group was given a piece of newsprint, several markers and a pair of scissors and told to draw either "a typical juvenile delinquent" or "a typical adult prisoner". After 15 or 20 minutes, the groups presented their Paper Dolls to each other.

In adapting this exercise to the seminar, I think it's probably best to do this as a group BEFORE the group has been to site. I also think that repeating the exercise at the end of the term, and then comparing the two Paper Dolls, is a good closure activity.

Peck (1978) can be assigned either before or after Paper Dolls: a possible journal assignment could be to have students reflect on their part in the activity after reading Peck.

For CD staffings, the assignment would be changed to draw a typical drug abuser or alcoholic.

Thinking about systems helped me give examples of systems in seminar. We did Paper Dolls and had everyone try to think of examples of systems. At first, everyone was pretty clueless about systems. Most of the examples kept to individual acts. I asked Mike to explain systems, but he didn't remember, so Stacey and I gave it a shot. I used the job system as an example. We read the Discussion Questions on the Mills (1959) article, which helped people to see things on a bigger level, and the Sociological

> *Imagination, but the discussion was not in as much depth as I had hoped.*
>
> *—Rick Smith*

Wheel Of Fortune

This activity was originally a coordinator Journal Assignment during the Fall '89 Term. Here are the directions.

1. Fill in the blanks in the Wheel with questions about information you would like to know about the people at your site (race, class, gender, etc). If you have time, you may consider how you would answer these questions yourself.
2. Assign your version of the Wheel as a journal entry.
3. Record seminar members' individual responses, perhaps on a newsprint Wheel. Refer back to it as part of a group closure activity in December.

> *I thought the Wheel of Fortune was particularly good because it allowed me to finally admit some of the prejudices I have been harboring all my life. I'm glad that I completed the Wheel because now that I've worked in the prison system, I realize how untrue a lot of my prejudices turned out to be.*
>
> *As for Peck, well, I think the Wheel of Fortune leads more to the sociological imagination than do the Paper Dolls. It could go both ways, but the questions on the Wheel lead directly to background that influences a prisoner's behavior, whereas in the Paper Dolls, some things about background*

may be overlooked, just leaving stereotypes.

—Kathy Garcia

The following two students respond to Peck (1978):

My psychological map predisposed me before I even went to the site. I was expecting to see good looking, well groomed lawyers with Shadoe Stevens voices standing in front of the jury, then ambling around the courtrooms gesturing and bellowing their case against defendants—seated precariously on the edge with every eye in the courtroom upon them.

I had this sort of map in my mind about criminal court cases. In reality, the lawyers look like everyday people, the judge looks like he doesn't really care what is going on in the courtroom, and the defendants look like they don't care what is going on either.

I also have the map in my mind that says bad guys always go to jail. All I have to do is pick up the paper to prove the map is wrong—drug dealers off on technicalities, murderers out on parole in a year. The list goes on.

One guy I saw today did fill my map image of a felon. He was dressed in the "orange felon overalls" and he got all upset when the judge didn't let him change his attempted murder charge to assault with intent to do great bodily harm. His lawyer seemed upset too. I guess if you approach a person sitting in a chair, lower a gun towards that person and shoot him in the leg, that isn't as serious as trying to murder him?! Oh, I forgot—he didn't mean to do it.

This guy did fit my map of a felon squeezing anything and everything out of the system—and acting cheated when he wasn't just slapped on the hand. Some things don't change.

—Gregory Pond

On my first trip to Maxey Green Oaks Center, I brought many preconceived notions with me. I imagined an institution looking very much like a prison filled with angry and often

times violent youths. However, my subsequent experience working at Maxey Green Oaks has shown me that many of the preconceptions—about both the institution and the individuals in it—were generally unfounded and incorrect. The time I have spent at Maxey has caused me in many ways to rethink previous opinions that I had concerning crime, criminals and criminal institutions.

Perhaps the biggest surprise for me at Maxey were the individuals confined within its walls. While I realize that each of these individuals has most likely committed at least one criminal, and probably violent act to earn himself a spot at Maxey—however, most of the kids at Maxey that I have come to know strike a person as anything but hardened criminals. Though a certain violent nature of wildness is apparent in some, many are friendly and eager to please. The question that keeps re-entering my mind is what could some of these kids have done to have wound up at a place like Maxey? Perhaps they are good kids at heart, act accordingly when in a controlled environment, but when placed in the violent, drug-ridden environment [from] whence they come, they adapt accordingly. This explanation, though, does little to explain the many kids in these same environments who do not turn to crime. Perhaps these kids do have a darker, more violent and criminal side to their character which they successfully hide when I'm around. Whatever the explanation, they certainly are not the type of kids whom I expected to encounter.

The Maxey Green Oaks Center itself was also a surprise to me. First and foremost, there are no bars. Despite being a maximum security center, it strives to be, and in many ways succeeds at creating, a remarkably humane environment. It is generally clean, has impressive recreational facilities, and small but fairly reasonable rooms for the inmates. Unfortunately, despite these facts, and despite a variety of counseling and services offered, Maxey does a poor job in reforming these youths. As I understand it, most of its inmates will find their way back into the prison system sometime after

> *they are released. Perhaps this is not Maxey's fault and there is nothing Maxey can do about these kids once they return to their old environment. Nonetheless, the sad fact is that Maxey is not fulfilling its role as an institution of reform.*
>
> *—Daniel Glaser*

A Visit To Archie Bunker's Place

Toni Caldwell wrote the script for this role-play. She and I first presented it at the Fall '89 paper meetings[3]. Coordinators reported using it successfully in their seminars throughout the '90-'91 academic year.

The scene opens as Archie is returning from a hard day at work:

EDITH: Archie, Archie did you have a nice day at work?

ARCHIE: Now Edith, don't go all gushy all over me just because you know that the man of the house is home from work. Can't a man get a beer around his own house without all this mush about how things went at work?

EDITH: (leaving to get beer for Archie) All right Archie, if ya don't feel like talkin' I understand. (returning from the kitchen with a beer—hands it to Archie)

ARCHIE: (sitting down with his beer) Well Edith, I just don't know what this world is comin' to. Some folks just don't see that all they have to do is work real hard and they will get what they want and need outa life.

EDITH: What folks ya talkin' about Archie?

ARCHIE: Ya know who I'm talkin' about, Edith. Old Black Joe down at the docks is all puffed up because he got passed over for the foreman's job. He's sayin' that it's because he's Black that he didn't get the job. I just think that he doesn't see that all he has to do is work hard and he'd get the promotion. If he didn't get the job then it's just because he didn't work hard enough. I'm tired of hearin' about all this stuff every time some Black or Mexican don't get the job they want. Life ain't no bowl of cherries and they just better get used to that. Like I said, they just oughta work a little harder. After all, Joe, he's only been there fifteen years. What does he expect, for the boss to give him the job just 'cause he's Black?

EDITH: I don't know Archie. I don't always think that workin' hard will get someone where they want to go. Seems to me I heard you say lot's of times that your boss don't like Blacks too much and that there are some things that Blacks just ain't able to do. Maybe Joe is right. Maybe your boss don't want a Black man in that position. Seems to me I heard you say that your boss thinks Blacks can't read good enough to be able to do the foreman type work. So maybe it ain't Joe's not workin' hard enough. Maybe no matter how hard Joe worked for YOUR boss he would never get the foreman's job. Did you ever think about that Archie? And if he don't read well, maybe his school wasn't as good as our school.

Unknown to Archie and even Edith herself, Edith has developed what C. Wright Mills (1959) call the sociological imagination. She is able to see that there may be more going on in Joe's situation than Joe's effort on the job which may be affecting his position in the company. She realizes that in addition to the affect that each person has on his/her own life, there are many other things that affect what we are and what happens to us. We are affected by perceptions, policies, laws, attitudes and decisions of others, as well as by the place we hold in society. She also seems to see that in some instances there is not much we can do to change the situation. For example, Edith realizes that if she can just get Archie to think about things, he MIGHT one day see the light and begin to develop his own sociological imagination.

Anyway, just a note on the Sociological Imagination: I like the Archie/Edith approach best! (Oh, and it's one of the questions on my Soc. midterm!).

—Kathy Garcia

The class seemed to enjoy the skit you put on, Joe, as they laughed at the way you portrayed Archie Bunker. I laughed myself, finding it extremely funny because such a role was tremendously out of character for you.

—Marc Zeplin

The Sociological Confrontation

Prentice Zinn created this cartoon and role-play which was widely used during the Winter '90 term. The cartoon is re-produced at the bottom of this chapter.

Coordinators generally like the Sociological Confrontation cartoon. The following are some pertinent comments:

> *I used the Sociological Confrontation cartoon in my seminar last week, and it worked out well. It definitely sparked conversation. My students thought, for the most part, that the cartoon was a little biased towards the individual.*
>
> —*Wendy Lassen*

> *Joe, we used the cartoon and although they thought it was stupid, I just think they were unwilling to admit that it was helpful. And, if it didn't help them, maybe it's because the group is small. I'm sure in a large group many won't comprehend the article and will need the cartoon to understand.*
>
> —*Chuck Ebel*

> *I did do the Sociological Confrontation. They seemed to like it. I had each of them read a role and then we discussed how effective it was in describing the theory. We concluded that it would greatly enhance the reading of the Mills (1959) article; that maybe if you read the cartoon before you read the article you might have a decent grasp on the premise of the theory. Other than that, it seemed like we just enjoyed the cartoon.*
>
> —*Kathleen Doherty*

> *Yes, I did use your clever cartoon in my last seminar. Considering that my group is larger than other groups, I had three people read the cartoon aloud. Using the visual aid with the humorous pictures made the activity interesting. After reading the cartoon, we discussed the sociological imagination by critiquing the cartoon, which led into a much broader discussion about the Mills (1959) article. After we discussed it,*

> *I went around the table and had everyone individually define exactly what they thought the sociological imagination meant. I think that this will be very helpful for their papers.*
>
> *—Jennifer Rabiah*

Suggested Journal Question

Obviously, the Wheel of Fortune is a suggested journal question. If you decide to do Paper Dolls in seminar, a follow-up question could be: "Reflect on your behavior and attitudes during Paper Dolls in light of Peck (1978)". Finally, a journal question on Mills (1959) could be "Describe three current troubles and three current issues in light of Mills."

NOTES

1. These Focus Questions are based on the current CD paper assignment, which all students in CD and CJ wrote during the '92/'93 academic year.
2. In past semesters, Coordinator Training meetings were often held on the first Saturday of the term. Sometimes Professor Chesler set the agenda, at other times program directors did the planning. Currently, program directors and teaching assistants meet with coordinators in their program area at the beginning and throughout the semester: Professor Chesler generally meets with coordinators in the middle of the term to review the Freire-based paper assignments.
3. The Sociology 389 teaching assistants usually meet with coordinators on a weekly basis in staffings but tend to have very little scheduled contact with students whose papers they grade. Sometimes, teaching assistants visit individual seminars to discuss the paper assignment, or hold large group meetings with several seminars at once. In the past, students were reluctant to visit the teaching assistant during office hours although this is required if students do not recieve passing grades on the paper assignment.

Chapter 5

THE GREAT DEBATE
Does Every Picture Tell a Story?

Fourth Seminar in Criminal Justice: What are Some Liberal and Conservative Perspectives on Crime?

The goal of this seminar is to provide students with an opportunity to identify their own positions relative to some liberal and conservative perspectives on various issues in Criminal Justice.

Focus Question: It seems as though Herrnstein and Wilson (1985) are a variation of the nature versus nurture argument regarding offenders. Where do you stand on the issue? How does this stand affect your participation in Project Community?

Yes, this topic actually did come up in seminar. The general feeling from the students was that environment plays a greater role in promoting criminal behavior. Whether or not this is the case, I think it's good that the students have this attitude, since they will therefore be more likely to believe that our efforts at Cotton will be beneficial to the inmates.

—Stacey Brown

I like this Focus Question a lot. It worked well in seminar. I wish that some questions could be more argumentative in nature to really stimulate conversation. Asking a student where he or she stands on an issue really doesn't beget critical thinking.

—Aaron Romain

The question helped me for some of the issues that came up during our Heath Wilkins debate. The group raised questions of rehabilitation and causal behavior. Aren't all criminals influenced by their upbringing? Even if a person can't help but commit a crime, they still need to be locked up. I think everyone in my seminar was against the death penalty or on the fence.

—Rick Smith

Walker (1985) is the basis for the Great Debate, one of two possible activites that could be used during this seminar. The text for the second activity, Heath Wilkins, will be presented in its entirety later in this chapter.

The Great Debate

Select two group members to read alternating paragraphs in the Great Debate. Instruct the two readers to stand at opposite ends of the room, and for the rest of the group members to stand in the middle. After reading the second and the fourth paragraph, have the readers stop. Ask the group members to move according to how the views expressed agree or disagree with their own. Give group members an opportunity to explain why they "voted with their feet".

After the Debate, briefly discuss the chart that relates psychology/ sociology with conservative/liberal, nature/nurture, and individual reponsibility/ social influences.

1. The thing that liberals don't understand is that some people are just plain bad. Some people simply lack the discipline and self-control to accept the limits that the rest of us accept. They are unable to subordinate their personal passions for the sake of the common good. That is what separates the criminal from the rest of us. Since they lack self-discipline, it is up to society to provide that harsher punishment to respond to continued criminal behavior.

2. Conservatives go wrong the minute that they claim that some people are born "bad." Human nature is shaped by social influences. Our primary concern should be to prevent crime by reforming society. We need to identify the sources of negative social influence at its real roots. We must eliminate discrimination and make real economic opportunities available to all. We must provide adequeate education to everyone. The only way to reduce crime is to reform the society which turns its people into criminals.

3. We are in the mess we are in for two reasons: 1) Too many people bought the liberal excuse that poverty causes crime when the real cause of both poverty and crime is that criminals lack the self-control to get a job and earn the things they desire; and 2) The liberals have succeeded in placing too many restrictions on the criminal justice system (i.e. Miranda warning, the exclusionary rule, the insanity defense, plea-bargaining). These restrictions mean that punishment is neither absolutely certain nor harsh enough to deter crime as it can and should. We need to give punishment a chance to do its job.

4. Punishment can never work because it does not affect the real root of crime which is society itself. Sure we should rehabilitate an individual who has been twisted by an inadequate environment. That rehabilitation might even require a prison stay in some few cases. But if prison is required, we should make it worthwhile by providng educational and

vocational training. Perhaps the reason conservatives cling to the idea of punishing the criminal is that they are unwilling to blame a society which has treated them so well for the crime problem. After all, any social reforms which would address the social causes of crime would threaten their comfortable place in society.

Following Up the Great Debate

Sociological	Psychological
Social Influences	Individual Responsibility
Liberal	Conservative
Nurture	Nature

Liz Rosenburg reported that the Debate went well in Trish Marsik's seminar where she was one of 14 students:

We had people at all different points in the (political spectrum).

Prentice Zinn wondered if the Debate activity might not intimidate a shy person. My thought is that you could give students an option to represent the opinion of a person they respect on the spectrum. Afterwards, this activity has the potential to be a community building experience as people share why that view/person is important to them.

Ron Ikens rewrote the Debate to address issues at site.

Anne Hardy assigned her students to write the view in extreme opposition to their own in their journal, then had students read their journals at the beginning of seminar. Later, students would talk about where they actually stood in the Debate.

Heath Wilkins

The text for the Heath Wilkins[1] case is at the end of this chapter. I have chosen to make the activity available here and not in the coursepack because it can be read quickly during seminar and the exercise requires people to be constantly referring to the text. The activity is fairly self-explanatory. In photocopying it you may want to omit the case decision from the second page. Omitting the decision allows you to end the activity promptly, by concluding the discussion with the actual ruling.

In staffing evaluations, Heath Wilkins was the most highly praised of the activities for the fourth, fifth and sixth seminars. "The class loved it," wrote one coordinator. One advantage of this activity over the Great Debate is that it allows people to role-play their positions, without being too typecast in the political stances which some students felt "were too extreme".

Suggested Journal Questions for the Fourth Seminar in Criminal Justice

Would you consider your stance on crime more conservative or more liberal?

How would you rule in the Heath Wilkins case?

Fourth Seminar in Chemical Dependency

The goal of this seminar is for students to apply the Disease Concept of Chemical Dependency in different contexts.

Focus Questions: Discuss the main point of Olhm's article (1981), that THIQ is "the biological culprit." This is a fascinating finding, however, how would this article explain the fact that not all children of alcoholics, or even identical twins where one is an alcoholic, eventually become alcoholics? Also, discuss the pro's and con's of this article—does it make sense to test children for this "flaw" in order to prevent alcoholism later in life?

The key reading this week is Olhms' "The Disease Concept of Alcoholism" (1981). Both suggested activities, Teach Your Children Well and Every Picture Tells a Story Don't it?, are meant to be directly linked to Olhms.

Teach Your Children Well

There are three parts to this activity. First, as a whole group, recap the main point of Olhms' article—"alcoholism is a chronic, progressive, incurable disease characterized by loss of control over alcohol and other sedatives"(1981).

Second, split into two groups. Each group is assigned the task of explaining the disease concept to a group of elementary children.

Third, bring both groups together and have them present their definitions. Close by discussing how the disease concept fits (or doesn't fit) with Mills' (1959) sociological imagination.

Every Picture Tells A Story, Don't It

In this activity, seminar members are required to collect advertisements for liquor during the week prior to seminar. At the seminar, the group will go through each of the ads and discuss what each ad's message is. After a message has been assigned to each ad, people can then talk about how these messages fit or don't fit with the disease concept. This discussion can be linked to Mills by concluding with Matt Kinney's question: "Who benefits from this arrangement?"

A version of this activity, applying it to codependency, has been done successfully in Chemical Dependency seminars over the past two years. This version, centering on the disease concept, seemed to work well in the Fall '91 staffing.

Suggested Journal Questions for the Fourth Seminar in Chemical Dependency

Based on the readings and the activity, how would you define the disease concept of Chemical Dependency?

NOTES

1. My thanks to the Constitutional Rights Foundation (1990) for permission to reprint this exercise.

The 8th Amendment
U.S. Government

Capital Punishment in the USA: Should Kids Who Kill Be Executed?

Introduction

Under our federal system of government in the United States, some crimes have been defined by Congress and they are enforced by agencies of the Federal Government. But by far the greater number of crimes have been defined and are enforced by the states within their respective jurisdictions. For example, at the end of 1988 our prison population included 42,738 federal prisoners, but more than 10 times that—561,190—were in state institutions. (From 1980 through 1988 our total prison population increased by about 90%, which has placed great pressure on our government and on public attitudes toward crime.)

In 1972, a determined effort was made by several organizations to persuade our state and federal courts that the death penalty was unconstitutional under the Eighth Amendment which "must draw its meaning from the evolving standards of decency that mark the progress of a maturing society." This effort was temporarily successful in California where the State Supreme Court held, on March 17, 1972, that the penalty was prohibited [*People v. Anderson,* 6 Cal.3d 628, (1972)].

The California Court noted that capital punishment had at that time been totally abolished in nine states and in about 45 foreign countries. It was also noted that nobody had been executed in the United States from 1968 through 1971.

Shortly after the *Anderson* decision, the United States Supreme Court stopped short of finding capital punishment itself to be "cruel and unusual." Instead, the 5 to 4 majority ruled that those individuals sent to death row by judges and juries must not be sentenced in an "arbitrary and capricious" way [*Furman v. Georgia*, 408 U.S. 238, (1972)]. This decision was followed by a period of uncertainty which, to some extent, continues today. In every death sentence case there are serious arguments and many delays in trying to determine precisely what facts and procedures will result in a death penalty decision which was not arrived at in an "arbitrary and capricious" way. In California, the *Anderson* case was overruled by a vote of the people who adopted a complicated set of rules and procedures to govern the position of the death penalty.

The Background

While the Supreme Court decided in 1972 that capital punishment did not violate the Eighth Amendment, in later cases it went on to rule that a death sentence was "excessive" (therefore, "cruel and unusual") when the life of the victim was not take, as in a rape case [*Coker v. Georgia*, 433 U.S. 584, (1977)]. The Supreme Court decided in 1989 that sentencing a mentally retarded murderer to death was not in itself "cruel and unusual [*Penry v. Lynaugh*, 109 S.Ct. 2934, (1989)]. In that same year, the justices also faced the question of whether sentencing juvenile killers to death was a "cruel and unusual" punishment in violation of the Eighth Amendment.

The case of Heath Wilkins became the center of a recent controversy about the Eighth Amendment. Wilkins grew up in a poor and chaotic family. His father was committed to a mental institution. His mother left Heath alone much of the time while she worked; she also beat him frequently. Heath began to burglarize homes. An uncle started him on drugs. He set fires, shot off guns at passing cars, and killed neighborhood pets. On one occasion he put rat poison in Tylenol capsules in an attempt to poison his mother and her boyfriend, whom he hated. Discovering his plot, they forced him to eat some of the capsules. Then they beat him.

After he was placed in a juvenile facility at age 10, Heath began to use drugs and alcohol heavily. He also attempted suicide several times. Sent home on probation when he was 13, Wilkins continued to use drugs and steal. He ran away from home, was locked up in a number of juvenile institutions, and finally was placed in a foster home. He ran away again and began to live on the streets during the summer of 1985. He was 16.

The Case

On July 17, 1985, Heath and an accomplice entered a convenience store in Avondale, Missouri. Heath later told authorities that he intended to rob the store and kill whoever was behind the counter because "a dead person can't talk." The person behind the counter was Nancy Allen, a 26 year-old mother of two.

While the accomplice held Nancy Allen, Heath stabbed her. She fell to the floor bleeding, but not dead. The two robbers had trouble opening the cash register. When Nancy spoke, trying to give them directions, Heath stabbed her three times in the chest. Nancy begged for her life. But Heath stabbed her four more times in the neck. He and his accomplice then left Nancy to bleed to death on the floor.

Although he was 16 at the time of the crime, Heath Wilkins was certified as an adult by the Missouri juvenile court. He then pleaded guilty to first degree murder and several other felonies in an adult criminal court.

At his sentencing hearing before a judge, Heath gave up his right to have a defense lawyer present. Several experts examined him to determine if he was competent to waive his right to counsel. Taking their reports into account, the judge decided Heath was competent. However, one state-appointed psychiatrist concluded that Heath "suffers from a mental disorder" that affects his "reasoning and impairs his behavior."

Be fore he was sentenced, Heath told the judge he preferred the death penalty to life in prison. "One I fear, the other one I don't," he said. The state then presented evidence in support of the death sentence. The judge decided that capital punishment was justified in this case.

The Arguments

There was never any doubt that Heath Wilkins murdered Nancy Allen in a particularly vicious way. The issue is whether the death sentence was a "cruel and unusual" punishment because Wilkins was only 16 at the time he committed the crime. The following arguments by the defense, prosecution and friends of the court on this question were made before the U.S. Supreme Court in 1989. (In Supreme Court hearings on important issues, groups and organizations with views and expertise on the issues often submit "Friends of the Court" briefs to help justices decide the case. The justices may or may not use these briefs to help make a decision.)

The main legal argument centered on whether "evolving standards of decency" had made capital punishment for juvenile criminals "cruel and unusual." The defense view pointed out that 12 capital punishment states specifically prohibit executing anyone who had committed a death penalty offense while under the age of 18. Another three states prohibit such executions for juveniles who committed their crimes under age 17. Now, there are an additional 14 states that do not permit capital punishment at all. Thus, 29 states would not have sentenced Heath Wilkins to death.

Those on the other side of the argument countered that 21 capital punishment states wither do allow the execution of juvenile offender or at least do not forbid it. In the view of those who argued in favor of the execution of Heath Wilkins and those like him, there is no consensus in the country today to do away with the death penalty for juvenile killers. According to this view, the states are still too divided to make this a "cruel and unusual" punishment.

Those opposing the death penalty for Heath Wilkins argued that judges and juries in the country rarely recommend capital punishment for juveniles who have committed even the most serious crimes. From 1982 to 1988, nearly 2% of all adult homicide arrests (1,772) led to the death penalty while only one-half of one percent of juvenile homicide arrests (41) resulted in a death sentence. Thus, according to this view, such sentences are clearly unusual today.

Those arguing on the other side said that the reason for the low number of juvenile death sentences is the fact that far fewer capital crimes are committed by those under age 18. In their view, the national consensus today is that the death penalty for juvenile criminals should be available, but only use in extraordinary cases.

Another argument against the death sentence for juvenile criminals concerned their level of maturity. According to this argument, adolescents are inexperienced, impulsive, subject to peer pressure, and prone to taking risks without thinking ahead. Because of these characteristics, those under 18 are less mature and not as responsible as adults. Therefore, according to this reasoning, Heath Wilkins and others in his situation should not have to face capital punishment because it would be an excessive penalty.

Countering this view, the other side argued that the death penalty for young murderers like Heath Wilkins is a highly individualistic affair. In Heath's case, he first had to be certified as an adult in a juvenile court. Then the adult court judge was required to review all the relevant facts about Heath's background, including his youthfulness, before condemning him to death. In a case as serious as first degree murder, this view argues that states should handle juvenile killers individually, not like anonymous members of an age group.

As you can see, the arguments for and against capital punishment for juvenile offenders are varied and strongly held. It will be left to the U.S. Supreme Court to decide the matter, and in so doing, give more concrete meaning to the Eighth Amendment.

For Discussion and Writing

1. The Supreme Court has ruled that deciding what a "cruel and unusual" punishment is depends on the "evolving standards of decency that mark the progress of a maturing society." What do you think this means?
2. A judge or jury who deliberates in a death penalty sentencing hearing must consider both *mitigating* (favoring leniency) and *aggravating* (favoring harsh punishment) circumstance. What were the mitigating and aggravating circumstances in the case of Heath Wilkins? After considering these circumstances, decide whether he deserved the death penalty.
3. Under what circumstances, if any, do you believe that juveniles should receive the death penalty?

For Further Reading

Streib, Victor. *Death Penalty for Juveniles.* Bloomington, Ind.: Indiana University Press, 1987.

When the State Kills. New York: Amnesty International, 1989. [Surveys the status of capital punishment in every country in the world.]

Activity

Is the execution of juvenile murderers "cruel and unusual" punishment?

Organize a moot Supreme Court hearing on the question above.

1. Organize the class into three role groups: attorneys representing Heath Wilkins, attorneys representing the state of Missouri, and members of the U.S. Supreme Court.
2. The two attorney role groups should prepare by finding arguments and supporting evidence, especially in "The Background" and "The Arguments" sections of the article. The Supreme Court justices should thoroughly review the cases discussed in the introduction to the article. These students should also prepare a list of questions to ask each side. All participants should be familiar with the facts of the *Wilkins* case.
3. Conduct the moot court hearing informally with the attorney groups alternately presenting arguments and responding to the opposite side as in a class debate. Those students playing Supreme Court justices should participate by directing questions to both sides.
4. At the end of the moot court hearing, one student from each side of the case should make a closing summary statement. The student justices should then meet to discuss and decide the question of the case by majority vote. Finally, they should announce their decision and give reasons for their individual votes.

THE WILKINS CASE DECISION

On June 26, 1989, the Supreme Court decided (5-4) that capital punishment for a person who had committed a crime at 16 or 17 did not constitute "cruel and unusual" punishment under the Eighth Amendment. The majority concluded that, "We discern neither a historical nor a modern societal consensus forbidding the imposition of capital punishment on any person who murders at 16 or 17 years of age" [*Wilkins c. Missouri* decided with *Stanford c. Kentucky*, 109 S.Ct. 2969, (1989)].

Chapter 6

RON, CHRIS AND THE LEGALIZATION DEBATE[1]

The goal of this seminar in Criminal Justice is for students to explore how a person's educational situations (residence, family status, nursery or day care experience, schools, college) may affect that person's access to treatment for drug addiction. The goal of this seminar in Chemical Dependency is for students to identify their position if drugs were to be legalized in the United States.

Focus Question: If what George Bush says is true, that "fundamentally, the drug problem in America is not one of supply but of demand" (1989), what policies make the most sense for curtailing demand? Do you agree with such policies? At your site, do you see evidence of programs that curtail supply or demand?[2]

> *I like this question, and when I used it last term, it sparked great discussion among the recreational drug user(s) in my seminar. (S)he felt that the demand would never go away, so recreational drugs should be legalized. At site, drugs are both abundant and demanded. I think in some respects, Bush is right, but only in the sense of a truism or cliche. Demand for drugs doesn't come from nowhere. It perhaps is like demand for cosmetics or clothes. As long as life is unbearable, and someone is telling you this substance will make things better, that substance will be in demand.*
>
> *—Rick Smith*

Fifth Seminar in Criminal Justice: Drugs & Crime—Is There a Link?

The Ron and Chris Activity is based on composites of seven cases I worked on during the Winter '87 term and relates directly to Shine and Mauer (1993).

Ron and Chris[3]

Before seminar, make a chart three columns wide on newsprint or on a chalkboard with the different "situations" (residence, day care, etc.) in the middle of the three columns. Select two seminar members to fill out the categories for Ron and Chris. Have the group generate answers for Ron and Chris alternately. For example, when describing "residence," the group might say that because Ron is poor, his family lives in federally subsidized housing, or "the projects". On the other hand, because Chris is rich, his family's home is nearly palatial, valued between $250,000 and $500,000.

Ron	Situation	Chris
Fed. Subsidized Housing	RESIDENCE	House worth $250,000
Female head of home ($9-11,000/yr.)	FAMILY STATUS	Both parents wrk($100,000yr.)
Left to fend for self stayed w/ neighbors	NURSERY/DAY CARE	Mother stayed home/best day care
Remedial/Vocational	HIGH SCHOOL	College Prep.
No one in family even has HS diploma	COLLEGE	Expected

Remember, these are high school students on my '87 caseload, suspected of breaking into lockers so they could obtain money for drugs. These cases are real. The school district is within its rights to expel both students, but has told both families that the expulsion will be delayed or reconsidered if they accept the recommendation to get the boys residential Chemical Dependency treatment.

1. Which family is more like to comply? (Chris' family)
2. What resources are available to each family? ($, time, insurance (i.e. treatment = $10-20,000 for 45 days))
3. What are some statistical outcomes? (Adult alcoholism treatment success rate = 75%; "graduation from juvenile justice system to adult criminal justice system" = 65%)[3]

Two "tough questions" arose when coordinators presented Ron and Chris to their seminars. Trish Marsik reported that one seminar member saw the exercise as "racist," stating that "the rich kid is White and the poor kid is Black." Whereas race and social class often overlap, remember that this exrcise is based on my caseload, and that all seven students are White. Coodinators tell me that students in seminar sometimes conclude that neither family will seek treatment. Again, recalling the actual cases, ALL the "haves" got treatment, while NONE of the "have nots" pursued the issue any further. Without referring to this in seminar, coordinators can answer that question with a question: "Whereas both families may object, one family followed through—which family do you think it was that did follow through?"

One coordinator really liked Ron and Chris because:

It brings the sociological perspective to a particularly understandable level.

Other coordinators had the following positive opinions on Ron and Chris:

...it does a good job at illustrating socioeconomic effects on treatment...It involved students, discussed concrete issues and opened the door for debate...It got to the heart of many issues this course addresses.

Suggested Journal Questions for the Fifth Seminar in Criminal Justice[4]

Describe your own educational situations, using the five categories from Ron and Chris. Are your circumstances more similar to Ron or to Chris? How do you see this affecting your services at site?

Fifth Seminar in Chemical Dependency: Should Drugs Be Legalized?

This week's activity, The Legalization Debate, draws from the arguments presented by Beale, Bush, Forsgren and Meadors (all 1989).

The Legalization Debate

Essentially, this activity is the same as the Liberal/Conservative Great Debate (Chapter Four), but with different content. Speakers representing pro and con sides in the Legalization of Drugs Debate stand on opposite sides of the room, taking turns stating their case. Initially, seminar members stand in the middle, halfway between the two opposing views. After points 2 and 4, students are to move towards the stand closest to their own. They are then asked to explain why they moved.

1. Americans agree that the biggest threat we are facing today as a nation is drugs. Who is responsible? Everyone who uses drugs. Everyone who sells drugs. Everyone who looks the other way. America is fighting a war against drugs. We must call on our most important weapons in this war, the ones that are the least tangible: self-discipline, courage, character, support from one's family, faith in God and in one's self.

2. A war on drugs? Have we learned nothing from history? Shall we return to the days of Prohibition? Why is no one talking about criminalizing alcohol, a dangerous drug in its own right? Legalization is the only answer: the drug war is simply not working. We continue to throw our money away, building more and more prisons to incarcerate drug offenders, and we still cannot keep up with the demand for jail space. Meanwhile, AIDS cases among IV drug users are on the rise and the issue of medical benefits of certain illegal drugs never gets addressed because of the drug war mentality.

3. Fundamentally, the drug problem in America is not one of supply but of demand. Every student in America, at some point, must choose to accept or reject drugs. But there is another choice that college students, as responsible adults, must make—whether to get involved in a personal way to end drug use or to look the other way. Legalizing drugs will not prevent pushers from killing other pushers, decrease the crimes committed by addicts to support their habit, or cut down the random, irrational violence from drug users who are under the influence. We must commit ourselves to staying away from drugs and work to keep them away from our friends. Peer pressure is what spreads drug use and peer pressure can help stop it. You can help stop it—if you get involved.

4. Taking drugs is a choice that the Bill of Rights leaves up to the individual, not Congress. The drug war "cure" is worse than the disease—are we, as Americans, willing to give up our civil liberties for a cause that clearly is not working? Let's look at Europe: The Netherlands and Great Britain have both implemented various legalization models, and both with positive results. The solution to the war on drugs? Legalization and education, education, education.

The new L-word (legalization) has crept into many different parts of my life in that I have brought up the dilemma to many different people. During the last seminar I had, we discussed the debate. No one took the position of legalizing drugs. Ward brought up the issue that the drug epidemic is a form of genocide in the ghettos—if such an epidemic of crack, ice or cocaine was in the suburbs that the government and the rest of society would win the drug war. He said that legalizing drugs was an apathetic attempt by the government to solve a problem whose roots are far too great to solve by simply legalizing the drug. Sarah and Amy took the position that legalizing drugs wouldn't necessarily lead to increased drug use and those who take drugs now aren't necessarily going to go out and become addicts just because it was legal.

Me? What do I think? I'm torn. What I really think is that we should quit worrying about the supply of drugs and focus on why there is such a demand for drugs. Are people's existences in such dire straits that they need a quick fix to escape for a while? But for those that are addicted, then what? Then we could treat them, right? One other aspect of the whole L-word thing is Bush doesn't include alcohol in his war on drugs. That in and of itself is a problem. But he couldn't now, could he? The alcohol industry in this country makes too goddamn much money on the drug, and he'd never survive such a conflict with industry. That bothers me quite a bit. Yes, I am glad he is focusing on the drug problem, but I doubt he is taking the proper channel and can only win at the number of people who will become complacent thinking he is doing enough to take care of the problem.

—Kathleen Doherty

The debate—legalization, decriminalization or what we think should be done. For this section, we split into two groups - one pro legalization and one con legalization. We set up like a panel on legalization. This was really fun—people got into it —even if they were arguing for something that they didn't necessarily agree with. People were talking and really examining what should be done about the drug problem. I don't know if we came to any earth—shattering conclusions, but we did have an interesting debate and a really good section.

When we had the debate in section, I was sort of surprised. Most of the people in my section were for legalizing pot. This surprised me. I guess I take for granted that people are against it because I don't use it. Stupid, I know People just thought that legalization would be the best way to deal with the problem. As far as the privacy issue—a civil liberty—I'm completely for drug testing in the workplace. I think that if you make an agreement that you're not going to use illegal drugs (i.e. when you agree to work for someone), you should also submit yourself to a drug test. I think an employer has the right to know. Call me conservative—but on the issue of drugs—I am.

—Jeanne Gray

Suggested Journal Questions for the Fifth Seminar in Chemical Dependency[4]

Where do you stand on the Legalization Debate?

NOTES

1. The two activities in this chapter, Ron and Chris, and the Legalization Debate, can be used in either Chemical Dependency or Criminal Justice seminars.
2. The Focus Question is the same for both Chemical Dependency and Criminal Justice and is only printed once in the text.
3. The 65% recidivism rate was quoted to me at the 1988 UM School of Social Work Alumni Conference by top ranking Department of Corrections officials. In the July 5, 1993 Ann Arbor News, Jeff Smith, the Director of the Older Adult Recovery Center in Chelsea, is quoted as saying, "the center's succes rate, based on surveys sent to former patients, has been 75 to 85 percent" for "about 700 patients" since 1986 (Serju, 1993).
4. In the past terms, as supplementary reading for coordinators I've assigned Hadley (1990).

Chapter 7

12 STEPPIN'
A Teleology on the Rocks

Sixth Seminar in Criminal Justice: Does the System Promote Racial Inequality?

The goal of this seminar is to raise questions among students about how race and gender may be affecting their interpersonal relationships, particularly at site and in seminar.

Focus Questions: Williams writes that the "dynamism of the self-as-reinterpreted-by-the-perceptions-of-others is a fundamental part of ourselves and our dignity depends on the uncontrollable, powerful, external observers who make up our society" (1991). Do you think that Williams persuasively demonstrates that American Blacks are self-alienated and discriminated against because of their definition as "other"? What do you feel about her assessment of the Howard Beach incident? What about the Bernard Goetz subway shooting?

> *I like the way Williams (1991) illuminates the absurdity of the Goetz shooting and Howard Beach incident point by point. She takes an excuse: most crimes are committed by Blacks. And counters it with a fact: 71% of arrests are white. Her style is compelling, the emotion behind is sincere and not self-righteous. Almost tragic. I think her central point is compelling, that of "dynamism of self as reinterpreted by others." In other words, when another person sees me, they in fact don't see me in the sense of knowing me, but only an appearance. The image in the mind of the other is a construct of stereotypes. For example, when I was in Mexico, I wasn't Richard John Smith, but a guero, or gringo. Or a pretty white boy desirable for marriage because of his obvious wealth and natural white beauty. Because of the elaborate system in which my being is perceived, these facts about my self cannot be wiped away, but only examined, using the critical consciousness.*
>
> *—Rick Smith*

Be! Aggressive!, Through the Eyes of the Other and the SAPAC Guided

Fantasy have all been helpful to past coordinators in facilitating discussion on the key points in Williams (1991), MacIntosh (1989) and Collins (1983).

Be! Agressive!

This activity, loosely based on this week's readings is actually four related exercises. The Agression Molecule (see chart) is another idea I borrowed from Chemical Dependency treatment. In the center of the chart is the word, "aggression." Extending outward are four spokes representing the physical, legal, psychological and social consequences of agression. Essentially, this is a brainstorming activity. The leader asks the group to name all the negative consequences of aggression that they can think of. As they come up with these consequences, the coordinator writes each one on the chart. The end result is something that looks like a complex molecule. At the point, the coordinator asks, "If aggression is so bad, why is it so prevalent in our society?" (To paraphrase one of Matt Kinney's favorite phrases, somebody must benefit!)

"Chair-ish" is the Word I Use to Describe" calls for students to role play three situations involving an empty chair.

"Why don't you take this chair? I really don't want to sit there."
"Okay—if you insist!"

"Excuse me, but I would really like to sit in this chair."
"Okay—if you insist!"

"Gimme that chair or I'll shoot you!"
"Okay—if you insist!"

The coordinator then discusses with the students the difference between being passive, assertive, and aggressive in each situation. The coordinator then suggests that, in addition to behavior, social factors such as race, class and gender may also be influencing where the line is drawn in each situation.

"Combed My Hair in a Thousand Ways, but I Wound Up Looking Just the Same" is another brainstorming exericse. After Chair-ish, the coordinator asks the group to list all the ways they can think of that their site uses to deal with aggression. During staffings, the list has included things like Positive Peer Culture, Art Therapy, Creative Writing, Group Therapy, Individual Counseling and Sports (basketball, boxing and weightlifting). When the list has been completed, ask the group what all the items have in common. In closing, suggest that primarily these strategies treat aggression after the fact, but that less emphasis is being paid to the larger picture, the role of violence and aggression in our society.

"***He Coached, Not Wisely, but Too Well."*** is an excerpt from the 11/12/88 Detroit Free Press that can be used to close this activity.

"Jim Donnelly...offensive coordinator for the Chiefs, a boy's team in W.

Palm Beach, Florida, was fired this week because he allowed his players to pile on the points as they rolled through an undefeated season...Rules of the Palm Beach County Youth League (for 10-12 years-olds) say that after a 17-point lead, the winning team must ease up and refrain from demoralizing it's opponenents...QB Michael Henly, 12, who engineers the Chief's triple reverses and sophisticated wishbone attack said he sees nothing wrong with punishing his opponents: "Football is supposed to be a mean sport. That's what football is all about. You shouldn't be punished because you're good."

The Aggression Molecule

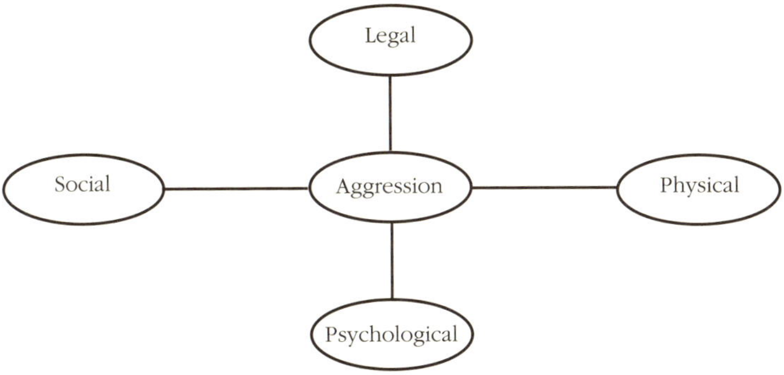

One activity I would change is the Agression Molecule. I felt the activity needed to be explained better. Give more opportunity to let people challenge, instead of stacking the cards to get the desired response.

Ron Ikens reported that Be! Aggressive! worked well for him all three times. He added a "financial consequences" spoke to the model.

For Kathleen Doherty, the most effect part of Be! Aggressive! was probably the story at the end.

Through The Eyes Of The Other

Read the following sentences slowly, taking long pause between the lines.

I'd like you to imagine yourself as a student at a university.

This can be any university in the country.

I'm calling it Imaginary University.

You're a student at this university, and your same sex and race can apply.

There are only ramps and lowered facilities due to the high percentage of handicapped students.

There is a white Student Services Office which is open on Thursday.

All residents' hall staff are people of color that speak English as a second language.

At this particular university, less than 5% of the professors are White, and there are predominantly Black female professors.

There are no white professors in your department and of the total 5% at the university, most teach upper level or graduate courses.

Some buildings are only accessible by wheelchair, so if you're not in a wheel-chair, you have to redesign your schedule.

Classes are held during Easter and Christmas, but not during Hanukkah, Passover, or Rosh Hashannah.

The other students complain that you do not integrate yourself into the community. For example, all of the white students sit together at a dinner table or in class. White students tend to join one of the three sororities or one of the three fraternities.

The majority of the students at this university are concerned that you, as a White student are taking their graduate student admissions.

It is perceived that you are accepted by virture of your race, and that's all.

And finally, people look at you strangely when you show open affection to members of the opposite sex.

Think about all these things that happened to you.

Okay, why don't we all sit up. How did you feel?

Michelle Blankenship thought that this activity was the highlight of her single best seminar during the Fall '88 term.

SAPAC[1] Guided Fantasy

Purpose: This exercise is intended to enable students to become aware of how roles of women and men would be altered if the past was different or if our socialization had a different basis. In gaining this awareness, it is expected that students will be better equipped to develop critical thinking skills and to use their sociological imagination.

Instructions: Have everyone lie down or get as comfortable as possible in their chair. Have them close their eyes. Ask them to relax as much as possible. Explain that you would like them to work on feeling what their responses are as they are guided through this exercise. Impress on the students that it is important that they try not to intellectualize this exericse. It is important that they stay with what they are feeling—what does it mean to a woman or a man.

> Imagine that we live in a world where the generic term for referring to people is reversed... "Woman," "Her," "She," of course all include both men and women. Think about the "future of woman-kind"—meaning both men and women.
>
> Imagine that the signers of the Declaration of Independence were all women. In fact, whenever we read about the history of our country, we are reading about the "founding mothers." How does this change your view of the world?
>
> Look at your schools. All of your teachers are women, the principals are women. The school crossing guards are women, and the coaches for the team sports are women. The main people you learned about throughout school are women and their achievements—the inventors, the fighters, the positive people in our lives—all women. Occasionally, someone will point out the "rare exception of a man" who made a positive contribution to our society. What does this look like? How does it make you feel? As a women or as a man, does it tell you anything about yourself?
>
> Think of it always being this way, everyday of your life. Feel the overwhelming presence of women and feel the non-presence of men. Men seem to be hidden. You hear stories about what boys do, but it's laughed at, snickered about. How does this feel? What does it tell you of the importance of being a woman or of being a man?
>
> Recall that everything you have ever read all your life uses only female pronouns—she, her—meaning both girls and boys, women and men. Recall that most of the voices on radio and more of the faces on TV are women's—when important events are covered, on commercials, on the late night talk shows. Mostly women.
>
> Notice that our government is headed completely by women. You have no male senator representing you in Washington. The President is a woman. The Secretary of State is a woman. The head of the Pentagon is a woman. In fact, remember back to the time that a man once ran for Vice President and how much that shook everyone up. Remember how they asked questions about what his wife must feel like? And who was going to take care of the children? Does the world look different, act different? How does this make you feel? As a women? As a man? Feel what it is like that women are leaders, the power centers, the prime movers. As you grow up, you are taught that man's natural role is husband and father. He fulfills himself through nurturing children and making the home a refuge for woman. What does this tell you about the importance of women? the role of men?
>
> Then think further, about the lessons you receive in school, throughout life, through friends and family members, through our religious institutions. The lessons you learn about the differences between men and women. The reasons why women are the power centers. How does this feel to learn that the obvious biological explanation for women as the ideal, the leader, the powerful, is her genital construction. By design, female genitals are compact and internal, protected by her body. Male genitals are

so exposed that he must be protected from outside attack to assure the perpetuation of the race. Biologically, he has evolved into this position because his vulnerability clearly requires sheltering. How does this make you feel as a woman? as a man?

Recall that you are taught that, by nature, males are more passive than females—they are socialized to wait for things to happen, to let women take the initiative. Women are the aggressors, they make the descisions, take action, go after what they want. Because of this men yearn for protection by women. They are taught that they are only "whole men" when engulfed by women, when cared for and protected. What does this tell you about growing up as a woman? as a man?

Of course, as you grow up, it is natural to have some confusion about your identity. To question some of these strict messages we have been taught. You struggle with the roles that are defined for you as a woman or a man by society. If the man denies his feelings of wanting to be protected and cared for, he is told that is "unconsciously rejecting his masculinity" Therapy is recommended to help him adjust to his own nature. Of course, therapy is administered by a woman, who has the education and wisdom to facilitate openness leading to male's growth and self-actualization. How does this feel to you?

To work on better accepting his role, males are told that they must understand their defensiveness. To do this, he is invited to get in touch with the "child" in him. He remembers his sister making fun of his gentials that "flop around foolishly". She can run, climb and ride horseback unencumbered. Obviously, since she is free to move, she is encouraged to develop her body and her mind in preparation for her active responsibilities of adult womanhod. The male vulnerability needs female protection, so he is taught the less active, caring virtues of homemaking.

Because of his raging envy, he also learns to strap up his genitals and to feel ashamed and unclean of his obvious inferior anatomical design. He is encouraged to keep his body lean and dream of getting married, waiting for the time of his fulfillment—when his woman gives him a girl child to carry on the family name.

You are who you are in society. Your gender has defined these lifestyle issues for you. When you look around you, it is reinforced everywhere. In your books, on TV—all the shows, advertising for every product from toothpaste to car wax. It seems that there is no escaping the fact that women are the power centers, the people controlling the world and men are simply to decorate and to nurture the children. How does this feel? What does this tell you about your place as women as a man?

Sit and experience this for a few minutes. Reflect on your feelings, on what you saw around you keep your eyes closed, just concentrate on this vision of the new world.

Stacey and I decided for our seminar to do the SAPAC Guided Fantasy as a discussion inspirer on gender roles and sexism. Everyone enjoyed the exercise and talked much. I was surprised that Jason, the poet, was more sexist that David, the soon to be law student. Once again, stereotypes fail. Neither Jason nor

> *David had heard of the glass ceiling or wage inequity. All the women had. Jason talked about the rights of men accused of rape, sort of. He related a story about how one of his friends was accused of rape because his girlfriend's "feminist" friends convinced her she had been raped although "in fact" she was only upset to have lost her virginity. We got into another discussion on biological determinism. David and Jennifer (everyone else but me) felt sexism was a result of the patterns of nature. They did feel that humanity, using the intellect, could overcome that force. Cool.*
>
> —*Rick Smith*

Suggested Journal Questions for the Sixth Seminar in Criminal Justice

Describe a situation where you were affected, first-hand, by stereotyping. This can be an observation that you have made, a personal reflection of how you've been treated or of how you've treated someone else.

Sixth Seminar in Chemical Dependency: 12 Step Programs—Cure or Cover?

The goal of this seminar is for students to identify their position relative to AA's 12 steps.

Focus Question: What do you think of AA's emphasis on individual responsibility and, in effect, guilt? The 12 Step Program has been criticized for focusing too much on the person, at the expense of larger societal pressures and dynamics: what do you think?

Powerless Over Fish Innards

During the Winter '90 term, I originally wanted each member of the staffing to summarize one of the articles on the 12 Steps (in the coursepack) at the beginning of our discussion. What happened was the Legalization Debate ran too long the previous week, so I could not make any specific assignments. I ended up doing the summaries myself. For each article, the author and title are on the top line: The first paragraph of each summary states why the author believes that 12 Step groups work; the second paragraph states the author's criticisms of 12 Step programs.

In staffing, I passed out the Powerless Over Fish Innards handout and gave everyone a chance to read the summaries. I then gave people a chance to ask any clarifying questions about the articles that they may have, and then moved the discussion towards having people talk about where they stood regarding the effectiveness of the 12 Step program.

The Summaries (All from the Nov./Dec. '88 Utne Reader)

Herman: "The 12 Step Program: Cure or Cover?"

They seem to work because "They pay serious attention to ordinary pain by requiring people to pay attention to it themselves....Working the steps one by one and repeating them indefinitely, gives people at least two things that neither science nor politics consistently seems to trust people with: a largely self-determined routine and permission to understand our problems differently at different stages in our lives, in ways that make sense to us even if they don't to anyone else." Criticism? Are all substances and activities the same? Non-addicts joining? Individual/political responsibility?

Bufe: "AA: Guilt and God for the Gullible"

AA works because it provides an important social outlet; alcoholics realize their problems are not unique, and the steps provide structure.

Create a structure without AA's religiosity/guilt/hypocrisy?

Perrin and Colman: "Is Addiction Actually a Misguided Move...?"

Something outside of us can make us whole but a problem arises when the "something" is substance in our drug-using society.

"Attitudinal healing"—power, peace, etc., are all inside you?

Peele: "On the Deceasing of America"

Hopelessness results from "creating a world of addictions (which) actually engenders more addiction."

Our children's hope: People (individually and as a society) are self-correcting through knowledge and experience?

Berenson: "AA: For Surrender to Transformation"

AA generates "planned spontaneous remission" on three levels: education, therapeutic change and transformation (community).

Schaef: "Recovery as Process"

"I find that they (criticisms) are usually made by persons who have not really tried the program or working the steps. The steps have to be worked everyday and repeated endlessly. Yet the levels on which one is working them change, and the perspective changes constantly as recovery proceeds. Recovery is a miracle."

Collett: "Step by Step: A Skeptic's Encounter with the 12 Steps"

"With group help, abstain from your compulsion—alcohol, sex or chronic credit card debt. Admit you can't do it alone. Straighten out your relationships with your fellow human beings by admitting your faults. Accept help from your higher power, defining him or her any way you want to. Do these things, help others and your compulsions will lift as if by magic.

Some people...think 12 Step groups encourage conformity and passivity. Perhaps that is inevitable given our generation's cultural history: rebellion, sex, drugs and rock 'n roll splashed over our lives in one big wave that looked like liberation...?"

> *We got into a very heated discussion about AA and other treatment programs. It was good because we covered the material before break. I don't know if people hadn't done the*

reading or what, but the discussion was pretty lame. Bill brought up again that our debate was kind of similar to the one we had in section.

—Jeanne Gray

During Powerless Over Fish Innards, some coordinators noted that some students in their seminars had some negative experiences with 12 Step groups. Jeanne Gray indicated that some members in her seminar said:

Those Utne Reader articles are the best readings in the coursepack!

Trust Walk

Cris Zerkel used this activity during the Winter '91 seminar. Basically, group members are split into dyads and one member of the dyad is blindfolded. That person is led around the room by his/her partner, then the roles are reversed. The Trust Walk could effectively initiate an in-depth discussion of the 12 Steps since blindfolded group members are meant to experience the need for other's help that the 12 Steps are founded upon.

Suggested Journal Questions for the Sixth Seminar in Chemical Dependency

"We must clarify what we mean by responsibility. The addictive meaning of the word means accountability and blame. Unfortunately, this attitude puts us in the position of being a victim and robs us of our power. It is only when we accept that we have choices, and we exercise those choices, that we can reclaim our lives."

—Schaef, 1990

I think that Ms. Schaef's distinction between responsibility and blame is important when looking at AA. While AA does put impetus for recovery in the hands of each individual member, it acknowledges the power of alcoholism as a disease, and does not dwell on shame, guilt, or blame. AA encourages its members to focus not necessarily on why they are what they are, but rather, on what they must do about it to improve their quality of life. There is no pretense that recovery will take place within a vacuum, distinct from a society where social drinking, and over-drinking are the norm. By stressing the importance of spiritual health, positive coping skills, and by providing a safe and supportive meeting place and social network, AA encourages it members to strive for sobriety in spite of societal pressures.

—Mary Jo Callan

How would the 12 Steps read if you wrote them? How have you seen the

12 Steps applied at site and in seminar? Have you observed any evidence that the 12 Steps actually work?

NOTES

1. SAPAC is the acronym for the Sexual Assault Prevention and Awareness Center at UM. My thanks for their permission to reprint this article.

Chapter 8

A FREIRE HOME COMPANION

Seventh Seminar: The PC Pedagogy— What is our Midterm Evaluation?

The goal of this seminar is for students to think critically about how their experiences at UM and PC may or may not correspond with Freire's perspectives on Banking and Liberationist Education (1970).

Focus Questions: What do the following terms mean to someone from a 100% Banking and a 100% Liberationist perspective: social change, individual change, education and service?

Social Change
Banking: What's left in your pocket after going to the bar.
Liberationist: Your life's work.
Individual Change
Banking: The only thing that counts.
Liberationist: A necessary product of your life's work.
Education
Banking: Puppy training for jobs.
Liberationist: A passion for the development of critical consciousness.
Service
Banking: What you used to get at the gas station.
Liberationist: A calling.

It might be interesting to ask people to brainstorm what they think these terms mean in light of Freire, but I tend to like contrasting PC and UM. It's a lot more concrete. Mark Chesler deserves one pint of Stucchi's ice cream for updating the second paper assignment. I think it cuts to the essence of PC. I can't wait to write it."

—Rick Smith

The activities in this chapter are based on the assigned reading for the week, Chapter Two of Paulo Freire's Pedagogy of the Oppressed (1970).

I have three reasons for introducing Freire at the mid-term. First, this allows people to re-visit their understanding of a "learning community": Freire's educational (and political) philosophy underlie the Kahn and Howard (1990) readings for the second seminar. Second, studying Freire gives people the opportunity to re-evaluate both their group norms and personal goals. Third, the activities are meant to help coordinators in writing their term papers. The paper assignments[1] for the Winter '93 term are included at the end of this chapter.

Freire On My Wayward Son

This activity has two parts. At the beginning of seminar, the coordinator splits the group into dyads and assigns each dyad opposing terms from the following list.

	Banking	Liberationist
Knowledge...	—is a gift —the teacher deposits —students know nothing	—emerges through dialogue —teacher/student and student/teachers in solidarity
Reality is...	—motionless, static compartmentalized predictable	—a process undergoing transformation
Education consists of...	—transfers of information	—acts of cognition
Thinking is...	—obviated	—critical
The focus of words is on...	—their sound	—their meaning
This system...	—mirrors oppressive society	—trusts people's creativity
This system is...	—reactionary	—revolutionary

The first part of the activity ends with each dyad presenting and explaining its terms for the whole group.

> *Freire's Wayward Son exercise was not exactly duplicated in my seminar. I did not think that my members would fully grasp the definitions of the words. So what I did was read from the lists given out in staffing and asked them to place the terms under their appropriate headings (Banking and Liberationist) instead of having them explain the meanings. I wanted to make sure they had at least a general idea of the differences between the banking system and liberationist system.*

> *Each of us looked at your handout and picked out a couple of dilemmas that were listed. We basically discussed them, like what happened in our staff meeting. They knew the concepts, not just the words I liked your list a lot—it's concise and gets the point across, allowing us further time for reactions and discussion. The nature of Freire lends itself well to natural and plentiful discussion.*
>
> *—Kathleen Doherty*

My original idea for the second part of this exercise was to refer the group back to the list of norms created during the second seminar and then ask, "How Freirean are we?" A frequent response, which also tended to limit discussion, was "We're pretty Freirean."

Once the seminar was clear on the differences between banking and liberationist education, Kathleen Doherty suggests that discussion then center on two questions:

1. What would the University of Michigan be like if it were based entirely on the banking model?
2. What would Project Community be like if it were based entirely on Freire's liberationist model?

During the Fall '92 term, seminars were divided into two groups with each group assigned one of Kathleen's questions.

> *The exercise in the staffing helped me with Freire a lot. It clarified a lot of confusion and also gave me great examples for each type of perspective.*
>
> *—Elissa Zelman*

> *The exercise we did at staffing was good because it gave us practical examples of Freire's theories. The idea of comparing his theories to the University of Michigan is something everyone can relate to. I think that almost every student has some problem or can find some fault with the University, as in anything else. Making a familiar analogy is helpful in understanding a tough concept. For my seminar, I used the same exercise, comparing U of M to Freire. I did give them the key words and we went over them until I thought they understood the concepts. We did the U of M exercise and it went very well. The students in my seminar thought that it was very good; I think they got a lot out of the whole exercise. They came up with some very good ideas and they explained them very carefully and correctly; they now have a good idea of what Freire's concepts and theories are about. Discussing Freire in this manner is somewhat of a liberationist technique because we are discussing the concepts and theories—I didn't just lecture to them about what they mean. They got a practical look at what their life could be like either totally banking or*

> *totally liberationist. In my paper, I think it will be helpful because it is an example of using a liberationist technique that worked. If it would have failed, it would have been a mark for the banking system. We all agreed that there needed to be more liberationist techniques in the University, although we also agree that the University couldn't be completely liberationist.*
>
> *—Monique Whitman*

Five Universal Organizational Elements

To focus on the second part of "Freire On My Wayward Son", during the Winter '92 term, I had coordinators address their remarks within the framework of the Five Universal Organizational Elements found in Chesler and Crowfoot (1989). Following are notes from the Winter '92 CD and CJ staffings.

U-M as 100% Banking

Mission: Our knowledge rules. Shut up and listen.	Teachers know everything. Students know nothing. Students are sponges.
Organizational Culture: Don't question. Obey. Conform. White, straight, Christian, male culture is obviously and implicitly superior.	Students never question teachers. Students never face teachers. No hands-on learning
Power: Decision-making is top-down, reinforcing the status quo.	Teacher makes all decisions. Students have no power. Teachers talk; students listen.
Structure: A pyramid structure with white males (administrators) on top; students, women and minorities on bottom.	Well-defined boundaries. Lectures; no discussions.
Resources: Guns; corporate, state, federal funds; tuition; alumni.	Papers that professors have written. Students made to buy coursepacks. Grants, federal funding.

PC as 100% Liberationist

Mission: Dedicated to reconciling the teacher/student—student/teacher dilemma.	To exchange ideas/knowledge by broadening the intellectual and experiential worlds of the participants.

Culture:	
Egalitarianism and freedom of expression are valued and honored based on trust and love.	Non-conformist, non-dictatorial, liberal, accepting of new ideas and change.
Power:	
Democratic group process of of decision-making.	Non-hierarchial, closely related to a network, horizontally integrated.
Structure:	
Transitive property of leadership.	Authority attained through evolution of a leader rather than designation (i.e. respect, merit, performance).
Resources:	
Everybody contributes everything.	Contribution of individuals; grants are possible, volunteers; state/federal funding.
—CD STAFFING	—CJ STAFFING

Mary Jo Callan thought that this version of the activity was particularly helpful because it gave people specific and concrete examples of how to apply Freire's pedagogy.

Suggested Journal Questions for Seventh Seminar

Review your goals in light of Freire. How would you describe your progress? What adjustments do you think are necessary? Do you have any suggestions on how we could make your Project Community experience more liberationist?

NOTES

1. 49% of a coordinator's grade in Sociology 395 is based on the program director's review of work done in seminar, site and staffing: 51% is based on the term paper written for Professor Chesler.
2. In addition to Freire (1970 and 1973), Professor Chesler also recommends Shor and Freire (1987) to students writing term papers for him.
3. Although not cited, Professor Harrison usually recommends Dewey (1962) to students writing papers for him. Professor Harrison is Project Community's faculty sponsor for Education 317, 310 and 610.

Mark Chesler
Assignment #1
Sociology 395, section 003
4028 LSA
747-3654

Guidelines for Project Community Coordinators' Papers:
The requirements for fulfilling this independent study course are twofold:

1. That you do a good job of facilitating your students learnings, of learning about education facilitation and leadership, organizing students' field efforts, etc. This requirement will be assessed and graded by the Project Community staff, and they will make input to your course grade.
2. That you undertake a serious written intellectual effort to review, reflect upon and generate a conceptual understanding of the role of experiential learning, of your role in facilitating such learning, and of the problems and opportunities in doing so. This requirement will be met by a paper, described below, that will be handed in to me and will determine your grade for the course.

The LSA College is quite clear that course credit (and grading) for facilitating other student' learning is not to be based upon such activity, per se, but upon demonstrated learning and intellectual exploration of such learning processes.

The paper should be rooted in a <u>review and application</u> of Paulo Freire's concepts of consciousness raising and liberationist education, as spelled out it <u>Education of Critical Consciousness</u> (1973) and <u>Pedagogy of the Oppressed</u>, (1970)[2] as well as other works. You are asked to:

1. <u>Describe</u> his concepts of banking and liberationist education, noting how these concepts do or do not fit your experience with pedagogies at the U-M and PC.
2. <u>Analyze or theorize</u> about why the University pedagogy and/or Project Community pedagogy is the way you have described it.
3. <u>Describe</u> some of your dilemmas, problems, and/or successes in facilitating experiential learning in Project Community.
4. <u>Analyze</u> the roots of these dilemmas (e.g. why do they occur or where do they come from) in yourself (ideology, skills, fears, hopes), your students (their ideology, skills, expectations, habits, hopes, the Project Community structure and culture (staff relations, sites, resources), and/or the surrounding University setting (Soc staff, LSA curriculum, University pressures, etc).

An outline of this paper should be shared with me by __________. This is not required, but suggested as a way of increasing the level of dialogue and exchange between us and advising you of my expectations. Note that an acceptable outline or draft is no guarantee of an acceptable final product...one does not subsume the other.

The final paper is due to me by __________. It can be placed in my Sociology mailbox (outside room 3012 LSA) or my CRSO mailbox (4507 LSA). I would be delighted to meet and talk with you about your ideas, problems, outlines, or drafts at any time throughout the semester.

Mark Chesler
Sociology 395, section 3
4028 LSA—747-3654

SPECIAL GUIDELINES FOR PROJECT COMMUNITY COORDINATORS WHO ARE WRITING FOR CREDIT AND WHO HAVE ALREADY WRITTEN THE FRIERE-BASED-PAPER

The groundrules for credit are already clear to you. Since you have already written the basic paper, we are ready to take the next step.

Closely related to the field-site work you and your students are involved in are four closely related terms that often are used carelessly and ambiguously. They are

- SOCIAL CHANGE
- INDIVIDUAL CHANGE
- EDUCATION
- SERVICE

Freire focuses most of his concern on social change, and his notion of education as a strategy to get there is quite different than the ways in which most of us discuss education, including those of us involved in Project Community who talk about Friere.

Our society, rooted in Western traditions of individualism and voluntarism, usually focuses on individual change as a strategy to solve most individual and social problems. But there is no necessary connection between individual change (e.g. in information, attitudes, values, behaviors, feelings), even the changing of many individuals, and social change (e.g. in patterns of resource distribution, allocation of wealth, structures and cultures of major institutions, etc.).

Many organizations, groups and people who are involved in delivering services to others consider themselves in the business of social change, but there are contradictions between the acts of delivering services within a stable system and creating social change of that system.

And finally, the tradition and individual change often rests on a base of the strategy of education as a way to achieve its objectives. But even massive education programs, which may or may not lead to meaningful individual change, do not necessarily lead to social change.

Write about the following questions:

1. Where are we and what do we do in Project Community...social change (of what), individual change (of whom), education (of whom), service (of what, to whom)?
2. If your site work were to seriously address social change as a goal, what would have to be different (in the site, in the students' activities, in your role and knowledge and skills, in the structure of Project Community and its location and relationship to the larger University)? Be concrete and specific about the hows and whats of this inquiry.

An outline of this paper can be shared with me by __________, and I would get it back to you within 48 hours. This is not required, but suggested as a way of increasing the level of interaction and dialogue between us. I would be glad to meet with you (preferably in small groups rather than one-on-one) at our mutual convenience.

Don K. Harrison[3]
Guidlines for Independent Study
Education 310 and 610
1360 School of Education
747-0618

The information contained herein has been developed to assist students who are interested in a an independent study for in one of the courses identified above. The student will develop and submit a written proposal describing the plan for an independent study. The proposal should contain the following information, minimumly.

1. Name of topic to investigate.
2. A statement of what it is that the student seeks to learn about the topic investigated.
3. A statement that describes the method(s) that the student plans to utilize to conduct the independent study.
4. The student should suggest how the independent study might be evaluated by the professor, e.g. pass/fail; satisfactory; letter grade, which must meet the requirement of the student's department or college, as well as University guidelines.
5. The proposal for the independent study should contain a complete listing of bibliography, the style which should conform to the latest publication manual of the American Psychological Association.

The proposal, containing the Name, Address, and Telephone Number of the Student, should be submitted for approval NO LATER THAN 2 WEEKS AFTER THE START OF THE NEW TERM. The student should telephone for an appointment to discuss the proposal, and to obtain final approval. The approved copy of the proposal will constitute an agreement regarding the expectations and work to be accomplished.

Chapter 9

HERE'S A STORY
The Stanford Prison Experiment

Eighth Seminar in Criminal Justice: How Do Their Social Roles Influence Correctional Staff?

The goal of this seminar is for students to experience the powerful connection between social roles and expected behavior during an activity based on Haney and Zimbardo (1970).

Focus Questions: Haney and Zimbardo write, "The causes of behavior, we have learned, are more likely to reside in the nature of the environment than inside the person. And although the operation of situational forces can also be extremely powerful"(1973). Do you agree with them? What do you think it is about the prison situation that makes people act the way they did in the experiment?

Both Part One and Part Two of Imagine You Are a Prison Guard are based on "Social Roles and Role Playing" by Haney and Zimbardo (1973).

Imagine You Are A Prison Guard

I. Introduction (to be read by coordinator)

The exercise's running theme is "social roles influence behavior" (SRIB)—prison guards being the specific case in point. The Stanford Prison Experiment is a good illustration of this relationship. Although we can't recreate the experiment here, what Matt and Joe hope is that this exercise will give you a little taste of what it was all about.

I am going to read some sentence stems, and I want everyone in the circle to respond to them as if you were a prison guard. It's important that you say the first thing that comes to your mind, that people respond quickly and that there are no long pauses for thought, jokes or other reactions during this exercise. As we go through the exercise, be aware of your own thoughts and feelings as we go along—you'll have a chance to talk about those later.

My idea of what a prison is came from...
What a prison really accomplishes is...

You can tell if a prison is working by...
All guards are ...
I want to be a guard because...
It makes me feel good to use my power when...
The ultimate aphrodisiac of power is...
I resent the public's image of brutal guards because...
I am angry when people see me as something out of an old Cagney movie because...
Outsiders are ambitious, arrogant meddlers in my business because...
I resent people sticking their noses in my business because...
The treatment staff is my enemy because...
It's important to keep the treatment people happy because...
On thing that shows the administration is drunk with power is...
The administration is really ignorant about...
What I hate about the way that the administration has undermined my authority is...
All prisoners are...
All women prisoners are...
All Black prisoners are...
If the public really knew how tough my job was, my pay would be...
I am pissed off about my salary because...
Prisoners who try to con me are...
I use my power on prisoners who...
I don't feel bad for prisoners who...
Prisoners deserve what they get when they...
Guards know more than anyone else about prisoners because...
I know more about how I treat my prisoners because...
When someone tells me how to do my job I feel...

II. Debriefing the Exercise

What was happening with you during this exercise? What were you thinking? How did you feel? Did these things surprise you? Remember SRIB.

III. Introduce Part Two

A. Read the newspaper article about the proposed program at Ferris State[1].

B. Pass out the worksheet and split into groups. Following the directions on the worksheet, each group then designs their own program similar to Ferris State's.

C. Bring groups back together to share models

1. What did you call the program? (Discuss image)
—"guard versus officer"
—this name is a big part of SRIB
2. Go through the factors individually—How well does the proposed program address each?
3. How does your program address our running theme, SRIB? Concluding statement: It really is an insidious problem, SRIB. At the very least, there are these dimensions to be dealt with. Where

does the role end and the self begin? How does the individual see himself or herself in that role? Are there larger insititutional and/ or socializing factors at work here and what is their impact on that role?

Worksheet for III

Your task is to create a degree program similar to Ferris State's at the University of Michigan. Students would enter your program at the beginning of their junior year, enroll in two years of course work, have a summer prison field placement, and then have a job waiting for them after graduation. In designing your program, keep in mind the experience that you just had, along with the following factors.

- Guards are sensitive about their public image, especially characterizations of them as being brutal and power hungry.
- Guards generally view the prison treatment staff as an enemy, but comply with them to keep open future alliances.
- Guards see the prison administration as being ignorant, as being drunk with power, and as making decisions that endanger them and undermine their authority.
- To guards, outsiders are ambitious and arrogant meddlers.
- Guards experience feelings of isolation on the job, and also feel accomplishment in reducing inmate stress by increasing inmate autonomy, certainty and privacy in individual interactions.
- Guards may have trouble dealing with the "isms"—racism, sexism, classism—simply because of the inmates' diversity.

The following reflections on Guards and Guards II are from journals and evaluations.

> *I felt the Guards activity worked well, nailing the issue and bringing up discussion.*
>
> *I like Guards because people's inner personalities were revealed.*
>
> *I thought the Prison Guard exercise was particularlry good because I'm interested in the [Stanford] Study. It really fascinated me that people would change like that.*
>
> *I liked the Prison Guard activity because it was interesting to see just how much people like to utilize their power over others. I already had these stereotypes from working at this prison, and this activity did nothing but reinforce those beliefs.*
>
> *... the activity still worked well. People identified program outlines similar to those we came up with in staffing. I tried to get people to think about what the relation was between their feelings on guards' power and what classes the guards-in-training would take. My reason for wanting them to consider*

> *this relationship was because some people didn't think guards abuse power; yet, they still wanted them to take classes, or have experiences, such as social roles/sterotypes, role playing of guard/prisoner, an intern-ship as a guard, and PC. Such classes/experience would teach guards to try to not abuse their power. Finallly, I asked the question, "Do you think the guards create the need to use their power (i.e. Do they inherently just want to abuse their power?) or do the prisoners put the guards in a position where they need to abuse their power?*
>
> *—Julie Mathews*

Suggested Journal Questions for the Eighth Seminar in Criminal Justice

Keep track of the roles you play in different social situations throughout the week—friend, student, sibling, child, lover, etc. To what extent is your behavior in each situation determined by your role? To what extent is it determined by your personality?

Eighth Seminar in Chemical Dependency

The goal of this seminar is for students to identify codependency as one specific application of Systems Theory (Napier and Whitaker, 1998)—that to some extent, having an addict as a family member affects all other parts of the Family System.

Focus Question: What connections can you make between systems theory and codependency?

The goal of this seminar is to introduce students to codependency. Prentice Zinn reminded me that codependency is a controversial issue and should be presented as such: that is why Haaken (1993), Epstein and Epstein (1990) and Lamb (1990) are in the course pack. I did not pursue this further because the criticisms leveled at 12 Step Programs also apply to codependency. The Eighth Seminar reading most directly relevant to the activities is Black (1982).

Here's A Story

This exercise again is taken from my experience in Chemical Dependency treatment. Basically, the coordinator starts by drawing a blank genogram (see diagram) on newsprint or a chalkboard of a nuclear family with two children. The group is first asked to give names and ages to each family member. The coordinator then writes this information on the genogram.

Next, the coordinator asks the group to assign role "hats" to each family member. For example, the father may be "the breadwinner" or "the disciplinarian" in this "typical American family."

After the group generates a fairly comprehensive list of roles, make one of the parents chemically dependent. Then go through the list of that person's roles and see who in the family is affected by the parent's chemical dependency and how. For example, if the father now is chemically dependent and "the breadwinner," his use may affect his job performance. The group may create a scenario that calls for the mother and the children all to "pitch in" financially, and this, in turn, affects each of their roles. This exercise is most effective when the coordinator takes the group through each role in detail.

Afterwards, the coordinator can have the group process the exercise both in terms of site and in terms of their own families.

> *Well another uneventful week...We did roles and Here's a Story. People really got into that—it was sort of funny then got sort of serious—especially when we brought it home to the site and the kind of stuff we saw out there.*
>
> *—Jeanne Gray*

"Here's A Story" Genogram

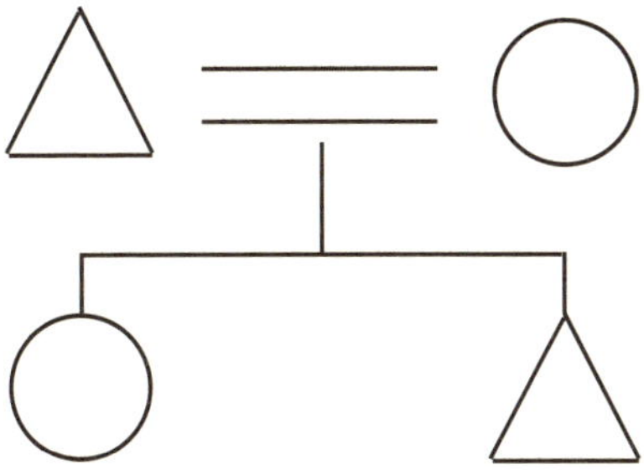

Every Picture Tells A Story, Don't It? (Codependency Version)

During the Winter '91 term, Cris Zerkel had difficulty running Here's A Story in her seminar. She quickly made the transition to this activity which did work well. In reflecting on the situation, Cris quoted seminar members who said, "People were reading way too much into this—over-identifying the hypothetical family in the activity with their own family."

In his stint as "guest Sociologist" during the Fall '89 term, Matt Kinney created the following activity. Before the staffing, Matt and I cut out about two dozen glossy magazine ads. In the meeting we split coordinators into groups of three or four and gave each group eight to ten ads. For each ad, the groups were directed to identify what the message was and then identify how this message supports (or does not support) a specific aspect of codependency.

The following comments come from coordinators' evaluations.

> *One activity I thought was particularly good was the magazine pictures—good illustration of how subtly codependency is incorportated into society.*
>
> *I like the magazine ad exercise because it was active and let*

us see how it [codependency] is 'alive' in society.

Satir-icons

This is a technique I've adapted for seminar from my work as a family therapist. Basically, the group creates a sculpture of a family with an alcoholic parent. During the Winter '92 staffings, I posed volunteers, one at a time, in a family sculpture portraying an alcoholic parent, his or her spouse, and three or four children. The activity is meant to be interactive: throughout, input on how each family member should be posed is solicited from all seminar participants. In processing the exercise, people are first asked to identify their thoughts and feelings about their role in the family sculpture, and then asked to connect these feelings and thoughts to some readings[2].

Tom Cook did this exercise with his mentees at site. Terri Newsome thought that it was the best of the seminar activities on codependency. Mary Jo Callan pointed out to me that it is very difficult for the Satir-icons not to have a very strong and personal effect on people.

Suggested Journal Questions for the Eighth Seminar in Chemical Dependency

Which of the family roles did you most identify with? What effect do you think this role has on your behavior today?

NOTES

1. Holyfield, "Legislator working on new training program for prison guards," in the September 7, 1988 Ann Arbor News. Basically, the program requires 3 and 2/3 years of academic work at Ferris State and a 16 week training program for a BA in corrections science and a post-graduation assignment in one of the state's prisons.
2. Banaszyski's "The Ties that Blind" (1992) is a brief description of how family sculpture works in therapy.

Chapter 10

AND THE POOR GET. . . A FAST CAR?

Ninth Seminar in Criminal Justice: Do the Poor Get Prison?

The goal of this seminar is for students to examine how class bias may affect arrest, conviction and sentencing procedures in the criminal justice system.

Focus Question: Reiman (1984) asserts that the criminal justice system weeds out middle and upper class people such that the prison population is comprised mostly of people on the low end of the socio-economic ladder. Does this resonate with your site experience, which macro-societal systems may be responsible for this weeding out process, and do you agree with his analysis?

The Reiman text readily lends itself to Kahn's barnraising idea.

...And The Poor Get Prison

This activity is straightforward, getting people to look at how the criminal justice system differentiates between the rich and the poor in arrest, conviction and sentencing.

On newsprint, write "arrest, conviction and sentencing." Split your seminar into two groups. At this point, you could designate a "rich group" and a "poor group" and have each group generate a list of how they are either weeded out or processed into the criminal justice system. Have the students record their ideas on the barnraising graphic. After 15 or 20 minutes, pull the groups together and have them present their lists. Another option is to make this a competitive activity of giving both groups the same assignment.

Chuck Ebel suggested setting up the Poor Get Prison as a competition, noting it would probably work well thanks to the good-natured rivalry between coordinators, a sign indicating that they were a cohesive, working group.

> *"The Poor Get Prison" went very well. Everyone brainstormed together and came up with great ideas. As one group read off their ideas, the other group listened and made comments like,*

'Oh yeah, that's true.' Thumbs Up!

—*Elissa Zelman*

From what contact I have had with the inmates at Cotton Correctional Facility, I would agree with Reiman. Looking around the classroom at Cotton compared with looking around the classroom at UM, it is obvious that the prison system weeds out the middle and upper class. Even more obvious is that it weeds out white people.

—*Stacey Brown*

At site the kids are definitely from the lower socio-economic class and are about 90% Black. In addition, the white kids at the County Juvenile Detention Center appear very poor. Reiman blames this weeding out process on Blacks being disproportionately poor, class bias and economic powers in the US. I agree that these macro societal forces affect who goes to prison.

—*Scott Waldbaum*

I like this question because it touches on the class based reality of the US, where equality is a cliche, but not a reality. Poor people are not equal under the law according to Reiman, and I agree. This question has a site application and provides another example of how systems influence the lives of communities.

—*Rick Smith*

A Reiman Barnraising

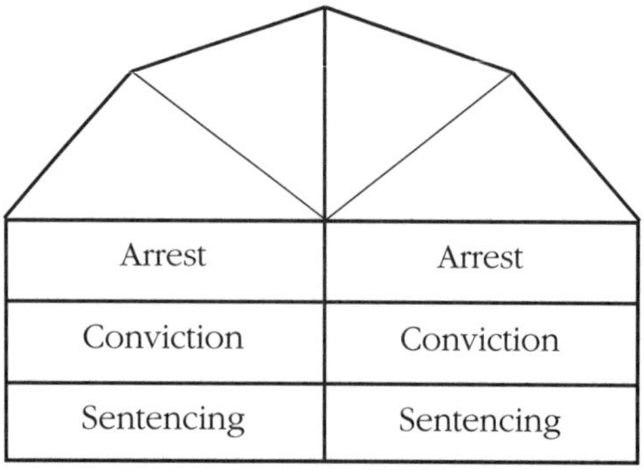

Suggested Journal Questions for Ninth Seminar in Criminal Justice

How does the Poor Get Prison's depiction of the criminal justice system fit or not fit with your observations from site? What further conclusions can you draw from this?

Ninth Seminar in Chemical Dependency: How Do Roles Develop in an Addict's Family?

The goal of this seminar is for students to apply the codependency concept in a number of different contexts—popular culture examples from music, TV and movies may provide interesting "case studies". This may spark discussion regarding the prevalence of "addictive thinking" in culture—and if such thinking is so widespread, is it necessarily a bad thing?

Focus Question: Some critics of the codependency concept have argued that it is a construct of Western psychologists and psychiatrists—who until quite recently have been mostly men. In other cultures, these traits of autonomy, independence and individualism are not so highly valued as they are in this country; therefore, being strongly impacted by other people, being emotionally "needy", valuing strong connections to other people is not pathological. What do you think? Is codependency necessarily the same thing as being dysfunctional or pathological (in the clinical sense)?

The key reading this week is in Black, "The Progression of the Roles" (1982).

Fast Car

This exercise is pretty straighforward I played Tracy Chapman's Fast Car[1] for the staffing and then had discussion. Here's A Story introduces people to family systems theory; Fast Car is an Adult Child of Alcoholics case study.

The discussion has two parts. Part One asks students to look at the song as Claudia Black (1982) would—a write-up of the main points is included below. Part Two asks students to take C. Wright Mills' (1959) perspective. Although we were not specific about it in the staffing, the discussion here could center on issues of race, gender and social class.

You got a fast car
I want a ticket to anywhere
Maybe we can make a deal
Maybe together we can get somewhere
Anyplace is better
Starting from zero got nothing to lose
Maybe we'll make something
You got a fast car
And I got a plan to get us out of here
I been working at the convenience store
Managed to save just a little bit of money
We won't have to drive too far
Just 'cross the border and into the city
You and I can both get jobs
And finally see what it means to be living
You see my old man's got a problem
He live with the bottle that's the way it is
He says his body's too old for working
I say his body's too young to look like this
My mama went off and left him
She wanted more from life than he could give
I said somebody's got to take care of him
So I quit school and that's what I did
You got a fast car
But is it fast enough so we can fly away
We gotta make a decision
We leave tonight or live and die this way
I remember we were driving in your car

The speed so fast I felt like I was drunk
City lights lay out before us
And your arm felt nice wrapped 'round my shoulder
And I had a feeling that I belonged
And I had feeling I could be someone, be someone
Be someone
You got a fast car
And we go cruising to entertain ourselves
You still ain't got a job
And I work in a market as a checkout girl
I know things will get better
You'll find work and I'll get promoted
We'll move out of the shelter
Buy a big house and live in the suburbs
You got a fast car
And I got a job that pays all our bills
You stay out driking late at the bar
See more of your friends than you do of your kids
I'd always hoped for better
Thought maybe together you and me would find it
I got no plans I ain't going nowhere
So take your fast car and keep on driving
You got a fast car
But is it fast enough so you can fly away
You gotta make a decision
You leave tonight or live and die this way

Fast Car Discussion, Part I

"While children of alcoholics are at high risk to become alcoholic, research also demonstrates children of alcoholics are often prone to marry those who are, or [who] might become alcoholic. In addition, my own research demonstrates that should a child of an alcoholic neither become an alcoholic, nor marry an alcoholic, emotional and/or psychological patterns develop which may cause problems for this person in adulthood. Adult children of alcoholics often have difficulties identifying and expressing feelings. They become very rigid and controlling. Some find themselves overly dependent on others. They feel no sense of power of choice in the way they live. A pervasive sense of fear and guilt often exists in their lives. Many experience depression and frequently do not have the ability to feel close or to be intimate with another human being. These factors all play a vital role in the professional and personal lives of children of alcoholics." (C. Black, 1982).

Father's Use:
—his drinking identified as a problem
—"mama went off and left him"
—drinking continues despite negative consequences, including work and physical deterioration
—is he using to feel euphoric or to feel normal

"At risk"—The Narrator's Use
—"speed so fast I felt like I was drunk"—familiar with drinking's effects; does she equate the car/relationship with use?
—Is she at risk? (genetic predisposition)—How does she reconcile her use with her father's?

Family Role
—The Responsible One (note how this relates to last week: narrator takes over mama's responsibilities, "I quit school/to take care of him")
—recreates family of origin dynamic with Fast Car driver
—other focused "You got a fast car": "I had to take care of him"

—out of touch with her feelings/needs/self?

Treatment
—12 step program (ACOA or Alanon)
—therapy (individual/group)
—in-patient treatment (1 week with Ann Smith[2] = $800)

"I rarely heard speakers (in 12 Step groups) mention directly the realities of economic inequality, racial bigotry or sexual coercion, even where these were clearly being described." (Herman, 1988)

I was surprised during the Winter '91 staffing when coordinators were familiar enough with the song to discuss it in depth without having it play at the meeting. They could readily connect the lyrics to the readings with little prompting from me. Todd Roeske told me that Fast Car worked when he did it in his group, but added "everything works in my group."

> *Since they were all familiar with the song, the lyrics worked well in showing how codependency was not just helping people, but was an extreme case of over-extending oneself and identifying oneself through others and their problems. One student brought up an example of a friend who had just gotten over a very serious relationship in which the two people literally lived for the other and were now sort of lost after the break-up. I compared it to drug ot alcohol detosification and called it "relationship withdrawal".*
>
> *—Mark Matthews*

Don't Cry Out Loud[3]

Near the end of her therapy, one of my clients quoted the following song lyrics for me as "The Theme Song for Codependency." She concluded, "That was me, before I found this program."

Don't cry out loud,
Just keep it inside,
And learn how to hide your feelings.

Anne Wilson Schaef (1986), in Codependence: Misunderstood, Mistreated, writes:

"Most of our love songs are about addictive love and are based on its assumptions—suffering, possessiveness, cling-cling relationships and externalizing our identity (that is, needing someone outside ourselves to establish our identity). Our culture teaches our teenagers to aspire to such relationships! They are taught to want someone who cannot live without them and through who they can find their identity; they are taught to see suffering as noble and accepted."

In responding to Schaef in a journal, Kathleen Doherty listed nearly a dozen songs, "off the top of my head" that made Schaef's point. This could be easily turned into a group activity. First, split the seminar into two groups, with each group brainstorming a list of popular song lyrics describing love and/or relationships. Second, as a whole group, discuss what the seminar views as each song's message. Third, relate these messages to the readings. Is Schaef right? Are these lyrics describing codependency? Finally, conclude by asking "who benefits" by popularizing these messages?

> *I couldn't help but listen to songs all week and try to pick out signs of codependency. I found a couple which were really interesting since they came from the male alcoholic perspective. They are a little less serious but suggest big-time enabling.*
>
> *Up on Cripple Creek*
> *She sends me*
> *If I spring a leak*
> *She mends me*
> *I don't have to speak*
> *She defends me*
> *A drunkard's dream if you ever did see one*
> *•Cripple Creek by The Band•*
>
> *She's got everything delightful*
> *She's got everything I need*
> *Takes the wheel when I'm seeing double*
> *Pays my ticket when I speed*
> *•Sugar Magnolia by The Grateful Dead•*
>
> *—Mark Matthews*

Parenthood

On the opposite page, is a family map featuring the characters from the 1989 Ron Howard film, Parenthood, starring Steve Martin and relating their roles in the movie to the codependency literature. Originally, I used the family map to illustrate how roles develop in an alcoholic family during a Fall '89 Mini-Lecture. Monique Whitman actually had her students watch the film and then discussed it in seminar.

Assuming that people were familiar with the movie, running the activity in seminar would be similar to Here's A Story. Begin by diagramming the family. Add in names and images from the movie. Conclude by relating these images to the readings.

Parenthood is not the only family from TV and the movies that demonstrates the roles described in the readings. I've read several reviews that call "The Simpsons" (Fox TV) "America's favorite dysfunctional family." Also, on "Sisters" (NBC TV), each Reed sister is cast as both an adult and an "inner child": on the show, a reoccurring theme is how alcoholism has affected the entire family.

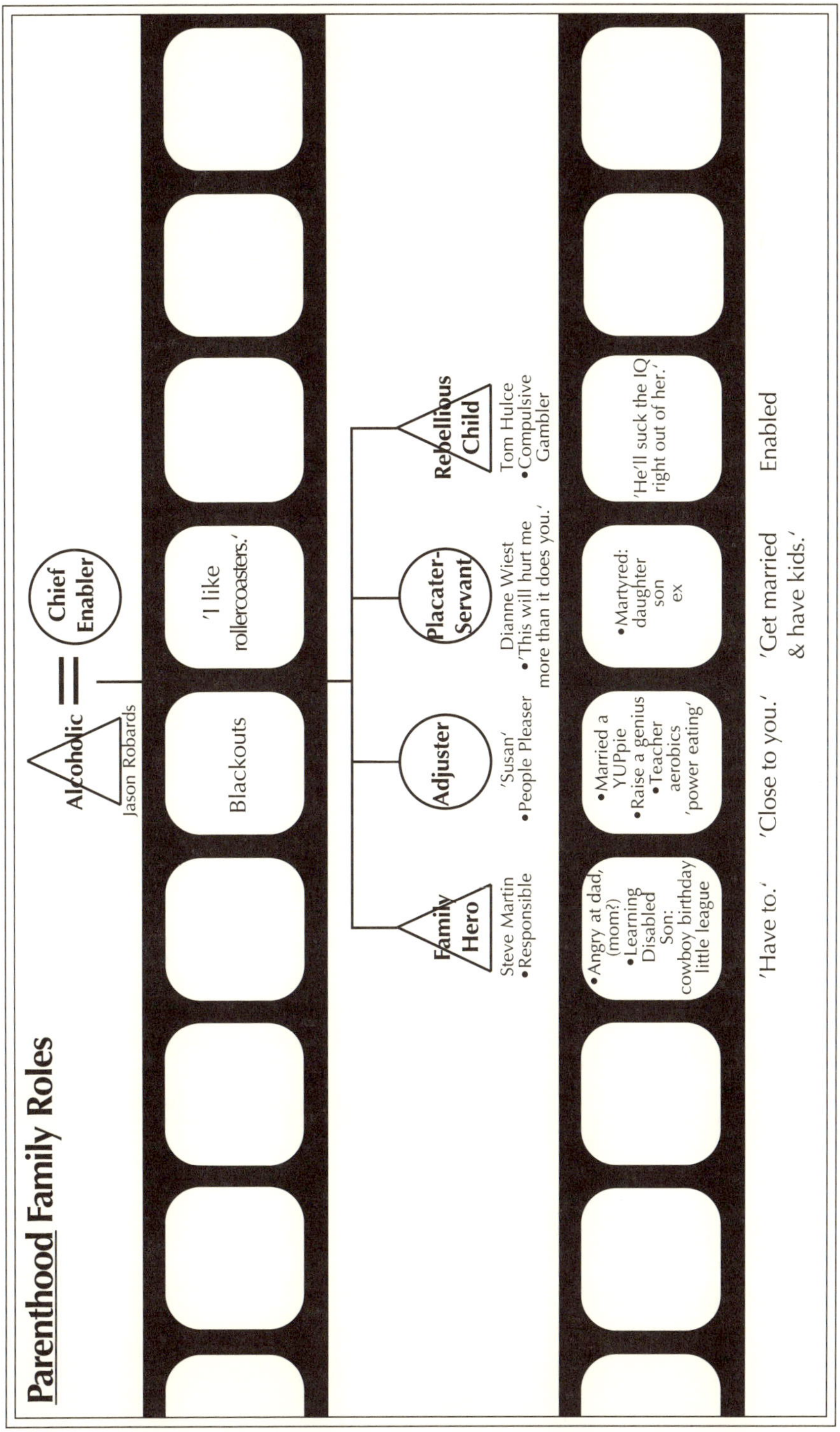
Parenthood Family Roles
Alcoholic
Jason Robards
Chief Enabler
Blackouts
'I like rollercoasters.'
Family Hero
Steve Martin
•Responsible
Adjuster
'Susan'
•People Pleaser
Placater-Servant
Dianne Wiest
•'This will hurt me more than it does you.'
Rebellious Child
Tom Hulce
•Compulsive Gambler
•Angry at dad, (mom?)
•Learning Disabled
Son: cowboy birthday little league
•Married a YUPpie
•Raise a genius
•Teacher aerobics 'power eating'
•Martyred: daughter son ex
'He'll suck the IQ right out of her.'
'Have to.'
'Close to you.'
'Get married & have kids.'
Enabled

Suggested Journal Questions for the Ninth Seminar in Chemical Dependency

How would you define codependency? Use three illustrations from your site, seminar or personal observation.

NOTES

1. "Fast Car"—by Tracy Chapman, Electra/Asylum Records, (1988)
2. In 1989, I attended one of Ann W. Smith's workshops, based on her book (1988). At that time, she was the director of an in-patient treatment program for co-dependency at the Caron Foundation's Family Services in PA: this cost was quoted to me by one of her former clients.
3. "Don't Cry Out Loud"—by Melissa Manchester, Arista Records, (1978)

Chapter 11

TAKING THE FRIEL INVENTORY DURING MARJORY'S MINUTE

Tenth Seminar in Criminal Justice: What Does Incarceration Accomplish?

The goal of this seminar is for students to discuss the relative effectiveness of incarceration's stated goals—rehabilitation, deterrence or incapacitation.

Focus Questions: Krajik and Gettinger (1982) are quite pessimistic about the effectiveness of prisons to significantly deter, incapacitate and/or rehabilitate. Do you think their conclusions are reasonable and what sorts of alternatives does their analysis imply?

> *I think that the best argument they present is the way in which rehabilitation is choked by bureaucracy and therefore ineffective while the prison turns into a school for learning crime. Perhaps all those trendy alternatives to prison would be a better solution.*
>
> —*Rick Smith*

Marjory's Minute

The activity calls for the coordinator to pick out three individual members of the seminar. Each is to make a political statement, up to one minute, strongly in favor of deterrence, rehabilitiation or incapacition. After all three people are allowed to make their statements, each will be given up to a minute for rebuttal. This activity was originally Marjory Gustke's idea. She demonstrated it for me when I visited her seminar during the Fall '88 term.

Rooming the House

This variation on Marjory's Minute expands the discussion to the entire criminal justice system. Split your seminar into three groups and assign each group one of the following: deterrence, rehabilitation, incapacitation.

Each group must answer the following question regarding it's assigned topic:

In the criminal justice system, who (which population) would you target for deterrence/rehabilitiation incapacitation? Why? How? When? Where?

Rooming the House

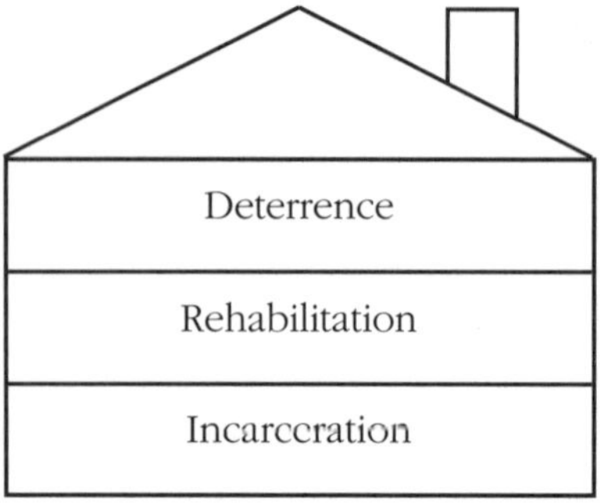

Call everyone together and have people present their answers to the whole group.

John Choi much preferred Rooming the House to Marjory's Minute. He reported that Rooming The House seemed to promote more discussion in his seminar than Marjory's Minute, which he described as "adversarial."

> *I don't believe prisons accomplish a lot as far as rehabilitation goes. So, the conclusions of the pessimistic authors are valid. Prison systems lack one important component. CARE. In generalizing, I will say that many staff workers at Maxey have shown lack of interest in the guy's needs. They aren't friendly, and it is obvious that many just look at the job as a means of earning a weekly paycheck. I believe that it comes from the social view of prisoners as "lesser" people than non-prisoners. Another reason for ineffectiveness in prison is cuts in budgeting for follow-up rehabilitation. I don't mean to completely put down Maxey. As proposed in the article, some rehabilitation takes place. However, these programs happen during the guy's sentence and not after.*
>
> *—Donetta Pedroza*

> *To respond to Donetta's experience, it seems to me that any care a well intentioned social worker has is soaked out by a bureaucracy and capitalist hegemony that gives little support to it's workers in the field. Ruby Daniel, my site contact at Cotton Correctional Facility, is extremely overworked. The prison could use at least five Rubies. I don't think any human being should be expected to spend 40 hours a week in a setting like that and continue to do a good job. Even 20 hours a week may be too much. We need a fundamental reorganization of work and NOTHING less.*
>
> *—Rick Smith*

Suggested Journal Questions for the Tenth Seminar in Criminal Justice

Which of the three purposes—deterrence, rehabilitation or incapacitation—appears to be the goal of your site? During this term, what have you observed regarding the process your site has made on this goal? How would you describe the relationship between the service we provide and this site goal?

Tenth Seminar in Chemical Dependency: Codependency—Any Personal Implications for Me?

The goal of this seminar is for students to decide whether codependency has any personal relevance for them after examining their responses to questionaires from either Beattie (1987) or Friel (1988).

Focus Questions: "Codependency teaches us that femininity is pathology, and we blame ourselves for self-destructive feminine behavior, letting men evade any responsibility for their violent and abusive behavior"(Lamb, 1990). What do you think of these criticisms of the codependency movement? Is codependency a gendered concept?

The text most related to the activities is Beattie's checklist (1987).

Codependent No More

This exercise is pretty straightforward. At the beginning of discussion time, I had everyone fill out the codependency test from Beattie (1987). We then discussed our thoughts and feelings about our scores.

As Jeanne Gray said, this exercise is meant to "bring it on home", that is, to have students investigate codependency theory on a personal level as it applies to them.

Regarding the follow-up to Beattie, Kathleen Doherty noted, "I just enjoyed listening to the discussion."

The Friel Inventory[1]

During the Fall '90 term, I edited Beattie's Questionnaire down to two pages so that people could have time to complete the Questionnaire during staffing and then reflect on their experiences as group. During the Winter '91 term, I substituted the Friel Inventory for Beattie because it is shorter and easier to score. All the Winter '91 Chemical Dependency Coordinators reported that the Friel Inventory initiated an insightful discussion in their seminars.

When Is A Door Not A Door? (the Chemical Dependency version) could also be used here. The sequence as I envision it:

1. Assign the Beattie Questionnaire as a journal assignment.
2. Process students' reactions to the Questionnaire during the first part of the seminar.

3. Ask students where they think these behaviors and attitudes may be rooted for them.

Note that the premise of this activity (see Chapter Twelve) is that major social institutions may actually promote codepedence.

Suggested Journal Questions for the Tenth Seminar in Chemical Dependency

Do you see yourself as codependent? Reflect on how this perspective may affect your service at site and your participation in seminar.

NOTES

1. I met John Friel at a conference in 1991: my thanks to him for his permission to reprint the Inventory (1988).

Assessing Co-dependency

To help indentifying the issues of Adult Children and co-dependency discussed thus far, we designed an inventory which we have been using for the past five years, both in research and clinical work. We also find that it is a useful tool for people to begin identifying for themselves the problems that they need to work on.

The Friel Adult Child/Co-dependency Inventory (Friel, 1985) is based on our developmental framework, and includes many of the core symptoms we believe define co-dependency. If you decide to answer the questions in the Inventory, we ask (1) that you answer as honestly as you can, with as much of your own denial put aside as possible for you at this time; and (2) that you fill it out alone and don't feel you have to share the results with anyone but yourself. It is very important that you begin focusing on yourself without worrying that anyone else is going to "find you out" or shame you.

To score the inventory, give yourself 1 point for every "true" response to all of the even-numbered items; and give yourself 1 point for every "false" response to odd-numbered items. You can have a possible score of 60.

In our research thus far, we have found scores from 10 to 20 indicate mild co-dependency/adult child concerns; scores from 21 to 30 to be in the mild-moderate range; 31 to 45 to be moderate-severe and over 45 to be severe. Rather than keeping score, though, we suggest again that you use this inventory as a means for self-exploration. And as we will discuss in the next chapter, we invite you to arrange for a one-session evaluation with a professional if you feel that you have some of these issues interfering with your happiness and sense of well-being.

Friel Adult Child/Co-dependency Assessment Inventory

Below are a number of questions dealing with how you feel about yourself, your life and those around you. As you answer each question, be sure to answer honestly, but do not spend too much time dwelling on any one question. There are no right or wrong answers. Take each question as it comes and answer as you usually feel.

1. I make enough time to do things just for myself each week.
2. I spend lots of time criticizing myself after an interaction with someone.
3. I would not be embarrassed if people knew certain things about me.
4. Sometimes I feel like I just waste a lot of time and don't get anywhere.
5. I take good enough care of myself.
6. It is usually best not to tell someone they bother you; it only causes fights and gets everyone upset.
7. I am happy about the way my family communicated when I was growing up.
8. Sometimes I don't know how I really feel.
9. I am very satisfied with my intimate love life.
10. I've been feeling tired lately.
11. When I was growing up, my family liked to talk openly about problems.
12. I often look happy when I am sad or angry.
13. I am satisfied with the number and kind of relationships I have in my life.
14. Even if had the time and money to do it, I would feel uncomfortable taking a vacation by myself.
15. I have enough help with everything I must do.
16. I wish that I could accomplish a lot more that I do now.
17. My family taught me to express feelings and affection openly when I was growing up.
18. It is hard for me to talk to someone in authority (boss, teachers, etc.).
19. When I am in a relationship that becomes too confusing and complicated, I have no trouble getting out of it.
20. I sometimes feel pretty confused about who I am and where I want to go with my life.
21. I am satisfied with the way I take care of my own needs.
22. I am not satisfied with my career.
23. I usually handle my problems calmly and directly.
24. I hold back my feelings much of the time because I don't want to hurt other people or have them think less of me.
25. I don't feel like I'm "in a rut" very often.
26. I am not satisfied with my friendships.
27. When someone hurts my feelings or does something that I don't like, I have little difficulty telling them about it.
28. When a close friend or relative asks for my help more than I'd like, I usually say "yes" anyway.
29. I love to face new problems and am good at finding solutions to them.

30. I do not feel good about my childhood.
31. I am not concerned about my health a lot.
32. I often feel like no one really knows me.
33. I feel calm and peaceful most of the time.
34. I find it difficult to ask for what I want.
35. I don't let people take advantage of me more than I'd like.
36. I am dissatisfied with at least one of my close relationships.
37. I make major decisions quite easily.
38. I don't trust myself in new situations as much as I'd like.
39. I am very good at knowing when to speak up and when to get along with others' wishes.
40. I wish I had more time away from my work.
41. I am as spontaneous as I'd like to be.
42. Being alone is a problem for me.
43. When someone I love is bothering me, I have no problem telling them so.
44. I often have so many things going on at once that I'm really not doing justice to any one of them.
45. I am very comfortable letting others into my life and revealing "the real me" to them.
46. I apologize to others too much for what I do or say.
47. I have no problem telling people when I am angry with them.
48. There's so much to do and not enough time. Sometimes I'd like to leave it all behind me.
49. I have few regrets about what I have done with my life.
50. I tend to think of others more than I do myself.
51. More often than not, my life has gone the way that I wanted it to.
52. People admire me because I'm so understanding of others, even when they do something that annoys me.
53. I am comfortable with my own sexuality.
54. I sometimes feel embarrassed by behaviors of those close to me.
55. The important people in my life know "the real me," and I am okay with them knowing.
56. I do my share of work, and often do quite a bit more.
57. I do not feel that everything would fall apart without my efforts and attention.
58. I do too much for other people and then later wonder why I did so.
59. I am happy about the way my family coped with problems when I was growing up.
60. I wish that I had more people to do things with.

Chapter 12

WHEN IS A DOOR NOT A DOOR?

Eleventh Seminar in Criminal Justice: How Can the System Be Improved?

The goal of this seminar is for students to identify how their site placement is connected to the rest of the criminal justice system: further discussion may examine how these connections should be improved.

Focus Questions: In your opinion, what are some of the weaknesses of the "Blueprint for Youth Corrections" (1991)? Try to think in terms of suggested interventions based on his goals of offender accountability, public safety protection and competency development.

In Criminal Justice, When Is A Door Not A Door? is meant to give students an overview of the criminal justice system by having them classify the various programming alternatives described in the readings.

When Is A Door Not A Door?

The activity begins with the coordinator drawing three doors on a chalkboard or newsprint. The top of each door represents an aspect of Adult Corrections—Alternatives to Incarceration, Alternatives With Some Incarceration, and Incarceration. The bottom of the door represents parallels of Adult Corrections within Juvenile Justice—Alternatives to Institutionalization, Alternatives With Some Institutionalization, and Institutionalization.

The coordinator then explains the differences between the six categories and asks students to describe and place the different programs in the readings in the appropriate category. Be sure to include your site in this discussion.

The activity hinges on the title's punch line. When Is A Door Not A Door? When it's ajar! Revisit the doors. When do the various programs appear to be most effective (i.e. when is a door a door)? Under which circumstances are they ineffective? (i.e. When is the door ajar)? Do you notice any trends as discussion shifts from one door to another?

Wendy Lassen thought that this activity "went well" during her Fall '89 seminar and confirmed that with Jennifer Rabiah, then a student in Wendy's seminar.

> *The When Is A Door Not A Door? exercise went great—probably one of the top two of the term. Seeing it all on the board and the trends of cost, restrictions, goals, etc., also added to the activity. It stirred up a lot of discussion and is appropriate for the end of the term.*[1]
>
> *—Josee Charvet*

One variation on this activity would be to start with a written list of the programs in the readings, and then have the seminar go through the list, classifying each program. Todd Roeske's opinion was that the first version of the activity would work better in his seminar.

> *I think that Schwartz's major weakness is that he doesn't address the cause of the youths' delinquency—which is the crime-ridden, inner city environment that the kids are surrounded by. His alternative programs do not offer a way for the youths to escape this environment. Meeting with a social worker every week is not going to stop any kid from partying with and getting in trouble with his old group of friends on the weekends.*
>
> *I don't know how realistic this is, but couldn't middle-class suburban families be persuaded to take individual kids in as foster children? Since most delinquents are trouble makers because of the intense peer pressure to commit crime among their gangs, couldn't we place young, minor offenders in suburban homes? If I had completed my degree and were working in my field, I would be willing to take someone in. Maybe it would be a trendy thing for yuppies to do.*
>
> *—Stacey Brown*

> *I think it would be a very trendy yuppie thing to do but it might not go over so well with people in various activist circles because it abandons the inner city. I think that the best way to reduce inner city crime is to rebuild the inner city. It's harder, but I think we deserve nothing less. When the city is cleaned up, perhaps meeting with a social worker every week would do some good.*
>
> *—Rick Smith*

Suggested Journal Questions for the Tenth Seminar in Criminal Justice

Reflecting on the When Is A Door Not A Door? activity, where does your site fit within the criminal justice system? How could linkages and services with other parts of the system be improved? What barriers can you see as impeding this improvement?

Eleventh Seminar in Chemical Dependency: What is Incremental Intervention?

The goal of this seminar is for students to identify how their site placement is connected to related services providing treatment for Chemical Dependency. Follow-up discussion may examine how these services could be improved.

Focus Questions: Given the idea of incremental intervention, how do the various systems such as the family, schools and courts seem to help or hinder the "flexible model" in dealing with adolescents who are chemically dependent?

In Chemical Dependency, students also classify programs in an activity similar to When Is A Door Not A Door? One Step Up and Two Steps Back is based on "A Flexible Model: Making The Action Fit The Need," Chapter Four from Muldoon and Crowley's One Step Ahead: Early Intervention Strategies for Adolescent Drug Problems (1986).

One Step Up and Two Steps Back

The chart (at end of chapter) is based on the Muldoon and Crowley (1986) text that describes "A Hierarchy of Interventions—Clarification of Behavioral Expectiation, Realistic Information, Personal Awareness, Changes In The Family System, Personal Change and Direct, External Control." The activity calls for the coordinator to first dialogue with students about what each level of intervention is and then have students cite specific examples for each level. Students should be able to talk specifically about their site experiences and relate those experiences to the model.

Regarding this activity, Prentice Zinn remarked that "I wouldn't change a thing in (my) seminar." Another Chemical Dependency coordinator told me that her seminar's discussion during this activity "pretty much followed what happened in our staffing."

During the Fall '89 Term, I created a Chemical Dependency version of When Is A Door Not A Door? based on excerpts from Schaef (1986). Schaef's premise is that many major social institutions, such as school, church and family, may actually promote co-dependence.

In this activity, the three doors now read School, Church (or Temple or Synagogue) and Family. Students are split into three groups and each group is assigned a door. Each group is asked to brainstorm a list where their institution promotes "healthy social norms" (i.e. when is a door a door?) and when it promotes co-dependence (i.e. when is the door ajar?). After 10 to 15 minutes, the individual groups report to the whole seminar.

After the groups report in, ask the seminar about the commonalities in each list and, "Why do you think the different doors are ajar?" Matt Kinney's question, "who benefits?", could be asked at this point to introduce Schaef's assertion that "the white male system is the addictive system"(1987).

One activity I thought was particularly good was When Is A

Door Not A Door? because it made me realize that things are not always what they appear to be as well as encouraged me to scrutinize things more harshly.

—John Sittu

Suggested Journal Questions for the Tenth Seminar in Chemical Dependency

Reflecting on the One Step Up and Two Steps Back activity, where does your site fit within the Chemical Dependency Service Network? How could linkages with other parts of this network be improved? What barriers do you see as impeding this improvement?

NOTES

1. Because this material is scheduled for late in the term, I usually encourage coordinators who are behind in the syllabus to make these readings optional so that students wrap up the term by reading Palmer (1987).

When Is A Door Not A Door? (Criminal Justice)

When Is A Door Not A Door? (Chemical Dependency)

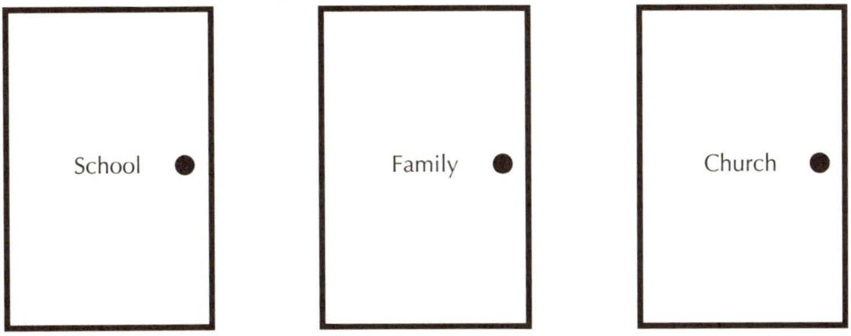

One Step Up & Two Steps Back Chart

Clarification of behavioral expectations
Realistic information
Personal awareness
Changes in the family system
Personal change
Direct, external control

Chapter 13

LET THIS CIRCLE REPRESENT[1]...

Twelfth Seminar

The goal of this seminar is for students to evaluate their PC experience in light of Palmer (1987).

Focus Questions: Using Palmer's "Community, Conflict and Ways of Knowing,"(1987) evaluate Project Community. How does the PC structure facilitate the type of learning environment Palmer advocates and how doesn't it? If you feel we haven't reached Palmer's ideal, how would you change things?

I chose to conclude the course pack with Palmer for three reasons. First, Palmer's pedagogy has some similarity with Freire (1970), which provides an opportunity for people to reflect on their group norms and/or personal goals as the term draws to a close. Second, Palmer emphasizes relationships and interconnectedness in his community: this emphasis gives people a chance to examine how other group members have affected their learning process. Combining this activity with Brown Baggin' It (Chapter Fourteen) appears to be an effective formal agenda for final seminars. Third, Todd Roeske has told me repeatedly that "Project Community is actually more Palmer-ian than Freirean."

We Don't Need No Education, We Don't Need No Thought Control

This activity has two parts to it. The first part calls for the coordinator to split the seminar in half and to give each group a newsprint-sized handout. One handout has epistemological terms on it (Objectivism —objective, analytic, experimental and trained schizophrenia) while the second handout lists pedagogical terms (Community—communal way of knowing, communal conflict, fear and love). The task of each group is to define each term and then to explain how the terms on their sheet relate to one another.

Wendy Lassen noted that "this is hard." During the Winter '90 staffings, I handed out extra copies of Palmer's article along with the worksheets. In Jennifer Rabiah's Winter '90 seminar, all the members of her group had their course packs with them: this certainly helped them with this part of the exercise.

> *Both Freire and Palmer talk about conflict, fear and love in the learning community. Through my experiences with PC, I can really relate to what they were talking about. I have seen the fear of feeling stupid in myself and in my students. I have seen the need for love and support. And I have seen the learning that results from conflicts. My group this semester has taught me a lot about these terms; thus, I have seen the importance of having them present in my own personal pedagogy.*
>
> *—Jennifer Rabiah*

Part two of this exercise asks for people to reflect on their PC experience in light of Palmer. One starting point could be experience, "according to Palmer, is our seminar a community?" The follow-up questions all relate to people being more specific about applying Palmer's terms to their experience. For example, "How have you seen love of learning and of learners demonstrated in our seminar? Can you give an example of a time when we supported each other through our fears? When did conflicts arise and how did each of us grow from them? Is it true that what we've learned together this term has been enhanced by our relationships with one another?"

The nature of this discussion may vary greatly from seminar to seminar. Some of the variation will be due to the material and some of it will be about how your group is dealing with closure. "Brown Baggin' It" is also about closure and relationships. It makes sense to me for coordinators to combine the two.

> *Joe, obviously the Kahn and Howard articles describe how a seminar should be, but the Freire and Palmer articles explain why this is "better" than the traditional method of education. Also, although all four authors help set up the seminar into a model, it isn't until the group has met and feels comfortable with one another that a learning community exists . It's in this area that site, seminars and staffing come into play. These three areas facilitate the ability to discuss things openly and learn. I think we've seen this throughout the semester in staffing. We felt comfortable, and as a result, share more views.*
>
> *—Chuck Ebel*

> *Significant group experiences through which and from which everyone in the group gains knowledge through working together, sharing with each other and support each other. This knowledge need not be the same for all members; in fact, it is more meaningful if it is not. Each person will have the benefit of everyone else's thoughts and their own. In this way, one is also building community. Everyone is working together for a common goal: The attainment of a goal in general. When building community, we are building camaraderie, helpfulness and joining of forces to reach our ends. My group was headed*

in that direction—began to feel the unity building, the ease at which people began to express their feelings and ideas and reasons, and the aid given to one another in times of need or misunderstandings. I especially noticed the acknowledgments by members of our group as a dynamic entity- many of them commented on the relatedness and dynamics in their journals.

—Wendy Lassen

At the Winter '91 staffing on Palmer, during the Mini-Lecture, I referred coordinators to Palmer's terms, but had them arrive at their own definitions of a learning community. During the last part of staffing, people reflected on how their experience in PC fit or didn't fit with their definitions. During the Winter '92 staffings, I split coordinators into dyads and encouraged each pair to reference Palmer as they defined among themselves what a learning community was. Each dyad then shared their definition. A discussion followed, regarding the similarities and differences in their definitions, as well as which parts of these definitions had and had not been realized during the course of the term. Several CJ successors were present at this staffing. Afterwards, Jeff Salinger remarked that the discussion exceeded anything he imagined taking place in his seminar. "Of course," Jeff noted, "it really helped to be in a room full of people who actually knew something about how to build learning communities."

Obviously, then, I would describe a learning community as Project Community. It's beyond a place for experiential learning and action and reflection. It's what Peck called "A Safe Place" (1987)[2] *where you can let down your defenses, learn boundaries and learn to heal yourself. Our staffing is a perfect example. Probably because you emulate it so well, we all know not to overstep our boundaries, we know to just sit back, listen and accept. Just like Peck describes the experience of the psychotherapists. It's never been so clear to me as it is in what he's written—I know you gave this to me before, but recently so many revelations have been given/shown to me that I didn't recognize its importance previously. Anyway, I really feel we created a safe place where we could open up and not be judged. I know we have all benefited from it too... When you're shot down in class for raising an idea that's different, it's not a safe, secure feeling. It's frightening and disheartening. You lose confidence and interest, and nobody benefits—not you, because you're too hurt or scared to care, and not others, because they're too closed to hear new ideas, too scared themselves to listen to anyone else put himself/herself on the line, or too in need of wanting help that they forget about listening and try to give advice and heal others.*

The staffings you run, though, are safe and open—even from the beginning, because you and Toni seem so adept at just listening, knowing when to step in and offer encouragement and advice, and accepting us for who we are so that we can feel safe. It's an important point that you don't try to make all the coordinators the same, that there isn't a concrete standard guideline to coordinating because we are different and need to feel good and confident about those differences so that in seminar we can be as accepting and as adept at creating a safe learning environment.

I think we are able to, although not to the extreme that we do in staffings. It's hard to try to create a safe learning environment on purpose. I've learned that on some level I've got to be conscious of it to keep on task, but mostly let things happen naturally. Many times I've bitten my tongue while someone was going on about something I disagreed with only to wait and hear someone else bring up another side and then another without threatening the first person. Is that real barn-raising or what? It all seemed so natural, and we were all enlightened and learned something from it. That's the result of overcoming my own personal issues, and like you, trying to create a safe place through listening and accepting. It's been the most important part of my education at Michigan.

—Cris Zerkel

If PC Were...

During the Winter '93 term, Randy Ross devised this activity, based on a column by Jack Gillard[3]. To initiate a dialogue on Palmer, people were asked to complete the following:

If PC were a __________ it would be __________ because __________.

I opened by saying if PC were a college basketball team, it would be Michigan's Fab Five because all of the talented and vested interests that work through this office. Pauline Gianoplus stated that "if PC were a type of food, it would be a salad bar because you take what you want and leave the rest." Randy Ross added that "if PC were a color, it would be green because that is what you get when you mix the colors maize and blue, which like PC, are a brilliant representation of all that is good at the University."

If PC were a food, it would be a chunky soup because you could eat it with a fork.

—Bush Helzberg

If PC were a song. It would definitely be by the Grateful Dead because, my what a long, strange trip it's been.

—Brett Jaffe

If PC were a garbage dumpster, it would be Mr. Rubbish because of the tidy manner in which we deal with some messy subject matter.

—Chris Wright

If PC were a computer, it would be user friendly because all of us are also user friendly.

—*Rick Smith*

I do think the PC structure helps facilitate the type of learning environment but it certainly could be changed to more closely resemble what Palmer describes. I think that we do not spend enough time at site. Although we try to minimize a hierarchy of responsibility, there still is one. A more equally emotionally invested group of individuals would lead to more creative conflict and learning. Maybe if the whole group applied for a site together and delegated responsibilities themselves and were completely responsible for evaluating each other, we could come closer to Palmer's environment. Also, maybe PC people could live together and share the responsibility of living.

—*Bush Helzberg*

It seems to me that Palmer's epistemology is what PC is aiming for, but as Palmer said, it will not work in a system that is objective. UM is objective. The underlying mode of knowing has stayed the same. But PC is an honest attempt. Another problem is that many PC students lack the love of learning that this way of learning needs. Some students just want easy credit and a good time. I would set higher standards to get into the program. Having higher expectations would really help.

—*Aaron Romain*

However, there is one aspect where PC is weak. Palmer says that 'there is no knowing without conflict.' I agree with him and we have observed in the past that our best staffings occur when the articles address a particularly controversial topic. In addition, my seminars last term were especially good because we had students who represented each point on the liberal vs. conservative continuum. I think that often our discussions in staffing assume the liberal viewpoint, and people with other opinions are automatically silenced because they don't want to speak against the entire group or appear un-politically correct. This is detrimental to the learning experience of all staff members. I think it's important to recruit a diverse staff and to encourage a diverse range of opinions.

—*Stacey Brown*

PC meets the learning environment that Palmer advocated because it meets his central objective that community must become a central concept in the ways we teach and learn. The PC structure helps facilitate the Palmer objective in many different ways. The most important, I think, is by allowing students to lead each seminar (rather than grad student TA's): this allows the revealing of "the complex web of relationships

> *between teachers and students." The structure of PC thus is set up to counter and destroy the objective, analytic and experiemental ways of teaching and learning and allows Palmer and community into the classroom. We try to retrain students through seminar and site experience to realize they cannot (or should not) "take pieces of the world and carve out for themselves a niche of private sanity in the midst of public calamity."*
>
> —*Scott Waldbaum*

Suggested Journal Questions for the Eleventh Seminar

- What final reflections do you have on your personal goals?
- How would you define a learning community and in what specific ways have you seen this definition demonstrated throughout the semester?

NOTES

1. "Let this circle represent what we can do together what we could not do separately." My thanks to AA member Tom F. for this quote. In general, AA meetings conclude when the members stand in a circle, hold hands and recite the Lord's Prayer: in New Mexico, I'm told that this line precedes the prayer—a fitting introduction, I thought, to students' closing reflections on community.
2. This journal is a reflection on a specific passage from Peck (1987), pages 67 and 68.
3. This column, originally in the March 3, 1993 Ann Arbor News, initiated a reader's contest. Gillard's first example was: "If Ann Arbor were a pinball machine, it would pop 'Tilt!' at any sign of social insensitivity."

Chapter 14

THE LAST CHAPTER MADE MY STOMACH HURT

Your Last Seminar

This chapter is written specifically for coordinators, to be read by them as they reflect on the semester coming to a close.

For the past ten terms, sometime in November or March I have lectured on closure. My aim in doing this is to remind coordinators that they may be having their own issues around closure. I believe that this awareness must come before coordinators begin to wrap up with their seminar and at site: in the seminar, people tend to primarily focus on closure at site.

Before the first edition of this text was published in 1990, I would lecture on some aspect of closure[1] during staffing and then have coordinators follow up by reflecting on closure in their journals. One coordinator remarked:

> *Sorry this plan is so strange. I'm really tired. I got up late. Anyway, how did I like [the closure lecture]? I didn't. My stomach knotted up, and I started feeling sick. I guess you are right, though, about how some people deal with things. I use avoidance. I am feeling much better now, though. I had a great weekend!*

During the Fall '90 term, I began assigning this chapter for coordinators to read and reflect on as part of the closure process. Then I would follow up by reading current coordinator journals aloud in staffings and then commenting on what appeared to be common themes.

> *Let me begin by commenting on last week's mini-lecture. I found your discussion of reflecting on our experience this term to be especially valuable. Since I am very task/goal oriented, I tend to finish some experiences and immediately say, "OK, what's next?", instead of "OK. What have I learned or experienced that might assist me in whatever comes next?" Generally speaking, I do not believe that the PC experience is one that anyone could leave without a considerable amount of reflection, but it is certainly important to be reminded to*

evaluate the experience.

—*Mary Jo Callan*

Typically, my coordinator staffs have chosen for their last time together to be a potluck or pizza party. Either at that party or at the last formal staffing, I give out Word Gifts or Nicknames to coordinators which recall aspects of our work together. In the text that follows, I have listed each staff member by academic year[2], along with his or her Nickname or Word Gift and some of their reflections on closure.

Fall '88/Winter '89

Marjory RELIABLE Gustke
Michelle AUTHENTICITY Blankenship
Don LONGSUFFERING Neal
Kathy ADAPTABLE Russell
Anne SCHOLAR Hardy
Trish DISCLOSING Marsik
Jeff LEFTY Maple
Kathleen LYRICAL Doherty
Tony REBOUND Smith
Utpala COMPETENT Patel
Dave EXPERIENCED Magee

I'm sitting here in the Michigan Union Grill, and I can't believe this is my last journal. My last everything. On Friday, I cried because I went to the bank and closed out my account which I opened in 1985. It was so sad since I'd been going to that bank with my dad since I was a little girl. If this minor stuff makes me cry I am going to be a mess on April 29th.

Last site? It was sad. We ate ice cream—of course! It was really hard to say good-bye to Rico. He gave me flowers I was very sad. I sit in my room and look at the flowers and think that after two terms of learning from him, this is all I have. In a way, these false friendships aren't fair. (Yes, I see myself as a friend and NOT A ROLE MODEL like some other coordinator told me I was!) Imagine a 43 year-old man who is so smart but can't read and write. He's been in and out of prison since age 12. He spent one and a half years in solitary confinement in Jackson. God, he's amazing.

I guess the most important thing I've learned from him is that I've been incarcerating myself. He says people are incarcerated in their minds, and I believe that. By thinking about things this way, I feel better about graduation. I know I can do anything.

—*Michelle Blankenship*

Anyhow, given what I've gotten out of the program in this last term (and it is the LAST term)—growth, growth, growth!, a deepened understanding of myself, a continuing education on how to listen (as well as how to be heard) and some wonderful support and conflict from a number of places—I give myself an "A" without a glance backwards.

Other stuff...this place (U-M) has the ability to make my heart virtually sing. I remember days I've walked across the diag so amazed by the vitality and wonder of this place. And yesterday, as I walked out of my very last class, I felt like I was putting that sheet music away, and it hurt. A lot. For all I hate this wretched, vile, oppressive, brainwashing place, I love it.

—Trish Marsik

Fall '89/Winter '90

Glen TEDDY BEAR Lansky
Phil CELLMATE Slotnick
Kathy CRIMINAL SEXUAL MISCONDUCT Garcia
Jennifer YOU'RE NOT THE TEACHER Rabiah
Jenny RED SHIRT Kellman
Karen Marsh and Donna Kennedy: THIS IS CONFUSING
Korey INSTANT REPLAY Miller
Sandy FLINTSTONE KIDS Choi
Sabrina I DON'T KNOW ANYONE WHO WORKS AS MUCH Booth
Amanda FAMILY Carlson
Mike JOE'S DINNER Shaw
Kris NECTARINE Merecki
Chuck WITH A LITTLE LUCK Ebel
Dora I DON'T KNOW ABOUT THIS, JOE Brantley
Marc CO-HOST Zeplin[3]
Liz SWIM SUIT Rosenburg
Wendy U-TURN Lassen
John KROGER COLE SLAW Fohrman
Todd GLUTINOUS BALLS Roeske
Jeanne NEW GRANT Gray
Prentice CARTOON Zinn
Laurence ORGANSKI Potlasch[3]
Kim CLEMENTINE Anderson
Jeff PANTS Maple
Kathleen LYRICAL Doherty

Last term when we wrapped up our PC site activities, it was really important to me. Leaving the men at the Huron Valley Men's Facility was difficult because of the rewarding experience for everyone associated with that site. It was like leaving a bunch of newly found friends. But, at the same time that I was sad, I was also glad because the term was finally over—and with the end of the term came the end of my first time coordinating. I was glad, because at that point, I knew I had coordinated successfully. Doing something for the first time always makes me anxious (as you could tell in the beginning of last term), but after it's over with and I realize that not only did I make it through, but I made it through successfully—I am very relieved.

As far as site is concerned, the thing that I thought was the most important to close with was to let the men know that we were not some "college kids" who were there for a couple of months just to watch some monkeys in their cages. I wanted them to know that we genuinely cared about them. In order to do this, I made sure that when I left I talked to the men in our unit and made sure they knew we appreciated them letting us come in and share in such an eye-opening experience. I let them know that working with them made me appreciate them as human beings, not just prisoners. In a way, I guess, I had to qualify our being there. Now that I think about it. I don't know whether this is good or bad.

—Dora Brantley

As far as site is concerned, I want to remember Rachel telling me about all her past experiences—ones I'd only read about. Needing to stay in an abusive relationship (or any boy-girl relationship for that matter), trouble in school because of trouble at home, wanting to commit suicide, running away, sex for love. People are really behind every one of those statistics that I read and that is alarming. I want to remember my feeling of being overwhelmed—how can any one person have so many problems? I want to remember the trailer she is living in—a home the size of what some people camp in for a weekend. How can you get privacy in a place so small and in a neighborhood that is so scary and beaten?

Project Community is, to date, my most rewarding, fulfilling and satisfying experience at U-M.

—Kathleen Doherty

Fall '90/ Winter '91

Jennifer CONSULTANT Taylor
Josee BOOTS Charvet
Kathy CRIMINAL SEXUAL CONDUCT Garcia
Rachel GRACE Story
Susan TABITHA Webster
Jennifer YOU'RE NOT THE TEACHER Rabiah
LaNeice RADIO Jones
Korey INSTANT REPLAY Miller
Julie ANYTHING IS POSSIBLE Mathews
Walter DEADHEAD Fisher
John MELLOW Choi
Andrew BLISTER Kramer
David FRUIT SALAD Oppenheim

Sabrina I DON'T KNOW ANYONE WHO WORKS AS MUCH Booth
Jenny RED SKIRT Kellman
Elissa SPECIAL CHIEF Zelman
Ira HEADLIGHTS Pintel
Ashley PANDEMONIUM! Andreae
Monique BACK PAGE Whitman
Kati MOM Hanna
Cris HOW AM I DOING? Zerkel

Closure is much more threatening for me this semester. The biggest reason is because this is probably my last Project Community experience for a while. I have really appreciated this one island of humane education amidst the sea of information transfer. I have left experiences that I truly enjoyed in the past but that makes it no easier.

—Todd Roeske

I think my biggest surprise this term deals with something that has affected seminar, site, staffing and myself. That surprise is the level of enthusiasm that I have seen in every area of Project Community. Being a coordinator this term, I have been able to see the workings within Project Community and outside at the Juvenile Detention Center. What I have seen is a wonderful group of individuals with an incredible willingness to serve the community and the eagerness to learn from the experience. My group in seminar and at site are so enthusiastic, and this benefits the discussions we engage in during seminar—it is obvious that the kids have a great time due to this enthusiasm. Yes, I have to admit it, this is a surprise. I thought that with all the responsibilities of being a coordinator I would get lost in all the stress, but this is not the case. I look forward to site every week and getting together with my group for a seminar. The enthusiasm that I have is sincere, not just a fake smile that is plastered to my face in hopes of fooling everyone that I am having a good time.

—Jennifer Rabiah

Joe, I must say that I'm dealing with lots of emotions as this term is ending, along with my college career, though at times the sheer pressure I'm feeling is enough to cover them all up. Of course, I'm thrilled to be graduating, but honestly, I am not as excited as I thought I might be. It's funny, but I really am feeling like I'll miss this place. I can't believe that it's taken me two years to find a niche here and now that I do occupy a comfortable place, it is time to go! Privately, I think I'll miss the whole PC experience. It's been wonderful for me to get involved with the program, as it has really shrunk the University down for me, making it a much warmer place.

—Ben Macrory

Fall '91/Winter '92

Toni LAUGHS WITH THUNDER Caldwell
Courtney HANNAH Loveman
Randy DICTATORIAL PROFESSOR WANNA-BE (NOT!) Ross
Jane LISTENER Klaes
Todd CONTRIBUTOR Berg
Tanisha VOLUNTEER Scott
LaNeice NETWORK Jones
Claudia TWILIGHT ZONE Phillips
Amy ALMOST Rotberg
Jon ROUND TWO Carlson
Tom ECCLESIASTES Cook
Julie SEMINAR CONSULTANT Zelman
Eric PEDAGOGY OF FEAR Maier
Greg PERFECTION Richards
Jenny FIVE! Kellman
Marcie FUN! Marcus
Mary Jo THANKS! Callan
Monique KNOCK 'EM DEAD! Whitman
Amy BUDDY Lynch
Terri 12th STEP Newsome

My last staff meeting was the most notable Project Community experience this week. Notwithstanding, the fact that this wasn't structured like the usual meeting, I know that I was much quieter than usual. I had trouble bringing myself to speak, for the feelings that I have about the group cannot really be done justice with humor or sarcasm, and I have trouble expressing myself without these tools. PC, the staff meetings in particular, were the big part of my life. I felt like I was saying good-bye to my family. Good bye was all I had, but certainly (it was) not enough.

—Eric Maier

Obviously, PC was one of the few places at school where I felt safe and free to be myself. Even then, it took me a while to let my guard down. But I think that somewhere around the third week this term, I started to feel really happy at staff meetings... Well, our last staff meeting was pretty sad. You'd think somebody died. It was pretty touching, and I think we are all going to miss PC a lot. I know I'll miss it a lot more than I even thought I would. It's funny, but I can distance myself from the kids [at site], but leaving you all behind is tough. I really can't say much more because it is still too close in my heart right now, and I haven't sorted it out yet.

—Tom Cook

Well I knew that the last meeting was coming soon, and I had been preparing for it, but still it seemed to come pretty quickly. It was hard to believe that this might be the last time that so many people who had shared successes and failures and joys and sorrows would be in the same room together. When I left the room that day, I was happy and satisfied that I had been a part of something so special. I stood outside in the rain and felt refreshed that something so wonderful had highlighted my time here. When I came inside I played some inspirational music by Melissa Etheridge that is very much related to the PC experience:

Everybody's got a hunger
No matter where they are
Everybody clings to their own fear
Everybody hides some scar

Precious Pain
Empty and cold but it keeps me alive
I gave it my soul so that I could survive
Keeping me safe in these chains
Precious pain

Maybe it's just my interpretation, but I think PC acknowledges that everyone has a precious pain and builds from that. The vulnerability is something that is very real and acknowledging that is key to creating a learning community.

—Randy Ross

Fall '92/ Winter '93[4]

Rick ONLY BE STRONG AND COURAGEOUS Smith
Stacey TCOB Brown
Scott MINOR INJURY Waldbaum
Donetta DISCO QUEEN Pedroza
Tracy RETURN Kollin
Amy MY PONTIAC! Rotberg
Bush WORLD TOUR Helzberg
Aaron IN YOUR FACE Romain
Jeff PC Salinger
Brett DYLAN Jaffe
Chris 187 Wright
Rachel RUSSIA Jellinek
Mark SELF-REFLEXIVE Matthews

I'm both sad and relieved that this term is coming to a close. Although the students have attended every site and nearly every seminar, there is a lack of enthusiasm in my eyes...I am sad to separate with (two people at site). I know one will be fine after the group is over and my missing him is purely selfish, but it happens. He was fine—too fine when he first came to the group...The other is fun to talk to. I truly believe he has the strength to stick through things and I feel that our group is therapeutic for him only because it is something for him to participate in and have an eagerness for. Somehow, my separation with him won't be as hard because I know he has stood on his own two feet since he walked into group the first day...

—Donetta Pedroza

Anyway, this is probably a cop out but I am not thinking about closure yet. Too much to do here before it's over. I know...this is a feeling in itself about closure...denial.

—Bush Helzberg

My feelings this term differ from most of '92 because I am graduating. I am obviously sorry that the term is coming to a close because I am not returning next year. This has been a difficult semester for me. I am finding it hard to concentrate on anything because I am so concerned about my future. I am having trouble finding a job and do not like this feeling of uncertainly. I am sorry if I have been a little "out of it" this semester. Project Community has been an important part of my college life which I will never forget. Becoming involved in PC was one of the best decisions I have made. It has had a strong impact on me.

—Tracy Kollin

Suggested Journal Question for Twelfth Seminar
(taken from the student's course evaluation)

Reflection is an important part of learning at PC. Many PC students use their journal to reflect on their weekly experiences. Please reflect on your entire PC experience this term, and articulate how it has personally affected you. In writing your PC "story", you may wish to include:

- significant things you have learned—about yourself, site, seminar group and/or the teaching/learning

- ideas and issues, thoughts and feelings, with which you have struggled

- what you will continue to ponder and/or seek answers to

NOTES

1. Depending on the term, I've focused my lecture on aspects of closure relating to Crisis Theory and defense mechanisms from the Growth Works handouts at the end of this chapter. My thanks to Sue Davis (1988) for her permission to reprint. During this time, I've also brought

in material from Kubler-Ross (1970) and her Stages of Denial, Depression, Anger, Bargaining and Acceptance.

2. My practice has been to give out Word Gifts or Nicknames once during the academic year, usually in the Winter. Over the years the pattern has been for my staff to consist of mostly first time coordinators in the Fall and mostly returning coordinators in the Winter.
3. My thanks to Laurence and Marc for contributing "Brown Baggin' It" as a closure activity. Basically, near the end of the last seminar, each group member is given a brown paper bag with her or his name on it. Group members are then instructed to take out several small pieces of paper and write down one or two things they have appreciated or liked about each of the other members of the group. These remarks are placed in the appropriate bag but cannot be read until after the seminar is over. The activity worked well for Marc, Laurence and also for their successors—Andrew Kramer, Julie Mathews, Elaine Murphy and David Oppenheim.
4. Toni Caldwell, Anthony Gilliam, David Marable and Jenny Kellman volunteered as site coordinators for various sections. Randy Ross, Mary Jo Callan and Rachel Meiland worked as Program Assistants.

Crisis Theory

Definition of a Crisis State

A crisis is any change that creates upset in an individual's equilibrium. The person then finds him/herself in a new situation where previous coping mechanisms and problem-solving techniques no longer work. More generally, a crisis can be either an event or an opportunity which forces an individual to make new adaptations to his/her new status. Crises come in many forms. They may be unanticipated, such as a loss of a loved one, a natural disaster, a new job, a challenge. Or they can be developmental: birth, puberty, leaving home, etc. Crises can also be situational: moving, holidays, or vacations. These examples illustrate that crises are inevitable, they are an integral part of living and growing. They need not be feared, for they can be mastered. The first step in mastery is being able to recognize and understand the nature of the crisis.

The characteristics of a crisis include the following: 1) there is always a precipitating event, sometimes this event may be minor in scope, or it may be a reaction to stresses that have been building up. 2) Crises are existential, the person has difficulty focusing on the past or future, which limits his/her perspective or objectivity. 3) The individual is in a vulnerable state, since his/her old coping methods of dealing with life are not functioning, he or she must create new ones. Finally, 4) crises are time limited, they usually last from one day to four to six weeks, but there may be tandem or overlapping crises which will extend the time frame longer.

While in a state of crisis, an individual generally feels isolated or confused. Since previous coping mechanisms and problem-solving techniques do not work, he or she is desperately searching for new ones. It is an overwhelming experience for anyone.

Once a person is involved in a crisis, he/she is able to become mobilized and then frees up energy which can be used to deal with the problem at hand. Intervention at this point can help direct this new energy in constructive ways and help that person advance and grow.

Stages of Crisis

D-1: *Denial*—Person denies that there is a problem.

D-2: *Deep Feelings*—Once denial has been broken and the person accepts there is a problem, deep or denied feelings about the event will surface (hurt, fear, shame, anger, sadness, gladness).

D-3: *Dependence*—The person will need support to cope with feelings at the crisis, there will be a need to talk, problem-solve with others, rely upon others.

I-1: *Independence*—The crisis has passed, the individual has learned new coping skills, they will feel secure in being on their own again. The person may shun dependence.

I-2: *Interdependence*—The ability to ask for help when it is needed, and also the ability to give others help when needed.

Crisis Assessment

1. *Event*

Maturational	life stage, developmental (puberty)
Transitional	role change (new job, school)
Situational	unexpected (suicide)
Disaster	natural (tornado, political (war)

2. *Vulnerable State*

Increase in stress	tension	
New coping	success/failure	
Disorganization	loss of support systems	
Subjective factors	events	
	• threats	• anxieties
	• loss	• depression
	• challenges	• hope

3. *Precipitating Event*
   "Final Star"—pushes person into active crisis state, event often is minor/negligible and misperceived.
4. *Active Crisis* (Time limit: 4-6 weeks)
   - coping vanishes or self-destructive coping appears
   - psychological, emotional, physical turmoil
   - aimless activity and immobilization
   - disturbances in body function, mood and intellect
   - exhaustion
   - shock crisis

Basic Rules of Crisis Intervention

1. **Listen**—let the client speak, be sure you hear what he/she sees as the problem crisis and what it is that they want from you.
2. You are a **listener**, **problem-solver**, **referral agent**, not a ***rescuer*** and you do not have all the answers. You can help the person by listening, pointing out alternatives, offering assurance, but you **cannot** assume responsibility for the person's problem or life.
3. Don't be **overreactive**—The first inclination may be to talk a lot and offer a good deal of help. The client must be able to take the leas and talk out the problem.
4. Be **empathetic**—Try to get to the **feeling** level. Is the person depressed, frustrated, angry: Get them to talk at this level and become more aware of how they are feeling.
5. Give **reassurance** and **hope** that the crisis will pass.

Group Rules

**MAINTAIN CONFIDENTIALITY
**MAINTAIN HONESTY, OPENNESS, AND WILLINGNESS
**OWN YOUR FEELINGS, THOUGHTS, AND OPINIONS

REMAIN INVOLVED THROUGH FEEDBACK AND CONFRONTATION LEVELING, RISK TAKING, AND GIVING SUPPORT
**NO ADVANCE GIVING, FIXING, OR RESCUING
**NO BLAMING
**AVOID ASKING QUESTIONS, INSTEAD USE:
"I feel, I see, or I think"
**SHARE YOUR OWN FEELINGS AND EXPERIENCES

NO GUM CHEWING, DRINKING, SMOKING, CANDY, OR WALKING OUT OF GROUP WITHOUT PERMISSION

Purpose of group

- To discover one's own positive and negative qualities.
- To accept one's own dependencies (chemical, co-dependency, food, work, sex, money, gambling, etc.) and to see the need for a positive, "sober lifestyle".
- To reduce the use of defenses (rationalization, justifying, projecting, blaming, humor, intellectualizing, explaining, comparing, attacking, withdrawing, silence, questioning, complying, threatening, denying, and minimizing).
- To identify and express feelings:
  MAD SAD GLAD HURT ASHAMED SCARED
- To identify what one has in common with other group members.
- To develop the ability to ask for what one needs from others.
- To learn new means of problem-solving in order to cope with life.
- To practice, try out, and model new behaviors and roles.
- As group members, we have a responsibility to confront the use of these defenses and help one another become feeling persons.

PART FOUR

Service-Learning Projects Affiliated with Sociology 389

Chapter 1

STUDENT INVOLVEMENT AT THE WASHTENAW COUNTY JAIL

By Randy Ross and Jenny Kellman

As I perceive history, it is not something that happens necessarily, but something that will be made, can be made, that can make or can refrain from making...History is made by us, and as we make it, we are made and remade by it.

—Paulo Freire (1970)

Introduction

The above quote is very significant to community service learning. In fact, it could not be more appropriate, because this experiential type of education demonstrates the capacity that individuals have to learn through experience. It is about real life, real people, and, most importantly, real situations. When one makes the commitment to this type of education, he or she is able to provide assistance to the surrounding community and at the same time be able to grow through personal insight and self-reflection. As individuals who make this commitment, we have the potential to create history, and the power to influence the future. The processes involved arc ever changing to meet the needs of the people involved and must continue to evolve while allowing us to grow with them. Project Community emphasizes this philosophy and should be affirmed for doing so. What follows is an account of the evolving commitment that Project Community students have shown to the Washtenaw County Jail (WCJ) and the inmate population there.

Washtenaw County Jail

The Washtenaw County Jail is located at the Sheriff's Department in Ann Arbor, Michigan. It is a maximum security facility that holds 280 inmates. The jail is run by a competent staff who work hard to keep the facility running safely and efficiently. The jail is highly regarded throughout the community and the criminal justice system because of its modern features, clean appearance, and services provided to inmates.

The Office of Correctional Services develops, implements, and supervises all of the services for the inmate population. The primary goal of the office is to impact and influence the offender in a positive manner in order to facilitate re-integration back into the community. Unofficially, the idea is to, within bureaucratic and time constraints, give the inmates some type of "edge" or life skill that will help them stay out of the criminal justice system. The office is guided by human interaction which is why community service learning and, in particular, Project Community has been successful and highly regarded at the jail. Except where noted, students have individually gone to the jail each week for three hours to earn two credits and for six hours to earn three credits.

Goals of PC at the Jail

The goals of PC at the jail, like any other PC site, are twofold. First, the students must have a meaningful site experience to which they can apply sociological concepts and past personal experiences. Second, we must provide necessary services that benefit both the agency and the clients. More specifically though, PC hopes that the interaction between students, staff, and inmates can break down barriers. These barriers include but are not limited to stereotypes about criminals and college students, differences between races and classes of people, and personal and bureaucratic obstacles that hinder self-improvement. While the means and services provided by Project Community (they will be detailed later in this chapter) have changed throughout the course of our involvement, we feel that we have been able to personalize and clarify the criminal justice system for students and inmates. At the same time, we have been able to ease the workload of the jail staff by providing services under their guidance and supervision.

Staff Support

Before this chapter can go on further to detail the specifics of "what we actually did" at the Washtenaw County Jail, we must first acknowledge the fact that Project Community's efforts have been met with much support, encouragement, and enthusiasm. The Office of Correctional Services has had two directors since PC's involvement began. Lucy Leist was the director when PC students first started during the Winter 1989 term. Cathy Wood took over during the Winter 1990 term and has maintained PC's presence within the office as an asset to the staff and inmates.

Myra Wilson has been invaluable to PC students' experiences as the office secretary. She sets up the interviews between students and inmates and ensures that both adhere to the rules. Jon Voelkner was instrumental in training and supervising PC students and introducing them to the policies and practices of the jail. Jon also provided the administrative liaison between PC and the jail when other administrative responsibilities made Cathy unavailable. Since Jon's departure, Jenny Kellman, one of the current MSW interns, has taken over his role with Cathy's approval. Throughout our involvement numerous staff, corrections officers, BSW and MSW interns, and trustees have aided in our efforts. PC acknowledges that sometimes service-providing agencies, though desperate for help in the form of volunteers or service-learners, are lacking in the resources, funds, or staff to train and supervise them. The Office of Correctional Services has tried its best to ensure that PC students are prepared and satisfied with their experience, and we thank them for that.

Student Initiative

The WCJ section, more than any other PC site, has been a symbol of what student initiative can accomplish. The Office of Correctional Services has always been open and responsive to students' suggestions on how to improve the quality of the services to fit the needs of all those involved. As a result, students have taken an active role in changing and updating the content and format of the information and counseling forms (Initial Needs Assessments and Pre-Release Counseling) administered through interviews between students and inmates.

During the Winter 1991 term students felt that they lacked the information and training that was necessary to adequately explain to inmates the services provided by the jail and other community agencies. Working with a resource card that was normally handed out to inmates, a small group of students began to do research on each of the agencies listed. The result was a comprehensive manual that included phone numbers, services provided, hours of operation, cost and other policies that varied from agency to agency. The number of agencies included was larger than what the original resource card had listed. The Inmate's Guide has since served as a training and information manual for students and as a resource for inmates. The original manual was edited and updated to keep up with changes in the service community during the Winter 1992 term by another group of students.

Orientation

Based on the course outline of Sociology 389 and the later starting date for the seminars compared to most University courses, it is important to begin site placement as soon as possible. Before any student begins his or her service work at the jail, the coordinator must arrange an orientation session for the entire group. This orientation should take place during the second week of seminars—preferably in addition to seminar rather than in place of the second seminar, if schedules permit.

Before students can come for orientation, they must first pass a security clearance. At WCJ, the Law Enforcement Information Network (L.E.I.N.) information (name, Social Security number, birthdate, race, and gender) is used to check for any outstanding warrants or previous arrests that may cause a security concern if they are placed with certain inmates. For all subsequent visits, students must show a picture I.D. (usually a driver's license and not a school I.D.) to the officer at the central command station in order to gain entry and obtain a jail visitor I.D. tag. It is important for the coordinator to obtain all necessary L.E.I.N. information and contact the director with that information prior to the orientation. During the orientation, students will be shown how to enter the facility and secure the proper identification.

The orientation is designed to allow students to become familiar with the facility and the rules and regulations that are in effect there. Some of the more important issues are what is appropriate dress and behavior, what is "safe" to discuss with inmates, what our role is in the office, what we can actually do for the inmates, and what items are contraband. For instance, women are not allowed to wear short skirts or dresses or any tight fitting clothes. Gum and pens are contraband items because gum can be used to jam locks and pens can be used as weapons, but pencils are allowed. Also, students should not reveal their last name or address for their own safety. Giving an inmate money or cigarettes or mailing a letter for them is not allowed. Inmates have accounts to which friends and family can add money so that the inmate can purchase snacks or personal items, but they have no need for money inside the jail, which is a non-smoking facility. Also, there are postal facilities on the premises for inmates' use. These may be things that a first-time visitor may not realize as being important safety and security concerns that need to be strictly adhered to.

After the briefing on the rules and regulations, students are taken on a tour of the jail. They are able to see almost the entire facility—booking, solitary confinement, attorney-client visitation rooms, the medical unit, the barber shop, the control centers, and the cell blocks themselves. The tour shows the stark reality of confinement as students are able to go on the catwalks of each block that run behind the individual cells. There is no privacy. Students can sense this violation of personal freedom, and, to many, it is an uneasy feeling. Nevertheless, it is important for students to understand the situation that an inmate is in when they come to the Office of Correctional Services.

Creative Writing and Art Therapy

During the first few semesters of PC involvement at the jail, there were a few different activities that students were able engage in with the inmates including creative writing and art therapy. The director was able to place students with inmates who expressed similar interests in writing and art. Both activities provided the inmate with opportunities to confront their inner feelings and bring them to some form of reality. Many inmates were not able or willing to do this verbally; so, the writing and art offered them a chance to release their feelings in a different way.

Mother-Child Visitation Weekends

During the Fall 1989 semester some of the students took part in the Mother-Child Visitation Program which took place (and still does only now without PC involvement) once a month on weekends. This was a chance for incarcerated mothers to visit with their children in a positive therapeutic environment. It was also an opportunity for students and volunteers to help the women develop positive parenting skills and ways of dealing with the emotional trauma of separation from the family during incarceration.

Initial Needs Assessments

Initial Needs Assessments, or intakes as they are often called, have been the most common activity for PC students to engage in at the jail—although their use like other activities has changed from term to term. The intakes consist of students interviewing inmates to probe the processes of incarceration and re-integration. Students question what the inmate has learned during incarceration and/or what services they need to have in order to learn necessary skills for functioning in society. The jail does offer services like General Equivalency

Degree (G.E.D.) classes, Adult Basic Education (A.B.E..) classes, Alcoholics Anonymous/Narcotics Anonymous (AA/NA) meetings, group and individual counseling and therapy, mother-child visitation, AIDS testing, and lectures on sexually transmitted diseases. It is through the interview that students can inform the inmate that these services are available to them during and, even in some cases, after their incarceration. The student can then make recommendations for staff follow-up and placement.

The Initial Needs Assessments form found in this text is the version that was updated during the Spring 1991 term following the recommendations of the students from the previous term and the completion of the first edition of the Inmate's Guide. Jon Voelkner and Randy Ross, the coordinator at that time, were able to implement the newer version with much success during the spring and summer before students began using it again in the fall of that year.

Another function of the Initial Needs Assessments has more to do with human interaction than information transfer. As a student in the first PC group at WCJ and eventually a coordinator, Rebecca Story recalls, "Lucy would often encourage the students to just sit there and talk with them, kind of as a sounding board, or a friend in a certain sense." Oftentimes, the PC student is the first person from the "outside" that an inmate speaks to, and thus, it is the first semblance of a "normal" conversation.

Pre-Release Counseling

During the Fall 1989 term, co-coordinators Rebecca Story and Mandy Carlson and CJ program director Joe Galura worked to design a supplement to the Initial Needs Assessment. The Pre-Release Counseling form served as a dual component with which PC students could be involved and offered follow-up for inmates who would go through both interviews. The pre-release worked to target offenders two to three weeks prior to their release. The purpose was to initiate their thinking about what they would do upon their release. The interview covers such areas as financial, employment, housing, substance abuse, and mental health needs. Also probed are thoughts and feelings related to avoiding re-arrest. With these ideas in mind the inmate can begin, if he or she has not already, to take responsibility for his or her actions. These tend to be attitudes and feelings with which some offenders may be unfamiliar and unable to deal unless they have some type of guidance and support. The session is also intended to inform them of any agencies in the community that may be of assistance during their re-integration.

In the Spotlight

In April 1992 ABC TV's "Good Morning America" decided to do a feature on community service on college campuses with the University of Michigan as the featured school. The WCJ section was chosen as one of three to represent Project Community's involvement to the nation. Despite the fact that the lights and cameras were a bit unnatural in the tiny cubicles inside of the Office of Correctional Services, corespondent Betina Gregory and her staff were able to capture the essence of what Project Community is all about—human interaction, service to the community, and thoughtful reflection that combine to

Washtenaw County Sheriff's Department
Correctional Services Initial Needs Assessment

***Note:** All blanks must be filled with pertinent information, "Yes," "No," or "Not Applicable."

I. Demographic Information

Date: _________ Completedby: ____________

Inmate Name: _________________ IB #: ____________________

Classification: __________________ Aliases: ________________

Date of Birth: _______ Age: ______ Sex: ______ Marital Status: ___

Ethnicity: ___________ Street Address: _________________________

Apt/Lot #: __________ City: _________________ County: ______

State: ______________ Phone #: _____________ Zip Code: _____

II. Legal Information

Charge/Judge/Court: I. _____ / _____ / _______

II. _____ / ____ / _____ III. ____ / _____ / _______

IV. ____ / ____ / _____ V. ____ / _____ / _______

Attorney: ___________ Police Dept./Arresting Officers: ___________

Previous Wash. Jail stay (Y,N): ____ Previously Arrested? (Y,N): __

Parole: Agent: _________________ Probation Agent: __________

III. Other Information

Employed? (Y,N): _______________ If "Yes," employer: ________

Health Insurance? (Y,N): _________ If "Yes," specify: __________

Social Security #: _______________ Last Grade Completed: _____

Receiving any social service benefits at this time? (Y,N): __________

If "Yes," specify: ____

Program Needs Assessment

*Answer Y="Yes" and N="No" for "Needs" column. If indicated, record "Y" or "N" in applicable columns.P

Programs	Need	Ref.	Enrolled	Completed	Comments
1. Education					
a. GED					
b. ABE					
2. Sub.Ab.					
a. AA					
b. NA					
c. ChemDep					
d. Ind.Thrpy.					
e. Grp.Thrpy.					
f. Fmly.Thrpy.					
3. Mntl.Health					
a. CMH REF.					
b. Ind.Thrpy.					
c. Grp.Thrpy.					
d. Fmly.Thrpy.					
4. Alternative Sentencing					
a. Inpt sub ab					
b. Oupt sub ab					
c. Inpt psych					
d. Outpt psych					
5. Child Visit					
6. STD Lecture					
7. Other					

Additional Comments: ______________________________

____

____

____

WCSD Correctional Services/JDV, CSB 04/30/91

Pre-Release Counseling

Name: ______________________________

Today's Date: ______________________________

Date of Release: ______________________________

Date of Birth: ______________________________

Charge: ______________________________

Significant Events

What specific events brought you to the county jail? ____________

____

What have you learned from your incarceration? ____________

____

What specific changes are you making to avoid re-arrest? ________

____

Personal Needs

1. Financial: ______________________________
   ____
2. Housing: ______________________________
   ____
3. Employment: ______________________________
   ____
4. Substance Abuse: ______________________________
   ____
5. Mental Health: ______________________________
   ____
6. Other: ______________________________
   ____

provide learning not found in textbooks alone. Even as the inmates and staff chanted, "Where's Joan?" they understood the importance of letting the nation know about the successes in corrections that usually get overshadowed by the failures.

Criminal Procedures

The Winter 1993 term saw a restructuring within in the CJ program area as the Court Watching and Washtenaw County Jail sections were merged into a new section called Criminal Procedures. Joe Galura and the co-coordinators, Jeff Salinger and Brett Jaffe, were hoping that the combination of the two sections would create a more thorough understanding of the criminal justice system. Students would be expected to follow a rotation which would include visiting the different levels of courts in Ann Arbor and going to the jail. Part of their new agenda that never materialized was a ride-along program with police. The resulting rotation meant that each student went to WCJ about three times during the term to do Pre-Release Counseling. The students were generally positive about their experience although the lack of time at the jail was cited as one of the drawbacks. One of the students, Marc Blackman said, "The pre-release format, on top of the time one had to reflect while in jail, were major contributors to an inmate's re-thinking process about where his or her life was headed." Josh Woods went on to say, "The jail experience was rewarding and enlightening for the students and the inmates—one that will not be forgotten."

Reflection

Reflection and communication are essential to the learning and understanding that take place in Project Community and especially in the WCJ section. Experiences and thoughts need to be challenged, supported, or just heard rather than occurring in a vacuum. It would be easy for stereotypes and beliefs to continue on unchallenged or unquestioned without forums such as seminar or journal writing. What follows is a poem excerpted from a student's journal based on her interaction with the inmates.

"Victims"

Big room, no windows.
He was escorted to my desk and I introduced myself.
He was reluctant. I was nervous.

His name is Michael.
He prefers to be called Michael.

I asked Michael what had brought him here.
He was hesitant. I was calm.

"B&E and CSC."

I pretend to understand and

during the course of our conversation
I do understand.

He showed me a picture of his daughter.
Lovely, adorable.
What will she think of her father
when she is old enough to understand,
I wonder.
Lovely Shamica—the light of Michael's life.

Shamica has changed him, he confesses.
Life will be better.
He's been a victim
and nothing is his fault.
He'll show us all, he confides.

Time works against us
too fast, for a change.
He doesn't want to leave.
He wants to talk just a little while longer.
Rules are rules are rules, I admit.
Perhaps we will talk again, I hope.

He asks me to escort him out, I consent.

I return to my desk and quickly jot down some notes—
Oh Michael, what's a nice guy like you...

"You're next," she yells.

His name is Marvin.
Just Marvin.
He didn't do anything, but when he gets out
life will be better, he swears.

-Debra Groddick

Process time is not only an important feature of staffings as noted in Off to See the Wizard but also an essential and effective learning tool for a seminar. Since site work is done on an individual basis, it is important to have an open forum to discuss events and issues in a group setting. It is important to nurture a "safe" learning environment in order for students to be able to share their thoughts and feelings. While the jail is a relatively safe in terms of personal, physical well-being, it can be a terrifying experience to even someone who knows that they can leave after a few hours. The shared learning that goes on in the seminar and, in particular, process time helps to form a more complete understanding of the jail and the criminal justice system.

There are always several key questions that emerge from the jail seminars: What do I do when an inmate doesn't want to talk with me?; How do I know if they are telling me the truth?; Will they get the treatment/services once this form is completed?; Are we making a difference in their lives? Sometimes the best response is that we really do not know. It is important to never take things for granted; we must always be asking and questioning ourselves, the inmates, and the institution to attempt to determine the truth of the situation and its outcome. Most of the results of our efforts are not immediately visible; however, there are some tangible results from our work. Thank-you notes and handshakes are the most common source of gratification. G.E.D. completion, sobriety, and the cessation of a criminal career are others, but then, as a service-learner, you can not go around and follow-up on every inmate to see what type of progress they have made. It is easy for a naive college person to believe that they have made a difference when in fact they may have just been conned. We can only hope that some day they will appreciate our honesty, sincerity, and compassion, and if they do, then we have done well. If they do not end up in the system again, then we have done even better.

Special Alternative

Beyond the core of readings and activities, students were interested in other related issues such as drug treatment programs, and state policies to build or not to build more prisons. One of the greatest sources of discussion during the Winter 1992 term was the issue of Special Alternative Incarceration (S.A.I.) —or prison boot camp as it is more commonly referred to. PC students were noticing during the Initial Needs Assessment interviews that several of the inmates were being sentenced to S.A.I. The inmates wanted to know if we knew anything about the boot camps; many of us knew nothing. So, partly out of a general thirst for more information and training that could be applied for the benefit of the inmates and also partly to satisfy our own curiosity about this military-style, shock incarceration, some of the students decided to find out more about S.A.I.

S.A.I. is modeled after the United States military's own training regimen of discipline, hard work, personal hygiene, and respect for authority. Sentences are generally sixty to ninety days depending upon the program and the state. Not all persons sentenced to jail or prison time are eligible for the boot camps as they have criteria based on type of crime and length of sentence. All persons who are sentenced to S.A.I. are given a choice between a traditional prison and the boot camp.

Cassidy Lake Boot Camp in nearby Chelsea, Michigan was gracious enough to allow students to view the daily routine from intakes to meals to work duties. Prior to the visit, views of the program ranged: cruel and unusual punishment; violation of civil liberties; immoral; a slap on the wrist; sending criminals back to the streets too soon; the right choice to overcrowding. After the visit, many of the same opinions were present—only more this time more emphatic. The boot camp program is indeed a shock not only for those sentenced to it but also for those who witness it. There was plenty of yelling and screaming and verbal abuse but no physical abuse (intakes are taped to ensure that guards refrain from any such contact) in an attempt to break the street image of the criminal.

Officials at Cassidy Lake, specifically Assistant Warden Bruce Curtiss and Inspector Ray, were very accommodating to our inquiries. They realize that the public has very mixed conceptions about what S.A.I. tries to accomplish and the means through which it tries to do so. Although there are skeptics, early figures seem to show that S.A.I. is able to lower recidivism rates with low cost and risk to the community. Inspector Ray pointed out that, like other programs, the positives and progress of treatment at the boot camp can be washed away without adequate aftercare.

Cassidy Lake was able to provide an informational video for students who were unable make the trip. This tape was also viewed by Jon Voelkner and Cathy Wood so that they could supplement their knowledge of the program and answer any questions from inmates and PC students. The video is now part of the Project Community video archives and is available for coordinator and student use.

Conclusion

During the Fall 1991 Mass Meetings, a challenge was given—a call to service. The jail section was looking for students willing to withstand the frustration and intimidation of working in a secured facility with adult offenders. It was explained that this section was not like the ones described before it—Maxey Boys Training School, Cotton Facility, or Western Wayne. There would be no games and no sharing of creative works; connections with the inmates would be fleeting and there would be little, if any, follow-up. We were there to talk and listen and offer advice to the best of our ability. There would be few visible rewards from our work, but there would be the possibility that a life could be changed and saved from becoming a career criminal or remaining an undesirable in society. The challenge was answered. That school year marked the highlight of Project Community's continuing legacy of involvement at the Washtenaw County Jail. It was not the first successful year and already we have seen that it will not be the last. We hope that others can develop a similar passion and conviction to service and that this piece will help others to grow and to become more aware of a world that so few people know.

Chapter 2

PRISON LITERACY

By Jeanne Gray and Scott Dent

Introductions

Jeanne: I inherited the prison literacy program in my new position as the partial program director of the Trained Volunteer Corps (TVC) at the University of Michigan. The two sites that we used were Washtenaw County Jail and Milan Federal Correctional Institution. Both institutions are maximum security facilities with strong educational components, and have provided good learning experiences for students who have them worked at them in the past. I came from the background of having been a student of Project Community for over a year, and coordinating for almost two years. I had only been involved with the juvenile justice system through coordinating a site a Maxey Boys Training School for one semester, so I was fairly new to working within the correctional system.

Scott: During the Fall and Winter terms of 1992 and 1993, I had the opportunity to participate in an adult literacy program at a Federal Correctional Institution in Milan, Michigan. The first term I participated as a student volunteer in the prison, and the following term I coordinated the student volunteers attending the federal facility in Milan as well as Washtenaw County Jail.

Our class consisted of two to three hours spent at the prison taken at various time slots throughout the week. In addition, we met for a seminar for an hour and a half each week.

Although we entered the prison as literacy volunteers, the issues raised by our experiences reached much further than how to communicate the rules of grammar and spelling. For many of us, the prison experience involved crossing lines of race and class as well as entering a correctional facility for the first time. Each of us had our own set of expectations, fears, and reasons for being there. Project Community allowed us a space where we fully realized our experiences.

Washtenaw County Jail

Jeanne: When I began working for TVC, only one of the two sites was being used actively (Milan Correctional Facility), by students involved in TVC. My first priority was to re-open Washtenaw County Jail as a potential site. I contacted the jail, and got the name of the educational coordinator, Gloria

Jadwin, called her and set up a meeting. She had worked with Project Community in the past, and was very receptive to the possibility of having students come out to the jail. She explained to me the way that the classrooms worked. Basically, there were two classes offered, Adult Basic Education (ABE) and GED preparation classes. The GED prep class provided tutoring for inmates that wished to take the GED. The ABE classes were more specific, covering all the basic disciplines offered in traditional educational settings.

She told me that classes met everyday, in three and a half hour time blocks, one in the morning, and one in the afternoon. The male inmates were separated from the female inmates, with the classes for females only being offered twice weekly. She explained to me that there simply were not enough female inmates to warrant more classes. The students would be interacting one-on-one with the inmates tutoring them in whatever subjects the inmates needed. Washtenaw County Jail houses inmates of two types. The first are inmates who have been sentenced for under one year, basically low level felonies and misdemeanors. The second type are inmates who are awaiting trial for further sentencing. The educational consultant told me that the average stay of an inmate is about 11 days. So, the educational planning is more geared towards getting the inmates prepared for their GED.

I was a bit taken aback by this information. I had envisioned my students working with the same inmate all semester. When I expressed this to Gloria she was sympathetic, but reassured me that the experience would still be rewarding for a student. This way, she said, the students would meet and interact with different types of inmates, at different levels of education. She also told me that because the program was so broad, students would be working with 45 year-old men who couldn't read, as well as college level 20 year-olds. She said that the disparity between the educational levels of inmates was a testimony to how our educational system was (or wasn't) working. I left the meeting feeling very confident that my students would experience and learn a great deal here.

The next step was contacting the volunteer coordinator at Washtenaw County Jail, Cathy Wood. Cathy basically explained to me the process by which one becomes a volunteer at the jail. A person needs to have their name, social security number, and birthdate submitted to the "LEIN." The "LEIN" is a nation-wide computer that cross-checks to see if the person wising to volunteer has ever been convicted of a misdemeanor or felony. If my students passed this, then they would set up an orientation with Kathy and Gloria to go over the rules and regulations for volunteers at the jail. After this, they would be able to begin tutoring.

Milan Federal Correctional Institution

Jeanne: This site presented an entirely different problem. There were four students placed there last semester, and although the site was good, it was problematic. For starters, the educational contact person was less than receptive to my phone call. She was uncertain as to whether or not she wanted volunteers again, but wouldn't get into specifics with me on the phone. She was reluctant to meet with me, but after I pushed the issue a bit, she agreed to do so. At the meetings she told me that she felt as though our program was run too loosely. She stated that the volunteers didn't have a set schedule, and that they were unreliable. She also said that she was never certain who the contact person was, and that when problems did arise she didn't know who to contact. She did not want women to volunteer at the site anymore, and if she decided to have volunteers again, she only wanted four men. These men would be able to volunteer during the morning classes from 7:00 to 11:00AM.

This posed a huge problem for me. I was very uncomfortable with her not wanting women at the site. I was also unhappy about the fact that she only wanted four volunteers. The site is almost one half hour away from Ann Arbor, thus we would be tying up four Project Community cars for a half a day each week. I was unsure about setting up a section with only four people in it, and began to wonder if the site was more trouble than it was worth.

In trying to decide how to resolve this problem, I read through some of the journals that had been written the previous semester. The students that were out there all had extraordinary experiences. Because Milan is a federal prison, all of the inmates were there for substantial periods of time. The students formed solid relationships with the inmates, and got to see dynamics of the corrections system that people on the outside rarely get to view. For instance, the hierarchy in the prisons between the teachers, guards and inmates was a huge issue for most of the students. They were witnesses to gross inequities in the system, and were forced to re-evaluate many of their prior beliefs about the corrections system.

For these reasons, I decided to meet with the educational director again and try and iron out some of the problems. Leanna said she was willing to give us another try under the following conditions. She wanted me to screen all of the volunteers. I needed to give her two contact people. The volunteers would only come once a week, one per day. She wanted a written schedule of who would be coming when. There was a strict dress code by which the volunteers had to abide, and finally the volunteers had to attend a four hour orientation. Quite a switch after the reception at the jail.

I also addressed the issue of not allowing women at the site. I informed her that I had worked at a corrections facility, and that I could help prepare the women for possible problems they might face. Leanna would not budge on this issue. Evidently, in the past when they had used women students, the classrooms got "out of hand." The women were harassed if they were dressed even the least bit provocatively. She stated that the inmates never got to see women, and when they did their attention spans were almost non-existent. She maintained that the classrooms were supposed to be learning environments and when women were present this process was inhibited. This left me feeling dismayed. I couldn't help wondering what these "uncontrollable" men would do when they were re-exposed to women. But as I was treading on thin ice anyway, I let the issue drop.

The classroom settings would be different then those at the jail. The GED prep class still existed but there was a "longer term" educational plan. The inmates actually took courses like history and English for semesters at a time. The college in the area had professors that came over to teach on a regular basis. It was possible for an inmate to gain an associate's degree while incarcerated. There was also an "English as a Second Language" course. Evidently, there is a high population of Colombians and Hispanics at Milan. She invited me to try and find a student that spoke Spanish to assist with the course.

Hiring Coordinators

Jeanne: For the two prison literacy sections, I needed to hire one coordinator. One coordinator was supposed to be returning, and he would be in charge of the Milan section, which is the section he had run the previous semester. So basically I only had to fill one position. The position had been posted in the School of Social Work as a work-study position, so I had received about five resumes. I contacted these people and set up interviews. I also set about the task of contacting the person who was supposed to return as a coordinator. Of these people who interviewed, I hired the person that I felt had the most experience working with groups. She was a first-year Social Work student and appeared responsible and organized.

Formatting the Coursepack

Jeanne: There was already one coursepack in existence for these sections. However, it covered all of literacy and had very little information about the prison system. I borrowed some reading materials from the Criminal Justice sections of Project Community[1] as well as using some reading materials that I had collected from the School of Social Work. Basically, I thought it was important to look at some of the issues that students were faced with in he prison system. For instance, the roles of teachers, guards, and prisoners is an issue that students consistently struggle with. Specifically, students struggle with the cruelty of the guards to the prisoners. So we included the Stanford Prison Experiment (Haney and Zimbardo, 1973).

Scott: In my seminar, a description of the results of the Stanford Prison Experiment was as a vehicle to discuss broad issues of control, the function of the prison system, and its effectiveness.

Jeanne: We also included many writings of Danny Martin (1993). Danny Martin is a prisoner that has done a lot of creative writing. His work about prison life is well written and informative about what it is like to be a prisoner. This is valuable, I believe, because it gives students the opportunity to look at a highly educated incarcerated man's view on the prison system. We also included a few articles on how to actually tutor. Students entering this class were apprehensive about their ability to "teach." So we used some materials from the Washtenaw Literacy Council—basic tips on how to tutor.

Scott: The creative writing of the inmates helped us break down the popular image of the men in prison as being barbaric, with nothing positive to offer to society; an image that dominated the orientation at Milan. The readings helped us discuss the politics and implications of the word "rehabilitation." The authorities at Milan used this term as if it was the prison's job to transform the men into "useful citizens." These readings helped us understand that the inmates had a great deal to offer society, and our role was one of helping them develop the tools necessary to express themselves in a more constructive manner.

Jeanne: With the assigned Sociology readings, i.e. the readings required by the Department of Sociology, we included an article which addresses the question of "nature vs. nurture" in an attempt to discuss common views about why people turn to crime. This is always a good discussion tool and was most effective when used later in the semester after students had a chance to really get to know the inmates that they are working with. We also used a chapter from Kozol's book Savage Inequalities (1991). The chapter is about inequalities in the Chicago school districts and works really well with the topic of education in corrections facilities.

Scott: From a more sociological standpoint, excerpts for Jonathan Kozol's Savage Inequalities led to some very animated dialogue on issues of public education in the inner city, societal guilt and social responsibility. This type of reading allowed our group to look at the inmates in a much broader scope, and led to important reflection on our own lives and things that many of us may have taken for granted.

Recruiting Students

Jeanne: Recruiting students for these sections was fairly easy. There were already five returning students so essentially I only had to recruit fifteen other students. To do this I contacted a new professor at the University. She was teaching a general Sociology course along with a Social Injustices class. I met with her to discuss the prison literacy class, and she was very receptive to me. She said that she thought that community experience as well as classroom education was valuable to students, and agreed to let me speak to her classes.

I spoke to each class for about twenty minutes. I briefly outlined what it was that the students would be doing. I spoke about the relevance to what they would be learning in the class. The professor spoke up at this point and said that the students could use their experiences in my class to write their term paper for her class. I also talked about the credit available for this work. Then I opened it up for questions. One student in the class spoke out and said that she had participated in Project Community. She was very excited about it, and recommended it highly. I stayed after class to hand out flyers and my phone number, and from this recruited the remainder of my section.

Orientations

Jeanne: Each institution had their own orientation prepared for the students, and I used one of our section times to complete this. Milan, being a federal institution, had a very lengthy orientation. It went over the history of Milan Prison. They also spoke to the students about some of the dangers of being a volunteer, and some traps to avoid. They spoke a lot about the population at Milan and the kinds of inmates that my students would be encountering. They used a "scare" tactic almost to remind the students about the seriousness of following the rules. They talked about the dress code and the importance of abiding by it. They also put the students through the "Uniform Crime Report" to make sure that none had been convicted of a felony. I had to write a letter of recommendation for the students. The whole thing took about four hours.

Scott: At the very beginning of our Milan Prison orientation, we were given a handful of definitions. The one I wrote down was: Rehabilitation—working with individuals and helping them change their behavior; preparing inmates for acceptance into society. We were told that although each staff member at the prison had a different job, they were working towards a common goal—to help rehabilitate the inmates. However, before the night was over, the officers would make it very clear that their goals were simply to keep their prison running smoothly and nothing more.

Along with other students in our group, my initial reaction was one of anger and frustration. The officer seemed to envision himself as a zookeeper who was dealing with animals rather than people. That was our orientation to the facility and our introduction to the officers and the guards. Each term, UM volunteers at F.C.I. Milan were given a sort of second orientation. On our first day, one of the teachers we worked with pulled aside and described the notable tension that existed between the education staff and the guards. She advised me to be careful of what I said to them, as they might use it against me at another time. It was almost as if they were working against one another. The conflict of interest between these two groups left me wondering what messages the inmates received. As student volunteers who primarily dealt with the education staff, we were able to avoid this tension for the most part, but its presence was known.

Jeanne: Washtenaw's orientation was entirely different. They started out by giving the students a tour of the facility. Then the students met the teachers with whom they would be working. They went over the dress code and the rules of working in the Jail. They went over general emergency procedures in case of problems. They opened up the orientation for questions. This orientation was very informal and lasted about one half hour.

I did my own orientation as well. I knew two Sociology TA's that had taught in correctional facilities. They came into the section and spoke for about half an hour each about their experiences teaching. I did this after the institutions' orientations so that the students could ask questions. This was very effective because I believe that many of my students left the "official" orientations feeling scared and overwhelmed. The two men that spoke later were very relaxed and reassuring to my students. They also weren't intimidating, so my students could ask questions without feeling scared. I highly recommend doing this for any section teaching in prisons, because it was comforting for my students to meet and interact with people that had done this type of work.

Formatting Exercises for the Class

Jeanne: Much of my exercises for the class came from the <u>Wizard</u>, and I changed them to fit the purposes of my section. For instance we did the "Paper Dolls"[2] exercise having the students draw their stereotypical criminal. I did this at the very beginning of the semester, kept the drawings, and did it again at the end. I had the class break into two groups, draw their "criminal" then come together and present it to the group. This is an extremely powerful exercise as it forces students to face stereotypes head on.

Scott: When I did "Paper Dolls" as a student, we came up with a terrifying man who matched every negative image of an inmate, right down to the swastika imprinted on his forehead. The activity is actually quite enjoyable, as it is designed to make fun of the stereotypes we place on the men and women behind bars. It is an important exercise because although it seemed very much a joke, I realized that I had internalized many of these stereotypes, and it was important for me to see how ridiculous it all was.

We also did the "Teacher-Student" excercise. In this exercise, students work with a partner and assume the roles of teacher and students. The teacher is to help the student get through a reading passage that is unreadable to the student. The teacher passage might read: The quick brown fox jumped over the lazy dog.

The student passage might read: T** Q***K BR*** *OX J**PED **ER T** *AZ* ***. This activity allows students to practice teaching skills, as well as understand what it might feel like to be illiterate.

Jeanne: With the Kozol readings we used the "Ron and Chris" exercise[3] from the Wizard. The Kozol readings are all about inequities in the educational system, and the "Ron and Chris" exercise is a very specific way to illustrate what the readings are trying to teach. People begin to see and understand how different school systems deal with "problem" kids. They also understand a little better why some people succeed and why some people fail in school.

Most of the readings will spark discussions anyway, without using exercise, but it is good to have them and to use them. As I said already, much of what we did resembled exercises in the Wizard, and we would shape them to fit our sections. Again, it is important to include in your sections a number of icebreakers[4]. People need to feel comfortable talking to each other about issues that they are faced with at site. Building community in your section will facilitate and enhance the learning process.

Scott: I firmly believed that in order to get past the surface conversation often found in the traditional classroom, it was important that each group member get to know each other and feel comfortable with one another. This was the process of transforming the traditional classroom setting into a learning community.

The first few meetings were primarily dedicated to allow the group to become comfortable with one another. These meetings were vital as they paved the way for future discussions which wouldn't have taken place amongst a group of distant students. Facilitating these early sessions was far more difficult than I had expected. We started off talking about why each one of us was volunteering at a prison. What had brought each of us to this first, organizational meeting? We then moved on to expectations—what did we each hope to gain from this experience? These initial discussions, and others throughout the term, helped group members feel comfortable in seminar. This allowed us to tackle more difficult issues that would come up throughout the term, such as social responsibility and crossing socio-economic barriers in community service.

One student reflected on seminar at the end of the term:

> *I enjoyed getting to know the people in my group and hearing about their experiences at site. I was very comfortable talking and expressing my opinions. Everyone really seemed to care about what they were doing and were interested in my feelings as well.*
>
> —*Patricia Dugan*

Some Site Related Issues

Scott: In order to volunteer or work at the Federal Prison at Milan, one is required to review and sign a 35 page program statement which includes a detailed list of how one is to conduct oneself while in the facility. The rule that pertained to our situation most was also the stress of the orientation: Don't get personal. We were always to maintain a professional rapport with the men with whom we worked. We were never to stray from the work at hand. To me, and others in our group this seemed not only extremely difficult but also counterproductive. Separating the learning process and the personal experience contradicted everything we had learned from Paulo Freire and others in articles in the courespack. How each volunteer is affected by these rules of conduct depends upon the teacher with whom they are working with. Although spending an entire session talking to one inmate would be discouraged, incorporating personal material into the learning process has never gotten me into trouble. Each situation is different.

Although many of the men were working towards their GED, there were a number of inmates who could not read or write and were working to increase their basic vocabulary. One exercise that I found very effective in this situation was suggested to us by one of the teachers at Milan. The exercise was simple. The inmate would speak of a past personal experience, anything they wanted to talk about. The volunteer would record whatever the inmate dictated word for word. The volunteer then typed whatever she/he had recorded. The exercise allows the inmate to see what they said on a hard copy. The student volunteer and the inmate would then go over the story together, and identify the spellings of new words which the learner could previously only verbalize. The exercise was effective because it was based on the inmates own experience and therefore held their interest. I had a lot of fun with this, as the men I worked with eventually began to ask me to help them write letters home. We were able to see the direct benefits of literacy while learning.

A common question that many of us asked ourselves at one point throughout the term was: Are we really helping them? Going into the prison and helping an inmate get through a GED workbook didn't seem to be a big deal. To most of the inmates, our two or three hours a week was a big deal. It represented more than just help with grammar, but a stranger from the outside who was reaching out to them. For me, the experience represented the establishment of a mutual respect. Certainly, I feel that student volunteers have a lot to offer inmates as tutors, but it is more the gesture of volunteering, the idea of the commitment, which leaves the lasting impression.

Final Reflections

Scott: One semester is an extremely short period of time to fully understand a new experience such as a prison. Seminar time is both valuable and easily wasted. It is important to get in touch with your site contact well before your first meeting. Information such as orientation dates and time slots available to volunteers is helpful to have before the first meeting. Other "business" items such as transportation and lab fees are easier taken care of immediately in an effort to begin attending site as early in the term as possible.

—Find out the employee/volunteer dress code at the facility that you are working with to prevent any situations in which new volunteers are confused with inmates.

—Maintain consistent contact with the volunteer coordinator at the prison in an effort not only to maintain a positive relationship, but also to check on attendance and any other situations that may arise throughout the term.

Emphasize consistent attendance to site. Inmates know when the students are coming in, look forward to it, and are disappointed when no one shows up. The students volunteers are making a commitment to the inmates which must be respected.

No single experience is the same. Working with and coming to understand inmates and the prisons brought out different reactions in each of us.

> *I learned a lot about how a different group of people view the world. I also got to help them with some things that are important for them to know. Sometimes just talking to the inmates was interesting and makes me think about a lot of things I take for granted.*
>
> —*Gina Zanotti*

> *I really enjoyed talking to the prisoners at site and learning their point of view on many issues. I also liked the feeling of really helping people; by helping them with letters for court, or listening to their problems.*
>
> —*Patricia Dugan*

For the most part, I watched and saw the rewards on a weekly basis in the journals and at seminar. After we had all dragged ourselves out of bed, driven out to site and spent a couple hours with the inmates, something happened. We felt really good. It felt good to make the inmates feel good. Help with grammar or spelling aside, the very fact that we had chosen to spend a few hours of each week with them was pleasing. We felt it in the warm receptions and the sincere good-byes. Inmates genuinely cared for the student volunteers because the volunteers genuinely cared for them.

NOTES

1. The current syllabus for Criminal Justice appears in Chapter One of Off to See the Wizard.
2. Examples of Paper Dolls can be found in chapter four of Off to See the Wizard.
3. Ron and Chris can be found in Chapter Six of Off to See the Wizard.
4. Chapter Two of Off to See the Wizard describes various icebreakers for seminar.

Chapter 3

"ONLY BE STRONG AND COURAGEOUS"[1]
A Conversational Cookbook on How to Conduct a Creative Writing Workshop in a Correctional Facility

by Richard J. Smith and friends

Introduction

I used to think it'd be a good idea for students to take a year or two off between their sophomore and junior year in college. Take a break from school and then come back with a real desire to go to school, to learn...Now, maybe it'd be better to hang out in a prison for some extended time instead. The guys I'm with all have a tremendous desire to be educated, to educate themselves. They're always asking me what's going on in school and they mean in school, not in life. They want to know what I'm learning, what I'm studying. I feel somewhat embarrassed then, to respond, "Oh, you know, the usual stuff." We should reform education in this country by sending students A Year Incarcerated before they take their Year Abroad.

—Hans Hwang, Fall '92 Cotton Section

How I came to be a PC coordinator

During the summer of 1992, I spent my mornings as a Diversity Facilitator for the University of Michigan's Summer Orientation program. I co-facilitated interactive exercises that engaged students in examining their relationship to a multi-cultural nation. Towards the end of the summer, we hosted an information tea for University of Michigan administrators interested in learning what the incoming students were like. After our panel discussion, Joan Scott, from the Office of Community Service Learning, asked if she could pass on my number to her suitemate, Joe Galura. She had noticed that I was a creative writing major, and told me that Joe needed a facilitator to conduct a creative writing workshop in a prison. I spoke with him that day: my life will never be the same.

Historicity

Cotton

Cotton Correctional Facility is Michigan's second largest prison. The largest facility in Michigan and the world (I'm not kidding), the State Prison of Southern

Michigan, rests across the street. Cotton has living quarters with four levels of security from minimum to maximum. It is handicap accessible and hosts a wide range of rehabilitation services from psychotherapy and drug counseling, high school and college completion, and job training. Ruby Daniel, Director of Special Activities, is particularly proud of the Project Community Creative Writing Workshop, because she claims that it encourages residents to participate in several of the other services and programs that Cotton has to offer.

Project Community has been a part of Cotton Correctional Facility since the winter of 1989. Joe Galura, program director for the criminal justice and chemical dependency sections of Project Community, put in a proposal for a group of UM students to conduct a weekly creative writing workshop in the facility that would culminate in the publication of a literary journal. Although none of the six coordinators of the section ever used the detailed syllabus Joe wrote for the proposal, the section remains one of the most successful and favorite of all those who have participated.

N-way[2]

About one month ago, I sat down with Joe Galura, Rachel Meiland, Stacey Brown, Bush Helzburg and Rachel Story, three other Cotton coordinators, for an N-way conversation. We agreed that Cotton was a very special site, because it is the one site where it is possible to form a learning community.

At the Cotton Creative Writing Workshop, the UM students are alone in a classroom with the Cotton students. The bars are gone, so are corrections officers and staff. The workshop is a very safe space for people to share their stories, and build relationships they thought they could never have. We discussed how it was a different world: not prison, not school—somewhere in between.

Let me introduce my predecessors. Mike Shaw was the first coordinator; his group christened the first journal Building Bridges. Mike has just finished two years in the Peace Corps teaching English in Africa. He was succeeded by Rachel Story,[3] who is now finishing a Masters in Public Health and moving on to Case Western's MD program. She spent two terms coordinating. The next coordinator, third world development major, Bush Helzberg, now works for an airline in Nigeria that specializes in airlifting local Muslims to Mecca for the Hajh. His group changed the literary journal's title to Captive Thoughts. One of the men in his seminar, creative writing major Todd Berg, filled in next term. Todd is now in law school at DePaul. Another creative writing major (they're a dime a dozen, you know) took his place the next fall. I had the unique distinction of never having taken Sociology 389 before coordinating and it showed. During my first term, the title shifted to Captive Cry's. (It was supposed to be Captive Cries, but our calligrapher decided to get creative with the spelling.) Last term I teamed up with Stacey Brown, a junior in the Business school. For that term, we ran two workshops: Stacey's group on Tuesday, mine on Wednesday. She will continue with the section next fall, co-coordinating with fellow English major, Jon Abramsom, a student from my Fall '92 seminar.

I gave this little history to show that the section drew from various backgrounds, and for many of the coordinators, was a life changing experience. What are the odds that seven random UM students could lead such exciting lives? I, too, get sick of the cliche that those who coordinate social work gain as much as those who participate. But you can observe, in our lives, and in yours as you conduct your program, that this cliche often rings true.

What Happened Anyway?

Social Change and Freire

The Project Community pedagogy draws heavily on the work of Brazilian educator Paulo Freire (1970). He spent a great deal of his life teaching Brazilian peasants not only to read and write, but to become full persons and to participate in the democratic process. In Freire's pedagogy, the goal of education is not job training, but individual and social change. He saw how social services at the time only served to sustain an oppressive hierarchy. The lower class were trapped in a helping relationship with the elite. By teaching women and men to read and think critically about the world in which they lived, Freire initiated a change in Brazilian society that is still in motion today.

I think that any program such as this should embrace social change as a value. The education that both college students and inmates participate in should cause an awakening in consciousness that leads to a transformation of the world. Keep this in mind while I tell you about how my year went.

Seminar Prep

I think that careful preparation with a willingness to see all plans fall apart at the last minute was the key to my year as a coordinator. I spent several weeks preparing for my role. I read a copy of <u>Building Bridges II</u> and <u>Captive Thoughts II</u>. I also read the weekly journal of my predecessor, Todd. That gave me a play-by-play of how a term as a Cotton section coordinator transpired. I also had several long conversations with my Program Director, Joe Galura.My staff training also helped initiate me into the magical world of Project Community.

My first big mistake was lack of communication with my site contact. I didn't speak to her until we filled the section. Consequently, after I had told everyone who signed up for my section that we would be holding site on Tuesday evenings, I learned from my site contact, Ruby, that we needed to hold site on Wednesdays. Fortunately, most of my fellow students were available Wednesdays, and freeing up Tuesday conveniently allowed us to hold our seminar at that time.

Each week I prepared a new seminar agenda and submitted it to Joe for comments. My first seminar agenda looked like this:

1. Introduction
2. Icebreaker-empty wallets or medicine wheel[4]
3. Course requirements:
    - two papers (Meeting w/TA tba)
    - attendance policy (valuing site)
    - journals (include creative work)
    - books/coursepacks
    - lab fee
    - transportation
    - set seminar meeting time (anytime before 10:30am M-F after 2pm T-F meet in the Michigan Union Grill? Anthony and David's idea.)

4. Discuss living learning community
5. Agenda for next week at site
6. Journal question for next week
7. Closing round (Howard and Kahn[5])

Joe thought it was a fine agenda. I intended the agenda to be very fluid. It was. We spent most of our time trying to find a weekly meeting time. The rest of the time I spent answering questions I didn't have answers to. I got the impression I wasn't heard. Considering that five weeks into the term, some of our best and brightest University of Michigan students were still shocked to learn that the course had assigned readings, I'm pretty sure that I had difficulty communicating the course requirements.

Another dilemma I had straight off was trying to square away a time for Ruby to orient us to the facility. She preferred to do it at a time other than Wednesdays, because she runs NA/AA[6] meetings that evening. Unfortunately, the only time all five of us were available was from 8-10 Friday morning. When the day came, sure enough, one of my bananas (that was my short lived attempt at a non-hierarchical designation that referred to persons in my seminar) slept in. Consequently, we were an hour late and Ruby was unable to do a complete orientation. We had to spend our first evening of site time completing orientation. To further complicate the dilemma, Christina lost her driver's license and was unable to enter the facility to participate in orientation. She had to spend our first workshop filling papers in Ruby's office while we ran the program without her.

The moral of the story is to get your act together, but if things don't always turn out, be prepared for the worst. Our first program was another example of this maxim. We had spent the previous seminar brainstorming exercises to do during our workshop. I designated Lee as our first facilitator because he was the only one to volunteer. Although we made it through the gate and to Ruby's office in time, Reed, Ruby's administrative assistant, couldn't find the call out for our students. Inmates need a call out in order to get a pass from housing to the education building. Ruby disappeared to do something mysterious while Taylor, Ruby's other administrative assistant, got us some paper and pencils. We started about twenty minutes late. Ruby introduced us and the course, preempting Lee's icebreaker. Lee started by talking about why he was at Cotton and what he wanted to gain from the experience. He then invited input from the group. One man asked if this was a calligraphy class to improve penmanship. Someone else said that he signed up because he thought women would be here. Finally someone suggested an in-class exercise. We all wrote a story or poem about "yourself" with each sentence starting with a letter of your name. Most everyone enjoyed that. We had some good laughs and feedback. Lee started a "complete the sentence" exercise and for next week everyone planned on bringing a poem based on that. About this time, Ruby came back and introduced Christina to the men. She had finally completed orientation. That evening, I left hoping we could do another icebreaker next week, because I couldn't remember a single name.

The rest of the term fell into a relatively smooth pattern. Each week we had a different in class exercise and each week some men brought in some material to read. We also had several dilemmas along the way.

Community Issues

Race/stereotypes

One of the initial burning questions that the men at the prison wanted to ask was what our motivations were for coming to Cotton and conducting the workshop. I waited for this question my first term. I had heard that one year, an inmate asked if the workshop was really a psychology experiment. When the men finally asked why we came to Cotton, we shared that we were all interested in writing and thought that visiting the facility would be a great learning experience.

One of the Black men also asked what stereotypes we had about inmates coming into the prison. We told him that we were scared at first, learning about prison through television and all, but were amazed when we met everyone. He also asked about race, and said that when he was at Purdue, he was taught to be pessimistic about race and asked us how our friends would feel if we were seen with a Black woman. Christina said she and her friends would be comfortable with an interracial relationship. Steve said racism was a problem on campus and pointed at underrepresentation of Afro-Americans at UM. He also added that conditions were improving. Another Black man asked why all of the Project Community students were white. I told him that other sections of Project Community had people of color enrolled, but in the case of Afro-Americans, many have work-study jobs and do not have the time to take the course.

Jen Chai, an Asian-American woman from the Winter '93 seminar, has this to say about prison stereotypes. We sat in on an Alcoholics Anonymous meeting as part of our orientation:

> *I couldn't believe it when Ruby left the room. I didn't think she was going to leave us alone with these "prisoners." Slowly, all my negative stereotypes faded away as I saw how the AA "steering team" took over. I thought these men would have all the hardened emotions and use double negatives and poor grammar when speaking. I imagined a bunch of leering, hard-nosed criminals, but all of these men were very intelligent, decent men with feelings and emotions like we have, and they have family too.*

I think that race is important to keep in mind when conducting a program in a prison, because often times, as was in our case, the clients will be predominantly people of color, and the volunteers will be predominantly white. Overrepresentation of Afro-Americans and Indigenous Americans (Native and non-European Hispanics) in our prison system is a chilling reminder of institutional racism in our country. In each of our workshops, we had a mixed racial group, and often times, due to the fluctuation of attendance, white inmates in the program were a minority. Facilitators should use the seminar and coursepack readings to educate themselves about race issues in the prison system.

Relationships

Cotton provides a rare opportunity to get to know clients on a one to one basis. I think it is important to draw clear boundaries on these relationships and not let anyone cross that line. During the N-way conversation, I learned that one term, a UM woman gave her address to one of the inmates. Corrections officers had to beat the slip of paper out of his hand and the woman was taken to the warden's office. She was barred from ever visiting the facility. If our program had not been so successful, it would not have continued.

Let me share some of our experiences getting to know these men. One woman, (Winter '93) who plans on becoming a public defender for Wayne county youth, writes about a rather unusual man who had been involved with several cults, from Scientology to Krishna Consciousness. She writes:

> *He has an incredible vocabulary and has [read] a wide range of novels...I found him (surprisingly) to be very intelligent yet psycho at the same time. He wishes he could blow up the world and start over. He also believes that 90% of the people in Cotton should be killed because they have no soul...He has been in prison for 38 years and I can see where he looses his drive and motive to succeed (sort of). He feels children should not have to grow up in today's world and should be destroyed.*
>
> *I also was able to speak with another man who is optimistic about his future. He wants to reopen a tatoo store in his hometown. I was glad to see some people do want to succeed in life. He has only been in prison for one and a half years.*

Jennifer Chai (Winter '93) describes what for her was a positive experience:

> *What was so weird was discussing the whole nature vs. nurture debate with an actual prisoner! Nick was pretty open with me, and told me about his upbringing and how he was in a foster home, and how he was neglected and at some points abused. Nick was in prison for breaking and entering homes and what was so unfortunate was that it sounded like it was the environment he was in that drove him to illegal acts. I bet if Nick was raised in [my hometown], he would turn out to be such a straight kid...There are some guys who just never learn and never reform. (Like that one man who's been in prison for about 38 years and would say he would still break the law.) Then there's men like Nick, where I can see a real positive attitude. Prison has definitely taught him a lesson, and reformed him into a "better" person.*

Another woman from the same workshop, Jennifer Schaffner, writes about the boundaries needed in working with people in a correctional facility:

> *After the class, one of the men...approached me and told me he really enjoyed meeting me...and he had thought a lot about me since then. He also told me he was getting out soon and wanted to know if we could keep in touch. I told him it was against volunteer rules to contact prisoners in prison or after*

> *their release, which he accepted. Although he seemed like a harmless man, and he didn't appear to be "hitting on" me, it still raised issues for me about the possibility of prisoners interpreting our attention the wrong way. I'm not scared that this man is going to stalk me or anything, but it did remind me that we have to be very careful.*

Jennifer stresses the importance of maintaining a volunteer/participant relationship in order to preserve personal safety.

Gender

Jennifer also raises the issue of gender. Although it is frightening for any person to enter a prison for the first time, it is especially frightening for a woman, who may already feel uncomfortable in a male environment, but are further aware that these men may be guilty of violence towards women.

In another journal, she writes:

> *It was a little awkward interacting with the prisoners because I am a woman. I tried to ignore the fact that men would occasionally make gestures in the hall to the prisoner sitting next to me, asking him who I was, etc. I hope it won't be a problem when we actually conduct our class, but I feel that how I choose to deal with it will make the difference between feeling comfortable and uncomfortable. For the most part, I am going to make gender issues as small as an issue for me as possible. Since I know I'm in no real danger, it isn't worth feeling discomfort about it.*

Another woman from the same group writes about a disturbing incident:

> *Another really shocking event happened when Alex brought in pictures for "Show and Tell." What did that man mean when I asked him to bring in the pictures he drew and he brought in these illustrations of men and women having sex in various positions?...He seems like such a nice, quiet, shy, innocent guy, (even though he is a prisoner). I can't believe he draws pictures that belong in The Joy of Sex!*

Christina, from my Fall seminar, also had several gender related issues. She had the disadvantage of being the only woman in a roomful of men every time we had site or seminar. She writes:

> *I'm treated as if I'm a non-person at site. I know that the prisoners listen to me, but I'm not sure how much they [consider] my opinion. Sometimes I feel as though they dismiss it.*

I hoped to have her facilitate the next site, but did not have a chance, because she missed the next week, which was our last workshop. The last day, she volunteered to "calligraph" the certificates of achievement, but I doubt this took care of her issue.

Not only did she have issues with her work at site, but during seminar as well:

> *I was upset with the last prison meeting, and it was no fault of any prisoner, or site for that matter...I was extremely irked by Lee. He may pretend to be poking fun, but sometimes he takes it a bit too far. He annoys me when he constantly refers to me as "defensive" and all of that.*

She writes about how throughout the term, Lee and Steve accused her of being defensive like all other women. They did this whenever she brought up a concern during seminar. If she didn't, they asked her if she was feeling defensive that day. For example, they asked if men whistling at her at site made her defensive.

She also writes:

> *Yesterday at seminar I thought was our best one...The fact that we were discussing gender issues was a definite advance. I don't think that all males feel the way Lee and Steve do, but I have to be honest that it is an attitude I've heard from guys before...No matter what anyone says, I have plenty of male friends who are just friends.*

At that seminar, Steve and Lee claimed that it was impossible for a man to be just friends with a "girl," because you'd only want to sleep with her anyway, and if you didn't she probably wasn't worth getting close to anyway. Christina protested, asserting that she had many male friends who were just friends. Steve and Lee insisted that although she couldn't tell, her friends really wanted to sleep with her. I presented myself as a counterexample, having many close female friends. I was granted my reality, but Christina was not granted hers. It did not help matters any that papers came back that week and all the men got a check plus while Christina received a check. Chortles about how men are smarter than women reverberated through The Tap Room, the student commons where we held seminar.

I write about gender, because if men in the seminar do not respect the women, the goal of building a learning community is severely thwarted. Our culture has a particularly offensive gender construction, and I find it inexcusable for those involved in service-learning to perpetuate it. Furthermore, at site, I think that it is very important for the men to have an opportunity to relate to women as peers, and not as only mothers or sex objects. Unfortunately, most of the time in my Fall seminar, neither the men at site or in seminar were capable of doing that.

Faith, Hope and Rehab

Race and gender aren't the only coursepack issues that manifest themselves in site and seminar. One week we had a long discussion about the success of rehabilitation, drugs and religion. Ironically, that week's delay in obtaining a room was the monthly urine drop. The maintenance room we used for our workshop had a toilet in it and Corrections Staff had chosen it for men to deposit their sample in the obligatory vial. One man had trouble coming up with a sample. We waited for him to finish a few minutes, but ended up starting before he finished amidst the noise and confusion.

Steve was facilitating that week and asked about religion in the prison. This was in response to Brother Birch's rewriting of the beatitudes that he shared in class. Brother Birch discussed Christ's plan for his life, relating it to NA. He said that when God wants him to walk out of this prison, no guard and no warden could stop him. Mattison said that he had a personal relationship with Allah as a Muslim, and could call Him up and talk to Him anytime. The two agreed that it is no easier or harder to practice any given faith in the prison, but being in prison does inspire soul searching. Brother Birch said that sometimes God allows bad things to happen in order to draw people to Himself. I noticed Steve and Lee bending over backwards in order not to divulge their Jewish background. The inmates asked and finally we all shared our faiths. Rusty, along with only one inmate was atheist. Everyone else was Christian except those noted above. Mattison asked Steve if he had faith in things he couldn't see. Steve said no. He asked him if he had faith his girlfriend would go out with him when he asked her. Steve said he didn't have faith in his girlfriend.

Next, Lee asked if anyone thought the prison system worked. (Obviously inspired by the coursepack readings.) Responses varied. Bracley thought prison was more rehabilitative in the 50's and more punitive today. Services today are not accessible, one has to work to take advantage of them. He felt that a lot of young inmates are subservient bootlickers and don't know the difference between fantasy and reality. He thought that drug rehab doesn't work, with maybe a 10% success rate. He felt that many inmates didn't belong here. Mattison agreed in that respect and not on the rehab one. He was ashamed that he lived in a country club (Cotton) while senior citizens back home lived in terrible conditions. Brother Birch felt that many end up in prison just to survive, that crime is the only attractive way to survive and prison is easier than the streets. He felt drug rehab worked in his case when he wanted to change himself, not because someone else wanted him to and that he had the support of a community (NA) to pull him through.

Rusty Barlow had this to say in his weekly journal about the above discussion:

> *I know what I would have had to say wouldn't have been too popular. I don't believe in God. And frankly, having been to rehab and AA, I can tell you that the long-term success rate is virtually not worth talking about...There's one thing you don't disagree with somebody about: their faith. You'll never change their mind and you'll always insult them. Now, I'll tell you that most faith turns out to be a lie, so I don't really have any, but I've noticed in other people that, even though it's a lie in the end, it really makes them happy along the way.*

I included this for two reasons: one is to talk about suburban capitulation, the other is to talk about the existential value of faith. Nietzsche, for instance, was very interested in believing lies in order to make life more exciting. Hopefully, I'll tie these and other ideas together in one big literary tour-de-force at the end of this paper. Rusty continues his existential analysis in another weekly journal:

> *I've been thinking a lot lately about the idea that we aren't doing anything to help these people...I don't know. We're definitely not changing the world and maybe teaching prisoners isn't so noble after all. But I think they enjoy having us, and I certainly feel welcome.*
>
> *I can imagine that, for the most part, being in prison is not good. Even if class is nothing more to them than a different way to spend time, I'd be pleased. From most of them I sense that they really want to be there, but from others, I sense that they just want to kill some time. Super I think reading and writing is a great way to spend time. So what if nobody is inspired to become a writer. So what if I don't become a writer. It's just a neat feeling to sit down a couple times in your life, read something which is somehow engaging and humorous, and know that you wrote it.*
>
> *The prisoners seem to want to write, to tell a story, or their own. Several of them, I've found to be very good. Some of them were very far from good. I'm not there to make anyone a writer...I never felt like I was teaching them anything other that that they could write and they need not keep their writing to themselves. Not everybody knows that.*

To paraphrase Rusty, even if running said program in prison doesn't amount to much social change, it's still a good thing because all those involved enjoy it. I think Rusty's right, although I believe that the potential for social change through this program is very real.

Christina Ellis had a more somber reflection about the "success" of rehabilitation:

> *I wonder what the men at site will do after they get let out from prison...If they have to fight to stay away from drugs and violence in the prison, how can they possibly go back to their same home environment? It's too easy to say they can just pick up and move to a new city...Most prisoners do not have the means to leave any town unless drugs are involved, but then the whole vicious cycle starts up once again.*
>
> *I would like a happy ending, but my [pessimistic] side tells me that none of those men—or maybe two or three—will really amount to much. It seems awful to say, but what else is there to say?...Nothing will help them unless they help themselves first.*

Although I suspect that the way the criminal "justice" system operates today, Christina is probably correct in observing the vicious cycle of drugs, poverty, violence and crime. I find her conclusions to be offensive. I don't mean to pick on her, the vast majority of Project Community students share her sentiments. She sees the phenomena as being separate from herself, as if it happened in some other world that she is not part of. Palmer refers to this as trained schizophrenia. Freire attributes this to the objectifying nature of an oppressive educational system. Both would say that our schools teach us to view important social dilemmas as occurring behind a vacuum sealed glass that can be talked about but only changed if the change occurs from within—perhaps through telepathy. Thus, the Republican-esque capitulation to individual change as the only way to social improvement. (She's not a Republican, either.) Obviously, this view is patently false. We have causal interaction with the world and the actions of suburbanite UM students have very real effects on the decay of inner-cities. One of the potentials for social change that I see in Project Community is raising the awareness of UM students, breaking them free of trained apathy and hopefully inspiring them to improve socio-economic conditions in their neighborhood and work to change public policy to facilitate social change in the city. College students are our future leaders and I am disgusted when I hear our future leaders moan crippled and weak that they are powerless to change the world around them.

Thank You!

Why don't I let one of our clients speak for himself. This man sent a thank you letter to the Project Community in response to the Winter '92 workshop:

> *This workshop has been a God-send for me. I have been writing poetry and songs for a lot of years now, and this has given me a chance to see how I would fare at prose, being able to stretch in many different directions thanks to the unique and great suggested topics.*
>
> *On a strictly personal level, being incarcerated and being a prisoner within myself as well, cut off from family and other loved-ones, some have died (my parents) and I wasn't able to be there. This has given me at least some venting room for the sorrow, anguish and rage within, as well as memories that are full, and that I am deeply grateful for striking at least some semblance of balance in my soul, letting me know that my whole life wasn't wasted.*
>
> *This workshop not only made an avenue for releasing the creative energies of our imaginations, it was also a buoy of sanity in a crazy situation. There was only one thing wrong with it as far as I can see: IT DIDN'T LAST LONG ENOUGH!*

If that's not enough, here's an excerpt from the thank you note the Winter '93 (my group) workshop presented to the UM students:

> *For those that dared to make a difference! Thank you for coming to share our time with us. We have appreciated every moment and have learned a lot from you. May you all find success in all that you do, as we wait patiently for our turn. It's*

> *people like you that make the world a better place. May God always bless you!*

He's right. It is people like us that change the world. People who care.

Exercises

Here's a greatest hits of creative writing exercises from the Cotton section.

Telephone Story—Have someone think of a sentence, preferably a silly sentence. Write it down on a sheet of paper and pass it along, having each person add one more sentence to the story. After it finishes going around the room, have someone read it aloud.

Dada Exercise—Based on the art movement in the 40's and 50's that considered that everything that happens in the world happens randomly. Each person fills out five cards, each with one descriptive noun on it, for example, Yellow Bugle. (no abstract nouns like "love" or "fury") Mix up the cards and pass them back. Have each person write a poem or a scene from these words as a warm up exercise.

Ten Things I Know About a Person—Pick two random names and write them at the top of two columns on a sheet of paper. Write ten characteristics under each name. Examples include the following: Drives a Porsche, Likes Moosehead beer, wears Fruit of the Looms, or doesn't get along with family. Collect the papers and pass them out to different people. Have that person write a scene in which the two people meet.

Freewriting—Bring in a tape of music or a poster of a famous painting or photograph. Have people write whatever comes to mind when they hear the tape or see the image. The trick is to keep writing until the time is up. In the case of the painting, one could write a paragraph describing what happens, has occurred or is about to happen in the poster. Often times, the songs spark a heated discussion. I wrote the following reflection when our Fall workshop tried this activity:

> *The Public Enemy song sparked a ten minute discussion on Race. An older Black man, college educated and a musician likened Public Enemy to the KKK. He felt that the Black community had itself to blame for a lot of their problems. "Every other ethnic group made it except us." Mattison and another felt that they were kept down by the system and could understand the anger in the rap. They argued that the family structure in the Black community is in deterioration. Another talked about growing up in East LA and moving to Hollywood, feeling like he let the Black community down as long as he got his. He learned one way of doing things in East LA, another in Hollywood. I noticed the white people dropping out of the conversation and steered onto the next song. Steve looked to me for support in that. "Write these ideas down. These are the problems we face today." I said. After our next song, the Enya*

> *piece, one Black man noticed that the white music was that of comfort—peaceful and soothing, Black music that of anger.*

Grammar Time—You may find a need to go over some fundamentals of grammar, style and punctuation. Don't be afraid to bring in a few worksheets and spend some class time refurbishing some basics.

Educational Materials—Bring in some poems, short stories, essays or even a video that you think might be interesting to the group. Discuss their value as literature and how one can apply said techniques in your own writing. The social ramifications of the work are sometimes even more interesting. They can be used to generate ideas for writing. One woman in my winter seminar writes about her experience facilitating this exercise:

> *We showed a movie about a young Black boy who wanted to be recognized as a man. Therefore, he went out and purchased a gun...I used the film to begin a discussion in class...They were opening up and explaining to us what it's like to be on the other side of the tracks. One man began to almost breakdown. He didn't cry, but he was really depressed because his fifteen-year-old brother was just killed by the police raid. He even told us how he almost blew his friend's head off. This had a very sobering effect for me.*
>
> *Often when I think of guns, I can forget that children begin to see them as a necessary element of survival. One man told me that to have a "piece" inside your jacket means that you have a heart. They didn't know who to trust, so they got a "piece" for self-defense.*

These exercises work well as homework assignments: Describe a color to a blind man, write about your hero, a childhood memory, your favorite place in prison, your most embarrassing moment, a dream, a secret, your future plans, or what it would be like to be an animal. Finally, assign a long term project, a polished story or essay, or a batch of poems. Keep the workshop thinking about the literary journal.

Advice

How to do a creative writing workshop in a prison in N-easy steps

Todd Berg (Winter '92) gives this advice in his coordinator journal:

> *I would like to remind my successor that it's okay to be scared of the experience that lies ahead. It's okay and it's natural and most likely it's what will keep you on your feet. It did me. Being a little bit (or a lot bit) scared makes you feel it would go away if you were only to work a little harder [planning]...And funny enough, with that extra work, the fear goes away and is replaced with confidence and a sense of accomplishment.*

In April, the coordinators of the Cotton section still in Ann Arbor, met with Joe for an N-way conversation about the site. Rachel, Bush, Stacey and I generated these bits of advice:

Talk to your site contact before you recruit students. Decide the dates and times you want to hold your program. Find out what information the facility needs for security purposes. The State of Michigan required name, birthdate, social security number, race and gender. Work out times for an orientation for the site with your site contact. It takes a few hours to learn the prison bureaucracy. Cotton required that everyone have a picture ID with an expiration date for entry into the facility.

Meet with your students, explain dates and times they are needed for the program and retrieve any security information necessary. Answer any questions and expect that many will not "get it" the first time around. Stress that everyone's contribution of ideas to the program is required. Make sure that respect for each other's ideas and contributions is a norm for both the seminar and the site.

Before your first workshop, brainstorm ideas for activities. Always have more than enough activities to fill two hours. Always do the exercises along with everyone else. Share your work too. Always assign specific homework assignments. Beginning writers want stimulus. Work out a rotation so that a different person in your seminar facilitates site each week. This ensures equal participation.

Make sure you debrief after each program. Think of ways to improve next time, even if the workshop went well.

Expect to learn a lot, have lots of fun and remember that the ultimate fate of the clients you work with is not your responsibility.

Remember social change and keep the hope alive!

NOTES

1. This phrase is repeated three times in the first chapter of Joshua in the Old Testament. The context is that Moses has just died and Joshua is to lead Israel into the Promised Land—a place where he has never been before. As Rick explains, unlike many other coordinators, he had not been a Sociology 389 student before coordinating—in fact, he had never even been to a prison before leading this project! I used the phrase repeatedly in our conversations and correspondence over the past two terms.
2. N-way is a term Rick invented for a group conversation: dialogue, strictly speaking is "two people talking."
3. Rachel Story was actually a Sociology 389 student during her first term in this project: Ben Macrory, an English major, was the coordinator.
4. Complete descriptions of these icebreakers can be found in Chapter Two of Off to See the Wizard. The Medicine Wheel is a variation of the Coat of Arms.
5. A reference to the readings and activities for next seminar: see Chapter Three of Off to See the Wizard.
6. Narcotics Anonymous/Alcoholics Anonymous.

Appendix

Selections from Building Bridges/Captive Thoughts/Captive Cry's

Dedication and Forward from Captive Cry's (Fall '92)

To the U of M Students:

In appreciation of your guidance, of your willingness to share your knowledge and the unselfish giving of your time. We the inmates recipients and benefactors of your favor wish to express our heartfelt thanks and gratitude for your participation. It's to you that we dedicate this journal of ours: Captive Cry's.

We being creations
Of our Creator
Inherit creativity
Through captive captions
We have thus created
Captive Cry's
WEB

Forward

Once again, Project Community attacks the walls of authoritarian pedegogies in order to foster community across lines of race, gender, class, sexual orientation, religion and whatever else you want to throw in there. This term was the best of my undergraduate years and coming to Cotton Correctional Facility was an important part of it. Not only did Christina, Lee, Steve, Rusty, Hans and I explore the boundaries of creative writing with the people of Cotton Facility, but we learned more than we could have ever learned through newspapers, coursepacks, television programs or political speeches. For me, I learned that people in prison are just like anyone else. (I was mistaken for an inmate twice, go figure.) I want to thank everyone at Cotton for welcoming us and providing an enriching learning experience.(Except the guard at the gate with the latex gloves.)

I also want to thank Rusty and Tammy for helping me type this thing. I want to thank Christina for getting her journal in every week. Todd, the previous coordinator for smoothing the path to Jackson. The Criminal Justice staffing, especially Joe and Pauline for all their work and support. Everyone at OCSL. Mark for sponsoring Project Community. Charlie for ideas on exercises, even thought we didn't use them. Ruby for bringing us to Cotton. Reed for coffee every week. Thank God for always giving us something off the topic to discuss. And my mother, who bought me the computer I typed this on.

Of course I have to thank everyone who contributed to *Cotton Cry's*. I had a great time this term and hope to come back again with a new bunch from Ann Arbor.

Until then, pedagogically yours,

Richard J. X.
(Yes, I did use a few pseudonyms in here.)

From Building Bridges (F '90)
"Blanks Away"
by Rangel

Blank, Blank, Blank
That's all I could hear
Blanking out the bad memories of my childhood years

Blanking was easy, it brought me great joy
But I wore out my blanking, like I wore out my toy
As I grew older it was harder to cope
With no blanks to help me, I quickly found dope

You talk about freedom, I had instant relief
Yes the world I had entered, could show me no grief
I had not way of knowing, I had no way to tell
the drugs I was taking, were my ticket to hell

Could I stop using, by blanking away?
There's one who still suffers, I call her my wife
She pays in the present, for the mistakes of my past
Yet she still stands beside me, and says our marriage will last

I give up on the hard life, on the darkness and pain
I'm no longer blanking or using cocaine
each day I'm aware, that's how it must be
As I face what life hands me, I set myself free

"Lifelines"

lifelines 1) An anchored line thrown as a support to someone who is falling or drowning. 2) A line shot to a ship in distress. 3) A line used to raise and lower deep sea divers. 4) One that is or is regarded as a source of salvation in a crisis.

There are four listed definitions of the word "lifeline' and perhaps more if we look into other sources. May these four suffice for what I would like to share.

When I first came to the institution, they talked of the many support programs. In reality, none were available to me. You go on a waiting list for everything, hoping there will be an opening. Being a quiet, reserved and inward person, I felt myself falling into this dark pit of despair, being swallowed up by the rolling, dark breakers of depression, my mind becoming incapable of even minor decision making skills. Then at the bulletin board, the lifeline was thrown. I didn't realize it as such, but by the second meeting I knew. Creative Writing—the term may have various meaning to each person involved, but I found it a many stranded lifeline. Lives woven together for a time to bring succor. Here are four of the strands: Ben, Jodi, None and Rachel—A caring, responsive, insightful and non-judgmental lifeline.

They came to learn, share and experience. By ourselves we were so aware of the inadequacies and shortcomings, but together we are made aware of strength in union. As they shared and cared, they became a valuable part of the lifeline of hope in me. They are a ship in control, pulling me to safety from the horrendous storms of my mental anguish and raising me to a place of light and stability.

The last definition on the list that we share is one I must use with care and caution. As we see each strand of my lifeline going on to fulfill their own destinies, can I dare refer to them, classifying them as a source of salvation? Was one more effective or important than another? Not so, each one supplying their gift, talent and skills of caring to me and becoming a means of salvation. A Jewish Prophet said: "Saviors shall come upon Mount Zion"(Obadiah 21). Saviors—more than one, lives bound together bringing change and love, hope and peace.

Thank you lifeline, my heart and mind smile again even in the midst of distress. Because of you I will survive.

May you be blessed with all of life's prosperity. Shalom.

Bob

From Building Bridges II (Winter '91)
The Latest Oracle of Delphi

One night, as I lay on my bed in that twilight point of consciousness between solid thought and the ephemeral ghosts of logic we call dreaming, I saw an image precipitated from the darkness of my mind's eye.

The image was that of a shard of glass. Not a thick, needle-like sliver, but more shaped of a wide dagger with no handle; the spire of some glass tower, broken, ragged at the base, and miniaturized to the size of a weapon. t was the kind of shape so often seen when someone shatters a window, all the glass breaking, pointing accusingly to the heart of impact. One the tip of this hung a single drop of crimson, possibly the result of an incident as just described.

Earlier that day there was an incident. What happened wasn't important; what mattered was the result. It was just one more time when the gulf between me and the rest of society was poignantly brought to light. One of those many trials in life, when after it was all over, I feel totally alone and apart due to the irreconcilable difference between us. I soon put the incident in its compartment for later analysis and went on with life. I had a feeling afterward that this incident is what brought on the dream.

Now dreams have a logic and cognizance all their own. When we see a phantasmal image, we all suffer from synesthesia, a crossing of the senses of the mind. So it was with this image. I will try to convey the feelings and understandings that seem to flow from my core and which only wore the picture I've described thus far like a man wears a name, even though there is much more inside. I will inevitably fall short of my goal.

The glass was an image of purity. A platonic form incarnate. I could sense bottled child's laughter in the glass. If it were to drop, the laughter would burst forth from each scampering piece of glass. If lightly struck, the glass would sing with crystal purity.

The life's blood, instead, was silence itself. Like a soundless tear flowing down a face, or was there a hint of a muffled sob with no one to hear it?

I was struck by the contrast of the two. Where one was cold, the other was warmth. Where one was hard and unyielding, the other formed and adapted as life itself will. One showed only the color of its surroundings like a chameleon; the other was always the color of passion, both hate and love. Nowhere could I find any aspect they shared. They were ying and yang. I could find no common ground.

Then it struck me! I was just looking too close, always comparing individual qualities. When I stood back and saw the two together, I realized that they,...no, not they, but it, was an expression of pain, of the pain of sorrow, of passionate pain. The pain that drives an artist to be spared. The pain that drives a warrior to victory. The pain that gives birth. The pain, the one thing, that binds us all.

The realization woke me. I laid there, in the dark, in bed, wide awake, and felt a single tear falling from the corner of my glassed over eyes. For that instant of pure emotional pain, I felt one with humanity. The moment passed. I wiped the tear away, rolled over and went to sleep.

From Captive Thoughts I (Fall '91)

"The Color Green As Described to a Blind Friend"

by Thomas A. Svacha

I would like to have you understand what the color green looks like. First I want you to clear your mind completely. Now, think, feel, taste and see the color green as I describe it to you.

Green, such a beautiful and wondrously radiant color. If I were asked to describe the color green with one word that one word would be LIFE. Hold out your hand. This is a leaf that has dried up and died. Its color is a dull brown, dull, meaning bland, lifeless and tasteless. Now, close your hand slowly and feel how it crumbles into dust.

Give me your other hand. Here is a fresh mint leaf. Gently rub it between your fingers. Feel how tender and moist it is. Smell it, let the sweet aroma of mint fill your senses. Now, close your hand and open it again. Notice how the leaf has not crumbled but has returned to its original form. This leaf so tender, so full of life, so very green.

Green is also the color which represents youth and innocence. It is fresh, it is alive and indeed the color of life. This is my description of the color green.

"My Favorite Place"

by Thomas A. Svacha

It's Friday.
I go through my routine,
just as I do every morning,
But today brings with it something special.
I can't help
but to feel good, filled with anticipation.

You see, tonight's the night
that me and my baby get together.
It's been a week since we've touched.
I've been thinking of tonight
all week long.

HMM!
IT'S GOING TO BE SOO GOOD!
I'M GOING TO POUND AND SWEAT!
I'M GOING TO KEEP WORKING IT
UNTIL MY MUSCLES ACHE.
I'M GONNA DRIVE HARD AND NEVER MISS A BEAT!
I'M GONNA STAY IN THE POCKET AND WON'T MISS A STROKE!
YES!
TONIGHT'S THE NIGHT YOU CAN FIND ME IN THE BANDROOM,
MY FAVORITE PLACE.
JUST ME AND MY DRUMS.

From Captive Thoughts II (Winter '92)
"The Number"
by Dione Slay

"Prison, is it the way, or the number?"

Receiving a six digit number to replace a birthright name given by your parents with careful and loving attention. Stripped of dignity and pride with little or no consciousness of faith. Close behind grieving solitude, forgotten by society who's objective was justice. However, was I wrong? Can I complain or was my name meant to be changed to the six digit number? Bars draped horizontally, diagonally embedded in sheets of steel and concrete from top to bottom, giving me a claustrophobic feeling to the core of my soul. Suffocating the thoughts of freedom. How can I understand? Can I change at all? Or can I replace my name for this six digit number?

Stacks of galleries with cells filled with hopelessness. A weep here and a cry there, hidden in the masculinity of pride. Anger builds up trying to adjust, but to no avail. I toss and turn and realize, "What shall I do? Death? No, that is not pleasing to the sight of God. Besides it is much too final. Strength? I need strength to cope, strength to live, strength to realize this six digit number."

Echoes return from the cries from within. Shade consumes the mind, taking away the bit of joy I've found in a thought. I got to sleep and find peace in my dreams, only to wake and find the nightmare, true, dreadful, and oh so real. I hear the call of my name or was it my number?

I can't seem to remember. However the door to my cell opens and I am tossed around to and fro. In a system of paperwork, files, charts and hassle by people in uniform who have forgotten the ways of humanity and mankind. Not being able to relate to anything but the six digit number. What shall I do? Is there nothing I can do? I tell myself, "Yes!"

There is hope and joy, a fulfillment of freedom. Peace, love, sharing, caring giving, a way out of despair and grief. Call on the name of the son of God, Jesus Christ, our Lord and Savior, whose blood was shed for what he believed in, the saving of souls and redemption of sin.

Believe in his precious name and you will realize you have a name and not a six digit number. May God Bless.

"The Inevitable Move"
by Caleb Smith

As my wings grow tired, I fight the last twenty-five feet upward to find the thermal draft that will allow me to glide, rest my wings and search the prairie below for the nourishment that keeps me alive and flying high.

In the vast area below we see the long black strips that carry the killers of everything that is beautiful and pure.

The noise that arises day after day has no doubt slowed the hunting ground.

And now the concrete grows closer and closer with each spring.

It is inevitable that I will be forced to leave my home, and find a new place to dwell and hunt.

It seems so unfair that I am forced from my home, to places unfamiliar to my eyes, I was raised here and have spent my entire adult life here.

And yet with each passing year come changes that I cannot erase.

And this land too becomes foreign to my eyes.

If I must see changes of environment, I prefer them to be free from the black strips that carry death, the concrete that generates only smog and noise.

Therefore it is inevitable that I seek the peace and serenity that is only offered deep within the mountains.

Yes the move is essential to my survival.

From Captive Cry's (Fall '92)
Untitled
by Jerréll Ashanti Gray

To anyone taking any type of creative writing class: I believe that it is a valuable asset for the future.

To me the obvious thing about my poetry or whatever I may write is the fact that it or they are totally inspired. This inspiration usually manifests itself as an equilibrium between the sacred and the profane—gemstones of innerself counterbalanced with the granite of life as it may be. My compositions are always fluid and natural, as convincing as landscapes collaboration with me or paper will always become a sheer delight (if you are a female) because my literary style is highly evocative in the visual sense. My love for poetry is expressed not only in my sensitivity to the way I feel, but also my power over what I write and think. My style of writing will remind one of water in the sense that it always retains its essential characteristics, what ever the environment. Whether elegant and luminous like dew dripping in a rain forest, or sensuous and insinuating like rapids roaring over stones, it is always "Jerrell's" unmistakable and unique poetic personality which captivates and affects the reader.

One phrase that comes to mind, salvaged from an otherwise forgotten education, is Ovid: "Great art conceals the method by which it is achieved." In this regard, I will always try to excel. No amount of magnification or close scrutiny can detect the seams of my creativity, since it is so intrinsically relaxed and uncontrived. The feelings that I communicate in my style of writing have a signature imagery all their own. With my poetry, if someone were to read it to you, with your eyes closed, ears listening to soft music being played between woofers and tweeters, as the warm breeze cascaded across your face, you would come to know that the mind deciphers this emotional code and one is effortlessly propelled along, listening to the beautiful expressions inside of this dialogue of imaginable overtones, spellbound.

I would like to extend my deep appreciation, to you for allowing me to express myself in this manner.

Thank you!

"Life is very much like a knife, you can grab it by the blade and get cut, or you can grasp it by the handle and cut your way through."

From Captive Cry's II (Winter '93)
The Warehouse
by Tony Lett

I'm now part of the stock here at the Warehouse.

Inventory at this warehouse is counted five times every twenty four hours 365 days a year. The warehouse keepers need to keep close check on their human inventory. It's worth $24,800 a year, can't lose any of that can we?

You know, the state is always crying broke.

You the tax payers cover our room and board.

Hell, we get free clothes (1 pair of shoes 2 shirts 2 pants 3 underwear 3 socks 3 t-shirts) free meals (if that's what you want to call them) three times a day. And a cot.

Education? Counseling? Help? Yeah Right.

As far as John Q. Public knows we've got it easy.

Easier than some of them.

Most of it's a joke.

There is a lack of love, understanding and compassion, on both sides, the stock and the keepers. Kindness is considered weakness.

Existing here basically reduces one's living skills to the animal level.

Most of the inventory here is salvageable;

But this warehousing system is designed with revolving doors.

What is taught and propagated in this vast store of humans is designed to keep old $24,800.00 coming back and teaching new $24,800.00 how to do the same thing, *come back.*

This is great for the state financially, Hell on the taxpayers though.

But how 'bout morally?

Use some of that money to teach us how *not* to come back!

I know that if we didn't come back, some people might lose their jobs. But then again there may be more jobs. Simply because of all of the *free* minds at work out there.

Maybe I could open a restaurant or even a chain, I could give an ex-con or ex-guard a job, (food for thought) you never know.

For now though, I'm here at the warehouse. I took the time to look up the definition of warehouse, just to make sure I haven't gone off on some kind of self-pitying tangent.

Warehouse: a building for the storage of goods or merchandise.

Storage being the operative word.

All that most of us here do, is be stored (some die).

I want to be restored.

But then who would generate that $24,800.00 annually?

I guess it's up to me, I have to restore me myself. I have to learn myself. If I'm allowed to do so by the warehouse keepers. If I learn to be self-sufficient and law-abiding, I become a threat to their livelihood. This is the reason why, when I try to do positive things and promote positive ideals for myself and others, I'm ordered not to. Obstacles are put up: barriers to becoming that acceptable, responsible and productive member of society.

Where did I go wrong? I thought I was put here because I failed at being acceptable, responsible and productive. Now I want to be that way, and I'm not allowed.

What's *wrong* with this picture?

Well, now I'm stored. When my time is up they will shove me back into society with the same tools for living that I left with.

No new tools; no new job; no new life.

Old tools—what am I to do?

You fill in the blanks:

T H E S A M E O L D T H I N G .

Yeah, that's right: And come back.

Faith, Hope, Love

by Brother Maples

"Love is the greatest of these."

We need a new love consciousness
in the spirit. Communicate with love and clarity.
We must try to love one another
as God loves us. God's love is unchanging
not arbitrary or conditional. It
supports us whether we behave lovingly or
badly. The challenge is to maintain
a loving center no matter how someone
else behaves. When we are loving, we
feel the inner harmony and peace
we are striving for. LOVE. It's
our purpose, this is why we are
created.

**Faith: sustains us in the midst of change.*
When changes occur meet it with Faith!
**Courage: Be strong and of good courage.*
Be strong and courageous, then you will be
prosperous and successful.

Chapter 4

A HANDBOOK FOR JUVENILE JUSTICE VOLUNTEERS

By Amy Rotberg and Tracy Kollin

Introduction

Juvenile delinquents and children at risk require special attention and care. Many of these youths come from dysfunctional families and often have been neglected and/or abused. Juvenile delinquents and children at risk are starving for positive attention, love, and relationships with people that care about them. Due to a lack of support and discipline from family members and the community, many delinquents have poor social skills and are often under-achievers academically. Often they have no direction in their lives or do not have the means to be successful in the real world. Troubled youths need someone to guide them to lead a happy, successful life free of crime. They need positive role models who care about them. Service-learning projects have tried to provide some of this care for numerous youths in need, with experiences that are beneficial for both them and the University students involved.

Project Community has discovered site placements in need of University students to act as positive role models and to interact with their youths. Project Community has also tried to recruit the dedicated and caring students these juveniles require. Through numerous, educational and enjoyable activities, students are able to lend a helping hand to the juveniles in need.

We are students who have been involved with Project Community for the majority of our college careers and we feel we have made a difference in the lives of the juveniles with whom we have worked. Many of these youths look up to us and are inspired by the lives we lead. We try to convey optimism to them by sharing a part of our lives with them.. We are not there to analyze these juveniles or reprimand them for their past history. We are there because we care —and most importantly to be their friends.

We have spoken with the various coordinators who have visited the different Juvenile Justice sites where Project Community sections are in place. With the information we gathered, we have compiled some general guidelines for all sites and specific words of advice for each particular site according to the age of the youths, the size of the group, and the seriousness of their problems.

Getting Started

To begin with, there are certain points that should be established before the students first visit their site. The seminar of students should meet at least two times before the first site visit to become acquainted as a group and to agree upon and develop what their goals for site and seminar are going to be. The key to a successful site is to form a cohesive seminar. If the students in the seminar respect each other and have similar goals, sites will run more smoothly. If there are problems between the students, it detracts from the issue at hand—the juveniles at your placement. We are not suggesting that every member of the seminar be best friends, but any personal conflicts between people should be dealt with outside of site. Project Community's goals are to serve as role models and to teach the youths positive social interaction If conflicts between students are apparent at site, it takes away from the goals we are striving for. These youths pick-up on every move that takes place; therefore University students should try to be on their best behavior.

Forming a cohesive group can be extremely difficult, especially because Project Community tries to recruit a diverse group of students. The more diversity there is, the more we can learn from each other. Yet, wen students are too different from one another, conflict may arise. People tend to disagree more on certain issues and how activities at site should be run. It can be beneficial to have various opinions, as long as arguments are not carried out too far. The coordinator should listen to each student's input in order to better the section, but when a decision needs to be made the coordinator should have the final say. While at site the coordinator or student running the activity must establish authority to prevent dilemmas. The students should continue to participate but should not try to be in charge of the group unless there is substantial reason to do so.

We would like to emphasize that authority must be established from the beginning so that students do not take advantage of the coordinators and the class. We suggest that every student in Project Community is initially given a syllabus of dates for coursepack readings, paper assignments and due dates, attendance policies, the goals of Project Community, the program director's and the TA's office location, office hours and phone number, and the phone numbers of the coordinators. This way there are no discrepancies about the guidelines of the class. This will enable a coordinator to focus more on bringing the seminar together and bonding with the juveniles at site through organized and appropriate activities.

A good relationship must also be established between the section coordinator and the site contact. Open communication is important in this relationship throughout the semester since the site contact is responsible for organizing so the students can attend the site. It is a good idea to call the site contact before each visit to discuss the planned activity. It is crucial for the site contact to constantly be aware of what is going on in case of any problems. However, the site contact should not become so involved that it prevents the coordinator and their seminar from having the freedom to conduct the activities.

Breaking the Ice at Site

To help both the University students and the juveniles the first site should always consist of an "ice-breaker" activity in which everyone learns each other's names and maybe something personal about one another. For the seminar members, such an activity during the first seminar meeting is also important. It allows everyone in the group get to know each other. If members of the seminar are comfortable with each other they can work together more effectively at seminar and at site. This may help the juveniles to feel more at ease also.

One example of an "ice-breaker" is called the **"Name Game."** Everybody sits in a circle. The students should make a conscious effort to spread themselves among the youths. The coordinator will start by saying his/her name preceeded by an adjective starting with the first letter of his/her name, for example "Talkative Tracy". The next person says the person who went before's name and adjective and then their name and an adjective. The third person says the previous two people's names and adjectives and then their name and adjective. This continues around the circle. This is easier to do with a small group but more challenging and fun with a larger group. These adjectives often stick with the University students for the rest of the semester. We are known at Maxey Boys Training School as "Talkative Tracy" and "Amazing Amy".

For youths with less serious problems who have the ability to talk about their feelings comfortably, **"Yarn Ball"** is an excellent ice-breaker. (The youth's emotional status is something that should be explained by the site contact before the initial site visit. "Yarn Ball" can be played after the "Name Game" or alone. This game is also played sitting in a circle. A person starts with a ball of yarn and throws it to someone else while saying his/her name and the person's name they are throwing to, while continuing to hold the end of the yarn. The person who catches the yarn has to pick an emotion out of a hat containing pieces of paper with various emotions on them such as happy, sad, angry, etc. He/she tells a story about a situation that involves that particular emotion. He/she then keeps hold of a piece of the yarn and throws the ball while saying his/her name and the person's name they are throwing to. The person who catches the ball says how they feel about the story while trying to guess the emotion the previous person was trying to express. The game continues in this manner until everyone has caught and thrown the yarn ball. This activity not only helps to learn everyone else's names, but also allows the youths to open up and "vent" some of their feelings. There is also a physical connection among the group at the end of the activity when everyone is holding part of the yarn.

Choosing Activitites

The coordinators along with the site contacts must use their best judgement when planning activities. Every site has different strengths and weaknesses that must be looked at. Age, academic level, gender, interests and the groups budget are examples of factors to be considered. Most of these activities are inexpensive and depending on the site, reimbursment for supplies can sometimes be provided. After orientation with the site contact and the ice-breakers, the University students should get a feel of which activities will be appropriate and which will not be. We are going to briefly explain various sites and the best and worst activities we have discovered. These sites represent a fairly wide spectrum of the numerous types of juveniles that are worked with and each activity should be used accordingly. However, students need to remember that just because a certain activity worked for a group similar to their group, it does not mean it will always be successful because each group is different.

There is no particular sequence of activities that we suggest outside of the ice-breakers and closure activities. However, we have found through our many semesters of experience, that some activities work best at specific points of the semester. Again every group is unique and must be evaluated individually. Some groups feel comfortable doing any activity at anytime. Other groups may need time to warm up to the University students, therefore activities dealing with personal issues and emotions should be saved until the group feels comfortable together or near the middle or end of the semester.

The University students must keep in mind that not all of the youths are going to be receptive to them or the activities. From our experiences, those youths who start off receptive, stay receptive throughout the term. Of course every now and then one of them will have a bad day and will not be as enthusiastic as usual. There are also juveniles who are extremely cold to the students and will not participate. An effort should be made by the students to help change a youth's negative attitude, but students must not take it personally if the juvenile does not respond to the effort. Often the juvenile has too many intense problems unrelated to Project Community causing them to misbehave and to have a poor attitude. If, after several attempts to try to get the youth involved, he/she does not respond, it may be best to leave the youth alone as long as he/she does not negatively affect the group. If the juvenile's maladaptive behavior is affecting the group, first a warning should be given and then dismissal from activities until changes are made. Another important way to help get the youths involved is to be sure that all of the students are always participating with full enthusiasm at all times. If the juveniles see the students participating and enjoying themselves, they may be more apt to join in.

Best and Worst Activities

We are now going to explain some of the best and worst activities and the various placements starting with Maxey Boys Training School. It is a medium security facility with one maximum security center. It is for boys between the ages of thirteen and twenty-one. We usually work with approximately twenty boys at a time. These boys have committed serious crimes and have numerous psychological problems. They have poor social skills, have difficulty interacting with others, and have problems acknowledging and talking about their feelings. Our goal at Maxey is to provide social interaction, positive role models, and enjoyment for the boys. According to Amy Rotberg, Tracy Kollin, Donetta Pedroza, Bush Helzberg and Marni Levine, the following have been successful activities.They can also be done with female youths.

The **"Banking Game"** has been a favorite with the boys at Maxey. Each boy picks an index card out of a hat containing his occupation, marital status, family size, monthly salary and monthly food allowance. Then they are each given a piece of paper divided into the twelve months of the year. The University students are at different tables, each representing a commodity—vacations, cars, houses and miscellaneous luxury items. There is also a bank run by a University student.

The coordinator runs the "Banking Game". The coordinator goes through each month allowing about ten minutes for each month giving the boys the opportunity to buy what they wish and/or deposit their money in the bank. This may seem like a short period of time at first, but you want to have time for all the months and you do not want the boys to spend all their money by March. They should learn how to budget their money for a solid year. They must also subtract their monthly food allowance from each months salary. Throughout the game each boy takes a turn to roll the dice. If he rolls an odd number, he has to pick from the "chance bag". This bag contains pieces of paper that either give or take away money from the participant. A person can win the lottery, receive an inheritance, receive a present, owe money for car damages, have to pay a parking ticket, etc., for various amounts of money. The University students must be aware of and assist the boys who have difficulty reading or adding and subtracting. Try to only assist the boys, do not do it for them. This promotes independence and self-confidence. This goes for all activities at every site unless there are serious problems or exceptions. Time should be allotted for each boy to stand up at the end of the year and say what his occupation and family status is, how much money he has in the bank, what assets he has acquired and any bonuses or troubles he ran into.

We found that the boys helped each other when in financial difficulties and budgeted their money well during the "Banking Game". This activity helps them with a task that is required in the "outside world", is a positive learning experience, and very enjoyable. It may also be beneficial to the boys by imagining themselves engaged in a positive life outside the institutional setting. The "Banking Game" is slightly complicated and may be most successful in the middle or end of the semester because the juveniles need to feel comfortable asking for help from each other and the University students.

An activity which promotes creativity is **Tye-Dying T-shirts**. You need white t-shirts for everyone, buckets of warm water, numerous colors of dye, and rubberbands. Newspaper should be laid out on the floor with the buckets of different colored dyes placed on top. The boys can use as many colors as they choose or groups can be limited to only about three or four colors. If the groups are divided, the shirts can later be used for team sports, each member of the team having the same colors. We suggest tye-dying in the beginning so the shirts can be worn throughout the semester for competitive activities. The creativity comes into play in the way the boys use the colors and the method they choose to design their shirt. The boys seemed to take great pride in the shirts they made because they create the final products on their own, and every shirt turns out unique. Many of the boys wear their shirts every week when we meet with them.

A University student can demonstrate the different approaches that can be used in dying the shirts. You can lie the shirt down flat, put the end of a pencil or your finger in the center of the shirt, twist the entire shirt into a ball around the pencil or finger and then place rubberbands tightly around the ball. You can also place rubberbands in random areas on the shirt. Many of the boys came up with techniques their own. After the rubberbands are secure, you dip different parts of the shirt into the various colors. Make sure to get the dye into the areas that are not visible too. Using a spoon or paper cup is helpful for pouring the dye into the hidden areas. You wait about ten minutes and then take the rubberbands off. It is interesting to see the variety of designs made because every shirt is unique. At the end, everyone helps clean-up the room. This activity allows for casual conversation to take place, promotes creativity and requires team work during clean-up.

Team sports such as basketball, volleyball and kickball are always enjoyable for everyone involved. Such activities should be optional so those who do not like to play sports will not feel embarrassed by being forced to do so. Those who do like sports love this activity because they are able to show-off their athletic ability. It is important to have a site staff member referee, so the rules are followed and the game stays under control. When playing basketball, relays are better than an actual game because they are less active and there is no physical contact involved. When played properly, athletics can be a positive release of aggression and promote good competition. It also encourages team work while allowing individual ability to be demonstrated. Sports are great because they can be done at anytime during the semester. We have found that alternating sports and creative acitivities from week to week seems to work the best because of the diversity of interests among the residents. Sports are easy to organize at last minute, making them good to use as back-up activities in case another one does not work out.

A great way to make the sporting events more exciting is to bring to site various University athletes. We have used this as a surprise event at the end of the semester. This activity needs to begin planning at the beginning of the semester for a few reasons. First, it is extremely difficult to organize all of the athletes' schedules into one time period, especially those in season. Second, the athletes must have approval from their coaches and the University Athletic Department because there are regulations about athletes making public appearances.

The residents become extremely excited and tend to stay on their best behavior for the University athletes. We try to bring in several different types of athletes to cover everyone's interests; swimmers, runners, football players, hockey players, basketball players, gymnasts, and baseball players. The youths obviously get more excited if the athletes are famous in their sport.

The activity begins with everyone sitting in a circle in a gym or recreation area and the athletes telling a little about themselves. The youths are then able to ask the athletes questions. We suggest discussing with the athletes ahead of time that they should not only focus on their sport but also the other aspects of their lives for example, the importance of their education. The athletes should also be familiar with the institution before they arrive. After the question and answer period is over (you may have to cut it short) it is a great idea for everyone to participate in various relays or sports. At the end of the session many of the the boys request an autograph signing period, so be sure to leave an extra five to ten minutes at the end and to have paper and pens available.

"Win, Lose or Draw" is another popular activity. The group is separated into two teams. There is one blackboard and one team goes at a time. One team member is elected to draw the word given to them by the judge (the coordinator). He then has two minutes to draw on the blackboard whatever he can to convey to his team the word he has been given. At the end of the two minutes, if the team has not guessed the word, the other team can "steal". They only get one guess, and if it is correct they get the point. Otherwise, nobody gets it. It is then the next team's turn, and the same scenario occurs. Everyone must take turns drawing. This activity promotes creativity, group interaction and postive competition. "Win, Lose, or Draw" is a good activity to do near at the start or middle of the semester because it causes individuals to give encouragement to their team members when drawing in front of the group. If a youth has difficulty reading or figuring out what to draw the University students running the activity can help out before the youth begins drawing. The students running the game can also whisper hints to a youth if he seems to be struggling during the game. This rids of any embarrassment for the juvenile.

Another activity which gives the boys a chance to express themselves creatively is **making collages**. Gather as many magazines as possible to bring to site. If necessary, the University students can rip out any inappropriate pictures to avoid problems. Everyone cuts out any words or pictures from the magazines that describe how they see themselves in the future. Everyone then arranges and glues their cut-outs onto construction paper. After the room is cleaned up, each person stands up and explains their collage. Some of the boys take it very seriously and construct excellent collages, while others do not. It is important though for everyone, including the University students to make collages so that everyone can learn about each other on a personal level. Making collages helps the boys to set goals for themselves, be creative and to express their thoughts about their lives. Like the "Banking Game" collages allows the residents to envision a life for themselves in the real world. Although collages helps everyone to get to know each other better, we suggest this activity for when the group feels comfortable with one another. From past experience, the best collages have been made when everyone opens up and expresses their feelings to the group.

An activity which teaches a practical lesson and can be done at anytime during the semester, is **job applications and interviews**. The students get job applications from different stores on campus and bring them to site. Be sure to blacken out the the question about their criminal record in order to avoid problems. Each boy is given an application to fill out with the assistance of the students. When they are finished, three boys either volunteer or are asked to be interviewed by a student individually in front of the entire group. After the interview, it is critiqued by the group. Once again, be aware of and help those who have difficulty reading. The boys get quite involved in this activity because having a job is something they often think about. It teaches them about applying for a job and it helps to build their confidence for the time when the opportunity to work arises.

If it seems as though your group is interested and willing to have a somewhat serious discussion, Donetta Pedroza found at Maxey Boys Training School, Olympic Center, that the following activity is perfect. This activity encourages the boys to think about the treatment of women. You find **three songs** that talk negatively about women. We have used rap songs. Everyone sits in a circle and carefully listens to the words of the song being played. When the song is over, four questions are asked and discussed one at a time. 1) How are women spoken about in this song? 2) Do you think what is said in this song is true? 3) Why do you think they speak this way about women in this song? 4) Do you think this song affects your views on women? You may only get through one song or you may get through all three. Keep in mind that you are not there to teach them but rather to stimulate thinking. Some people may become defensive but you must keep the discussion as a discussion, rather than allowing it to escalate into an argument.

It is important for the boys to feel as though they also have something to teach you in order to help build their self-esteem. Playing cards is something they spend a majority of their free time doing and most of them are very good at it. You can either devote an entire session to playing cards, or you can end a few of the other activities thirty minutes early and spend the remaining time playing cards. We recommend the second choice because two hours of cards can become fairly boring. When this activity is used for the last half an hour of several sessions, it leaves the boys with feelings of pride and self-confidence because they were the "leaders" of the activity. Like playing sports, playing cards is an excellent back-up activity in case another activity unexpectedly ends early or if one fails.

An activity that has been attempted each semester but has not always been successful is **"movie night"**, in which you rent a movie and show it to the boys, provided that a VCR is available. You have to be careful with the movie you choose. Our recommendation is "Stand and Deliver," but make sure the majority of them have not seen it already. If another activity falls through at the last minute, renting a movie is an easy back-up plan. One concern about "movie night" is that there is no interaction occurring and they could have the same experience watching a movie without you and your group there. If there is time at the end, a discussion about the film may compensate for the lack of contact during the viewing.

Another activity that was attempted but was unsuccessful, was making **music videos**. It was disorganized and Maxey Boys Training School did not have all the necessary equipment. It would probably be a great activity if the necessary video camera, tapes and tape players were available. However, having an activity fail while at site is disappointing for everyone, so be sure you know exactly what the activity requires.

Washtenaw County Detention Center, where Tracy Kollin and Scott Waldbaum were coordinators, is similar to Maxey except that they have both boys and girls. It is a center where juveniles who have committed crimes stay until they have their trials. Tracy and Scott do the same activities as those done at Maxey. The one difference is that the residents are not under any strict supervision and are therefore not as well behaved. The youths were not always willing to participate in the planned activities. When an acitivity did not work, the juveniles were always willing to play cards or basketball.

Another site where Donetta Pedroza and Chris Wright coordinated is Wayne Youth Mentors. This site-placement consists of an even ratio of approximately seven University students to seven youths. The youths are in this program because they have committed minor crimes or are considered to be at risk. Many of them come from dysfunctional homes. The site is divided into two groups, eight to eleven year olds and thirteen to fifteen year olds. Project Community's goal is to build the juvenile's self-esteem and encourage them to behave in a more socially accepted manner.

The older group does not have structured activities. Most of the time at site is focused on group discussions about subjects such as drugs, gangs and safe sex. The University students need to prepare appropriate questions relating to these topics in order to spark productive discussions. Most of the site visits consist of question and answer sessions.

An activity that is conducted with the younger group is **"Family Portraits**." One child stands in front of the group and chooses people to represent his/her family members. He/she then places them in different areas of the room. The family members the child feels closest to are placed closer to them and the ones he/she does not feel close to are placed further away. A discussion follows each childs turn. This activity has been successful in getting the children to open up and talk about the problems that exist in their families. Patience is necessary with "Family Portraits" because some of the children may have a difficult time opening up about their families, especially because many of their families are dysfunctional. It may be best to do this activity near the end of the semester.

An activity that helps bonding within the group is **"Human Sculptures."** Everyone is divided into groups of three. Each group appoints an artist, a sculpture and a model. The artist stands in the front, facing both the sculpture and the model. The sculpture stands in the middle, facing the artist, with their back to the model. The model stands behind the sculpture, facing the artist. The model assumes an "interesting" position. The artist has to fix the sculpture to look exactly like the model. There are judges who determine when the team has completed the task of making the sculpture look exactly like the position of the model. The team who finishes first wins. There are several rounds with different positions and the role of each person can change. We suggest doing this activity at the beginning of the term because it is simple, exciting, and brings people closer together.

An indirect way of having a discussion on a specific topic is by having a **"Talk Show."** One person plays the host and three to five people are the guests. The rest of the group is the audience. The host interviews the guests by asking specific questions on the topic chosen. The audience can also ask questions and/or express their opinion. If a video camera is accessible, it is a great idea to film the show as though it were live, on the air. This is a fun way to have children discuss various issues and voice their opinions and can be done at anytime during the term.

When working with younger children, it is important not to do activities that are too childish for them. They may only be eight to eleven years old, but they become extremely defensive when they are not treated with respect. Speak with the site contact and the children themselves to discover what activities they enjoy.

The final site placement we will discuss is Special Friends where Chris Wright and Bush Helzberg also coordinated. This involves females between the ages of sixteen and eighteen who are wards of the state. Project Community works with two to six adolescents at a time. The site contact prefers that the activities engaged in take place outside the residence in order to get the girls out and about and doing something different than their daily routine. It is a difficult task to find activities outside their home that do not require money. Once again, the role of Project Community is to represent positive role models while providing entertainment.

Playing pool is an activity the teens have enjoyed. Project Community uses the pool hall in the student union. You divide the group into teams of two and set up a tournament. Prizes can be given for first, second and third place. Everyone has a great time while interacting with one another and working together as teams.

During the winter, if there is adequate snow on the ground, **sledding** can be a successful activity. You need to find a good, safe hill and several sleds. Rules should be established about the manner in which they can go down the hill (one at a time, facing forward, etc.) so that injuries are avoided. This is always enjoyed by all.

During the warmer weather, going to a park and having a **cookout** is enjoyable and relaxing. Each person should participate in the cooking because it enhances interaction within the group. After everyone is finished eating, everyone should help clean-up. Then you can either sit and talk or play a sport like basketball, kickball or frisbee. You should allow the girls to help in the decision of what food is being cooked and the activity that follows the meal to make them feel included and to be sure they are interested in what is going on.

One activity that was not successful was **walking around downtown** Ann Arbor and the University's campus. The girls were not interested in going into any of the stores or buildings and had negative attitudes. A more structured activity usually works better because they are provided with the enjoyment instead of having to create it themselves.

Wrapping Up

The end of each semester for any site is extremely crucial. Many of these youths may not show it, but they become considerably attached to the University students. Once the semester ends though, contact is usually forbidden to continue. We suggest the last site visit consist of several things. Food and refreshments could be provided by the University students. While enjoying the food, have a discussion reflecting on the past semester, the good and the bad. Finding out what activities they did or did not enjoy and why, can be very helpful for future groups. During this final visit you may learn how much the youths appreciate Project Community.

Autograph books are a great way to remember people by. Everyone staples together paper like a book, with a construction paper cover with their name on it. Then all of the University students sign the juveniles books and the juveniles sign theirs. People usually write about what a great semester it has been and everyone wishes each other good luck for the future. If there is time, the youths like to perform various talents for us, like singing and dancing. All of these activities are great because everyone departs with a good feeling.

It is sometimes difficult though to walk out the door for the last time. It makes it easier if students remember what a wonderful experience they have had and the impact they have made. These youths will never forget them just like we will never forget the juveniles we have encountered throughout the years.

Chapter 5

THE GROWING TREE
Working with Children From Addictive Homes

By Jeanne M. Gray

Introduction

The Growing Tree was inspired in part by Luanne Donner, one of the primary directors of what used to be Huron Oaks Drug Rehabilitation Center. Huron Oaks Rehabilitation Center was an inpatient/outpatient facility that serviced youths and adults in need of treatment for chemical dependency. Since Huron Oaks opened it has changed forms several times due to changes in insurance policies and funding to finally become part of McAuley's Center for Mental Health. The treatment module remains the same however, and the primary belief is that the whole family has been affected by the individual's use, and thus needs to be treated.

Components of the therapy include a three-day treatment program in which the whole family is involved. Sessions include intensive discussions about family dynamics and how they are affected by chemical dependency. They also discuss how family dynamics perpetuate the chemical dependency in the individual. The treatment center rests on the belief that chemical dependency is a disease, and should be treated as such.

The Growing Tree

From this belief comes the Growing Tree program. The Growing Tree (TGT) is a treatment module that consists of sessions that meet twice weekly for six weeks. TGT works with the children, adolescents, and siblings of people that are in treatment. The ages of these children range from three to fourteen but the average age, when I was there, was about eight. There were usually about ten kids in each section, with about four staff. The staff consisted of two Huron Oaks staff and usually three volunteers.

I started volunteering there during the summer of 1988. I'm not entirely certain how I became involved, I was just looking for something different to do, and I ran into this program. The aspect of this program that really drew me to it was the whole family concept. The fact that they didn't see family dysfunction as being one member's responsibility or problem, made a lot of sense to me. I knew a few people that had been through different forms of drug rehabilitation, and hadn't been very successful. One of the reasons that I believe that they weren't was because the treatment was only centered on the individual.

The program was different and interesting for a number of reasons. When TGT was first introduced to me, I couldn't believe that it was important to treat four year olds. They were just babies, what could they possibly know about drug abuse? I remember my surprise when a five year old drew a crack pipe for me, and began to understand the necessity of treating the entire family. The other aspect that really drew me to the program was the educational component. TGT is very proactive in that respect, it teaches kids not only about what chemical dependency does to their family, but also what it does to the individual, and helps kids to take steps to stop the cycle of chemical dependency in his or her family.

What Students Actually Did

In order for someone to understand how we formed our group and the issues that we discussed, I need to give you a brief description of what we actually did during the treatment sessions. For each major issue or theme, the kids were placed at tables according to age with one or two facilitators. The topic was "taught" through a series of drawings, plays or puppet show in which everyone played a part.

The first issue that TGT tries to handle is teaching kids how to keep themselves safe. The first activity is drawing or coloring. The group facilitator sets up a scenario—for example, "have you ever been in a situation where someone has tried to get you to drive with them when they have been drinking?" The kids will draw a picture of a similar situation, and then share it. The group will then brainstorm around different ways to respond to this. The second activity is usually a puppet show with a similar theme. The kids practice taking safe actions—like telling a parent "no" or leaving the house and going to a neighbor that they can trust. Primarily, the kids are taught to "network" or find safe places that they can go, or locate safe adults that they can turn to.

Another important aspect of TGT is teaching kids about the role changes that occur in a chemically dependent family. When a member of the family system is chemically dependent, the whole family structure breaks down. Typically the children will take on unhealthy roles to try and return the family back to homeostasis. For example, if a father is chemically dependent, a child may not believe that it is smart to act like a child. Thus they take on the role of the inoperative parent to try and compensate. The activities for this session are centered around educating kids about these roles, and the unhealthiness of them. Again, this takes place through puppet shows, drawing, and family sculpting activities.

The other major component of TGT is education about what chemical dependency is, and how it affects individuals and family members. Using the disease concept,[1] kids are brought to a greater awareness about chemical dependency and their own predisposition to becoming chemically dependent. The kids are shown that chemical dependency is a disease, and is not anyone's fault. The facilitators discuss peer pressure, and how to cope with it. They also discuss different ways to have fun without using drugs. They teach the concept of co-dependency,[2] and give concrete examples again, using interactive puppet shows and plays.

Forming the Coursepack

There is an inordinate amount of information about chemical dependency circulating in society. Consequently, finding articles to fill the coursepack wasn't that hard. What was difficult was deciding what to use. The director, Joe Galura, asked me to help formulate the coursepack by reading some of the major authors on chemical dependency and co-dependency. I weeded out some articles that I thought matched the content of TGT, and he incorporated them into a coherent coursepack.[3] Much of the information that I got came from Huron Oaks. The agency with which you are working probably has an ideology from which it derives its treatment module, and will be able to provide you with ample information.

Forming the Group

I was asked a semester in advance to coordinate the Growing Tree section. Joe and I agreed that the volunteers/students should be screened before being able to participate in the section. The reasons behind this were pretty simple. The students would be dealing one on one with children that are in high stress situations with little supervision. Frequently the kids we work with in addition to dealing with the issues surrounding chemical dependency, are also abused. We needed to be sure that the students that we used were fairly mature and could handle emotionally-charged situations. Consequently before a student could participate, they needed to have an interview with both myself and Joe.

They also needed to go through volunteer screening at Huron Oaks which proved to be somewhat of a hassle. The volunteer training process was a series of meetings held by the Huron Oaks staff that basically delineated the entire program. Then the volunteer coordinator would decide who could volunteer and who could not. Besides being a large time commitment, this put us at a slight disadvantage. What if the students that we had cleared through our process didn't make it through that of the volunteer coordinator? It is essential to find out the volunteer requirements of the agency with which you are placing students before you actually place them. After a few tense meetings and phone calls, we managed to work out a happy medium.

I recruited my roommates, Monique Whitman and Lydia Soboleski, and my friend Jennifer, who was a psychology major. Four other students also signed up for the course. Seven people for this project seemed like a manageable number: one student had a special interest because she had grown up with an alcoholic mother. Three students went out to site on Tuesday nights, and four on Thursday nights. I went out to site on Thursday nights.

For the first meeting our group met in a classroom. This was a little stuffy, and we all agreed that meeting in the student union would be more conducive to creating an informal atmosphere. Our meetings lasted approximately one and a half hours, and we met once a week. The structure of the meetings went something like this. We started with either an icebreaker or "highlights and lowlights." "Highlights and Lowlights" is an exercise where people in the group very simply share the high point of their week, and the low point of their week. I'll talk about icebreakers later. Then we usually did a structured exercise that tied in the readings for that week. At TGT, the kids are asked to color a lot, so

I did that as well with my group.

The exercise that I remember as being the most powerful was the "stereotypes" exercise.[4] This is where you break your group into two groups and have them draw the "stereotypical" drug user, with markers and poster board. After ten minutes they come back and share their drawing with the group. This is very potent because it gets people to confront their stereotypes about chemical dependency head on, in a very light fashion. It also opens up the group to looking at why these stereotypes exist, and what views are prevalent in our society.

I handled the reading material in a discussion format. At the first seminar I passed around the schedule. Everyone put their initials after a certain week, with the understanding that they would lead the group that week. Usually people would go over the articles briefly that the group was supposed to have read, then have questions prepared to spark discussion. I think that this format works well for several reasons. For starters, it takes the coordinator out of the "teacher" position. Rather then just having one person lecturing all the time, different people are leading the group each week. It also provides a sort of positive peer pressure in the group to do the reading. You can't have a good discussion if only two people have read the materials, and if the group members know that sooner or later they are going to have to lead a group, they are more likely to come prepared.

Another way to combat the problem of people not reading is by assigning journal questions pertaining to each reading. For me, this was a last resort tactic. I liked having the journals be a reflective time for my group. I rarely assigned journal questions for the group, and if I did they were centered around the discussion that we had during seminar. Usually though they were about site, and some issue that they faced during the week. Journals can be a very powerful communication tool. What a student might not say during section they may say in the journal, and I think that it is important to put as much back into the journal as the student has put in. I almost always "answered" back the journals with a brief note or comment about what the student had written about. In evaluations at the end of the semester, my group members said that they really appreciated this, because it showed them that I was interested in what they said, rather than just assigning busy work.

At this point during the section we usually addressed issues of business, like paper assignments, or transportation problems.[5] Then we would finish with reflective pieces about what had happened at site that week. The group members really got into this, because they only got to see half of the program by only going out to site once weekly. They were very interested in what the other members were doing, and it helped to build group cohesion. A person would share a problem that they were experiencing, and the group would support and make suggestions on how to make the situation better.

The dynamics of our group were very interesting. I wanted to build a tight group primarily because of the high stress situations that the group members are faced with. I wanted the group members to be able to turn to each other with their frustrations and fears about what they were facing. I also wanted the group to be a place for people to "vent" the emotions that they were experiencing from working with damaged children. During our first section we did an exercise that gets people to start talking about what they are feeling. The format is fairly simple, you start out with a statement. "I feel (blank) about (blank) because of (blank)." One woman said, "I feel scared about site because I don't know what we are going to be doing." This opened up the first session considerably because then everyone jumped in and expressed the same concern. I had spoken to them all about the program, but this forum allowed the students to ask specific questions.

Never underestimate the power of icebreakers. In our group, over half of the members knew each other. So, I didn't spend a lot of time doing introduction stuff. This was a huge mistake. The group members that didn't know each other felt alienated, and held back from participating for the first few weeks. The group members that did know each other didn't have a comfortable way of reaching out to the other members. The icebreakers would have alleviated much of this discomfort very simply. In the most recent group that I coordinated I did icebreakers for the first four weeks. Each time the icebreaker got a little deeper into who the person is, and what they are all about. Making the icebreaker fun is a light way of getting students to talk about themselves and take risks that they otherwise probably wouldn't.

The icebreakers that I have had the most luck with are very simple.[6] During week one I usually do the "Shield of good qualities." This is explained in the Wizard, and is a good way to start off a group. The group members are asked to "brag" about themselves by talking about the things that they are good at, and the things that they are proud of. This exercise generally leaves people feeling good about themselves, and the other members. Week two we usually did the "introduce your neighbor" exercise. This exercise consists of pairing up group members that don't know each other, and having them ask a series of questions. Then they have to introduce each other to the group. Week three we usually do the Johari Window (explained in the Wizard). This is a great exercise because it allows students to disclose information about themselves in a safe format. It also is a low pressure exercise—a person can get as personal or as impersonal as they want during this exercise.

The coordinator really sets the pace for all of these icebreakers. I made the mistake of assuming that since four of us were already friends, the group would naturally form. I learned that a group doesn't just "happen," it needs to be nurtured and supported. Every individual in the group brings their own separate knowledge and person to the group. It is the task of the coordinator to help develop it.

Choosing a Successor

I am a strong advocate for choosing a coordinator out of the existing group. Throughout the semester one or two people will emerge as being extraordinary, and really excited about the project. By having the next coordinator be someone who has already been through the program, they are familiar with the materials and the site. They have already done most of the exercises and know what works and what doesn't work. They will also have suggestions on how to make the program better. I left my project to the hands of Monique Whitman, who made a very competent coordinator the following two years.

Some Pitfalls to Avoid

1. Don't assume that you are going to know everything. Before my first seminar, I was in a frenzy for about fifteen minutes. I thought "what the hell am I going to teach these people about chemical dependency, they probably know more than me." A truly good coordinator doesn't teach the group, just facilitates it.

2. Don't assume that just because someone is your friend that they are going to be accountable. Check on them the same way that you do all your other group members. One of my "friends" was scamming most of the semester, and I didn't realize it until one of the other group members pointed it out.

3. Be prepared to deal with emotions. You are working with a damaged population, and the chances of a situation at site hitting home to one of your group members is high. Make the group a safe place for people to bring the stuff that they are feeling. You can open this up by sharing a situation that you yourself have struggled with when working with this population. For instance, I shared the example of how hard it is to watch a kid go home with a parent that you know is abusive. The whole group feels this, and needs to be able to talk about it.

4. Have fun with your group. The more you enjoy the group, the more the group will enjoy their experience.

NOTES

1. For discussion activities on the Disease Concept of Chemical Dependency, see Chapter Five of Off to See the Wizard.
2. For discussion activities on Codependency, see Chapters Nine, Ten, and Eleven in Off to See the Wizard.
3. The current syllabus for Chemical Dependency appears in Chapter One of Off to See the Wizard.
4. Examples of "stereotypes" can be found in Chapter Four of Off to See the Wizard.
5. OCSL provides University-rented vehicles for students' site visits.
6. Variations of these Icebreakers can be found in Chapter Two of Off to See the Wizard.

Chapter 6

ALCOHOL PREVENTION AND INTERVENTION IN ELEMENTARY CLASSROOMS
A Step Beyond "Just Saying No"

By Mary Jo Callan

A Project History—Past and Present

Project Community's "A Step Beyond 'Just Say No'" is sponsored in conjunction with Catherine McAuley Health Systems. Originally titled "Just Say No", it was designed using many of the principals from the D.A.R.E. (Drug Awareness & Resistance Education) Program, in which law enforcement officers spend up to six weeks with upper elementary students, with much of the focus being on peer pressure and refusal skills education. An important rationale for beginning this type of program in upper elementary grades, is that this is the age that peer groups become very important and influential to children, and the need for peer acceptance and approval is high. Unlike D.A.R.E., "Just Say No" was not intended to be comprehensive, but to serve instead as a brief introduction to substance abuse-related issues, relying on follow-up by teachers and parents. Also unlike D.A.R.E., "Just Say No" used University students who are able to appear more like an older sibling, rather than as an authority figure. Presentations typically lasted about an hour and involved a variety of mediums including lecture, video, and role plays.

A typical presentation would begin with a video which introduced the concept of peer pressure and illustrated its various forms. At the conclusion of the video, University presenters would review each type of peer pressure portrayed in the video including: "friendly pressure," "I dare you pressure," "indirect pressure," and "heavy pressure." After doing a cursory review of the video, presenters would typically solicit responses from students regarding motives and consequences for drug and alcohol use. The concluding part of the presentation was devoted to role plays. Skits included student volunteers, depicted in a situation where they had to resist one of the four types of peer pressure highlighted in the earlier video.

Presentations were and continue to be arranged by the section coordinator, who contacts area schools to explain the goals and focus of the program. Although most schools already have some type of substance abuse education in place, the intent of the program is to serve as an effective compliment to an existing curriculum.

The course structure, readings and requirements are the same as other Project Community Chemical Dependency sections, discussed elsewhere in this volume. Students who wish to enroll in this section must arrange an interview with Project Community program director Joe Galura, and also with Gary Clark, the Catherine McAuley program liaison. The primary purpose of these meetings is to gauge the student's attitudes relating to substance use and abuse. The project encourages involvement of individuals who are genuinely committed to its goals.

Unlike most Project Community sections, students in "Just Say No" travel to different sites each week. This enables them to experience a variety of children from diverse backgrounds. This also creates the unique challenge of tailoring each presentation to fit the needs and comfort level of each class. The section is well suited to students who plan to pursue a career in education, or who have a strong personal interest in substance abuse prevention and intervention.

From Refusal Skills to Coping Skills

When I first became involved with Project Community's "Just Say No", I wanted to learn more about why kids use drugs and alcohol. I hoped that I could assist them in their attempt to avoid the value conflicts and pain which often accompany substance use and abuse. As I became more involved with the section, and more invested in the pedagogy of Project Community, I began to have reservations and questions about "Just Say No." With the support of Gary and Joe, I set out to improve it, and make it more consistent with the mission of Project Community. The remainder of this section details the changes, along with rationales for those changes, which I have made in this prevention program during my tenure as coordinator.

One of the most valuable components of Project Community is its non-traditional, liberationist pedagogy. It strives to equalize the relationship between teacher and student, by viewing students as active contributors, rather than passive recepticals, of knowledge. As a teacher and a student, I understand that the process of learning is as much, or more, important than the content of what is learned. With this in mind, the structure and goals of "Just Say No" seemed to be in direct conflict with those of Project Community. As students in the section, it was our job to "present" or impart our knowledge about peer pressure and alcohol to the students. We would stand at the front of the room and preach about the dangers of drugs and alcohol. When we did solicit responses from students, we already knew the answers which we would deem "right", and would return a "wrong" answer with, "Well, that's not really what we had in mind." The presentations set out to teach children uniform "recipes for success," rather than empowering them by encouraging critical thinking about choices involving peer pressure and drugs and alcohol.

The current program attempts to empower children. Project Community students act as facilitators, attempting to create a forum where children can speak openly about issues surrounding drugs, alcohol, and self-esteem. We encourage children to ask questions by creating a safe situation where they may do so anonymously. Rather than "presenting" an established set of facts and soliciting predetermined "correct" responses, University facilitators provide only a foundation of information, on which students will build. Children, as well as adults, are much more likely to learn and value that which they helped create. The primary goal of "Just Say No", was to teach children refusal skills, so that they would be able to resist peer pressure; especially when it involves drugs and alcohol. I have serious reservations about the premise that children begin using because they do not know how to "say no?" While refusal skills are important, they cannot realistically be expected to have long-term effectiveness when taught in a vacuum; we can not ignore coping skills and issues involving self-esteem; we do a disservice to children and society when we pretend that resisting peer pressure is as simple as exercising a little bit of will power. The current program incorporates some basic refusal skills into a curriculum which encourages the healthy development of self-esteem, and its role in the choices people make. I believe that both of these components are essential to any potentially effective prevention or intervention program, as children must ultimately rely on internal cues when making choices about drugs and alcohol. Long-term effectiveness of any alcohol and drug prevention program will be achieved only when children can see a legitimate reason to be invested in their own well-being.

Suggested Activities

The attached outline for facilitators and a Suggested Activities booklet for teachers is a compilation from various sources of activities. These activities are believed to be effective in combatting alcohol and drug abuse by fostering healthy coping skills and self-esteem, as well as teaching kids refusal skills. Each activity is geared for children in grades four and five, though most can be adapted to fit various age groups. The intent of the Suggested Activities booklet is to make it easy for teachers to follow-up the initial presentation by saving them the time of having to collect related activities on their own. It is given to the teacher at the time of the arranged presentation and should be used as review and reinforcement. Most activities can be plugged in to an existing curriculum, because they take very little time to complete. The booklet is rather eclectic in approach, but I believe its general framework lends itself well as an introductory tool to get elementary school students to think more critically about the feelings they have toward themselves and the choices they make. It includes activities aimed at increasing student awareness about their feelings, attitudes, and self-esteem, as well as role plays used with some success in the former "Just Say No" program.

I believe that it can serve only as an introduction to these important issues. The program is short, with the initial presentation and discussion taking about an hour. Follow up activities are left to the discretion of the classroom teacher who must find time to incorporate it into an already full curriculum. Also, no single program can significantly change the self-esteem of a child or her/his attitudes about drugs and alcohol without the active support and reinforcement of parents, school, and community. Coping skills, as well as feelings of self-worth, be they healthy or unhealthy, are learned throughout a lifetime. It is my hope, however, that this program may serve as a starting point.

Suggested Activitites

A Step Beyond "Just Say No" Program Goals

At the conclusion of this program, the student will be able to:

1. Explain what self-esteem is and why it is important.
2. Identify ways in which healthy self-esteem may be strengthened or weakened.
3. Identify what peer pressure is, including its various forms.
4. Understand and implement techniques to resist different forms of peer pressure.
5. Understand how healthy or unhealthy self-esteem may affect their choices involving drugs and alcohol.
6. Be aware of possible consequences of drug and alcohol abuse.
7. Be aware of "safe" adults or older youths, who may assist them in making healthy choices about drugs and alcohol.

Some Information About Self-esteem

There are many variations on the definition of self-esteem.

Since this program is aimed at elementary aged students, the definition of self-esteem should be somewhat simple, in hopes that more complex information will be added later.

Let us say that self-esteem is made up of the overall thoughts and feelings we have about ourselves. Everyone has self-esteem, and it may be either healthy or unhealthy. Healthy self-esteem is important as it affects the way we look at life and the choices that we make. People who feel good about themselves are more able to accept responsibility for their actions and deal with challenges in healthy ways. Our self-esteem is developed throughout life, and is influenced by how we are treated by those around us, including parents, siblings, teachers, and friends.

Activity 1

"I am lovable and capable"

This lesson serves as an introduction to the concept of self-esteem. It helps students understand that the things we do and say to each other affect the way we feel about ourselves. This is a good starting point as it can help to build the foundation for a safe and supportive classroom environment.

"Nothing else matters half so much...to reassure one another, to answer each other...perhaps only you can listen to me and not laugh."

—*Ugo Betti*

Lesson Explanation and Procedure

(approximate time: 20-30 minutes)

This lesson was designed to draw an analogy between our self-esteem and an invisible sign each of us wears saying, "I Am Lovable and Worthy". Each day, people do and say things to us which can either build up our signs, making us feel more lovable and capable, or rip apart our signs, making us feel less lovable and capable. Of course no one can always be lovable and worthy in every area, at all times. The better our "signs" are treated, the more likely we are to accomplish more and get along better in life. Self-esteem can easily be tied into the idea of this "I Am Lovable and Capable" sign that everybody wears. The following story should be read to students to enable them to see the importance of self-esteem. The story may easily be changed, with the point remaining the same. It is hoped that students will become more sensitive to each other when they realize the power of their actions and words. This lesson may be introduced by referring back to the initial presentation, in which the concept of self-esteem was introduced. Explain that this activity may help students to understand this idea better.

As the story is told, it is important for the teller to actually wear a sign which reads, "I AM LOVABLE AND CAPABLE." This can be a piece of paper which is taped to your shirt, so that as you read about the character in the story, you may tear or add onto your sign to illustrate the point.

After telling the story, break students into small groups (preferably 2-4 students), and have each group complete the following (allow five to ten minutes):

—Discuss with each other examples of when their "I Am Lovable and Capable" signs were either torn or added to, within the past few days.

—List three ways to tear someone else's sign, and three ways to add to it.

Then bring class together, and end the lesson by once again connecting self-esteem to the "I Am Lovable and Capable" sign which are worn by all of us.

An optional assignment to follow this activity: Have each student spend a couple of days trying to build up the self-esteem, or "I Am Loving and Capable" sign of someone in their family, and write a paper, or tell the class about the experience.

A Story About Roger

Roger wakes up one day and the first words he hears are his sister's yelling, "Come on stupid, if you want me to drive you to school, you better hurry up" (rip). He jumps out of bed, and runs down the hall towards the bathroom, but his mom beats him to it and says while closing the door, "You should have taken a shower last night instead of having your face stuck in the tv" (rip).

When he arrives at school, he sees a group of girls, including Debbie whom he has a crush on. As he walks by them, he hears them whispering and laughing (rip). After lunch, he passes by a little boy who has tripped and dropped all of his books. Roger helps the boy to his feet, helps him pick up his books, and assures him that there is no reason to be embarrassed. The little boy says, "Thanks a lot for your help" (add a piece on to the sign). But helping the boy makes him late getting to class. He tries to explain to his teacher but she says, "Just sit down Roger, I don't want to hear any silly excuses" (rip). During class, he gets back a geography quiz from the day before (rip). In science, the teacher calls on him but he gives the wrong answer (rip). After school, he sees Debbie walking by herself, and decides to ask her to the school dance. Debbie says that she would like to go with him, if her parents give her permission (add a piece on to the sign).

His mom picks him up from school and takes him to his basketball game. As the game begins, he notices that his mom and sister are both in the stands.

This is the first game his sister has ever come to, since she usually has her own basketball games (add a piece to the sign). He plays a pretty good game, but with the score tied and only a few seconds left, he fouls an opposing player, sending him to the free throw line. The opponent makes a free throw and Roger's team loses the game (rip of a couple of pieces). On the way home after the game, his sister says that he did the right thing when he fouled the other player, and that she would have done the same thing (add a piece back on).

When he gets home, he eats dinner, and begins on his homework. Having received his report card earlier that day, Roger's mom say to him, "After the grades you got on your report card, you better be doing your homework" (rip). He goes up to his room, and before he falls asleep, his mom comes in and says, "I'm sorry that I was so hard on you, I'll try to spend more time helping you with your homework" (add a piece back on). Roger says, "Goodnight" to his mother then drifts off to sleep.

Activity 2

Everybody Up

This initiative activity challenges participants to cooperate with each other. Its primary purpose is to help foster the creation of a supportive, open learning environment. Other goals include: increased student interaction, communication skills, problem solving, and decision making.

Lesson Explanation and Procedure
(approximate time: 10 minutes)

Begin by breaking the class into groups of two, with each group having members of approximately the same size. Each set of partners sit on the ground facing each other so that the bottoms of their feet are opposed. Knees should be bent, and hands tightly grasped. From this sitting position, the duo must try to pull themselves into a standing position. If success is achieved, groups may add on other partners and increase the number of participants until the whole group is working together to stand.

Actvity 3

The Leaning Circle

This activity may be used to follow Everybody Up as it encourages not only group cooperation but also trust. Its primary purpose is to foster the development of a safe learning environment.

Lesson Explanation and Procedure
(approximate time: 10 minutes)

This activity is for the entire class to attempt together. Participants join hands in a circle and extend outward until everyone feels some pull on their arms (participants feet should be about shoulder width apart). Have the group count off by two's all the way around the circle. On the count of three all "one's" will lean in to the circle, and all "two's" will lean out of the circle. While leaning, participants should not bend at the waist. The idea is for everyone in the group to lean in or out without letting anyone fall. All group members should be given an opportunity to experience both positions.

Activity 4

Characteristics of a Friend

Children at this age have a strong need for approval and acceptance from friends. This activity is intended to help children think about some healthy characteristics that a friend might exhibit. It encourages group cooperation, as students must work with others to successfully complete the activity.

Lesson Explanation and Procedure

(approximate time: 20-30 minutes)

Break class into small groups with three or four students in each. Distribute a copy of the form below to each student (or use it as an example for them to recreate). Students will work with their group to fill in, and rank in order of importance, characteristics of a friend. All members of the group must decide on where to rank each characteristic in order of importance (give students approximately 15 minutes to work within their groups).

Have students complete the rest of the form individually, including evaluating which characteristics which apply to themselves.

Discuss the necessity to compromise when working in a group. Ask students whether they would come up with the same answers if they were working by themselves.

Characteristics of a Friend

Directions

1. As a group, decide what are important characteristics of a friend. List them.
2. As a group, rank the characteristics in order of importance. Put a number 1 next to the characteristic you think is most important, etc.

Characteristics of Friend Describes Me	Ranking	
1. ______________________	______	______
2. ______________________	______	______
3. ______________________	______	______
4. ______________________	______	______
5. ______________________	______	______
6. ______________________	______	______

After the group has completed directions #1 and #2, complete the rest by yourself.

1. Place a check by each characteristic that you feel describes you.
2. If you were to do this activity alone, what changes would you make

____

____

Activity 5

Self-discovery

This activity is intended to help students discover themselves, including strengths and weaknesses. It is important for children to understand that everyone has weaknesses and that nobody can be good at everything. When worked on, weaknesses can serve as challenges to strengthen character.

Lesson Explanation and Procedure

(approximate time: 20-25 minutes)

Have students respond to the following questions. This may either be assigned as homework, or completed in class. Once students have been given an opportunity to complete each question, invite them to share with the class.

1. The one thing that I have done that I am most proud of:
2. My most annoying habit is:
3. A future goal I have is:
4. The dumbest thing I have ever done is:
5. Three things that scare me are:
6. The place where I feel happiest is:
7. My favorite memory is:
8. One of my best qualities is:
9. My favorite people are:

Activity 6

Problem Solving

This activity helps children develop problem solving skills, by giving them an opportunity to practice making decisions.

Lesson Explanation and Procedure

(approximate time: 25 minutes)

Divide the class into small groups. Assign each group a problem to explore, or have each group come up with their own problem. Have each group list some consequences that may result from this problem, as well as some solutions. Have each group list some possible sources of help which they might seek to solve the problem.

Give each student a "What would you do if..." scenario describing a hypothetical problem (see examples below). Ask them to complete each question.

"What Would You Do If..."

A group of your friends were teasing a classmate, and asked you to join in:

What is the Problem (if any): ______________________________

Choices:

1. ______________________________
2. ______________________________
3. ______________________________

Consequences:

1. ______________________________

2. ______________________________
3. ______________________________

Resources:

____

Decision:

____

Your friend asked you to go to his house after school to drink beer:
What is the Problem (if any): ______________________________
Choices:
1. ______________________________
2. ______________________________
3. ______________________________

Consequences:
1. ______________________________
2. ______________________________
3. ______________________________

Resources:

____

Decision:

____

Activity 7

Recognizing and Dealing with Conflict

This activity encourages children to talk about the physical and emotional symptoms associated with conflict, and helps them explore new ways of dealing with it. It helps to develop decision-making skills, and enhances healthy coping skills.

Lesson Explanation and Procedure

(approximate time: 20 minutes)

As large group or small, have students contribute to the definition of the word conflict, as well as some examples. Help students to describe some of the physical symptoms (tight muscles, butterflies in stomach) and emotional symptoms (short temper, irritability, preoccupation) caused by conflict.

Have students choose an issue that might create a conflict, and assist them in exploring ways to deal with it using the following steps to make a reasoned decision.

Identify the conflict: ______________________________
Choices:
1. ______________________________
2. ______________________________
3. ______________________________

Consequences:
1. ______________________________
2. ______________________________
3. ______________________________

Decision:

For homework or during class, have students write a story which includes a conflict, and a way to resolve it.

Activity 8

Refusal Skill Role Plays

Role playing is an entertaining, interactive, and concrete way for children to actually see what various forms of peer pressure looks like, as well as to practice possible techniques to resist it. They can also provide an opportunity for children to practice appropriate behaviors to deal with other problems and conflicts.

It is suggested that role plays be focused on near the end of the unit, since this will enable students to draw upon their knowledge of self-esteem and consequences of drug and alcohol use to analyze each skit.

Lesson Procedure
(approximate time: 10-15 minutes for each skit,
depending on how many students volunteer to participate)

For each of the role play activities, the classroom teacher or group facilitator should introduce each refusal skill with an explanation of the role play to follow. This person should also model each role play by serving as the main actor. After modeling each role play, and achieving the desired outcome, student volunteers should be chosen to serve as actors. Once the role play is begun, it is important to encourage each participant to remain in their roles until the desired outcome is achieved. Each role play is somewhat general and may easily be adapted to become more specific to the needs of a particular class.

After the completion of each role play, the entire class should be invited to comment on the perceived effectiveness of the main actor's behaviors, including suggestions on how the he/she might achieve a more effective outcome. Each play may be repeated to enable multiple students to get a chance to play the main actor.

"Asking for Help"

This skit depicts the main actor asking a friend for advice about an upcoming party at a mutual friend's house. It is expected that there will be alcohol present.

Steps for Main Actor to Follow:

1. Decide what the problem is (be specific as to who and what are contributing to the problem, and what its effect is on you).
2. Decide if you want help with the problem (figure out if you can solve this problem alone).
3. Think about different people who may be able to help you, and pick one.
4. Tell that person about the problem and ask her/him to help.

"Know Your Feelings"

This skit depicts the main actor feeling embarrassed when peers call him/her "chicken" after refusal to use alcohol.

Before beginning this role play, the teacher or facilitator should write the list of possible feelings (see step three) on the board.

Steps for Main Actor to Follow:

1. Tune in to what is going on inside your body to enable you to understand what you are feeling (some examples may be blushing, tight muscles, butterflies in your stomach).
2. Decide what happened to make you feel that way.
3. Decide what the feeling may be (some possibilities include anger, fear, embarrassment, joy, happiness, sadness, disappointment, frustration, anxiety).
4. Think about different ways to express your feeling and pick one (consider healthy ways to express feeling such as talking about it with someone you trust, telling the object of the feeling about it, walking away from the situation, or delaying action).

"Standing Up for Your Rights"

This skit depicts the main actor refusing a friend's request to steal liquor from his/her parents. It attempts to teach students to be assertive, rather than withdrawn or aggressive.

Steps for Main Actor to Follow:

1. Pay attention to what is going on inside of your body to let you know that you are anxious and need to stand up for yourself (remember that some cues might be tight muscles, or butterflies in your stomach).
2. Decide what happened to make you feel this way (some possibilities might be that you being taken advantage of, treated badly, teased).
3. Think about ways you could stand up for yourself (you might try seeking help, or saying how you feel).
4. Choose a direct and reasonable way to stand up for yourself and act on it.

"Responding to Persuasion"

This skit, which was introduced during the original presentation, depicts the main actor dealing with a good friend's high-pressure argument to try drugs. It attempts to help students learn to distinguish their values from those of their peers.

Steps for Main Actor to Follow:

1. Listen to the other person's ideas on the topic.
2. Decide what you think about it (distinguish your ideas from the ideas of others).
3. Compare what he/she said with what you think (remember that your idea about the topic is just as, or more, valid than the other person's).
4. Decide which idea you agree with and tell the other person (you might agree, disagree, postpone a decision, or suggest an alternative idea).

Activity 9

Attitudes About Alcohol

This activity gives students an opportunity to learn to identify some personal and societal attitudes about alcohol.

Lesson Explanation and Procedure

Prepare for this activity by asking students to list the first three words that come to mind when they think of alcohol (it may be helpful to assure the students that the list is only for themselves to see, as they may answer more honestly).

For homework, encourage students to view two television commercials and to collect at least two magazine advertisements for alcoholic beverages, to prepare them to discuss the attitudes about alcohol use as portrayed in the media (some common observations may be that it makes one look macho, sophisticated, happy, powerful). Have students get in to small groups. Within each group, have students create two collages of alcohol advertisements, one which promotes the use of alcohol, and one which shows the dangers. Have students discuss and evaluate the information in both collages (because there are very few ads depicting the dangers of alcohol, you might begin discussion by asking which collage has more ads, and why).

Activity 10

Perceptions

This brief activity is meant to emphasize the fact that alcohol and drugs alter moods. They do not solve our problems or change the situations in which we find ourselves, but merely change our perceptions.

Lesson Procedure

Select a student volunteer to stand anywhere in the classroom and describe what he sees while looking straight ahead. Ask this student to move to various places around the classroom, and continue to describe what she sees. Invite other students to speculate about what the purpose of this activity is (Only the view, or perception, of the volunteer student has changed. Everything in the room remain the same).

Activity 11

Student Journals

For those of you who don't already, have your students keep daily or weekly journals. This is an effective way to get to know a child, and to make him feel important when you respond to his journal writings. It is also effective in helping students to express their feelings.

Lesson Procedure

Stress to students that journals will be kept confidential, with only the student and teacher reading them. Also encourage honesty, with the understanding that there are no "right" or "wrong" answers. Use some of the examples listed below as journal topics for your students. Choose them randomly, or decide on an order that works for you.

- If I could have one wish it would be:
- My favorite TV show is: Because:
- The hardest part of school for me:
- The worst thing about being me is:
- I get angry when:
- I feel sad when:
- My best friend:
- I hate it when:
- I love to:
- The best thing about being me is:
- The other students in this class:
- If I were the teacher I would:
- I like to be with people who:
- I am a good friend because:
- When I grow up I want to:
- I don't like people who:
- The best part of school:
- I wish I could change:
- I feel scared when:
- I am happiest when:
- When I get home I:

Suggested Outline of Activities for University Facilitators

I. *Introduction of Facilitator(s) and Program*

II. *Questions*

1. Distribute blank sheets of paper to each student, and explain that they may write down any questions they might have about the issues discussed. Stress that they need not use names, in hopes that they will feel more safe to ask questions.
2. Explain that you will collect all of the papers, with or without questions, near the end of the program (this helps to maintain anonymity of students who ask questions in the event that there are few asked).

III. *Role Plays*

1. Create transition to this activity by asking questions which probe student exposure to drugs and alcohol, in a way that is non-threatening (e.g. Ask how many students have friends, or acquaintances who have experimented with alcohol).
2. Set up the "Responding to Persuasion" role play, located below, in which students respond to pressure from a friend to try drugs or alcohol. Continue with role plays until every interested student gets a chance to participate.

IV. *Brainstorming*

1. Ask students to name some reasons why people drink or use drugs, while writing their responses on the board. Stress that there are no "right" or "wrong" answers.

2. After you have received several responses, divide the class into small groups of three to five students.
3. Assign each group to narrow the list of reasons from the board into the five which they think are most common. Also ask them to come with five alternatives to using drugs or alcohol.
4. Have each group share their lists, while you tally up the total of votes for each reason on the board (the most common responses are usually related to peer pressure, escapism, and curiosity).
5. After the tally is complete, draw students' attention to each of the top five most frequent reasons which pertain to issues of self-esteem (e.g. peer pressure and escapism both easily tie in with self-esteem). Ask students how each reason might be affected by the way a person feels about themself.
6. Ask students if they have ever heard of self-esteem. Ask them what it is and what it involves (supplementing additional information if necessary).
7. Tie the idea of self-esteem into the choices a person makes.

V. *Questions and Answers (time permitting)*

VI. *Concluding Comments*

REFERENCES (for the suggested activities)

Borba, Michele.(1989). Esteem Builders: A K-8 Self-Esteem Curriculum for Improving Student Achievement, Behavior and School Climate. Rolling Hills Estates, CA: P Jalmar Press.

California Task Force to Promote Self-Esteem and Personal and Social Responsibility.(1990). Towards A State of Esteem: The Final Report of the California Task Force to Promote Self-Esteem and Personal and Social Responsibility.

Channing L. Bete Co.(1983). What You Should Know About Self-Esteem. South Deerfield, MA: What You Should Know Video.

Clemes, Harris, Bean, Reynold, and Clark, Aminah.(1990). How to Raise Teenagers' Self-esteem. Los Angeles: Price Stern Sloan.

Gerne, Timothy A., and Gerne Patricia J.(1986). Substance Abuse Prevention Activities For Elementary Children. New Jersey: Prentice-Hall

Goldstein, A.P., Reagles, K.W., and Amann, L.L.(1990). Refusal Skills: Preventing Drug Use In Adolescents. Champaign, IL: Research Press.

Kirschebaum, H., and Glasser, B.(1982). Skills for Living, Second Edition. Columbus, Ohio: Quest National Center.

Stauffer, Gary A., and Alvarez, Tony.(1992). Personalized Prevention Training. Unpublished Manuscript.

Chapter 7

AN AFTER-SCHOOL TUTORING PROJECT
Planning, Change and a Working Model

By Joan Scott and Carmen Wells

Introduction

The Tutoring Project began as a community-university partnership based in the housing project. Three years later, it shifted location to become school-based, while still serving the same children.

We have included a discussion of our initial planning process, the challenges faced and some important implications of the change in location, and the "working model" for 1993. Also attached are suggested games and activities. Carmen Wells, student coordinator in 1993, authored the model and activities sections; Joan Scott, Project Community staff, provided initial history and the discussion of project evolution.

History of the Project
Phase 1—Planning

Why and when a new community service project in a service-learning program begins is a matter of three important factors that come together to provide an opportunity. Sometimes the idea can be in the mind of a program staff person or a student for a long time, but until at least two of the pieces come together, it isn't likely to happen. It could be forced, but it would not have an authenticity that I believe is necessary when working with communities. The factors sound simple: 1) a need expressed by the community, 2) the human resources ("volunteers") who desire to be hooked up to help meet that need and provide the service, and 3) the financial and staff support, both at the community end and the college or university end to keep the project afloat.

The Community

The Hikone-Angell School After School Tutoring Project began with a call in August of 1985 from a social worker working with residents at a low-income housing project on the city's southeast side. She and a co-worker, incorporated as a two-person agency (hereafter referred to F.S.S.), were attempting to develop on a shoestring budget a program of community supports where none had previously existed. The city had given them the use of one housing unit as a "community center." One expressed desire was an afterschool program for kids. The children at Hikone needed academic support and friendly "role model" mentoring. They were already struggling for school success, and in Fall of '86 they were going to be bussed to a school in a neighborhood of university-related professionals, as part of a major school district restructuring plan at the elementary level. The other minority children at the new school were mostly from families of international university students. The particular housing project was also known in the mid 80's as a place where drug trafficking was a problem and families were at risk. Could we help? Could we find students who would commit to weekly contact with the children and to assist with school work? The shape of the program was yet to be developed. Yes, we were interested. Being in on the ground floor of the planning provided an opportunity for us to build, with community input, something that was tailored to community needs.

The Volunteers

Piece two fell into place almost concurrently. The social worker put me in touch with one of their volunteers, Tom[1], a Resident Advisor at a large dorm on campus. Bursely Hall was beginning to develop an interest in and structure for promoting student volunteering. Tom thought he could get Bursely students involved at Hikone. The dorm leadership and housing office saw community service as a tool for building connections and community within the dorm, as well as a means of contributing to the community. The social workers, Tom and I agreed that it would be wise to devise a pilot service program for Fall term, not connected to our for-credit seminar program, planning to add it to our credit options in Winter term. Volunteers would be drawn from Bursely Hall. It would become a dorm project. Holding the seminar in the dorm would be an added attraction.

Supports

Now piece three was worked on. The support structures existed through our office, the support from the dorm council, and the social workers. A little money was available; transportation to the site was "creatively" arranged. Logistics were worked out.

Planning Together

Over the next several months, Hikone residents, Bursely residents, the social workers, and our office all shared in shaping the first year's program. Dreams had to become realistic goals. The residents and social workers dreamed of a four day per week after school program. Tutoring would be part of it, but not too narrowly defined. The parents expressed the most concern about getting help with school work; social workers and I cautioned about the need for keeping the atmosphere relaxed and "not school-like," and for incorporating and accommodating the need for active movement and play. Some monies were available to F.S.S. through the Housing Commission and the city for supplies and resources.

During the Fall pilot, 6 Bursley students worked with twelve students from the project twice weekly, with some assistance from a social work intern working with F.S.S. Tom coordinated the University students' involvement. The Bursley students carpooled (somewhat of a problem) on their own to the site. The children targeted were school-aged. They arrived from school by 4:00, stopping at home long enough to leave school things before coming to the

Center unit. Following a period of settling down, announcements, and "playing around," the tutors and children focused on homework or skill building. About 5:30 food was brought out- a light meal provided as part of city grant funding.

As we planned for the Winter term, with the goal of offering course credit for this project as part of our Sociology 389 umbrella program, a series of issues were considered. Some were site and service related and some pertained to the learning goals for the Project Community students. All concerned principles of good practice for service learning.

1) Who would facilitate the weekly seminars and coordinate the site activities? Project Community's methodology and philosophy is significantly different from traditional courses. Fellow students attend weekly support and preparations sessions in order to prepare for this leadership role. Tom had not considered himself in that role, but with a co-coordinator from the Bursely R.A. staff to share the responsibility, he agreed.

2) What course readings and approach were appropriate and how did this fit academically with what we were already doing? Fortunately, this new project could fit reasonably well into the orientation and structure of the already existing sociology-of-education grouping of projects and coursepack. (More broadly defined, it might have just as well been oriented toward "youth at risk" issues.)

3) The Hikone youth in the program were all children of color. How crucial would it be to recruit University students of color into the program? How might we maximize the number of students of color from Bursely? Although the social workers assured us that help is help and that the color of the students was not a primary issue for themselves, the kids, or the parents, we all recognized that there were very compelling reasons to have Black tutors involved. The issue was not just about what happened at site, and whether people could relate, but also how experience had shaped the understandings and assumptions of the white upper middle class students, and how that would need to be balanced and challenged in discussion sessions. Tom sought the help of the dorm M.P.A.'s (Minority Peer Advisors) with getting the word out in the dorm, and we allowed for an informal goal of balance in the racial makeup of the group. (Note: in credit-bearing courses, one can not make race an "official" criteria for admission to a course.)

4) As mentioned above, Bursely instituted an emphasis on involvement of its residents in service, and developed several options for projects they could do together. All except the Hikone Project carried no course credit. Would we be competing with them for students, or would the offering of course credit and reflection opportunity be a significant draw? Would we mix for-credit and not-for-credit students in the Hikone project? What effect on coordination would that have? Would "volunteers" be required to attend seminars for the planning and community building and group process goals? We decided that last was

very important, particularly as service might be affected. Since the site had multiple needs, and program dreams, the compromise was to channel the "just volunteers" to other times with younger children, supervised solely by the staff of F.S. S. If we could not sign up a minimum of 12 students for the course (maximum 14, dictated more by the manageable size of seminars and transportation logistics than site need) we would work out a way to include several "volunteers" in the reflection and planning components of seminars.

5) Next, we explored transportation options. Although Project Community leases vehicles every term for project use, with cost for that partly covered by a lab fee, we could not make available two wagons twice a week at the needed time that year. Creative networking on the part of the F. S. S. staff resulted in an agreement that a van in use by another community center would also transport our students one of the two days. Back-up was Tom's car. (Since few first and second year students who live in dorms have cars, relying on student vehicles is not a good option.)

6) How would decisions about service issues be made, and by whom? This was clearly a collaboration, and the Bursely students, the site staff, the Project Community staff person, and the Hikone parents all valued the shared decision-making. However, it needed to be clear that the people on site—the F.S.S. staff and their parent consultants, had the final say about what was happening on their site. Our student coordinators needed to develop with the F.S. S. staff a system for ongoing evaluation and communication. We could suggest, offer, and work, but in the spirit of community empowerment, we were guests in their community, serving their needs.

Phase 2—Implementation

For the next three terms, approximately 14 students went to Hikone twice weekly as part of the service-learning tutoring project.The format remained similar to the pilot term. A wonderful spin-off was that one of our early coordinators remained involved with Hikone as a volunteer, recruiting and coordinating students to be involved without course credit in a big brother/big sister program and in a morning pre-school care program. Students who enrolled in our after school project and made a commitment to one of these as well were eligible for an additional course credit.

Orientation

The preparation our students received for the project. They needed orientation not only to learn tutoring strategies and resources (enough at least to feel comfortable), but also to address the following questions: Who are these children? What is their life like? What are my assumptions about them and what are their assumptions about me? The F.S.S. staff and a Hikone parent visited the seminar to help explore these issues. The support of the Principal of the elementary school, who participated in an on-site orientation of our students was a definite plus. Her enthusiasm and obvious interest in the children, indicated by her visit to the housing project, showed the children and tutors that they mattered. She stayed in touch with the F.S.S. staff about the needs of the children, and arranged for potential teacher contact for our U of M tutors.

Linking with Residents

As part of preparation, our U of M students visited the children's homes, meeting the parents or guardians of the children they would be tutoring. The goal was establishing trust and gaining the commitment of the parents to the program. After all, 14 students would be coming into the neighborhood at least twice a week. We wanted both residents and students to be comfortable. Many tutors developed the habit of dropping in to say hello if a parent or a sibling was home, or if the child did not show up at the Center.

Initial problems and challenges

Success creates it's own problems. By the end of the second full term of work at Hikone, our coordinators had identified several related concerns:

1) Too many people were crowding into the small rooms of the unit. The twelve tutors often felt overwhelmed by 25 or more kids, who were easily distracted by each other. Although the original plan called for working with school-aged children, four and five year olds were coming with older sibs to the center. Their needs presented a different agenda. Attempts made to limit their access during this time, or to assign a site staff intern to be with them, were not truly successful. They wanted to be included with big sibs. In the second year, partly to relieve space pressure, the junior high students in the group were tutored at their school instead of at Hikone. The tutors working with those students were dropped off by those going to Hikone, and then later rode the late school bus with their tutees to Hikone to join their colleagues. This was more efficient use of space and tutoring time; the challenge was keeping those tutors feeling connected with the Hikone community and with what their friends were doing.

2) There were insufficient tables, chairs and supplies for kids and tutors. The coordinators and site staff raised money for supplies from Bursely students brainstormed sources of furniture, and reorganized supply space.

3) The project lacked sufficient space for group games and large muscle activity, which challenged the coping skills of children and tutors alike. Children became restless and sought ways to let off energy. In good weather, outside space was used in the few warm months of the year.

4) Because of conflicting needs for Project Community cars, transportation for tutors continued to challenge creativity. Some tutors met their charges at the elementary school, which was within walking distance of campus, and rode with them on the school bus to Hikone. Another carload drove. The ride back had to be in shifts. The tutors commented

that while riding the bus with 40 yelling kids was not joy, the experience gave our tutors a sense of what the children take in daily as they ride through well-to-do neighborhoods on the way to the relative poverty of Hikone.

Initial Joys

The community was extremely receptive of the university students, welcoming them into their homes and their space. The community had felt isolated; they welcomed just about any interactions the college students offered to their children, but were particularly glad to see their kids getting academic support. The children, though not always easy to work with, rewarded the tutors as children do, with affection and small bursts of accomplishments. School staff indicated that they felt that the time spent on schoolwork was well spent, and they saw the value in the special attention received. The investment of the Coordinators and many of the students was phenomenal: several stayed involved with our project or the community, on site, for the remainder of their college career. As mentioned above, the personal involvement of the Bursely students led to the establishment of a couple of additional volunteer options at Hikone.

Phase 3—Major Changes The Project "Matures"

Almost simultaneously, two changes with lasting effects occurred. In summer of 1987, the F.S.S. social workers negotiated with the new Principal of the children's elementary school to have the after-school tutoring program take place at the school rather than at Hikone. Though the decision certainly made sense for many reasons, we at Project Community were taken by surprise, having had no part in that decision. Alternative solutions to space problems might have been explored. Two local churches are within easy walking distance of Hikone, for example. In the Fall, the partnership between the social workers dissolved, and a new organization, Community Action Network, (CAN) emerged under the leadership of one of the two. There were effects and implications from both events worth considering, though the first was by far most important.

Although the split between the partners of F.S.S. was difficult for the organization and its funders, and the persons involved, their commitment to the community did not waiver. Our Coordinators were not privy to the problems, but knew that there were some. To the credit of those involved, our staff was not drawn in. The agency's programs were able to be continued or rebuilt. We mention it here simply to illustrate that it is possible for service collaborations to weather agency storms and transformations as long as one's mission stays fairly clear. The chief impact on the after school tutoring program was that the shift in leadership of the agency meant adjusting to new lines of communication and to a more organized style.

The place change ultimately changed the nature of the program, not so much in the time spent with the children, but in conceptual ways. It changed the nature of the partnership. It is important to understand that life rarely stay the same and that history can provide a basis for insight. Whether based in the home community of the children or in the school, the project can be excellent, but acknowledgably different in some important ways. We feel that it is helpful to planners to be aware of the implications of the difference.

The benefits of using a school building, with a supportive Principal were immediate. We had far more usable work space in which to spread out. The number of children was controlled, since only those who enrolled with parent permission were present after school. Access to the children's teachers was, at least theoretically, easier. A cart of age-appropriate learning resources and learning games was available, organized by the Principal. Transportation became a non-issue, as tutors walked to the school. Finally, the Principal, and theoretically, teacher resource persons, would be more available for the orientation and training of tutors. From the perspective of the CAN staff, the shift also freed up the use of the small community center for other pressing needs two afternoons a week.

However, as it became school based, the locus of authority and control changed for the Project Community students and the connection to the community. In addition, a valued part of the original conception and intention-the direct input of the parents of the children being served—disappeared from our point of view. It could be argued that it was still present, but it is filtered through other school structures and processes.

The program became subject to the expectations of the Principal, as she became the person through whom we worked. As a school-based program, the buck stopped with her over use of space and equipment, discipline, supervision, and how time was appropriately spent. The tutoring project needed to conform to certain limitations and expectations. At our end, the question, "whose program is this?" had to be thought about. Coordinator's and Project Community staff's roles, scope of authority, and communication lines had to be adjusted. Within a year of the change, Hikone staff and parents were no longer present at group planning and evaluation meetings with the Principal, Project Community coordinators and staff. Eventually, though they still served as liaison with the families of the children in the program, Hikone staff were not known to the university students. For Project community staff, coordinators, and tutors, a sense of distance from the Hikone community and the lives the children led beyond school crept in. In stark contrast to the intense involvement with the community of the early years, our students began to raise critical questions about the separation.

The place shift altered funding sources as well, since School District and city Recreation and Education monies were available for some supplemental, after school on-site programs such as this. One result of this was that in the Fall of 1991, we were informed that a Recreation and Education employee, supervised centrally from outside the school but working in consultation with the Principal, was available on site as the link between the school and the tutoring program. She was to assist with logistics and with managing the children. While this seemed helpful and was seen as needed by the Principal, particularly since she could not always be in the building, it initially created a confusing overlap in roles. It also had potential to diminish the authority of the coordinators and university students, and their sense of investment until communication and responsibilities and roles were clarified.

A third major change occurred when momentum for the project fizzled out as a Bursely dorm project in the third or fourth year, and it began to be advertised for open enrollment along with other Project Community open sections. This change had two consequences. First, if there were no interventions (and some terms there were none), the make-up of the tutor group reflected the makeup of the university, that is, mostly white. Second, the jump-start to a sense of community and friendship that was possible when students shared a dorm community was no longer present. Both situations required thoughtful attention each year.

Between the Fall of 1987, when the program moved to the school, and the present, approximately fourteen children each term have been in the program, some for three or four years. In many cases, siblings followed big brothers and sisters. Formats have been experimented with, but the basic structure of snack, group time and individual time has not altered a great deal. Improvements have been made from experience and specific combinations of needs. The following section details the structure and happenings of the successful 1993 Winter term, which we and the school staff think can provide a good benchmark for the future.

A Coordinator's Perspective Introduction—Overview of the Program

The Angell After-School Tutoring Project matched upper level elementary students, third, fourth and fifth graders, from Angell School with University of Michigan students who elected to participate in this project. The age of the elementary students was particularly chosen because they were approaching middle school and would especially benefit by the goals of this program. Throughout the Ann Arbor Public School District, there have been continual projects implemented to improve the learning skills of children who are more at risk of losing interest and falling behind in school. A program such as the tutoring project can help these targeted children. One of Project Community's goals was to help children who are at-risk to develop necessary academic and social skills which will stay with them in the future. Our hope is that this program will increase the level of development for these children.

Throughout the many stages of planning and implementing this program, some key factors were kept in mind. These factors included: the time frame which we had available (how far can an hour and a half session be stretched, who these children are)—their specific needs to which the program has to be sensitive, and after-school arrangements (what time the bus comes, what other programs will be sharing the school or the bus with these children in this program). Some of these issues may seem small, but thinking of the dynamics of the program and what outside variables will affect the children involved are important to keep in mind when planning for success.

Because this is a course within UM, Project Community was almost guaranteed that the university students who elected to participate would have an interest in this service project as well as its sociological aspect to education. So many of these tutors became a part of this program because they wanted to help the community. One problem arose because most of these students had not worked with elementary children in this capacity. Many did not know how to handle certain situations unique to a program of this nature, for example conflict management relative to these children. This needed consideration when we planned tutor orientation.

Project Community does not help with the selection of children; the Principal of Angell School ultimately decides which children should be in the program. They are selected either by parental request, student request, or through the recommendation of the teacher or the Principal. All parties were concerned for potential problems in labeling the children, for example, singling these kids out from the other elementary students.

Set-up of the Program

The overall design of the program has not changed dramatically over years. Parts have been altered to make the sessions run more smoothly, address needs, and to enhance the learning of the students. Following is a breakdown of the major areas of the tutoring project with a brief description of the operations. These areas include orientation of the tutors, goals and duties, the initial meeting between the tutors and the children, the daily structure of the semester, how the building was used and new implementations.

Orientation/Training

Although orientations have occurred each term, we realized that they could be improved. The UM students needed more of a sense of who these children were and what could be done to enhance their learning. The Principal felt that there needed to be more of a structure to the children's learning activities and a more extensive training of the tutors. In the Winter term 1993, the tutor training was a two or three session orientation. It included a breakdown of the roles and expectations of the tutors as well as time to do some lesson planning and goal setting for the term. During this time the students were coached, or "trained", on how to be effective tutors for these children. This sometimes proved difficult. While these were university students fully capable of listening and taking in the information, the implementation would not occur until the tutors and Angell students worked face to face, and all found that practice and adjustment is what really makes the difference.

The coordinator of the tutoring program, along with the director, took responsibility for putting the initial in-service together. Also during this time, the Principal of the school as well as the coordinator of the Ann Arbor Public Schools After-School Program for Angell School were involved and spoke to the tutors about what their expectations were, gave helpful suggestions, and answered questions. Also during this inservice, time was allotted to develop program planning, structure educational games and to determine the personal goals and expectations of each tutor.

Basically it was a situation where the coordinators provided the tutors with the information, encouraged them to draw on their own resources, and had faith that, with action and reflection, a successful and rewarding program could be implemented.

Goals and Duties

One element of orientation was the development of realistic goals, which would be carried out throughout the term of the project. These goals were based around the needs and safety of the students, the expectations of the tutors and the level of emphasis that was placed on academics. Some of the more basic goals were as follows: to provide learning resources for the children, to help them improve study and organization skills—including planning for short and long-term assignments, to improve confidence levels of student to promote better learning, to encourage all actions to be carefully thought out, and to encourage cooperative behavior at all times.

The goals were designed to fit within the boundaries of the tutors' and coordinators' roles for the program. As mentioned previously, the elementary students are chosen or recommended to be in this program through a number of channels: their specific teacher, their parents or the Principal of Angell School. Generally, these are children who have a lot of needs, but there has been a mix of students depending on who the program is thought to help. Angell, because of its location near a major university, caters to a number of diverse families who are drawn to the community for either educational or employment purposes. Many of the children from these families tend to be directed into programs such as this.

The university tutors have to commit to three hours of site experience each week. They are also expected to attend another hour and a half of seminar time in order to fulfill part of the course requirements. The other credit requirements include weekly journals, full participation in seminar, and a comprehensive term paper integrating the sociological aspects of this program discussed throughout the term. At the beginning of the term, attendance is strongly stressed for the UM students as well as the Angell students in order to build a strong mentorship bond between the two groups.

The First Meeting with the Students

The project was set up to let the Angell students benefit from the UM tutors as much as possible. At the beginning of the term, each elementary student in the program was given the opportunity to have a voice in the child-tutor match-up process by socializing with all of the tutors, then indicating what their three choices of potential tutors were and who they would like to work with for the remainder of the semester. We chose the system of matching the specific children up with the university student of their choice rather than randomly pairing up the tutors and students, because it gave the students a feeling of control of the situation. In the majority of cases, the students received either their first or second choice. This outcome worked to affect the development of a positive mentorship relationship between tutor and elementary student.

The above process was done at the end of an informal get-acquainted session with the university student tutors and the Angell students. The majority of the session included introductions, icebreakers, and shared information about the expectations and excitements for the semester. Holding the session in the school's auditorium gave the program good space for some moving around and gave the students an opportunity to really get to know the tutors.

Sample Agenda

The following is the time agenda of a typical day at Angell After-School Tutoring:

3:15—the tutors arrive ready to meet the children when the school bell rings for dismissal
3:25—the school bell rings, the tutors are waiting for their students at the door of the school when they come down from their classrooms.
3:30-3:45—snack and one on one social interaction with
their tutor in either the Art (designated homework) Room or the Computer Room.
3:45-4:25—tutoring, either the homework room or the computer room
4:30-4:55—group game
4:55—clean up and get ready to leave.

The schedule remained pretty much the same throughout the semester and the whole group felt it was a comfortable schedule to follow. It was also flexible enough to allow a student-tutor team to skip the group game in order to finish homework or to solve a conflict with another student. The important thing to remember is that there is only an hour and a half to work with twice a week. The priority is to make the most of the time.

In order to form the two groups which determined where to study and learn for the day, the Angell students were for the most part split up equally, with a few exceptions. These exceptions were made when certain students distracted others or school teachers gave out assigned homework at the beginning or the end of the week. They were also split up in order to cut down on overcrowding in one specific area and to give the tutors enough room to effectively work with their student.

The program is fortunate to have access to a good portion of the school. In addition, Angell School provides supplies such as paper and pencils and access to the library for added learning. With the ample work space as well as the supplies provided, students were able to accomplish much of their school work without the problems of being interrupted by other children.

There were twelve students selected to be in the program this past Winter term 1993. The students were divided up into two separate groups. Half did homework on one day while the other half participated in educational computer games. The school's art room was designated as the homework room and there were two school computer rooms. If a tutor and student team were assigned to either homework or computers for the day, they were to report to their respective room for that day. On the second day of the week, the two groups switched assignments; if group one was in the homework room on Tuesday, they were assigned to the computer room for the Thursday of the same week and vice versa. Exceptions were made for those who had homework due to their teacher at different times of the week.

For the second half of the session, the group came together and played educational whole group games, which the tutors were responsible for formulating. These games were based on math, spelling or logical problem solving and also group interaction. We spent a good part of our time improving the students' skills in working with a team. These games gave us a good opportunity to stress this area.

As a side note, students were highly encouraged to participate in the group games, but if a situation arose where students needed extra time to finish a homework assignment, the student and tutor team were exempt from the game time. A student was not excused for things such as free play with their tutor or another student. This group-time was just as important as the homework time and participants of the program knew that all of the activities were required.

Use of Angell School Facilities

Angell Elementary School was a good location for the link with the university; it was within walking distance from central campus and easy for the tutors to get there. Because the program took place after school hours, the project had access to many of the school's resources. One good resources was the library which the children were allowed access to for free reading as well as the use of resource books for their homework. Additional rooms included both of their computer rooms, the art room (which was used for study/ homework time), and the main auditorium.

All of the mentioned rooms worked well for our purposes, and there was always the option of extra quiet study space at empty tables in the upper level hallways. This after-school time period also allowed for the tutor and their Angell student to have close contact with some of the teachers, if they were in the school building during that time. The teachers were always a good resource for homework-specific questions and occasional discipline problems. Teachers never turned down a tutor's 'cry for help' during the sessions.

When a child had difficulty settling down, or disrupted their own work and other children around them, discipline became a problem. This happened many times throughout the semester, and the conflict was handled either by the tutor of the particular child or by the coordinator. We stressed the importance of the tutors initiating the responsibility to resolve conflict with the students whom they were working with, mainly to establish respect between the tutor and the student. If the elementary student was unresponsive to the tutor's attempt, then the coordinator, the teacher, or even the Principal stepped in for additional support. Many times the problem could be solved without the additional support.

Secluded places were available to resolve conflict within the school. In addition, the tutors had access to some of the teachers who were more readily available during this time.

New Implementations

With every new year there were suggestions to make the program more effective. This past term was no exception. Next, you will see some of the new ideas which were tried in order to improve the Winter 1993 Tutoring Project. Later, you will see what the tutors and coordinators of that term suggested for the following year. I hope they all can be of some help in building your program.

At the beginning of the term, some new procedures were implemented in order to bring more continuity to the tutoring project and to help with the enhanced learning of the students. These included an added staff position to the project and different targeted training for the tutors. In addition, the training sessions were revamped, which was outlined previously.

Initially, the Principal of Angell handled the duties of shopping for the snacks and the coordinator was the liaison to Angell School staff. Because of developments within Community Recreation and Education, an adjunct of the

Ann Arbor Public Schools, a support staff person was hired to fill this role and relieve the coordinator from those duties. During the Winter Term 1993, I filled the role of coordinator and building supervisor at the same time while also freeing the Principal from shopping for snacks. I had been the building supervisor in the Fall 1992 term and smoothly made the transition to both positions the following term.

This was very convenient and allowed the lines of communication to be more open than in years past. The building supervisor and the coordinator, being joint roles, opened the avenues for freedom within the program that would not have been possible if there were more staff members involved. In addition to the dual roles of the new coordinator, another duty was to design the "improved" training session for the university students, along with the director of the project.

Many of these University tutors were inexperienced with elementary school-aged children, and needed greater sensitivity when working with children from multiethnic backgrounds. We needed to incorporate specific targeted training around these issues at the beginning of the term as well as throughout the semester. This was to help erase some of the boundaries which would have kept a distance between a tutor and student from different backgrounds.

Because most of these children are of color, primarily African American and Latino American, and because of the majority of the tutors were European American, the coordinator and the administration had to recognize this situation as potentially problematic and to try to work with the issue before a conflict developed. However, conflicts did arise and were dealt with on a one-to-one basis.

Educational Games

The purpose of designated game time was to help develop the students' social and listening skills while building academic skills through challenging games. I asked the tutors to develop educational games to play with the students during the group game time. For the most part the games were new and challenging to the students and highly enjoyed by them. We even had requests by the students to play the games during one-on-one time with their tutors.

Following are some of the games the tutors formulated which highly motivated the students academically and socially. These are only a few of the great games which my tutors developed on their own either from scratch or by modifying other traditional games. I encourage you to try these games with young students. In my group they proved to be successful in teaching both classroom content and group skills.

Children's Jeopardy!

The group is divided into two teams. On the board, a Jeopardy! board is drawn, with four category headings and five point slots below. We assigned equal points to each slot, for we felt if we made the questions progressively more difficult, some children would find it unfair. (This is the best method to use if the children are of differing ability levels). We used the categories of spelling, math, history, and miscellaneous trivia. Each team sends one contestant to the board at a time. Each team takes turns choosing which category to receive the question from. A category is chosen and a question is read. The contestant who answers the questing correctly earns points for their team. The game progresses along in this manner until all the slots under each heading have been solved. If a question is asked and neither contestant can answer, neither team gets the points. The team with the most points after all the questions have been asked wins the game. This game provides children with practice in spelling, math and other subjects, in an entertaining fashion.

Spelling Game

—This game is designed for students to learn and spell words that have particular characteristics such as a common beginning or prefix, ending or letter(s).

—Groups of three or four students will probably work best. Each team requires at least one student to have pencil and paper to write down the words given by the team. Students must be reminded that they are working as a team: they must share their answers but not give them away to the opposing team. The members of the team are required to make sure that the words are spelled correctly by the recorder.

—The game begins when the moderator gives the category. For example:

List words that begin with the letters “sp”.

—space, spoon, spiral, spank, spell...

List words that end with the letters “ing”.

—running, crying, writing, sitting, talking...

List words that have the letter “z”.

—zoo, zebra, buzz, ooze, zip...

—Teams can be given a time limit of two to three minutes.

—When time is up, the moderator checks the spelling of each team’s list and crosses off any misspelled words. Any words that appear on more than one team’s list are also crossed off so that the each team has a unique list of words.

—Each team is given one point for each word on their final list granted that a person from each team can spell a chosen word from that team’s list of words. The word is chosen by the moderator and spelled by the team’s appointed speller. If the word is not spelled correctly, then the team receives only half of the number of words on their list in points.

—The game continues for as many categories as desired.

—Other suggestions for the categories are:

—those with double letters: three, mess, nun, that...

—those with triple letters or more: beginning, Alabama...

—beginnings: BL, BR, CH, CL, GR, RE, SN, ST, SP, TH

—endings: ED, LY, S

—letters: QU, W, X, Z

Scattergories

This game went very well, with little running about, and the kids seemed to enjoy it a lot. It is fairly simple, and can be expanded quite easily to take up more time.

The way we played:

—The students are divided into equal groups (we had three groups of four).
—Each group is given a list of the categories (I have included the categories we used), and a sheet of paper.
—A letter (also included) is drawn and written on the board. The teams then have 3 minutes to write down a word for each category that begins with the letter drawn.
—When 3 minutes is up, each team tallies up how many words they got (a tutor to each team is a good way to keep it fair) and totals are written on the board (one point for each word).
—Continue with next list in the same manner. The team that has the most points win.

The game took about 20 minutes to play, but could be expanded to a half hour or 35 minutes by:
—having individual teams read their answers aloud to the whole group or
—creating one or two more lists of categories for a couple more rounds.

1. A boy's name
2. Cities
3. Things that are cold
4. School supplies
5. Pro sports teams
6. Breakfast foods
7. TV shows
8. Vegetables
9. States
10. Things you throw away

1. Jobs
2. Cartoon characters
3. Things you drink
4. Musical groups
5. Desserts
6. Things on a map
7. Athletes
8. Things in a refrigerator
9. Farm animals
10. Things at a beach

1. Colors
2. Sports
3. Song titles
4. Birds
5. A girl's name
6. Things in a kitchen
7. Villains/Monsters
8. School subjects
9. Excuses for being late
10. Ice cream flavors

Evaluation of the Project

With a program such as this it is often difficult to know right away whether it was successful. In other words, how do we know that what we did had an effect on the children, either positive or negative? Has it really made a difference, for any of these children, to participate in this program? As I said, this is a difficult question to answer but there may be a number of key indicators and people to consult with who may take the guess work out of this.

One indicator would be whether the children are happy participating in the program. Over the course of this past term, there were a few students who grew to dislike the program and constantly disrupted the rest of the students. Behavior like this was not tolerated, so after we knew that they genuinely did not want to be a part of the program, they were let go; however, most students were happy there. Another indicator of whether a child was benefiting from the program was if they made efforts to learn by either listening to the directions of their tutor, or actively participating in problem solving homework assignments. Many times when these two guidelines were not followed by the student, this usually showed a lack of interest in the program.

Among the consultants are the Principal of Angell School, the teachers of the participating students, the parents, and of course the Angell students themselves. But how can this group of people be key indicators? They can give feedback necessary, both positive and negative, in addition to constructive advice given by the educators in the school, and based on this information, we can determine the success of the program; it was definitely a success for most students.

At the end of the program, there was time for the Angell students as well as the tutors to complete evaluations to help us improve the project for the coming terms. There was an opportunity to gain feedback from the elementary students and the UM tutors, as well as the coordinator of the program, the director of the program and the Principal of Angell School. From all of these inputs, the message was clear; this program was much needed and appreciated and efforts should be put forth to continue the program.

Reflections

The basic structure of this program was developed over a number of years to be custom built to the specific needs of the Angell students. Some of these needs included maintaining a 1:1 tutor-student ratio, providing undivided attention to each student, and moving the program from the Hikone Housing Project to Angell school in order to have access to greater work space and learning tools such as the computers, the classrooms and the library. Of course, the needs of Angell students may not be the same as other elementary students, so it is necessary for each different program to look closely at its unique dynamics to develop a program that suits the specific needs of their children.

Throughout the year, I have been involved with the project, there has been an enormous push to take into account the needs of each child and shift the program accordingly to accommodate them. This push is characteristic within all of the administration—the Principal, the director, as well as within myself as the building supervisor and finally as the coordinator. We all have a common goal of increasing the childrens' education.

In addition to meeting the needs of the students, the Angell Project had administrative needs to be met. These included providing university students with an opportunity to work in a community tutoring program for course credit, teaching these college students the dynamics of the American educational system—hands on—from a sociological perspective, and providing the tutors with a seminar to discuss the connections which were made between the two. All of these factors needed to be taken into account. Again, the main focus was to meet the needs of the children as well as the needs of the administration.

Many hours have been spent at the beginning of each semester, as well as throughout, to improve the project. This has been for well over ten years and new implementations are still occurring. That gives you an idea of the amount of time and energy that is put into a program of this nature for the benefit of young students. Be aware that developing a tutoring program will not happen over night. Do not get discouraged, as I sometimes have, if your program does not run as smoothly as planned. This process takes a lot of time.

Over the course of the past year, my position in the Angell School tutoring project has changed and in turn so have I as a person. With each step I have gained more and more experience in helping elementary age students, participating with community service learning projects, as well as actually being the coordinator of a program. What I have learned from the Angell students, as well as the other university students, is immeasurable. I will take this knowledge with me onto another level and into my second year of this project.

I am very excited to move onto another year working with this project. The importance of consistency is so great to children at the elementary school level, and I feel this project can really work toward encouraging young students in their educational pursuits. For myself, this is one of the most positive contributions I can make at this time toward educating the future generations. My hope is that there can be more programs such as this in the near future which will benefit children at this formative age.

NOTE

1. A fictitious name is used to protect privacy.

Chapter 8

SALSA...LATINO TO LATINO...
A Tutoring/Mentoring Project

By Esmerelda Cadena, Areli Cavazos-Kottke, Amy Holmes, Christy Ochoa and Joan Scott

The service-learning project discussed below is somewhat unique because it was student originated. It aimed to address issues inherent in the struggle toward multiculturalism in society and in the university, the student initiators immediately sought a way to link it to the curriculum, and it remains a four-way partnership with the student organization, Sociology 389 through Project Community of The Office of Community Service Learning, and the high school which is the site of the service. What follows is a transcription of a recorded interview in the Spring of 1993, after three terms of involvement.

Participants in the interview discussion are Areli Cavazos-Kottke and Amy Holmes, who were initiators of the project (Areli was also an official project director for the grant received) and Christiana Ochoa and Esmerelda Cadena, who served as coordinators, (Christy for two terms and Esmeralda in the third term.) Joan Scott, staff advisor and a Program Director for the Office of Community Service Learning (Project Community), is the interviewer.

Background—In The Beginning...

J. Tell me a little about SALSA, and what motivated the SALSA organization in the Fall of 1991 to try to do a service-learning project.

AC. I think it all started back in the Spring of 1991. We were at the end of the term, and we had a meeting, and we were thinking SALSA doesn't have a service project...

J. Hang on a minute. Our readers need to know what SALSA is.

AC. SALSA stands for Socially Active Latino Student Association. It was started eight years ago at the U-M by Latino students. We weren't interested in just being "social" in the party sense as an organization.

AH. It's really difficult...Should student organizations be for social or political purposes? It's been a somewhat divisive issue for organizations on this campus. If you're "socially active" does that mean you're political? The question comes from white students really. Of course to be socially active in the sense of being involved with social concerns and society is to be political in some ways. This also includes social consciousness. Some people want to be socially active, but not political!

J. What motivated SALSA to develop this tutoring project?

AC. It was an idea that was brought up with a lot of enthusiasm in the Spring of 1991. As the Fall came, we started our meetings, new people approached and the subject of the service project came up. Not a whole lot of people had enthusiasm, but Amy and I were the movers and shakers of the project, and we wanted it to happen. It was a dream of ours for SALSA, and we knew that if we started something others would follow. Sure enough, we started dividing into committees of issues we wanted to address in SALSA in '91-92, and we came up with a service project that targeted Latino students. We had several potential communities in mind.

J. Let's stop at this point and focus on the questions and concerns you had when you first began considering doing the service project—even before you got to the point of exploring possible communities. Before you got to that point, what were your concerns?

AH. Oh, I see what you're asking, you're trying to take us back another step. One thing we discussed was, how could we have a project that would serve Latino communities outside the U-M? How could we get U-M students involved with communities, giving something back to the communities, being role models for others? What would be a project that would give individuals that experience and also give SALSA (the organization) a purpose, a project?

J. How did you go about planning for it? You mentioned having a special group form a committee.

AC. We got six or eight people involved in planning, because we had to have enough to cover all the bases.

Goals and Resources—And Planning in the Real World

J. Let's talk a little about the service goals and resources. Tutoring/ Mentoring programs can be shoestring, barebones operations, or they can be more elaborate. A lot depends on what resources, financial and otherwise, are available, and what structures you operate within. Let's talk about goals first, and then about the resources you considered. What were the hoped for outcomes and goals? What did you want to build into the project as components and why?

AC. We started with a lot of goals and a lot of hope—not only for the tutoring/ mentoring, but that we could really feel that we were family (with the mentees). We wanted to have a potluck, interaction, workshops at the school,...We wanted to focus with them on identity, their future. We wanted this project to be a two part project. The first part would start with mentoring and tutoring, and the first year would have included the tutees choosing a project to do such as theater or their own tutoring at the junior high or at the elementary level. We had BIG goals!

J. This might be a good place to focus for a bit on the students you hoped to work with. You wanted to work with Latinos. What do you think are the particular needs for Latino students? What about the kids you ended up working with...what are they like and why is there a need in this specific mid size southern Michigan city?

AC. Part of the reason that we ended up at South City[1] is that the Office of Minority Affairs and the Office of Admissions have developed college clubs in different high schools and middle schools, but not there. Contacts had been made at one time in the high school there, but they weren't interested, we understand. We were interested in connecting with a high school that had a lot of Latino students. There were already connections, from U-M, established with Western High School in Detroit, and there was another project at a middle school in Detroit, so we wanted to target a school, that for whatever reason, the regular institution hadn't been reaching out to.

J. What did you see as the need of the Latino students in the educational system?

AC. We are always hit with the issue of why history has so many things missing. We want our Latino students to have pride in their history and themselves, and in their history in this country. That was another one of our goals. I think there is a need for more Latinos to go on to higher education. We could target students between a 2 and 3 grade point to get them motivated to go to college or even just to stay in school. They need the extra boost to get through high school and to get them thinking about what might be ahead after high school, whether it be college or more training or a job. Also, the students we were targeting were persons whose families, many of them, came from migrant work, who weren't from Michigan and had problems with language.

J. Do you think that Latino students at the high school get much support?

E. No. Just this term we heard that issue raised...that there was racial discrimination and that "people don't pay attention to us". It's that blatant. Personally that is one of the reasons I got into it myself...being Hispanic myself and coming to U-M and seeing how few Mexican-Americans there were here at the University. I want to help these people whom I identify with.

AC. There is such blatant racism, but there is also a bias in the institution of education itself. They (the kids) are treated differently. Even among Hispanic high school students if there are any of the students with higher

GPA's the teachers and counselors put more emphasis on them and pay more attention to them than to the others.

J. Where did you think resources might be available (thinking back to the goal setting and planning stage)?

AH. It is hard to remember. The problem was SALSA had no budget.

AC. We didn't have any money, but Amy came to me and said the U-M was looking for students to apply for a Presidential Initiative Fund grant. We didn't have much time to write it. Something like that—luck. We just picked it up and ran with it.

J. What is the Presidential Initiative Fund?

AH. Money from the Kellogg Foundation was available through the provost's office as part the Michigan Mandate—President Duderstadt's program for development of diversity. There was a student competition. It had to be a new project, a student initiative, and it had to have a diversity component. We weren't sure at first what they meant by diversity, whether they wanted diversity among the U-M students in the group or would it count to be working with an ethnic group.

AC. We learned it had to involve interaction between Latino and non-Latino students in the U-M. We had to write the grant in a way to allow for that.

AH. To us it seemed that doing a project that might bring more Latino students into the University setting contributes to diversity. Helping more people achieve the possibility of higher education seemed important to us. SALSA's goals were to have Latino college students working with Latino high school students. The funding source's primary goals were a bit different. We did want other students to feel welcome to work with Latino students and the funding source goals forced us to work toward this goal...which was probably a good thing, and it forced a more mixed seminar interaction, too.

J. When you got talking with the community—the folk at South City—what was the reaction to the idea at the high school? To what extent did you have to adjust your goals or ideas there?

AC. We'll never forget this. There were problems initially. I was chosen to call the contact we had, a school counselor, herself Mexican-American, Ms P. She was very enthusiastic. She supposedly talked to the Principal and she arranged a meeting with us and other counselors. The Principal of the high school was very concerned—suspicious of our motives as "outsiders." He felt he hadn't been consulted as he should have been, and he was not wanting U-M students to come down and "radicalize" his Latino students. He wanted tutoring, but questioned the workshops. He seemed concerned about encouraging the kids to be socially active—

that it would be riling them up. We had to convince him we were "OK" and had to restructure our goals to satisfy him.

J. Also, about the Principal's concerns—I'd like to interject something. This is a point at which I'm convinced that the link with Project Community, with its record, became helpful strategically. Supposedly, he'd heard some "horror stories" about college students doing organizing that made him uncomfortable. It's probably important to recognize how much it mattered to him that Project Community had a good record with service projects. He was very direct. He wanted to know who we were, and why he should trust us or you! I remember wondering, after spending an intense half hour on the phone with him convincing him that you all would be excellent representatives and role models, and would respect his concerns, what I'd done!

AC. The compromise was tutoring and mentoring and letting go of doing identity workshops and social awareness stuff at the school. We also had thought we wanted to work with drop-outs, but realized we contradicted ourselves by talking about working with kids with between a 2 and 3 GPA, maybe, going on to college How could we target both? So, we really didn't target the most serious potential or actual drop-outs.

AH. We were reminded that the students dropping out often weren't there at school to be tutored and the distance between campus and South City made it difficult to work with those students.

AC. We would have had to have focused on a much smaller group and to have worked more intensively with them. Another thing we changed is we had wanted to get more involved with parents. We didn't have the money or time to give this kind of extra, intense effort so far away. It didn't happen. The Principal also didn't want us to tell a non-Latino they couldn't be a part of the tutoring if they wanted to be. We said we'd take care of that and hoped...We never had to confront the issue, though! That's interesting, really.

J. How did you go about recruiting the Latino high school students and getting support of parents?

AC. We sent a letter to the parents to let them know what the project was all about, and the letter was in Spanish and English. The parents signed it and send it back. It is important to get their support and trust. Ms. P. had the names of students. Some were referred from teachers, some she picked as ones who might benefit.

AH. We went down and met with Ms. P. and the other counselors. Whatever we needed to be arranged at the school needed to be done through her. She helped greatly in setting up the program, once the Principal said okay. We really learned a lot about school politics.

The Service-Learning Connection

J. Let's talk about the course credit for U students. We got it hooked up with Project Community as a service-learning project. What did that mean for the project?

AH. We expected there could be problems with recruiting if it were just volunteer. Credit meant more of a commitment. Doing it this way meant students could handle it as part of their school life, not something extra. Also the reflection component was important—helping people understand what they were doing. Also, it was important to me for this to be institutionalized, because I knew that the minute people who started it leave, the project could fall apart.

AC. We wanted to leave a legacy with SALSA. Project Community allowed us to really be in charge of it, yet helped us keep our goals straight. We always had a fresh supply of people, and we wanted to keep it our program, which is why we didn't take it to the Office of Minority Affairs.

AH. Students are coordinating the course and service projects, and that is an important part of Project Community's philosophy. Students have input and control. We are not just the agents of an office that has its own agenda, and the issue of it being more permanent, for me, was important.

J. As one who has been both a student in the project and a coordinator is there anything you would add, E?

E. Actually, I think it is good it was part of Project Community, because I don't think, for example, I would have heard of it otherwise. It might not have existed! I went to the first SALSA meeting in the Fall and heard about the class.

J. What networks did you use to recruit U-M Latino students?

(All) Flyers. Festifall, the outdoor organizational recruiting festival, with the SALSA table. "Alma Latina", a newsletter, was just getting started on campus, and we put an article in there. It was also in the Michigan Daily, a student paper.

J. I remember you sending a mailing directly to Latino students, too.

AH. Yes, the first term we sent out fliers to the dorms, directly to Latino students, and we were impressed, because they came into the office carrying the flier! It made a difference to do a personal mailing to people.

E. That is the way I have heard about almost anything on campus or in Project Community—word of mouth or by invitation.

Implementation—It's Really Happening!

J. Let's talk about implementation. What did the program actually look like when you started?

AC. The seminar was being held along with two site visits a week—Tuesday and Thursday. We were there about 1-1/2 hours each day, plus driving time—another hour each way. We had two coordinators in our first term (Winter '92) and a different group of tutors went down each of the days. We met in the cafeteria or in the library right after their school day ended. The time commitment for us was from 1:00 to 5:00.

J. How many students were involved?

AC. Initially, in the first term, we targeted 20 high school students, because we had 10 tutors. We ended up with about 12 students at South City who were faithful. A lot of that had to do with sports and other after-school commitments. When a student didn't show up, we attempted to call them and the parents to let them know. This helped bring kids back and let them know we cared.

J. Tell me about this year's structure-1992-93? What had worked? What changed?

E. We had the same structure, except we went out different days. There was only one coordinator Fall term, 1992, but there were two coordinators in Winter—same amount of kids. We changed the tutoring days due to feedback about when the kids' homework assignments were heaviest. One thing that was learned Fall term was that only one coordinator for a project like this places too great a burden on that person. Christy did a great job, but was very happy to share the responsibility in Winter. There are so many site details.

J. What about Campus Day? We haven't mentioned it. It was a big event for everyone!

E. We wanted to give them an idea of what university life is like so we had a special Saturday trip to U-M for the South City students each term. They [the Campus Days] were different each term, and my perspectives were different each term. Fall term I was a student, and Winter term I was a coordinator. There is a big difference when you are trying to plan and organize activities! It was my responsibility to handle the logistics this Winter—pickup, return, time, activities, parent and school permission, social awareness activity, and who would be involved from U-M.

J. For some of the kids even community college may be a big step?

E. Many may have the potential for more schooling. We want them to think about school—community college, technical, four year like here. For all three terms, we had a tour of campus.We invited someone from Admissions to talk about goals. Members of SALSA (besides members who might be in the seminar) visited with the South City students. We showed them the video "America Me" this last term, and we had a great discussion. It brought people from a Latino sorority and fraternity, the SALSA group and the kids together for a discussion.

J. This Winter you had a special guest resource person at Campus Day as well?

E. My brother! He'd had a lot of trouble in school and came from a similar background. He'd been in trouble with the law and had quit high school, and then went back. I thought the students could relate to him.

J. How did the high school students respond to Campus Day?

E. They really seemed to enjoy it. We also showed them the dormitories and broke down into small groups. I think they enjoyed the personal attention.

AH. I remember after the movie everyone looked at everyone and everyone seemed very moved. The U-M students had difficulty beginning the discussion, because it was so powerful. A couple of people began talking about their own experiences. The high school students talked about their own pressures, feelings, issues of gangs and choices about life. It was fascinating to me that the U-M students were talking about systems and "big picture" issues, and the high school students talked about their life —family issues and other very personal issues. The high school students confronted the U-M students, only 4 or 5 years older than they, about what was going on in their lives. It was very interesting.

For example, there was a high school student living in an apartment with a friend, and the U-M students said that didn't happen in their experience when they were in high school. Another South City student was worried about where he was going to live next term...with his grandmother maybe. It was really intense.

(All) After doing three Campus Days, we learned a lot. The first one wasn't as well organized. Things needed to be set in motion a lot earlier, and even then there are bound to be changes. Guardian permission slips have to be gotten out, signed, and returned. Transportation and drivers have to be lined up. Ms. P. helped at the school end. People have to be very committed. It's a real hassle if the U. students and resource people aren't responsible about following through. You have to check and recheck.

J. You can't just show up and take the students away for a day!

(All) Right. Yeah.

AC. The first semester, also, we had an end of the year party at South City, and we gave away t-shirts. This created a real sense of solidarity.

AH. The shirts said "South City High School—UM Latinos Unidos—Learning From Each Other 1992". They were really nice.

E. We heard about that, and we wanted to do it again, but didn't really get to it-know where it was done. We should remember about it!

Evaluation and Advice

J. Lets talk about evaluation from the high school and student's perspective as well as your views.

AH. We have talked a lot about our experiences, but it is important to talk about the student's experiences. The Principal's fear was that suddenly the Latino students at the high school would be radicalized. He doesn't seem to think students already know about differences, or recognize them.

E. They are experiencing racial segregation and prejudice as it is. They are told all the time they are different.

AC. Even though our stated goals changed, and we didn't have all the workshops and awareness things that we wanted to have, I think they happened anyway! We had wanted to help form a Latino student union, and of course, couldn't. We heard that the kids, on their own, wanted to organize a Latino club and ended up with a minority club, a compromise with the school, but it was something. Why did that happen? Did we have an effect? We didn't say "Do you want to form a student union?", but something happened anyway. We hope we had an effect.

J. What have the high school students said about U-M student involvement? How do we know it has mattered to them?

E. A quick summary of the evaluations that I read that the students filled out indicated they not only appreciated that someone was helping them with instruction, but that U-M students were driving an hour each way to come. They felt special and important. Ms. P. had some idea about mentorship, and I know for myself I've kept in touch with the students that I tutored, and others have too. I would have liked to have seen more of that.

J. How did you monitor the effect of the program? What tools did you use?

E. &
AC. The students and, supposedly also the teachers, filled out an evaluation at the end. So did U-M students. What we would like is something from the teachers at the beginning about what students need help with, then

in the end, and maybe something in the middle. They could indicate how the students have improved. We wanted that, but got very little feedback from teachers. This might be resolved by writing a letter. That way teachers would be aware of students being tutored and of how to contact us. Our own evaluation [from the U-M students] showed we'd like more connection with teachers. We got good feedback from the students.

J. Well, this is one challenge that you face for the future. A suggested improvement. What other challenges do you see?

E. The school staff involvement in general. For example, we never saw the Principal all year. We needed to feel more school support. We'd also like to see that interest transfer to the Latino students at the high school. As said before, we felt there might be some favoritism, where the counselor focused on students who are doing better in terms of getting them fee waivers, scholarships, testing and class selection. We feel many of our students had little guidance. We understand there are too many students per each counselor. What I don't understand is why these students are being cheated.

J. This can be a sensitive issue...

A. It is important because it always happens. Paulo Freire has a thing about this about training people to be leaders, but not training the community as a whole.

J. What kinds of challenges exist within the structure of the project? What sort of advice would you give to someone else who wants to set up something similar?

AC. You need to have a lot of patience with others who do not have your perspective or patience!

E. It takes a lot of time and persistence. You have to be willing to keep trying to get in touch with people, connect with the school, and let people know you're there—and you care.

J. That sounds like a recognition that the site staff are very busy folk and you are only a side-part to their concerns—so the message is don't get discouraged. Are you recommending broadening the basis of support at the school, as well?

E. Yes. As mentioned before, the U-M students feel invisible. It is after school, few teachers are there, and the Principal is gone or busy. It wasn't a very motivating environment. The second term, we used the library. It was better than the cafeteria, where the janitor would come by and ask us to move so he could clean.

J. Recognition and support from the community is important?

E. Yes. It helps with keeping tutors more motivated. Maybe at one of the early teachers' meetings in the year someone could explain to the staff what the program is so janitors and maintenance staff know we belong there. They asked us for our hall passes!

AC. The other issue is that we'd like to have a potluck with kids and their parents in the end or beginning to involve them more. Maybe we could have it at a local church.

J. Are there any last thoughts you want to add?

AC. I think if someone starts something like this they need to know it's a lot of work, time, along with a lot of rewards.

J. What are some of the rewards?

AC. Reading the evaluations and seeing good results. Seeing grades and progress reports of the kids improving Having good things said about us. What was neat is that it happened in such a short period of time. Seeing students think beyond just a job after school. Friendships made. The possibility that over the long term we made an impact on their lives.

E. There was one challenge that came from involving non-Latino students in our U-M group, that relates to friendships. There was some barrier, with the non-Latinos, to developing quick friendships, in terms of the mentoring with the South City students. They don't have the same background, the same issues.

J. I remember you telling me about the silence you encountered in seminar when the topic had to do with education and social class. Is that related to what you just said?

E. There are differences in social class background, in general, between the U-M Latino and non-Latino students, and sure, between the South City Latino students and the non-Latino tutors. The kids would expect it. There was resistance among our students in talking about the issues of social class. It's awkward. Everybody gets hesitant when it seems obvious that some of the non-Latinos come from a higher social class. As Coordinators, we weren't comfortable about how hard to push the conversation, though we think people would gain from more openness.

AH. Being confronted with our own social privilege, whatever it is, is very awkward. It's a challenge to work with those issues. I have seen that in the pilot classes and other things I've been involved with. The makeup of seminars does make a difference and communication is hard. It's a real problem not just here...how do we get through to being able to do it?

E. Another challenge we have in the seminar is coordinating the Latino perspective with the more general or broad issues about education from a sociology perspective that were in the coursepack. A lot of the writing focuses on Black experience with education. We had a supplement to the coursepack that was used by all the Project Community projects that were part of the "Education" program area. It would be easier to have it integrated for everyone, but I don't know it it's realistic.

J. Issues are more often written about and examples used in terms of Black and White. For some seminar-project groups, the issues of achievement or equality are more relevant in terms of Black experience with education, particularly here in the Midwest. This is a tough question.

E. It is surprising, too, that for some of the Latino students who are in the U-M, their own history is invisible It's like they don't want to know... would rather not talk about it.

J. The younger ones? Right from high school?

AC. People do change after they've been at the U a while. They get more willing to look at the problems, the struggle.

AH. I still believe that this kind of learning or opportunity is really important, and this kind of discussion that we've just had at the end is really important...be sure you get this down, J!

AC. And we need to keep this project going, too. Which means we need money to do the extra things with the kids that make it different, because the U. doesn't do that in the usual classes.

J. We have to stop! This has been great.

NOTES

1. The city and high school names have been changed to protect privacy.

Appendix

(What follows is added from written communication from Christiana Ochoa, who was a Coordinator for two terms but could not be present for the interview.)

On relationships with SALSA:

"Although help from SALSA was certainly appreciated [on Campus Day], I feel that SALSA has to promote the Project and consciously make an effort to [stay] more intimately involved in the activities and planning..." [as the project continues].

On Campus Day:

I believe that Campus Day is an opportunity to have the sort of investigative/introspective goal-setting and identity workshops that SALSA had initially hoped for but that we are not able to hold at the high school.

On the Seminar:

"The seminar was more successful the second term that I was involved. The students in the seminar agreed that the supplements help a great deal in bringing together their experiences at site and the sociological readings that are in the main course pack. I would encourage...[keeping] the supplement updated and to add new readings on Latino-specific educational issues. Also, I would recommend that fully half of the seminar be allocated to site issues. Processing the experiences that we had at site was truly our greatest learning tool.

On the Service and Site:

During the fall term we tutored in the cafeteria, which was disruptive and too casual. In the winter we moved to the library annex and found an atmosphere more conducive to tutoring as well as to making solid social connections. The librarians are very supportive of our work and only ask that we stay moderately quiet.

It is important that all of us involved in the project were so enthusiastic. I think our energy helped to prove our dedication. It is essential that coordinators, volunteers and tutees be willing to give time, energy, and emotion to make a project like this work—especially when the institution where you are tutoring is not as supportive as it could be. My hope is that through our display of dedication we will draw more involvement and enthusiasm for the education of Latino students at South City High School.

(Christy's communication echoed similar comments and suggestions to those expressed by the interviewees, about stronger communication links with teachers and the Principal.)

Final thoughts, Evaluation:

"Past coordinators, tutors, high school students, and Ms. P. all agree that if we are looking for a large quantity of students receiving tutoring help, the project is not very successful. There were rarely more than ten students at a single session and in the course of a year we probably tutored 40 students at least once.

However, we also all agree that the program is improving and that the contacts that we have made between U of M and South City high school students are very important, and the true measure of the project's success. It is impossible to see [all] the results, because the [effects] of tutoring and social interaction are not necessarily immediate."

Summary of Some Important Threads Present in the Discussion, from the Perspective of the Staff Advisor

1. It is really true that a couple of dedicated people can make things happen. Areli and Amy were absolutely right that "if we started something, others would follow." Sometimes that is what it takes. But their continued persistence and taking of responsibility throughout the planning and start-up was also crucial. Staff can assist and suggest but can not "make it happen" in this kind of collaboration. It takes student/organization ownership, and continued transferring of that ownership to new members.

2. The students got a quick course in "turf and protection", and in the politics of working with university and the community. They learned that what seems excellent and obvious from their perspective may not seem so to others. They learned that they had to adjust their objectives, and that maybe that was not bad, even though they may not agree with the reasons.

3. To make a project like this successful takes dedication from people at all levels. The coordinators found that they had to put much effort into making sure that the university students really followed through with the extra plans and responsibilities with which they were charged. Making very sure that everyone understands and commits to all the aspects of the project at the outset is crucial. A prime example is getting commitment from the U. students to the Campus Day participation, to giving up a Saturday, <u>at the very beginning of the term</u>, and getting it in their calendars.

4. Student volunteers really want to feel supported by the community in which they work. It needs to be visible to them. (This is not just true of students. It boosts morale, period.) And this support is also felt, then, by the recipients of the service.

Chapter 9

THE MIGRANT LABOR CAMP PROJECT
"Through Others' Eyes"

By Amy Holmes
Introduction by Joan Scott
Journal Excerpts from Charles Grose, Kari Lehman, Christiana Ochoa, Jeremy Olen and Shannon Pitcher

Introduction

In the Spring of 1989 Project Community/Sociology 389 at the University of Michigan began what is at this writing a five-year adventure in cross-cultural learning. Beginning with very modest goals (to learn about ourselves and about the migrants from the migrant workers' experience, to step into their world respectfully, and to provide real service in the form of recreational and quasi-educational experiences for the children of the camp) the project has expanded to include ESL (English as a Second Language) tutoring with adults, and in the summer of 1992, targeted work with adolescents. Also in 1992, activities with children intentionally became more educational or "horizon expanding" in their focus. A small venture grant for the 1992 summer from Michigan Campus Compact was extremely helpful in allowing us to build on the experience of the previous years, and to develop the new direction.

Michigan is host to approximately 45,000 migrant workers in the Spring-Summer months, with some staying into the Fall. The great majority are Mexican-Americans. They work on the strawberry and vegetable farms and in the fruit orchards. They come from Texas and Florida, in extended family groups, and as single men, often returning to the same camp or area year after year. Unless one lives near a camp, they tend to be an invisible population.

The camp which the students visited is in south-central Michigan, in an area which grows a variety of vegetable crops. The grower who owned and operated this particular camp raised pickling cucumbers. As migrant camps go, the conditions there were about average, with approximately 75 residents housed in trailers and barracks-type structures. A smaller, more primitive camp was nearly adjacent, and our students worked with residents of both, plus some adults for ESL tutoring in a camp a short distance beyond. Washroom facilities were barely adequate. Surrounding the living trailers was the dirt parking area, and field. There was no play equipment. A trailer brought in by the Capitol (Lansing) Area Literacy coalition provided the only covered meeting space, with its small rooms, and some reading resources.

In the summer of 1992 seven enrolled-for-credit students and six "volunteers" (some from the previous summer's credit group) traveled the fifty-five miles each way to the camp at least once a week from mid-June, by which time the camp residents had arrived, through August. Many in the group became even more involved traveling out on their own at other than group times.

The students began meeting weekly for seminars in May, Spring term, using the first weeks before the migrants arrived in orientation, exploration of assumptions and introduction to issues. Seminars continued weekly throughout the summer, with readings, discussion, planning time, personal reflection, and an integrative paper.

A major factor in the success of the 1992 season was the dedication and intelligent, sensitive leadership of Amy Holmes, the student coordinator. Amy had coordinated the project in 1991, and the bridges and relationships she established and the ideas she had, as well as her critical thinking and course resources allowed us to go beyond what we had previously done. Also to be credited is Toni Caldwell, a teaching assistant for the Sociology Department, who became actively involved in the seminaring and in pushing the students' sociological understandings.

What follows is not meant to be a comprehensive outline of the development of the project, or of suggestions for persons interested in doing something similar. It is, rather a compilation of commentary by Amy, and excerpts from students' journals, on themes that were of importance to the group. These taken together tell the story of an important journey of learning.

Reflection on Experience

Beginning

The project began with two seminars devoted to initial group development and expectations, and seminaring process; two more formal orientation sessions; and a planning workshop. Discussion of site logistics was of course necessary also.

Most of the Mexican and Mexican-American migrants are Catholic, and the Catholic Diocese in Lansing has had some outreach to them. They host an orientation at Christo Rey Community Center in Lansing, for persons involved with the Diocese's volunteer efforts with migrant workers. We had been assisted with entry into the camps through their contacts when the project first began, and have since attended their orientation. At that event we were made aware of some of the social and health services available to migrant workers, and to some of the current issues regarding migrant workers in Michigan agriculture. The students electing to do ESL (English as a Second Language) tutoring also participated in a training run by the Capitol Area Literacy Coalition, which was specifically geared toward work with Spanish language speakers in the migrant camps. The Literacy Coalition, through its Migrant Camp Outreach Program staff, has been very supportive of our presence and goals since we began working with them in 1991.

The planning workshop for students electing to work with children and youth, though well planned, needed, ran into some problems when an expected resource person, and some of the students were unable to attend. That became the first lesson for the summer in "adapting"! The components of the workshop became part of the content of the next seminars. There were eight parts that made the whole of what needed to be thought through:

1. "What do we want to accomplish?"
2. "What do we know and what will we need to know more about?"
   a. The site
   b. Material resources available to us
   c. Agency resources available to us
   d. Our own talents and personal resources
3. Presentations from agencies and resource people connected to the project explaining resources available
4. Brainstorming ideas
5. Mapping out ideas in calendar form, and dividing responsibilities

In seminar, we listed and discussed our expectations for the volunteer experience, and what we collectively knew at the outset about migrant camps. We discussed hopes and fears for the experience. We also listed and discussed what we thought migrant workers at the camp might expect of us, and what they might already know about us. We considered what we thought might be hopes and fears of people at the camp concerning this project.

Playing a "sticker game" was helpful. People chose stickers corresponding to categories of identity characteristics from a list of categories (examples included gender, race, ethnicity, religion, student or non-student, socio-economic class, region of origin, family, urban or rural background, etc.) which students considered to be factors that might affect their volunteer experience and interaction with people at the camp, the way they would be perceived at the camp, or the way in which they would experience the volunteer and study experience. Students could choose three stickers, and then, going around in a circle, each student explained the three stickers he or she had chosen.

In the second seminar, a discussion about participatory seminars and an introduction of some of Friere's ideas about teaching and learning (1970) led to an exercise which illuminated personal differences in how people deal with conflict, and the roots of our feelings. We then discussed how this might affect the seminar and the group dynamics. We closed with "What we will need from each other" to make the project successful.

People had varying reactions to the group development and group process sessions. Some people felt they were very helpful and important, while others did not like discussing themselves in relation to the group or the project. Some participants thought we were just doing group development to fill in time. As a facilitator, I felt that people's uncomfortable reaction to discussing themselves in relation to the project, and to discussing group dynamics, was an indication that they had never done this sort of thing before rather than an indication that the exercises are not worth while. I continue to believe that the personal reflections and intra-group communication sparked by the group development exercises and orientation sessions are an important part of both the learning process of this project, and the development of effective and sensitive volunteers.

> *When I first walked in the room and was determined categories I was reminded of the many times that I have experienced such things failing miserably. However, in retrospect I am quite pleased with how that meeting went. In a class like this one*

that depends heavily on building relationships and developing trust between students, this exercise was quite useful in breaking through the barriers of bashful silence that many of us have.

—*Christy Ochoa*

Something handed out by the DSS worker during the orientation gave me an idea for a neat project. They had a little pamphlet in Spanish about health services. It would be nice to create a booklet about something like nutrition and eating right in Spanish targeted for the migrant workers. Right now I'm thinking for my paper that I would like to explore what it takes to set up literacy programs in developing and Third World countries. My interest in this stems from an interest in going into the Peace Corps after graduation.

—*Charles Grose*

I took this class partially because both of my grandparents were migrant workers until they settled in Saginaw. As I understand, the conditions have not changed.

—*Shannon Pitcher*

I am not sure what I expect from this course. I expect to meet a lot of interesting people who have had many different challenges and experiences in their lives, and still do. The children will have not had a stable environment in which to grow and learn. So we will be something stable for a short period in their lives. In this period of time we will become attached to the children, and they will be attached to us.

This will be a growing experience for me. I am not used to working with children. But when I become a social worker I would like to work with youth at risk. Also, this will be a growing experience because any time people work together, they learn something.

My fears are many, more so than my expectations. I fear that the volunteers will not get along together, that we will not be beneficial to the children, that I will have a difficult time interacting with the children.

—*Kari Lehman*

And after one of the first camp visits:

Plenty of kids! I think I might have trouble trying not to be tempted to just play with them rather than doing what I am supposed to be doing—teaching English.

—*Charles Grose*

On Adjusting Our Expectations

Many of the university student volunteers had some initial adjusting to do in their expectations for how the learning environment should be organized and run. In the children's program, we were dealing with a largely out-of-doors environment in which to organize activities, were organizing activities for kids on their "play time," and were dealing with a community whose lives are unpredictable from day to day during the growing season. In the adult ESL program, we were never sure of just how many or which students would come for ESL tutoring. And with the youth project, all we had was an idea, we had no idea how we would get teenagers interested in hanging out with us, and maybe doing a little thinking about education. Some days when we arrived at the camp, most people were gone, either to town or because of a long picking day. Other days, there were as many as twenty two ESL students looking for tutoring at one site, or, often, lots of kids, sometimes including six or seven kids who had just arrived at the camp and did not know any of the other kids, or us. The atmosphere of the kids activities might have appeared to an outside observed to be chaotic. But we learned to deal with semi-chaos in the world of the kids "play/fun/learning" time, keeping things under enough control to clean up messes and make sure everyone had a fair chance at trying things, but letting the kids have enough freedom to keep them interested, and let them run out their after-school energy. We always had to think on our feet. The adjustment was a growing experience for those volunteers who had gotten used to the ordered and stately world of the university.

> *The first time I went to the camp I was nervous because I had never been there. But I was also nervous because it was my turn to organize a project. So I was going to have them [the kids at the camp] do self portraits either with paints or crayons. But I had never been in a teacher position before, nor was used to little kids, so I was terrified. The project was a disaster...the kids got paint everywhere. All they wanted to do was squeeze paint out of the tubes and mix all of the colors together. Then I got smart and I put the paints away and got out the crayons. Everything went much better.*
>
> —*Kari Lehman*

> *I went there not knowing what level student I was going to have, not knowing how long a lesson to prepare, [and] thinking that all the info that I needed on a student would be in a file in the trailer. When I got to the camp it became very obvious that he trailer had no file on students (that is being set up this week), that my student was an advanced English speaker, and that the lesson that I had prepared was not only too short but also basically worthless. I learned a lot that day. I loved it!*
>
> —*Christy Ochoa*

The Big Question

From the time we began our planning and orientation, we discussed our "big question" of summer: Did we in fact, or should we, have something to teach children and youth at the migrant camp? Or was our purpose, on the other hand, to go out with planned "fun activities" for the kids? The schedule of activities which evolved over the summer in the end included both purposes in its variety. During many of our weekly site visits we organized activities which we expected would be fun and would provide younger children with something to do during the evenings. We almost always played a few games of make-shift volleyball or kick-ball during a given site visit, and we had at least one project organized for the day. These were usually arts and crafts oriented projects, though we did expand into the sciences by showing the kids how to do home science experiments. The kids initiated the development of a play which they were going to write themselves.

Our approach was a mixture of our goal setting, planning, and initiation of projects, and of following the lead of the children and youth at the camp. This approach worked well. During our first visits, we largely hung out and let the kids dictate what would happen. They introduced us to their routine of kick-ball and volleyball games (as well as their rules and versions of these games!). We fit ourselves into their activities, and the patterns of organization of their mini social world. The kids knew a few of us from the previous year, and were immediately warm, loving, and eager to make us a part of their games, and of their lives at the camp. After the first two visits, when we pulled into the camp in the car the kids came running from all directions, often shouting our names and sort of cheering. It was quite an ego boost for the volunteers to have people (the kids) seem so glad to see us, although it was embarrassing at the same time as we wondered just why they were cheering our names, and we puzzled over what we possibly had to offer them that they got so excited about.

We did want to be organized, partly to vary the routine of playing kick-ball and exploring make believe worlds, and perhaps also because organizing activities gave us a sense of purpose. If we were bringing activities and materials into the camp, then we felt as if we had something to offer. (Ironically, while the activities were successful, part of what we had to offer, it seems, was simply our friendship. But at the time it was hard to believe that our friendship was really worth anything.)

I do think that the activities were a positive experience for the kids at the camp. First of all, there is truly little to do in the evenings at migrant camps. The camps are often isolated and have few facilities. Except for television (without cable, of course) "what to do" for kids is whatever they can invent with sticks, bikes, and maybe a few rubber balls or broken or second hand toys. The kids we worked with were extremely enthusiastic about coloring, reading books, and doing arts and crafts projects. The books and materials we were able to provide were materials which were not available to them at the camps. And, we provided the organization for activities, and instruction in how to do particular projects.

Some of our activities were specifically, intentionally educational. We planned with the hope that knowledge or skill or interest gained would transfer to school achievement. Many of the children were eager to sit down and read with the volunteers, either one on one or in small groups. The kids that could read in English took turns reading out loud, and for those younger children who could not read, the volunteers read slowly passing their finger underneath a word as they read it. We tried to discuss what was happening in a story after a few pages. Usually, we didn't need to work hard at initiating the discussion. After reading a few pages in English, the kids often broke out into a lively discussion of what was happening in the story, speaking in Spanish or "Spanglish," a mixture of Spanish and English, and in this case usually a Spanish conversation with English words interjected. The tutors who did not speak Spanish were sometimes uncomfortable not being able to understand when the kids spoke Spanish, but it was clear to many of us that the kids were eager to learn about everything in life, and that it was important to let their enthusiasm for learning develop, and to in fact nurture this enthusiasm, letting the kids express themselves in whatever language or manner was natural for them (if it wasn't disruptive to other kids, or against their parents rules.)

Those tutors who did speak Spanish worked on helping the kids to develop their skills in oral and written Spanish. We had a few bilingual books, and we tried to read these with the kids. For some children, it seemed like reading in Spanish was a new experience. They were surprised that pronouncing the written words came out as a story or sentence in Spanish. It seemed, though this was speculation on our part, that in their lives Spanish was something they spoke, and English was something they read in school.

One of our great resources was about a hundred copies of a "Mexican-American Coloring Book." As the younger kids colored, we read the stories in the book out loud. In one case, I was reading with a five year old friend who was coloring a picture of the meeting between Cortez and Monteczuma. He declared (in Spanish), "These [the Spaniards] were the good ones, and the Indians were the bad ones." As I sat there with this little lively kid who I had known for about three years, this kid who was Mexican-American, from Mexican ancestors, was mestizo with more than a little Native American, probably Aztec, blood in him, I was disturbed. "Is that what they are teaching you in school Alejandro," I thought, "That your ancestors were 'the bad ones'?" That can't be great for a kid's self image or future development. I then realized that maybe he had gotten this idea from seeing old westerns where the villains were always Indians on horseback. "Why do you think the Indians were bad?" I asked. "What did they do that was bad?" "Well," Alejandro replied, "Cortez was a good man, but then he turned bad and he killed a lot of people. And the Indians were good, too. But they also killed some people." O.K., I thought. I'll leave it at that. Alejandro is five years old. A second success of the "Mexican-American Coloring Book" was that some of the eleven and twelve year old kids got the idea of writing a play telling the story of Pancho Villa, and later the story of the braceros. They were going to write a play, make costumes, and have their little brothers and sisters play the bit parts in the play. They did produce a small script for the first scenes of the play. But a few weeks into the project many of the eleven and twelve year olds went to work in the fields, and were too tired and busy in the evenings to complete the play project.

Another example of the balance of fun and educational activities was the science projects. We had asked the kids to write a list of activities they wanted to do over the summer. One of their interests was science projects. So, we looked for home science projects we could use. Our first attempt was two "experiments." We talked with the kids about what we were trying to accomplish with the experiment. We decided, among all of us, that the process was to see what happened and then try and explain why it happened. We first mixed baking soda with colored vinegar and watched the results. The ten to eleven year olds were able to engage in a discussion of the fact that a reaction was taking place between the two materials. The younger kids just thought that the bubbles of CO_2 were great, and many called for their friends to come and make "volcanoes." We then used vinegar to neutralize grape juice, which took the color out of it. I remember kids from five to twelve years old jumping up and down (literally) and each wanting to try the experiment, and then try it again. I left them to their own devices after a while, and the experiment soon became an adventure in mixing anything they could think of until the mixture had become a brown-purple mess. But the kids loved it. As an educational tool, the activity had a ripple effect. Some of the older kids remembered other "experiments" they had done in school, and quickly demonstrated them for the younger kids.

Over the rest of the summer, every once in while a few kids would ask, "Can we do an experiment? When are we going to do an experiment?" I had left the jars and bottles we used for water and vinegar with the kids, and when we came in subsequent weeks five and six year olds would come running up with the jars full of all kinds of things and yell, "Amy, Amy, look at my experiment!" Wow! I thought. It may not seem like much, but if these kids think it is fun to do "experiments," then maybe that will help them be enthusiastic about science in school. At least, it was great fun, which is a quality of an activity which we grew to appreciate for itself.

As it turned out, most of us had a wonderful time doing projects, organizing sports games, doing educational activities, and organizing special trips for the kids. This brought us to our second question: Were we doing this project for the benefit of migrant workers, or more for our own enjoyment, benefit, and as a learning opportunity for us? Both sides of this coin presented us with ideological and moral dilemmas. If the presence of us, a bunch of young people with little experience in the world and without even a completed bachelor's degree to our names (in terms of formal training) was supposed to benefit migrant workers, did that mean that we thought we were somehow "better" than the people we would be working with? If, on the other hand, we were doing this project for our own benefit, were we then exploiting a group of people in order for ourselves to learn, grow, and advance in our careers through interaction with them? This is a question I don't have the definitive answer on, but I think our experience showed that the project was mutually beneficial.

> *They think it's real funny that their friend with the "pelo largo", [me], is taking out the garbage from the trailer. They follow him to the dumpster, egging him on despite his threats to throw them in. His load emptied, he chases them just as they had hoped for. They scream and laugh as this man runs through their camp like some kind of intruder.*
>
> *Intruder.*
>
> *Sometimes he wonders what is he doing here? The ESL*

> *experience will look good to the Peace Corps. Playing with the kids is more fun than he usually has on a Monday night. The ride up with his classmates is really bonding. But who asked him to come? Do the want me in their lives? Around their homes? Playing with their kids?*
>
> *Intruder.*
>
> *The little boy he refers to as "maestro" is on his back. He is a horse now, galloping to the boy's laughter. They see a big wooden spool. An idea flashes through his head. Soon the boy is off his back and walking on the spool as it rolls. Some more ohs and ahs. But they hear the voice of his father in Spanish. The horse doesn't understand, but from the tone and the immediate response of the boy getting off [the spool], it might not be good. For all he knows [it could be]: "Why is the gringo jeopardizing my son's safety?"*
>
> *Intruder.*
>
> *He is not sure at times; but the hug and the smile of a little kid, and a nod from the women he is tutoring, gives hope they want him there.*
>
> —*Charles Grose*

On Trust

One of our major tasks, and our greatest triumph, was developing trust between ourselves and the community which we wanted to work with. By trust, I mean the kind of trust that would allow them to feel comfortable participating in our program, and would allow them to feel comfortable about having their children participate in the program. We were timid at first, and unsure of ourselves. "What right?" we kept asking ourselves, "Do we have to be here?" Maybe they don't want us here....they must be wondering what the heck we are going to do to their kids....this is never going to work. But it did work. Over the course of my two summers, I saw us develop a relationship in which we felt comfortable, and in fact felt supported, by the migrant community. Teenagers were starting to look forward to organizing a program with us. And, to our great shock, by the middle of our 1992 summer families were entrusting their ten, eight, and even two-year-olds to us for all day out-of-town trips. And this, despite the evening when we got caught in a rainstorm and arrived home after midnight with the youth group to a gathering of panicked parents, and the day when we were shut up in the literacy trailer by rain and a certain five year old inadvertently slammed his cousin's fingers in a door. "How," we kept wondering, "does this community continue to trust us and accept us here?" Part of that, surely, has to do with the culture of the community, and the circumstances in which migrant workers live. It is the families that we worked with, and their enthusiasm and willingness to accept us, trust us, and put rules and parameters on our plans when necessary, that we have to thank for the success of our project. From our end, it was, I believe, our dedication, enthusiasm, humility, and honesty about who we were and what we were doing that contributed to the development of trust between us and the community, and to the success of the project.

An important element of our experience was the role we defined four ourselves at the camp. The kids that we worked with initially called us all "miss," "sir," or "teacher." We all felt a bit uncomfortable with these terms of authority, both because of their formality, and because they seemed to signify that we had something to "teach," which brought us back to our question of our purpose at the camp. We asked the kids to call us by our names. While this seemed strange to the kids at first, they quickly got used to it, and soon only called us "miss" or "sir" if they forgot our names. The "teacher" role, however, stuck. We were operating out of an old trailer which had been donated to the Capitol Area Literacy Coalition. The migrant community quickly named the trailer "La Library," presumably because there were a lot of books in the trailer, and when we arrived in the camp the kids always spread the news to their parents, "my teacher is here." Usually then they asked, "Can I go to the library?" This role of teacher was what the community labelled us. It seems to have been the role that they could define to explain our participation in the camp and our role in the lives of the children there.

> *What are we doing at site? I just play with the kids! Just kidding. I do not tutor and I do not educate the teenagers on options open to them. I just play with the kids. And yet I feel like I am part of [a] social service...The migrant families have been exploited by the system. We represent North Americans. Although many of us come from culturally diverse backgrounds, we are "Americanized." We attend college, we have jobs, we know how to work the system. I believe that we are establishing rapport with the migrant workers. We are developing a relationship with them where they are perhaps learning to trust us. I believe that establishing this type of relationship with their children is critical to the relationships and responsiveness we will receive from their parents...This trust is certainly hard earned. To improve their life style and protect themselves from being exploited the migrant workers need help. They see people who seem to care about their rights, their health, and their children. Establishing this trust is a social service in itself.*
>
> *—Jeremy Olen*

> *I have often written how I feel that the service we seemed to have provided the Migrant Workers was that we were helping by entering their isolated culture, (this isolation and even ignorance has caused them problems,) so that they might learn to trust other people to help them learn skills to benefit their situation, i.e. health care needs, legal options, English, etc...I have some reservations about the development of this trust. I sometimes worry that we are not doing them such a favor. Looking from their perspective I feel like they are happy with the way they are. It goes beyond this because I know that their mistrust and isolation has protected their culture. As they change by integrating and using English and the American system, I worry that, like other cultures they will lose their*

> *cultural identity and become "Americanized." A friend of mine once told me not to worry about this because the Chicano culture is a strong one and even if they do lose it a little it may be necessary for their benefit. I question this in a sense, because when it comes down to it I feel that people have reason to only trust those of their own culture. Integration can leave a group of people very vulnerable. At the same time the need for immediate solutions to problems like health care and protection from exploitation is necessary. So, in conclusion, we do what we can and will see what happens. One person can become social analyst but not much of a social influence.*
>
> *—Jeremy Olen*

The journal question was: Why might a migrant worker not seek legal help from Michigan Migrant Legal Services (or another social service agency providing services to migrant workers)?"

> *Beginning with a child's first experience with racism and carrying through a migrant laborer's constant struggle for anything resembling parity with the rest of the labor force, this sector of the population is separated from mainstream society. A large wall of distrust is inevitable built by a community that has continually been abused by the society in which it lives and for which it provides essential labor. It would be unrealistic to expect a migrant community to trust the legal system which is so centrally located in the inequalities that migrants face.*
>
> *When I think about what [we discussed] last week I am able to break large issues down to a more personal level. [We talked about] how long it has taken for the people at the camp to trust us; That the programs that we have been pulling off successfully would not have been possible last year. When I apply that knowledge to the legal services available, it becomes clear why so few utilize those services. We have been going out to the camp every week of the summer for three previous years. During those visits we have had personal (vs. strictly professional) contact with both adults and their children. We do not pose a substantial threat to the employment of the workers.*
>
> *If it has taken three years for us to measurable break through some of the cultural barriers that have been created by years of oppression and exploitation, I cannot imagine anyone expecting that migrant workers would fully utilize the services of an agency that does not visit them regularly on a professional let alone a personal level, has a very specific and explicit agenda, and does pose a substantial threat to their employment status through its ability to anger an employer.*
>
> *—Christy Ochoa*

On Chicano/a History in the Southwest and Class Structure

Talking about social class on a personal level, like talking about race on a personal level, is not easy. It is a lot safer talking about others, particularly if one has grown up privileged, and a lot safer not examining too closely one's own participation in the class structure. Seminar dialogue was emphatic, but not truly revealing, even though the group had developed some trust among members. Social class issues were becoming real to the students, because they could see them, and had to talk about them, but they nevertheless tended to be "out there."

> *As I read articles and statistics about Latinas in the United States and how they became the dominant portion of the migrant labor force, I become both educated and enthused. The more I read the more I want to read. The more I learn the more I want to get through the training and onto the camp. It is a very good experience to be this enthusiastic about a class. I feel almost as if we don't meet often enough...we don't learn fast enough. This is very exciting for me.*
>
> *-Christy Ochoa*

> *I just finished reading the article, "The Homeland, Aztlan." It was really disturbing. This article talked about how the Anglos (White people) came into the Americas and exploited the people and took over the land. Since they had guns and were barbarians, Anglos just marched into the New World intimidating and tricking the people that already lived there. In Texas they set up a government then demanded taxes that the people already there could not afford, so this legitimized the reason to boot these people off of their land.*
>
> *Now, when I think about this it really makes me angry how one group of people could treat another group of people that way. First of all the Anglos did not own the land, so how can they set up laws and taxes? If anything the native people should have put taxes on the Anglos for coming on their land. But that is the difference between Native Americans and Anglos. Native Americans share everything while Anglos take everything, yet Anglos have the audacity to call Native Americans, Mexicans, and Blacks animals. Anglos should be ashamed of themselves.*
>
> *What also really bothered me was that now Mexicans that were pushed off their land are trying to come back, and Americans are calling this an "invasion." How can Americans be so blind? I guess it's to their benefit to not see anything though because then they may have to be responsible for what is going on.*
>
> *Another situation that really scares me are the maquiladoras—the American factories in Mexico. The pay is*

very low, the conditions are horrible, the women must work long hours. How can heads of corporations live with their consciences knowing that they are exploiting and causing people to suffer so much? I guess it's all in the name of money.

It's very frightening to think of these women having to be exposed to so many chemicals and straining their bodies so much. All for what? Then I do not even want to buy a TV or clothes unless they are made in the U.S. for fear that someone had to go through so much for my pleasure.

It just does not seem right that we can allow each other to treat each other so badly.

—*Kari Lehman*

I do think, though, that the Marxist approach [to defining class structure] has a great deal more value than the strata approach...I think that because the Marxist approach does involve much more complex or integrative definitions of the economic groups in a society, that it immediately has advantages that the strata approach can not offer. As the article said, [Marxist definitions] tend to group people by their [class] interests more than by their income levels. It seems much more accurate, even in the United States where few more than academics even acknowledge that there is a Marxist approach, in classifying or grouping members of our economic society.

What I think is best about the Marxist versus the strata approach is the ideology that it carries with it. What I think the author in the article ignored, however, is that the strata approach also carries an ideology with it. Certainly there is some reason that the United States has refused to adopt the terminology of Marxism.

—*Christy Ochoa*

On Education

I believe the class structure is very related to the education of Mexican-Americans. Many have to drop out of school to work When they are in school, there are language differences unrelated to how they can perform. Teachers have (lesser) expectations of them because of their skin color. And for the most part, George Washington has little meaning to them. Because Latinos, in general, live in communities with a lesser tax base, have families where the young must help provide income, speak a language different than the white-based system, are confronted with teacher biases, and have a culture and history of their own, they are not able to receive the same education as whites in America.

—*Charles Grose*

It surprises me that in a capitalistic society we have not

> *realized the necessity of excellent educators and education for our children. Then again maybe it should not surprise me. We all know that the school system is set up so that kids get tracked into lower level classes so that they can fill the jobs of the proletariat. That was the rationale a century ago; maybe even thirty years ago. Today, however, the workers of the United States are needed less and less in the fields that require little or no education. Computers are taking those jobs. In order for the educational underclass to remain a productive part of our workforce we must make sure that they are no longer purposely regarded and tracked as an underclass and instead are trained and prepared for the same tasks as our educational elite.*
>
> —*Christy Ochoa*

> *One reason that these kids are dropping out is because the schools are overwhelmed. They are over-crowded [in poor areas] and lack the funding to provide adequate educational resources like textbooks and lab equipment. I can back this up with my own experiences in high school in Detroit. Often times we did not do experiments because we lacked supplies. Our teacher gave us extra credit for bringing in paper towels because we did not have any. Our textbooks were old and falling apart. When a student is in this type of learning environment, learning becomes frustrating. Tax money should be evenly distributed to all school districts. It's not fair to discriminate against one district because the people do not have a lot of money. Education should be an equal opportunity for everyone.*
>
> —*Kari Lehman*

On Language

In our discussion, it became clear that for non English speaking people, language can be a political issue connected to identity, history, and opportunities.

> *It is too bad that Americans [U.S] expect everybody to learn our language. I think bilingual education should start in elementary school for all Americans. In certain communities where there are large percentages of minorities, like in Florida, school should be universally bilingual with not only the teaching of extra languages to the students but of certain subjects in different languages. If history is taught in Spanish, it will both accommodate those who are just either learning Spanish or English.*
>
> —*Charles Grose*

Language was a big issue for volunteers. For those who felt comfortable with speaking Spanish, the volunteer experience was a great opportunity to practice Spanish skills. For others to be confronted with a situation in which they could not understand everything which was being said was a challenge, and a real learning experience. A number of students expressed that while it was sometimes frustrating not to be able to understand everything, they felt that the frustration was a good experience, as it showed them a bit of what it must be like for those adult migrant workers who speak little English to survive in the English speaking environment of Michigan during the summers.

Many of the student volunteers were surprised to find a Spanish-speaking environment in rural Michigan But having adjusted to the concept of migrant communities being Spanish-speaking communities, students were even more surprised to find that the camps, especially the social environment of the children and youth at the camps, was actually bilingual. While many adults at the camp were fluent in Spanish and skilled at reading and writing in Spanish but had limited English skills, most of the youth at the camp spoke both English and Spanish nearly fluently. Many of the teen-agers at the camp had been born in Michigan, and had been travelling in the migrant stream between Michigan and Texas all of their lives.

The most surprising language issue observed by volunteers was that, especially among the younger children (toddlers to twelve year olds) who were still developing language skills, "Spanglish" was their most common language of communication. They seemed to, basically, speak Spanish, probably the language they learned from their parents and the environment around them. However, they were also learning English words, especially for things they mostly talked about at school, or that they heard about from the television. I remember one child during a volleyball game exclaiming, "Hey, si tiras ese ball arriba del house, se va a caer al otro side." At another point in the game, one young friend said to his brother, "Oye, ese era mi side." While older children clearly divided English and Spanish most of the time, they were aware of the phenomenon of Spanglish. They joked about saying things like, "Mi Dad me dio..."

These children live a bicultural existence. They constantly travel back and forth across physical and figurative borders, from the political borders dividing states and countries to the border dividing their home culture from the dominant culture of their schools and popular media, to those cultural, ethnic, and racial boundaries they may cross daily during their summers in Michigan on short trips from the grocery store to the migrant camp. Migrant communities are, in a way, like internal colonies in a country or state. They are separated physically from the areas in which they exist, and they are like a production plant, with an internal organization in which workers and growers each fit in slots which produce a final product which is sold to the outside world. Within the camps, Mexican-American migrant workers carry on their own culture, while the camps rest in a larger Anglo-dominated culture which enters the life of the camp through schools, the medical care system, social service agencies, and workers' contact with stores and other institutions of the outside community. The children and youth of migrant camps particularly seem to have synthesized their two cultures, the Mexican and the Anglo, into something which is their own. Recognizing their invention of a mixed culture by celebrating it's language, "Spanglish," seems to be a healthy way for children and youth to cope with the stresses of understanding two cultures and languages, when one set comes from the colony in which they live, and one from the colonizing society in which they are often asked to survive.

Volunteers in the adult ESL project found that many adults in the camp were eager to take advantage of the opportunity to study English with a tutor. After long days in the fields, sometimes from 7:00a to 9:00pm, people were still willing and eager to sit down for one to two hours with a volunteer and study English skills. There was even one family who for a few weeks studied English from 10:00pm to midnight, and then got up every morning at 7:00am to go to the fields. During some weeks, it was simply impossible for people to study English with the tutors. Their work and personal schedules simply didn't allow time for the classes. Or, unexpected weather or growing patterns of crops made work hours uneven and unpredictable. While volunteers fully understood this situation, it could still be frustrating. Volunteers would arrive at the camp ready with a lesson, and find no one to tutor. It was difficult to talk about this frustration, as again volunteers had to question of themselves, "Who am I doing this for? If I am doing this for the benefit of migrant workers, and they are doing what is best for themselves, then can I be frustrated when there is no one to tutor? If I am frustrated, does that show that really I am doing this for my own satisfaction?" In the end, volunteers lived with their occasional frustrations, and found alternative ways to be active in the activities at the camp when no adults came for ESL classes. Part of the lesson was that life is unstable and unpredictable for migrant workers, and, in working with the migrant community, one has to learn to be flexible and adjust to the unpredictability of life at the camps.

For some of the Mexican-American university students participating in the project, the experience, and especially the issue of language, was a personal journey. I recall one humorous, but revealing, incident. Shannon, one of the university volunteers, and Tony, a ten-year-old at the camp, had gotten into a conversation about identity. Shannon's grandparents on one side of her family came from Texas to Michigan as migrant workers when they were younger, and eventually settled in Michigan. Shannon felt a strong sense of being Mexican-American, and had just returned from a huge family reunion with the Mexican-American side of her family when she and Tony got in this discussion. The conversation went as follows...

Tony: You're not Mexican.
Shannon: Of course I'm Mexican.
Tony: No you're not. Do you speak Spanish?
Shannon: Well, you got me with that one. That's the one thing I can't do. But what about you. You have awfully green eyes. You aren't Mexican either, with your green eyes and everything.
Tony: Yes I am, but you're not Mexican.
Shannon: Yes I am.
Tony: No you're not.
Shannon: Tony, why do you keep saying I'm not Mexican?
Tony: You're not from Texas. All Mexicans are from Texas.

Another interaction:

In good fun but heartfelt, between a volunteer, Charlie, and a ten year old child at the camp, Alonso...

Charlie (in broken Spanish): Por favor, senorita.
Alonso: What was that? Hey, say that again...
Charlie: Por favor, senorita.
Alonso (in a haughty, "tough" voice): Hey, don't mess with my language.

> *My Spanish is very rusty, but it was challenging and interesting trying to communicate with the children, who all know English.*
>
> *—Charles Grose*

> *We visited one camp trying to recruit some adults [to the ESL program] (with no luck unfortunately) and we ended up having the younger generation translate for them. I can see how this might be a pattern in many of their relationships with English speakers.*
>
> *—Charles Grose*

> *If I had been told in advance how unprepared I would be for my first lesson at the camp, I would have been completely freaked out!...I went to the camp the first day prepared to teach someone who knew very little English. Instead, the person who I am teaching is an advanced student by ESL terms...To the credit [of the people who did the ESL tutor training], the work they did to give us confidence in our ability to teach helped immensely to keep me calm and sure that I would make it through the first lesson...Juan knows about as much English as I know Spanish. We have similar problems in word placement and verb conjugation and have nearly equally limited vocabularies. I think that this helps me to identify with why he wants to learn English and also with the types of lessons that he needs to improve his confidence with the English language. At our second lesson I was much more prepared to teach him what he wants to learn...I am having a great time with this.*
>
> *—Christy Ochoa*

On Racism and Diversity

We had quite a diverse group of people in the course. There were a number of Chicana/Mexican-American students, and a balance between numbers of men and women, and numbers of white students and students of color in the class. Talking about racial and ethnic oppression was difficult, as it nearly always is. We tried to establish an atmosphere in which we examined our own identities as they relate to our perspectives on the society in which we live, and how our very different experiences influence the formation of different ideas. We tried to learn to listen to each other. And, we acknowledged from the outset of the class that, given that we live in a society where structural conflict is widespread and manifests itself today in outright conflict among groups of people, we were likely to experience conflict among the participants in the class. We discussed conflict, and tried to establish an atmosphere where conflict could be acknowledged and productively as a method for learning.

> *Cultural Diversity is when people have respect and understand and learn from each other's culture. One culture is not better than another. All cultures have their good points and their bad points. When we go to site we must be open to cultural diversity.*
>
> —*Kari Lehman*

> *Cultural Diversity is sometimes hard to deal with. When people of different cultures and socio-economic backgrounds get together, often they do not see eye-to-eye.*
>
> —*Shannon Pitcher*

> *When I went to a flea market I bought two balls to bring to camp and my mom and grandmother also gave me some little toys for the children. They (my mom and grandmother) were very glad that I took this class and so am I because I think I am learning a lot. Through all my struggles, and when I "make it" I will never forget where I came from. I may have never worked in a field I can appreciate the struggle and hard work of these people, my people. Because wherever you come from the struggle is great, from the fields to the urban ghetto. All people of color must fight to advance themselves and return to aid others.*
>
> ——*Shannon Pitcher*

> *My largest impression from the day [the "college day" visit to the University] was the blatant racism that the art museum guard woman on the second floor [of the art museum we visited] displayed...Tony, [an eleven year old kid from the camp] mistakenly touched the stuffed Samurai and this woman who had been following us around the entire time we were in the museum finally had her opportunity to display her discomfort that had already become obvious to many of us, with these Spanish speaking youth. She leaned over and (in a very e-nun-see-a-ted English) told Tony "NOT TO TOUCH." AARRRGHH! I agree that he shouldn't touch and I know that those people are hired to be jealously protective of the art pieces on display but the voice in which she reprimanded him was unmistakably full of connotations. I know that I shouldn't be surprised, but that museum has hundreds of young people visiting it every month—I'm surprised they haven't better learned to deal with them.*
>
> —*Christy Ochoa*

> *I was looking at the article about Hispanic/Anglo Cultural*

> *Differences...It occurred to me that no wonder people make stereotypes about each other. We do not understand each other at all. We perceive each other's actions differently; we misinterpret the meaning of each other's actions...(the articles on cultural differences and the "cycle of racism"] also helped me to look at some of my own racism in myself. Even though I may consider myself a very open-minded person, I do have some prejudices simply because I live in a racist society...As a white person and a member of a "first world country" (if countries should be defined in this way), I contribute to the systematic mistreatment of other people simply by having and accepting the privileges that I have in this society. What can we do to stop the cycle of racism?*
>
> *—Kari Lehman*

> *My first day at the migrant camp I was not surprised at what I saw. In fact, it reminded me of the poor conditions of the Indian Reservation up around Central Michigan University that I visited...The houses were in poor condition, weeds and grass were overgrown between the houses, wet laundry hung on ropes between the houses and there were the laughs and cries of barefoot, dirty-faced children. It made me think- how could the U.S. government support such a system that allowed people to live in such poor conditions, virtual poverty and then exploit these people for their economic labor? This is 1992 and the United States still supports an economic system that exploits people of color. These people could be my family 40-50 years ago when my grandparents worked as migrant farmworkers. It angers me that these people, my people, are treated in such a manner...We talked about the exploitation of people of color, and some white people [in the class] blamed these people for their situations, when Mexicans rely on this work for their very survival. Don't people see what's going on?*
>
> *—Shannon Pitcher*

On Working with Adolescents at the Camp

In addition to all the activity that has been described concerning the children's program and adult ESL tutoring, we formed a youth group over the summer. Working with teen-agers is difficult in any population. But it was especially hard in these circumstances, as most of the teen-ages we knew worked long hours. On many occasions, they expressed to us that they would like to plan and participate in activities, but sometimes their work schedule simply didn't permit this. The other problem was that most of the teen-agers saw themselves as adults. It was difficult, then, to figure out how to invite them to be part of a group, which seemed a lot like a "school thing" or a "kid thing." We ended up being successful in forming a group among the 13-15 year old range. The 16-17 year olds we knew participated in a few activities. At the end of the summer, as the group was beginning to become more formed and more interest was developing, it seemed as if, had we been given more time we would have been able to pull the 16-17 year olds more into the program. Really, it sounds strange to talk about "pulling people into the program." While we to some extent guided and gave a vision to the purpose of the youth group and the activities that would be planned, to a large extent the list of activities, and what the group chose to do, were the creation of the youth themselves. We offered suggestions and a list of ideas that we had thought of when we presented the idea of forming a youth group to the kids, but they chose the actual activities. The following is a list of special activities carried out with the youth group at the camp.

1. Ice Cream" run to a local ice cream parlor
2. Trip to Lansing to see a movie
3. Baseball game against an amateur Lansing team at a local baseball diamond
4. Showing of "Stand and Deliver" in a backroom of the local elementary school during an evening when the school was being used as a clinic for migrant workers. (We also planned to see the film "Homeboys," but ran out of time.)
5. "College Day" Visit to the University of Michigan and the Ypsilanti Water Park
6. Visit of a representative from the Office of Admissions of the University of Michigan to the camp to answer any questions students had about possibilities for higher education, and other career decisions
7. Closing pool party at the apartment complex of one of the co-coordinators from the Capitol Area Literacy Coalition with which we were co-ordinating efforts in the area of ESL tutoring

Organizing the activities was a struggle. The kids' schedules were very unpredictable, and the weather of a given day often dictated whether they would have to work late, or whether they would be able to participate in an activity. There were no phones at the camp, so we could not communicate by phone, but had to just guess what conditions would be like when we got there. All of this had to be coordinated with the complicated schedules of our volunteers. We began the program with fun activities, like going to see a movie or organizing a baseball game. We were clear with the kids from the beginning that the program should be partly fun, and also partly education-oriented, whether that meant direct involvement in education activities, or whether that meant taking a look at our society and their futures within that society. The latter is the route that we took.

For the film showing at the clinic, the kids chose the theme of gang violence as a theme as an issue in their lives which they wanted to see a film about and then talk about. We brought both the film "Homeboys" and the film "Stand and Deliver," but ended up only having time to watch the latter. We had a group of young men from a camp with which we had less contact, who were between 16 and 19 years old, attend the movie. I had stopped by the camp to invite them to the movie, but was actually a bit surprised that they came. Three of them were from families who had lost their fathers to car accidents, so they were the senior men of their families, and major breadwinners. It was difficult for us and for them to figure out a place for them to fit into the program we were developing.

I think the group did identify with the movie. I remember watching a scene from the movie when one of the main characters has an awful time trying to get medical care for his sick grandmother. In reference to the medical care system, a couple of the guys laughed and said, "Asi son," "Yep, that's how they are." The movie delivered a message which was along the lines of what we wanted to communicate to the group. It portrayed a group of Chicano youth living in a lower income urban ghetto who, with the aid of an innovative teacher, take and pass the AP Calculus exam. And this despite resistance from teachers, administrators, and the Education Testing Service who claimed that it was impossible for them to accomplish this.

The culmination of our project was the visit to University of Michigan campus, and the follow-up visit by an admissions counsellor to the camp. Our aim was not to convince students to attend the University of Michigan, but simply to show them the possibilities that lie open in attending college, and to communicate to them that we believed that they could be successful in the University, in a community college, or in a training program. We did not "preach" to the group, or tell kids that they should attend college. We simply had a discussion over pizza about what each person would like to do when they grow up (including sharing our own aspirations), then we took them around the campus, showing them what was available and answering any questions about "what it would be like when and if" they go to college. The group of 13-15 year olds that went on the trip showed a lot of interest in understanding what college would be like. I remember one young woman who, near the beginning of the summer had told me that she would like to get a cosmetology certificate. During the campus visit, she began to talk about her interest in computers and discuss how she could develop this in college.

A very interesting observation can be made for some of the young women, the computing center at the University seemed to serve as a "link" that made them feel comfortable with the environment. They said that they had used computers at school, and when we sat down at the University computers, the familiarity of the computer seemed to help some envision themselves in the University setting. For some of the young men, a couple of trips to the video machines in the University Union got them talking about being at college. I remember particularly one young man who had insisted at the outset that they only reason he was coming on the trip was to go to the water park, and that he was all set for his life with his plan to work in the fields. He joked around sometimes about starting up his own gang. By the end of the day he suddenly told us, "You know, this is a cool place." This kind of moment was what told me we were on the right track.

Endings

Earlier in the semester I and others questioned our roles at the camp. We were there to play with the children, to talk to the children, and to learn with the children. I thought that we were there to do educational lessons, but how can you force learning on youth who were in school or working the fields all day? That just wouldn't feel right. However, I think our purpose came forward when we took some teen-agers to [the University of Michigan] campus. This is when their eyes lit up at the size of the buildings, at all the computers and at the large pictures in the Art Museum. The idea was to show these children that there is something more to life than the fields. The migrant field system is a hard one to break [out of] and in an age where there are fewer and fewer jobs many Mexican-Americans rely on the fields as a way of life.

> *[We] were talking after the day was over and said that the outreach was the most important thing...This I believe because one boy who was asked about college had said he would probably drop out [of high school] before he got there...But after the visit to the UM campus, he though college could be a "cool thing." This is a start I think that the program in the future should [have a] longer [college day], for a total day, maybe a stay in the form next year...Our day was cut short because [we had to combine] the campus tour and the water park [because] the picking of pickles was about to ensue the following week [and the teen-ages would all have to be in the fields seven days of the week.] So, this flexibility was a necessity.*
>
> *My day was made when I saw the kids talking about their futures, about the possibility of college, and about education—it made everything (all of the work with the kids) important.*
>
> *—Shannon Pitcher*

> *After the first time I enjoyed going to the camp. The kids were so sweet and all they wanted was someone to play with. I think the best time that I had with the kids was college day...They were so curious about everything! They went into the museum and were fascinated by everything. And they were so much fun to be with. But on this trip I learned how one girl had dropped out of school because her family moved around too much. The reality stuck me. Here we are showing her a college campus. She may want to come, but she has already given up. I learned a lot from this experience. In seminar I learned that tall countries are special even though we label ourselves first world and some other countries third world. I realized at site how people are no only oppressed the city, but also migrant workers have been historically oppressed...And I realized that money is not everything, it does not a make a person good or bad. These children were so poor, but they were sweet, kind, smart, generous and they watched out for each other. So I really learned a lot this summer. I am very happy that I participated in this class. Thank you.*
>
> *—Kari Lehman*

> *Recently, I had a family reunion—the Guerrero family—and we celebrated the 50th anniversary of our family's settlement in Saginaw, Michigan. My great-grandmother and grandfather, all of her 15 sons and daughters were migrant workers. They travelled from Mission, Texas every year to pick*

various farm fruits and vegetables; the work was hard, the living and working conditions were terrible and my family was cheated of earnings and life.

Well, it is fifty years later, but not enough has really changed despite the efforts of Ceasar Chavez. Laws have been passed, but not well enforced. The American government has not been responsive to its own people, but then neither have the American educational or employment systems...

The mainstream American society allows it to happen. When you do nothing then you condone it because often the personal is political. Mexican-Americans currently do not have the power to get out of their oppression and are often blamed for their situation. However, as the Mexican-American population grows at a great rate the oppression will stop, but the system so far has left the Mexican-American population crippled and many times uneducated.

—Shannon Pitcher

The 'sociological imagination' is seeing how the unique historical circumstances of a particular society affect people and, at the same time, seeing how people affect history"(Mills, 1959). As I analyze my overall experience this spring and summer this line from Mills stands out in my mind...As we combined historical and current information with actual social interaction with a different group of people I feel that we became social analysts according to Mills criteria. We have learned intellectually and observationally how historical circumstances have effected a people and how a people have affected history. On a broader scale we are affecting history ourselves in the sense that we are travelling new grounds in relations with a particular group of people that are not used to trusting Anglo society. We became a particular set of circumstances. I feel that I have learned a great deal. Regardless of the social service that we seemed to be providing I developed an ability to locate my perspective in a different frame of reference...The combination of understanding anothers' situation and interacting with them at the same time provided me with an excellent medium in which to culture this skill. I learned a great deal...Not only about their history and cultural identities but a little about their outlook on life relative to my own. I do not believe that this has necessarily changed my outlook in any drastic way, but perhaps has made it more flexible.

—Jeremy Olen

I thought the movie "Crazy from the Heart" was a great example of how an artistic endeavor can have much sociological educational value while still be entertaining. The way the script portrayed the many stereotypes we have in our country about race and occupation, as well as the stain that results when the expectations because of these stereotypes are not met, was excellent.

I also like when I find experiences that counter what I usually think. As we watched the film last Friday, I found all of us ragging on men who watch football on TV. However, these are people too, and the stereotype we have of them as beer drinking, couch sitting, full-bellied pigs is just as wrong as what others might conceive Latinos as. (I learned, not very happily, a new derogatory term for those people; beaners).

What has this class done for me? To me? How did I change? What did I learn? I like that these questions won't be answered on a 4.0 scale with a grade. Still, I want to mark, evaluate the experience with something traditional, some process that is familiar to me so I can compare it to other classes. I know I'm a different person than I was in May. How much was from being up at the camps I'm not sure.

One reason I took the class was to try to get a taste of what the Peace Corp. would be like. I realized that it would be more than I had originally thought. 3 hours with them a week had a big impact. What would 24 hours, seven days a week for two years be like. One thing I learned was that I didn't have to get used to them, but they had to get used to me. I was the intruder, and in many ways I learned what the minority experience was like, where my language, my jokes, my methods, my ideas, my experiences were not common or even that important.

—Charles Grose

One of the heartbreaking realities for me of the summer program was that it had to end, and end all too soon. After our University visit, we started to talk among all of us, the kids from the camp and us "kids" from the University, about the possibilities for the youth program in the future. We talked about writing a grant proposal and having fund raisers for the project. We talked about the kids launching a program for making the camp environment more enjoyable for their families during the summers by organizing volleyball and basketball tournaments, and maybe a dance. We talked about setting up internships for the next summer for the kids, according to their interests, through the Hispanic Chamber of Commerce in Lansing. But the summer was ending. We had to go back to start the school year at the University full-time, and the kids started to leave for Texas one by one. It was just as they say it is in the migrant life. We came one day, and one family was gone, off to no one knew where. I came one Saturday to say good-bye to some teen-agers I had been particularly close to, only to find that I had missed them by a few hours.

What did the younger kids perhaps get out of the program?

I remember talking to Alonso, a ten year old friend, about the then upcoming November Presidential elections. He wanted to act like he understood the whole thing, and we gently sorted out who was running with who, for what positions, and how the party ticket system works. Perhaps there was a bridge there for a young man living in a community alienated by language, mobility, and culture from such institutions as voting and presidential elections.

I also remember Alonso's father asking me about what I was studying, about what kind of job I could get with my degree, and about how I was paying for college, and how financial aid and working to pay for tuition work. We also talked about people I knew who found a college close enough so that they could take classes and live at home, or at least visit home a lot.

I remember Yadira, a quite sophisticated little five year old girl telling me that she wanted to be a teacher then she grows up, just like me. And I remember Alonso telling me, as we sat on an old mattress behind his trailer looking for alligators in the cloud formations of a beautiful sunset, that he would like to be a scientist and travel to Egypt to do research. "But," he said, "Maybe not. I would miss my family a lot."

And I remember how I introduced Alonso's five year old brother Alejandro, a particular buddy of mine, to the idea of doing experiments. Concoctions of all sorts became a passion of his, and he led me to his secret "laboratory" between two bushes many times during the summer to show me his latest bottles and jars of "experiments."

Most frustrating of all, it seemed that after two summers of developing trust between us, and enthusiasm for the program, just as we were on the verge of being able to do great things, the time was up, and the kids had to move on. We found out through talking to people that due to some controversy between growers, food processors, and the Farm Labor Organizing Committee, many of the families we had gotten to know had decided that this part of Michigan was too risky of a place to come to next year. They didn't expect to find secure work, so were not sure they could afford to return. So, our bubble for the next summer (temporarily, at least) burst. But that was a true lesson for us. This is the way their lives are, we told ourselves. This is part of their dilemma, part of the reason they are alienated from many institutions of our society, part of the reason this group of people is locked into this extremely marginalized sector of the economy, working from generation to generation in the same excruciating, unstable, and low-paying work. And, this is why social service agencies often can't or don't reach out to migrant families.

So much was learned, and so much was felt.

PART FIVE

Service-Learning Projects Not Affiliated with Sociology 389

Chapter 1

THE SERVE BOARD
A Model for Student Leadership in Service-Learning Programs

By Anita Bohn and Claudette Rowley

Introduction

Project SERVE is a student-run department at the University of Michigan that works to encourage student involvement in community service and social action. The SERVE Board, entirely made up of students, works together with student committees to plan and implement all of our programs and services, as well as to determine our directions and priorities. Through programs such as Into the Streets, SERVE Week, SERVE Work, Alternative Spring Break and Alternative Weekends, SERVE Board members strive to heighten student awareness, increase community involvement, and raise social consciousness through direct service and social action.

Our History

The University of Michigan has a long tradition of student involvement in the community. For more than thirty years, students have had the opportunity to work in the community through departments such as Project Community and Project Outreach, which offer service-learning courses which can be elected for academic credit. In addition, student organizations have existed that are involved both in specific community issues, and in community service in general. In the late 1980s, Project Community recognized the need for an office that would work to build the community service movement on campus through developing and coordinating opportunities for students to be involved in community service and social action, and through networking with the variety of student-led service opportunities.

In 1988, with a start-up grant from the Presidential Initiatives Fund, Project SERVE was born. In the beginning, Project SERVE functioned simply as an information and referral service for students who were interested in volunteer opportunities in the community. A director was hired as the first full-time administrator.

During the 1989-90 school year, we began to add programs such as the Volunteer Fair, Campus Service Day (which would become SERVE Week) and Alternative Spring Break. At that point, work-study staff was added to support the office.

As our third year began, and both programs and numbers of students continued to grow, it became clear that some sort of structure was needed for the student leadership that was growing in Project SERVE. Therefore, during 1990 and 1991, a group of eight students comprised what was to become the SERVE Board the following year. They met as needed and worked together on all of the programs. That year also marked the beginning of our deliberate efforts to network with other student-run service organizations. A UM Service Network was developed as a means of bringing together those student organizations who were working in the community. Students also began to be involved in state and national organizations such as COOL and the Michigan Campus Compact.

In our fourth year, programs continued to improve and expand at an unbelievable rate. In 1991-1992, the Board developed a formal structure with specialized roles, and weekly meetings. Board positions fell into one of three categories: program co-chairs, liaisons, or support people (such as the co-chairs and the PR Chair). The Board consisted of 19 members, each with a time commitment of 10-15 hours per week.

Our fifth year brought the need for another layer of student involvement in the development and implementation of our programs. In 1992-3, 30-35 committee members were recruited to help with the work for which the Board members were responsible. We also expanded our programs to include SERVE Work, a support and information service for students interested in careers in social change. In addition, we added Issue Coordinators to our Board in an effort to add a more serious reflection component to our programs, and to ensure more effective placement of students.

In 1993-94, 23 Board members and 64 Committee members will continue the work that has developed over the five year history of Project SERVE.

Our Mission

Our mission: *To foster, through community service and social action, a student movement at the University of Michigan that thoughtfully addresses the challenges that we face as a society.*

Project SERVE is committed to:

Social Change—Our primary goal is to work toward a more just and peaceful society and toward an end to the social problems and issues that we face as a society. Our vision is of a community that values children and the elderly, provides quality education and health care to all people, respects all people equally, protects the environment, and is free of violence, hunger, homelessness, AIDS, poverty, and racism.

Student Leadership—Project SERVE is coordinated by the SERVE board and its committees, which are composed entirely of students. They are responsible for developing and implementing all of our programs and services as well as for determining the directions and priorities of SERVE. We believe student voice and leadership are essential in building this movement toward social change.

Empowerment—We strive to empower students to work toward real solutions to community problems through their involvement in community service and social action. We also commit ourselves to programs that

empower the communities and individuals with whom they work.
Building A Movement—In order to address social change issues, we must work together with all who are committed to social change. We are dedicated to building a diverse and inclusive campus movement; to networking and collaborating, both locally and nationally, with others (especially other young people) who are working to solve these problems; and to working with faculty, staff, community agencies, and community members to build quality service experiences.
Heightening Awareness—Our response to social problems is dependent upon educating ourselves and others about those issues. We are committed to raising awareness of social issues both on campus and in the larger community.

Our Meetings

The SERVE board meets once per week for an hour and one half. Board members facilitate the meeting and take minutes on a rotating basis. During the first part of the meeting, board members and the director give their updates about programs and activities. The second part of the meeting consists of a group discussion based on a topic that the facilitator has suggested. Past discussions have ranged from our individual responses to homelessness to Project SERVE's potential involvement in Martin Luther King Day on the University of Michigan campus. General Board meetings are held twice each month, while one meeting per month is dedicated to small group meetings and one meeting is spent working together on a community project.

Our Training

Training occurs through a retreat which takes place in September before classes start and through an office orientation. The two day retreat is an opportunity for new SERVE board members to get to know each other and to build group cohesion. During the retreat, we focus on visioning, goal setting, and planning. Board members also meet in smaller working groups in order to brainstorm ideas and possibilities for the upcoming semester.

Through the office orientation, board members become acquainted with the computer systems, the phones, the resources available for students, such as volunteer and career opportunities, and the ongoing office duties.

SERVE Board Descriptions

Qualifications—Each board member must be committed to service and social action as a means of addressing societal problems and creating social change. S/he must be dedicated to the process of working as part of a cooperative, non-hierarchical team. Enthusiasm about working with diverse groups of people is essential as is creativity, energy, and imagination. In addition, s/he should be able to motivate, inspire, and lead others, as well as be skilled at group facilitation and cohesion.

Into the Streets/SERVE Week Co-Chairs

Into the Streets—Into the Streets is a national initiative designed to introduce students to thoughtful community service and to provide a learning experience that will challenge them to volunteer on a regular basis. At the University of Michigan, students go Into The Streets of Ann Arbor and Ypsilanti to work on issues such as hunger, homelessness, the environment, children and youth, the elderly, and community revitalization.

SERVE Week—SERVE Week, which occurs in the spring, celebrates community service at the University of Michigan. The week is aimed at promoting direct service, as well as encouraging and recognizing student involvement in the community. In the past, this week has included clean-up projects, fund-raisers, and recognition and awareness events. SERVE Week is sponsored by a coalition of student organizations involved in service. Two co-chairs are responsible for organizing Into the Streets and SERVE Week.

Duties and Responsibilities—For ITS, the co-chairs responsibilities are numerous. Initially, they work to organize and promote the program which takes place each November. The aim of the program is to bring together individual students and student organizations in a collaborative community outreach effort.This effort includes issue-specific orientation and training sessions, a direct service project, and programs that are intended for evaluation and reflection on these activities. Other responsibilities include recruiting and working with participating organizations, issue coordinators, and site leaders, coordinating kick-off events, promoting the program in efforts to recruit participants, coordinating follow-up activities with all participants, evaluating and documenting the workings of the program, and providing feedback for planning future ITS programs.

In order to organize and promote SERVE Week, the co-chairs recruit a diverse group of student organizations to sponsor events during the week. Other responsibilities include serving as advisors to the organizations, coordinating publicity and recruiting for the week itself as well as for the specific events, exploring fund-raising and sponsorship resources to provide funding for the event, and providing feedback for planning future SERVE Week programs.

SERVEWork Co-Chairs

SERVEWork is a referral and support service for students who are interested in pursuing careers, internships, and long-term volunteer opportunities in non-profit and social change organizations. The center includes resource books, information from local, state, national, and international social change organizations and current job listings.

Duties and responsibilities—The co-chairs recruit and work with SERVEWork coordinators to organize all aspects of the program including selecting and maintaining contact with appropriate local, national, and global organizations, keeping current job postings and information, identifying and securing appropriate resources and publications, exploring fund-raising and sponsorship resources for SERVEWork, creating awareness of these opportunities on campus through promoting the center, considering creative ways to promote careers in social change, working with other career resources on campus (i.e., Career Planning and Placement, International Center, and individual academic units), evaluating and documenting the program, and providing feedback for planning the future of SERVEWork.

Alternative Spring Break and Alternative Weekend Co-chairs

Alternative Spring Break—ASB addresses problems such as hunger, homelessness, crime, drug abuse, poverty, racism, violence, health care, and environmental destruction. In addition, it addresses the need for students to become involved in thoughtful action toward the resolution of these problems. In 1993, over seventy students participated in seven spring break sites. These sites included working with the Sioux Nation in South Dakota, working with BEAKS, a program that aids birds injured in environmental disasters, and going into Detroit to spend a week with SOSAD (Save Our Sons and Daughters), an organization which works to eradicate the violence against children in Detroit.

Alternative Weekends—Like ASB, Alternative Weekends provides direct service experiences to students. However, this service occurs over a series of weekends which are organized throughout the year. Training and reflection will take place both on-site and during the weeks between the service weekends. Alternative Weekends is a newly conceived program which will be implemented during the 1993-94 school year.

Duties and Responsibilities—ASB and AW co-chairs are responsible for working with a team of student site leaders to plan and facilitate all aspects of the ASB and AW programs. Specifically, the duties of the co-chairs include selecting appropriate issues and sites, coordinating logistics (i.e. housing arrangements and work schedules), securing transportation, exploring fund-raising and sponsorship resources to fund the ASW and AW activities, promoting the program and recruiting participants, evaluating and documenting program events, and providing feedback for planning future ASB and AW programs.

Residence Hall, Greek, and Co-op Liaisons

The Residence Hall Liaison works with a team of residence hall coordinators to encourage residence hall involvement in community service and social action. The Greek Liaison works with liaisons for the Interfraternity Council, the Panhellenic Association, and the Black Greek Association to encourage Greek involvement in community service and social action. The Co-op Liaison works with liaisons from each co-op and the from the Intercooperative Council in order to encourage involvement in the community service and social action.

Duties and responsibilities—Each liaison recruits and works with a team of coordinators to support existing service programs as well as to implement new service programs. S/he also facilitates on-going communication between Project SERVE and the co-ops, the residence halls, and the Greek systems, and enlists the participation of members in SERVE's programs and events.

Cultural Outreach Coordinator

The Cultural Outreach Coordinator works with campus and community cultural organizations to encourage a multi-cultural response to social problems and to address multi-cultural issues through service and social action.

Duties and responsibilities—The Coordinator works with the Cultural

Outreach committee to network with cultural and multi-cultural student and community organizations and facilitate on-going communication between SERVE and these organizations. S/he also develops and coordinates awareness/ education action projects in conjunction with cultural events and celebrations on campus such as Martin Luther King Day and Hispanic Heritage Month.

Public Relations Chair

The PR Chair is responsible for all promotion and publicity for Project SERVE and its' individual programs and services.

Duties and responsibilities—The PR Chair communicates Project SERVE's activities and programs to students, faculty, staff, and community agencies. Other duties include assisting with the development of SERVE's promotional materials, writing press releases and maintaining contact with campus and local print, radio, television, and other media resources, investigating and initiating options for promoting the SERVE office, resources, programs, and events, and editing and coordinating the production and distribution of Project SERVE's monthly newsletter.

Issue Coordinators

The Issue Coordinators work with committees to maintain contact with current community service sites in each area as well as to develop new sites. They are active in the areas of hunger/homelessness, education/literacy, women's issues, environmental issues, children/youth, health/mental health, and the elderly and disabled. The issue coordinators follow up with students interested in volunteering in their issue area or in a specific agency. In addition, they provide reflection opportunities, and promote campus awareness programs around the issue or problem.

Our Challenges

Although the SERVE Board functions effectively as a team, the Board does face some ongoing challenges: 1) the need to continually develop the reflection component of our office and our programs, 2) the need for more office and work space, more financial support, and more paid staff support 3) the need to constantly re-energize ourselves, and 4) the need to keep our sense of urgency about social problems and the need for continuing change.

The SERVE Board is striving to make reflection a higher priority within the organization as well as for the participants in SERVE's programs and volunteer experiences. Through reflecting upon actions, attitudes, and emphases, SERVE will be an even stronger, more effective organization both in terms of the quality of its programs, and of the students who are reached and who participate. Reflection also enables SERVE Board members to process their experiences as a part of Project SERVE as well as process the outcomes of activities and programs that they have initiated.

One huge challenge that SERVE faces is a lack of work space, and financial and staff support. Despite these conditions, SERVE has continued to prosper and grow to a board of 23 people and nearly 1000 program participants. In order to continue to grow, however, SERVE will soon need to acquire more work space and financial and staff support.

SERVE Board members have recognized that at times the work that they do can become routine. At times the logistics of program planning can distract people from the real reasons why they do what they do, the importance of it, or the meaning behind it. Past board members have discovered that continuing to work in the community is one method of remaining focused on SERVE's purpose. As a result, the SERVE Board members work together in the community once per month in place of the weekly meeting. Board service projects are one way of sharpening and regaining focus.

At times, the SERVE Board has struggled with the relationship between community service and social action. Social action implies a greater sense of urgency, a desire to question, and to create more awareness and activism. While community service is vital to the people who are served, the SERVE Board is invested in promoting student involvement in social action and community problem solving.

Our Reflections on Student Empowerment

In Project SERVE, new program ideas are initiated by students. Students identify needs, brainstorm ideas, and develop programs that fit the need. Most of our programs, including SERVE Work, the Issue Coordinator program, and Alternative Weekends all began when one or more students recognized a need within either the student community or the larger community, and worked to develop an answer to this need. Although the director of Project SERVE acts as an advisor and source of support and information, SERVE's growth and development are a direct result of student initiative.

Within the University of Michigan, students are primarily conceptualized as "those who do not know and need to learn". They are often viewed as receptacles to be filled with knowledge imparted by professors. Within an organization such as Project SERVE, however, students are viewed as those who know and can teach each other. Because of SERVE's non-hierarchical approach, students are empowered to develop their own thoughts and ideas for their own benefit as well as the benefit of Project SERVE, the University students that it serves, and the larger community that is also served.

In order to accomplish this, staff must insist on actual student leadership. Too often, students are used as clerical staff or as program staff that just carry out roles and responsibilities that are determined by faculty and staff. Students must be able to not only carry out programs, but also to make decisions about the directions and priorities of the office. A cooperative, consensus-based environment is also necessary. This often is more frustrating and time-consuming than hierarchical models, but it is essential in trying to truly empower students.

During the 1992 SERVE board retreat, board members were asked to reflect on why they personally are involved. The following are excerpts from their writings:

> *Personally, I'm involved in trying to save the world because, basically I think I'd feel worse if I didn't. I got stuck with a mind that <u>sees</u> injustice, <u>sees</u> suffering, <u>sees</u> waste, <u>sees</u> a lot of things and does not forget them. If I had the ability, as do many, to*

not see or not remember, I could just work on being happy, independently of the world's problems. But I do <u>see</u> the problems and somehow they tie into my own happiness. The trap in trying to save the world is cynicism and giving up because the problems seem so insurmountable. I am constantly fighting to avoid such a trap.

The mark of service to me is what it springs from, where it arises. If it is an overflow of love—where love cannot be contained, so must be shared—then it is service. So I am involved in service because I feel love. With love comes the desire to end others suffering and bring others joy. The same action could be service one day and something else the next. I also have found that through service I connect with people—I learn from and with others—giving and receiving blur.

Personally, I am involved in service because I need to find my road, define my purpose. I want to change the world and allow everyone their rights to basic elements of life—love, shelter, food. These should not be privileges and it seems they have been usurped from many. I wish to increase the awareness and create a medium for attitude change.

Personally, I am involved in social action because of my very strong and overwhelming belief in people. I believe and try to see the good in people and I seem to have a never ending compassion that allows me to always find a reason to care. I think that our global village can be one of peace and happiness if we begin to question our socialized beliefs and our actions and attitudes. I believe that each individual can add to a collective action to empower us to reach new heights in all aspects of our lives.

Personally, I am involved in community work because I am called to community with both local and global life, and with that comes responsibility not only for celebrating that community but also for helping to find solutions to community problems. My peace and contentment are bound up with those of the community.

Chapter 2

BURSLEY COMMUNITY VOLUNTEERS

Dormitory Based Service Projects

By Chellie Ferczok

Bursley Community Volunteers (BCV) is a student-run volunteer organization located in Bursley Hall, a dormitory located on the North Campus of the University of Michigan. During the 1993-1994 academic year, the program will manage eight different volunteer committees. Bursley Hall has a unique staff: As a part of their job description, all resident advisers (RAs) in Bursley are required to co-chair at least one of the committees. Co-chairing consists of overseeing the planning and administration of the committee, as well as actively volunteering. This provides a special introduction to community service and additional leadership experience for the staff members, as well as setting a precedent to encourage residents to get involved. Further publicity efforts include a display at freshman orientation and the campus organization festival (Festifall), fliers, brochures, bulletin boards and a mass meeting. While all University of Michigan students are encouraged to participate, the majority of active participants are Bursley Hall residents. Each year, BCV introduces over 250 volunteers to community service options in the Ann Arbor area.

Bursley Community Volunteers strives to provide volunteer opportunities which offer meaningful service to both the volunteer and the community. Our programs are a combination of independent committees and involvement with other organizations. This allows us to offer our services wherever the greatest need exists. The BCV office keeps information on other non-BCV volunteer programs available as a reference for students interested in volunteering for programs other than those offered through Bursley Community Volunteers. Because of this flexibility, BCV is able to provide a wide variety of volunteer services to interested students and the community we live in.

Bursley Community Volunteers was established in 1981 when former building director, Caroline Gould became concerned about the ever increasing discrepancy between the have's and the have-not's in our society. She was amazed by the quantity of usable goods that was thrown out by students at the end of every year. Hoping to find a way to redirect some of the energy of her residents, she met with the resident directors and challenged them to have every resident donate a single quarter and a piece of clothing to Ann Arbor's homeless population. The following year, a second program was established, the goal of which was to reach out to our community's closed-in elderly. The next program to be included was a big sibling program for minority children living in low-income housing in our community. From these original programs (all of which still operate), we have grown to seventeen different programs currently being offered. Each year the commitment of staff has increased. Many of the original resident staff members who were involved in BCV have continued to demonstrate their strong concern for human rights and community service as they have pursued their professional careers as doctors, teachers, and social workers, as well as in countless other fields.

The staffing of Bursley Community Volunteers has changed considerably over the years. Originally the program was run at Bursley, independent of staff requirements. Most of the resident directors were involved, as well as some of the highly motivated resident advisers. As the program grew, increasing numbers of resident staff members expressed an interest in actively chairing a group. It was at this point that a full-time coordinator was hired and co-chairing became part of the job description for staff at Bursley Hall. This remains the structure under which Bursley Community Volunteers currently functions. Volunteering has become a special part of the Bursley staff experience, and the majority of the RAs involved are very enthusiastic about making the commitment.

One of the fundamental beliefs on which Bursley Community Volunteers was founded that we attempt to maintain is that if you can spare one hour a week, we can find a constructive way for you to use that time. We try to expose the truth about free time—there is really no such thing. BCV attempts to show that any problem, even those which seem insurmountable, can be broken down into smaller pieces and thereby be solved. We work hard to find opportunities that fit the desires and time constraints of our volunteers. Our program has grown and changed along with the needs of our community and the interests of our staff and volunteers. We pride ourselves on connecting dependable, enthusiastic volunteers to the community and are rewarded by establishing lasting contacts and offering meaningful service opportunities to our volunteers and those we work with. BCV provides a unique experience for both students and staff of Bursley Hall.

Volunteer Opportunities

After signing up for (a) particular committee(s), the volunteer attends weekly or bi-weekly meetings with the other volunteers and the committee co-chairs. Because this is a student-run organization, the volunteers are encouraged to play as active a role in the program administration as they desire. Meeting time is used for a variety of activities depending on the group. Some examples are making bulletin boards, planning outings, tutoring, brainstorming, etc. We feel that the volunteer experience provided through BCV provides a means of rounding-out the education gained at the University. Students are given the opportunity to actively pursue solutions to pressing social problems. This sense of caring and responsibility will stay with these students long after their years of college are over.

The committees of BCV change slightly each year in an attempt to best meet the needs of our community and the interests of our staff and volunteers. A brief description of each of the eight committees BCV will be sponsoring for the 1993-1994 academic year follows.

BACCHUS

This is BCV's first year of involvement with this national alcohol abuse prevention program. BACCHUS was established on the belief that "college students can play a unique and effective role in encouraging their peers to reflect on, talk honestly about, and to develop positive habits and attitudes toward...alcohol use or non-use." Our volunteers will sponsor weekend mocktail bars in the cafeteria, hold substance-free parties during televised sports events, and create a variety of activities aimed at educating our peers and preventing alcohol abuse within the college community.

BEAR

Bursley Environmental Awareness and Recycling (BEAR) was established with the goal of trying to raise the awareness of the entire community about environmental problems and encourage active participation so that we can heal the wounds which we have inflicted upon the Earth. BEAR develops environmental "thoughts for the month" which are simple things students can do to help prevent further destruction of our Earth, designs a large bulletin board which is aimed at more global measures for environmental protection, hosts speakers to help educate ourselves about issues, participates in river clean-ups, and promotes a campus-wide "trash-a-thon," a fund-raiser during which volunteers collect pledges based on how many pieces of garbage they clean up and a variety of other activities.

Big Sibs

Our volunteers are committed to the enrichment of the minority youth population in Ann Arbor. Community service efforts include culturally and socially enriching the lives of minority youth through increasing their awareness of higher education and its significance, as well as instilling pride, academic excellence and subsequently helping to prepare them for the future. This program sponsors weekly activities that promote positive goals and act as reinforcement for academic success. Volunteers interact with the youth one-on-one to help work with individual needs of the child as well as in small groups to help encourage positive group dynamics. Activities include tutoring, study tables, films, trick-or-treating, tours of the University, trips to Bursley and numerous other experiences.

Closing the Gap

Closing the Gap is a program which reaches out to senior citizens. We make weekly visits to two Ann Arbor Housing Commission Apartment Buildings and provide those residents with an opportunity to meet and interact with college students. Our goal as a volunteer committee is to try to bridge the gap between two very different generations. We work to find common interests between university students and senior citizens by planning activities which both groups will enjoy. In the past, these activities have included concerts, crafts, dinner at Bursley, discussions and movies.

Habitat for Humanity

Bursley Community Volunteers works with the Huron Valley Chapter of the national Habitat for Humanity. Habitat is a national volunteer organization that builds and refurbishes homes for those in need. There are several projects underway in the Ann Arbor and Ypsilanti area, and BCV provides about fifty volunteers to the various sites to help with construction. No experience is necessary so a wide variety of people are able to get involved. This is only our second year working with Habitat, but it instantly became one of our most popular groups. In the future we may look toward establishing our own chapter of Habitat for Humanity in hopes of completing additional homes in less time.

Helping Hands for the Homeless

Helping Hands works as a two-part volunteer organization. One part supplies overnight volunteers to the Ann Arbor Shelter Association. At the shelter, volunteers perform a range of duties. They check people in for the night, assign beds, answer phones, talk with clients, and help move clients along in the morning. Before volunteering at the shelter, interested individuals must attend a one hour orientation session sponsored by the shelter.

The second part of Helping Hands involves raising money specifically for the local homeless. Bursley residents are able to donate returnable cans and bottles by leaving them in the bathrooms. Volunteers collect these returnables, return them, and then donate the money. This money is used to provide basic needs for the homeless shelter and also for things such as security deposits on apartments.

Inmates Outreach

Our volunteers provide tutoring for those inmates at the Washtenaw County Jail who are pursuing their high school equivalency diploma and need extra help in basic high school skills. Students go through an orientation at the jail before beginning their volunteer work. By helping these individuals to receive their GED, we hope to help give them an extra chance when they return to society. As students at the University of Michigan, we realize that we are among the most privileged in our community. This committee gives us a chance to give back something meaningful to those less fortunate than us and put our skills to good use. We have received consistently positive feedback from the jail and have helped numerous inmates gain the skills necessary to successfully complete their GED examination.

Students for a Humane Society

Our students work with the Humane Society of Huron Valley and provide a wide variety of services to the Humane Society. Activities include helping rescued and abandoned animals, walking, comforting and playing with cats and dogs, adoption counseling, giving tours, recycling, school/nursing home visitations, clerical work, and much more. This committee is one of our most popular and provides a chance for students to interact with animals in need, while many of the volunteers are missing the pets they needed to leave behind when they came to college.

Making It Work

The key to making a residence-hall based volunteering program such as

Bursley Community Volunteers succeed is to have a dedicated group of staff. Whether a program is structured as a part of residence staff job descriptions or run independently, a lack of enthusiasm can easily work against all the positive energy behind your programs and eventually prevent you from achieving your goals and helping the community. Another factor of key importance is selecting which groups you will include in your program. A careful balance must be obtained between community needs and volunteer interests. BCV tries not to replicate the same thing that is already happening or receiving ample funding. While we do send volunteers to many established sites, these are all places which we feel are in need of the additional volunteers with which we can provide them. In order to provide the widest perspective possible, we try to keep a listing of other popular volunteering options available in our office for people interested in programs (such as hospital volunteering) that we do not currently offer.

We receive a great deal of feedback from the committee co-chairs which allows us to address problems as they arise. Each co-chair completes a bi-weekly evaluation (either written or oral) in which a description of the past two weeks' activities is given, any problems or concerns are expressed, and requests for funding or other assistance are made. These evaluations are kept on file and compiled at the end of each semester to help provide a more comprehensive view of the strengths and weaknesses of each individual program. In addition to this, each committee submits a semester report in which they (with the help of their volunteers) provide an overview of their program. We feel this sort of dual evaluation (individual and group) allows us to maintain the most accurate view on how the groups are functioning. This documentation then serves as valuable information for the next group of staff which will assume co-chair positions the following year.

Recruitment and placement are ongoing processes within Bursley Community Volunteers. Staff co-chair assignments are made well in advance to allow time to more fully educate the chairs about committee responsibilities before the actual volunteering begins. RAs are provided with a description of each of the committees, from which they rank their top five preferences. Most programs have three or four co-chairs assigned to them, with each person in charge of a specific aspect of administering a successful committee such as volunteer contact, community contact, secretary, publicity chair, etc. Early in the fall term, advertising begins for our mass meeting, and staff begin to talk with their residents generally about BCV. Fliers are posted throughout campus to attract interested students who live outside of Bursley Hall. We have a display board at freshmen orientation which lists our programs and office phone number and has copies of our brochure. This helps introduce students to the range of non-formal educational experiences available to them at the University of Michigan. Bursley Community Volunteers also sets up a booth at Festifall, which is a day-long showcase of campus organizations. These efforts provide us with a diverse and committed group of staff and volunteers. Although we are located in Bursley Hall, our volunteer opportunities are available to any student who is willing to make a one semester, one hour per week commitment to community service.

The operating expenses for Bursley Community Volunteers are quite reasonable. With the exception of the coordinator's salary, the program is completely self-funded. The hall council provides the organization with monthly allotments (currently $500) which cover the needs of the individual committees, and the expense of leasing and operating our volunteer station wagon. In addition, each of the committees organizes at least one fundraiser per year. In the past, we have received grant and University funding for specific programs and activities. These sources combined provide sufficient resources for a quality volunteer experience for all those involved, allowing us to offer dependable service for the clients and organizations we assist.

Bursley Community Volunteers has been a very successful program, but one which requires a great deal of planning and commitment. One element which helps to make our program a popular option is that Bursley Hall is located on the North Campus of the University of Michigan, isolated by a bus ride from the rest of campus. BCV allows students a constructive way of spending their time. Students living on central campus have a much greater variety of social activities available to them, and as such a residence-hall based volunteer organization may not be as popular a program. A dedicated group of staff is required to keep the quality of programs consistently high. Because Bursley RA's are required to serve as co-chairs, BCV is guaranteed ample staff for our programming. This may be more difficult if resident staff is not involved. Careful planning can provide options for addressing situations which do not exactly fit the template of Bursley Community Volunteers. After over ten years of providing community service to a constantly changing community and its students, we have gone through our share of both positive and negative experiences but we have persevered and grown as a result of each one. By remaining dedicated to the reasons behind providing volunteers to the community, you can make a program such as ours work, whatever your situation is.

Chapter 3

SERVEWORK
A New Career Center for the Social Change-Minded, and Non-Profit-Bound Student

By Craig Regester, SERVEwork Co-Chair

SERVEwork is a new career center at the University of Michigan that offers support and resources for students interested in pursuing jobs, internships, and long-term volunteer opportunities in the non-profit and social change sectors. The center is one of many programs that forms the entirely student-run community service organization, called Project SERVE. This organization has been working for over five years to promote and encourage student involvement in community service throughout the University of Michigan and greater Ann Arbor community.

The original idea that led to the establishment of SERVEwork was inspired by University of Michigan junior, Jane Klaes, during the fall semester of 1991. She had sensed a distinct void of a resource center on the University of Michigan's campus that encouraged and guided students seeking jobs in the non-profit and social change career sectors. While the University's traditional Career Planning and Placement center offered some resources in these areas, the help they provided was minimal. After a small amount of preliminary research, she had uncovered that another group of UM students had sensed a similar void in the mid 1980s, and established what was called the Alternative Career Center. Located in the Residential College, the center provided resources on various state and national non-profit organizations that were not available elsewhere on campus. Unfortunately, however, it had limited success due to its infrequent hours, and lack of institutional support from the larger university. Furthermore, after the students who had created it graduated, the Alternative Career Center dissolved.

SERVEwork grew directly out of the efforts of those students who had created the Alternative Career Center. With the help of three other University of Michigan upperclassmen, the observed need for a new non-profit resource center quickly transformed into a coherent plan of action. First, for the idea to turn into reality, the SERVEwork team needed money. Second, the initial money would be needed to subsidize an initial mass-mailing soliciting information from local, state, and national non-profit organizations from all over the country. The Residential College supplied a mini-grant during the Winter Term of 1992 to help defray the costs of an over 350-address mass mailing. Project SERVE provided staffing and financial support as well. The names and addresses of the organizations were taken from the dusty boxes of the former Alternative Career Center. Not surprisingly, some of the organizations no longer existed, some had moved to other locations, and some remained just the same. Of the roughly 400 mailed requests-for-information, approximately half of them eventually responded.

This initial mini-grant was followed by a much larger request for a Venture Grant from the Michigan Campus Compact. While SERVEwork received some funds from the annual Project SERVE budget, significant start-up funds were needed in order to get the center rolling. The start-up costs included money for: up-to-date books and resource guides for the SERVEwork library, subscription costs for monthly journals like EarthWork and Community Jobs, and office supplies such as binders, posterboard, and plastic sheet protectors. The grant also requested money for a proposed Alternative Career Fair planned for the spring of 1993. SERVEwork was fortunate to receive the full grant request of $4100.00 near the end of the 1992 Winter Term. Around the same time, Project SERVE added two new co-chair positions to its student-run board, to oversee the creation and establishment of SERVEwork during the 1992-93 school year. This institutional support provided assurance that SERVEwork would not become a "four-year experiment" like the earlier Alternative Career Center. SERVEwork would be here to stay on the University of Michigan Campus.

In the fall of 1992, the two co-chairs of SERVEwork began soliciting help from other interested students around the University of Michigan campus to participate in the establishment of the center. An eight-student team was eventually organized and began meeting regularly in mid-September 1992. From the beginning, each member of the team chose an issue(s) personally interesting to them and their own career tracks. The student issue-coordinators, as they were called, were responsible for contacting, researching, and organizing information from local, state, and national non-profit organizations that focused on their specific issue. Some of the issues included: hunger and homelessness, the environment, community organizing, religious-affiliated groups, and public health organizations. By the fall of 1992, SERVEwork had already received about 200 responses from the original mass mailing.

Once each issue-coordinator chose their designated area, the primary task ahead for SERVEwork was to envision all the services the center sought to provide, and how to go about providing them. After a few discussion meetings, it was decided that SERVEwork would provide four main services to interested students. These were: issue-folders, a resource library with books and monthly journal subscriptions, current job postings, and referral and support.

Each issue-coordinator was responsible for summarizing the non-profit agency information sent to SERVEwork, and organizing it into issue-folders. Thus, the "hunger and homelessness" issue-folder included summaries of non-profit organizations from around the country working on this issue. The "environment" issue-folder provided information on non-profits working in this area, and so on with all of the different issues. Though probably one of the more labor-intensive tasks of the issue-coordinators, the summaries eventually evolved into one of the more accessible and helpful resources SERVEwork provided to the student community. Each summary includes all the essential information non-profit organizations need to communicate to prospective employees, including: address, contact person, and how and when to apply for a position. Often non-profit organizations send a huge envelopes of information to interested parties, when actually only one page of information is sufficient. SERVEwork's issue-coordinators labored throughout the semester to consolidate and organize this information to make it more easily available to interested students.

The student-issue coordinator team and SERVEwork co-chairs, also collaborated to organize a resource library offering other relevant information about the non-profit and social change work sectors. Since the non-profit world seems to be constantly changing and growing, SERVEwork felt it was important to purchase the most up-to-date literature on the non-profit sector. After researching catalogues, and old books from the Alternative Career Center, an extensive list of potential resources was created. The list was then screened-out by members of the issue-coordinator team, and a final list of resources was created. Some books were ordered through mail-order, and others were purchased at Border's, the local bookstore. In planning the SERVEwork library, the student-team sought to include resources that would not only supplement the issue-folders, but also provide information giving historical and contemporary context to the social change sector. Some of the books ordered contained profiles of non-profit employees from different organizations around the country, and other books provided a more narrative picture of the history and development of non-profit work. Some of the more important books included:

1) Good Works: A Guide to Careers in Social Change, edited by Jessica Cowan. New York: Barricade Books, 1991.

2) Alternatives to the Peace Corps, eds. Becky Buell, Victoria Clarke, Susan Leone. California: Institute for Food and Development Policy, 145 Ninth Street, San Fransisco, California 94103.

3) Profitable Careers in Non-Profit, William Lewis and Carol Milano. New York: John Wiley and Sons, Inc., 1987.

4) America's Non-Profit Sector, Lester M. Salamon. Foundation Center: John Hopkin's University, 1992.

5) Great Careers: Fourth of July Guide ..., Devan Cottrell Smith. Garrett Park Press, 1990.

6) Volunteerism: The Directory of Organizations, Training, Programs, and Publications. Harriet Clyde Kipps, ed. R.R. Bowker, 1991.

Furthermore, monthly publications (Community Jobs and Earthwork) provided a consistent resource for current employment opportunities around the country. All in all, the SERVEwork library provides a range of resources and information adequate both for the first-year student just beginning to think about the non-profit world, and for the graduating senior ready to find a job with a specific non-profit organization.

SERVEwork also provided a bulletin board with up-to-date information on current job postings from local, state, and national non-profit organizations. During the initial mass-mailing, SERVEwork requested that all organizations send current job postings as they became available. As a result, throughout the

1992-93 school year, SERVEwork regularly receive job notices. Since most students are interested in finding jobs as soon as possible, this resource was utilized more than any other at SERVEwork. Unfortunately, because many non-profit organizations run very tight budgets, it was difficult for most of the smaller organizations to send recent job postings. Indeed, most of the postings SERVEwork received came from the Federal Domestic Action Agency, and other larger organizations like Green Corps, City Year, and Teach For America. Hopefully, this service will be expanded for the 1993-94 school year.

The final service SERVEwork provides students is referral and support from the issue-coordinators. Because the SERVEwork issue-coordinators spent so much time researching and organizing information from non-profit agencies throughout the year, it seemed logical to include their names and phone numbers in the issue-folders. SERVEwork encouraged all students who visited the center throughout the years to schedule a time to talk further about their area of interest with the appropriate issue-coordinator. The issue-coordinator team felt it was important to provide a "human element" to supplement all the books and other "paper" information found at the center. The issue coordinators were available to talk about anything from specific job postings to the politics of social change. Unfortunately, however, this service was rarely utilized by students who visited the center.

Reflections on SERVEwork

SERVEwork finally had its grand opening during the beginning of the Winter semester, 1993. The grand opening was a two-day event that attracted over 200 people, including many students, administrators, and a few professors. Since its opening, SERVEwork has attracted a consistent flow of students—most of whom, it has been observed, stay at the center for a substantial amount of time. While SERVEwork doesn't attract as many students as the more traditional Career Planning and Placement center, it has clearly been a helpful resource for a small group of concerned students, and will undoubtedly grow over the years.

Considering SERVEwork is still less than a year old, there is much to be learned from the past, and changed in the future. The creation of the SERVEwork issue-coordinator team was a very successful way to distribute, organize, and summarize the "loads" of information received from non-profits around the country. Unfortunately, like in any student organization, it was very difficult to schedule regular meeting times that all students could attend. As a result, after many failed attempts to plan bi-weekly planning meetings, it was decided that work would be assigned in the most independent manner possible.Thus, each issue-coordinator became responsible for their issue-folder, and the group decided to meet only once a month. Communication was facilitated among the group by the two co-chairs. I found that sending letters was consistently a more reliable form of communication than the telephone.

SERVEwork's biggest failure during its first semester on the University of Michigan's campus was its inability to network regularly with other resource centers on campus. While the SERVEwork co-chairs did meet on one occasion with staff from the Career Planning and Placement Center, more consistent communication and referral would have benefited both centers. SERVEwork also could have communicated better with the University's International Center, the School of Natural Resources, the School of Public Health, and the School of Social Work. These other campus resource centers would have benefited from SERVEwork referrals, and SERVEwork could have learned from their experiences as resource centers. Networking will be a much larger focus of SERVEwork in the coming years.

SERVEwork would also have benefited from keeping detailed records of the students who visited the center. By tracking these students, SERVEwork could learn more about how the students heard of the center, whether it was helpful to them, and what resources they utilized most. SERVEwork also could have more regularly referred student visitors to the appropriate issue-coordinators in their prospective field. In the future, SERVEwork issue-coordinators should have weekly office hours posted in the center so that interested students can talk with them at these times.

SERVEwork future issue-coordinators could further benefit the center by finding new and creative means for communicating with some of the smaller non-profit organizations around the country. As already mentioned above, SERVEwork needs to find ways for smaller organizations to more regularly send current job postings. It might be a good idea to make regular phone calls to organizations once a month to inquire about the most recent job postings. Furthermore, SERVEwork would benefit greatly by researching other monthly journal subscriptions like the Non-Profit Times. The regular publications that were used served as a strong supplement to the current job postings.

Finally, SERVEwork should establish an annual Alternative Career Fair to help promote the non-profit and social change sectors as viable career tracks. While this idea had been originally planned and budgeted for in the Venture Grant SERVEwork received, there was not enough time during the hectic planning of the grand opening to create such a fair. The former "Alternative Career Center" was very successful during its four-year existence in planning and organizing an annual fair. Many of the larger national non-profit organizations attended the fair. Furthermore, there were speakers and seminars which provided a vast range of perspectives, opinions, and experiences about working in the non-profit and social change sectors.

Ultimately, an Alternative Career Fair would help contribute to the fundamental goal of the SERVEwork career center—educating the student-body about the many non-profit organizations working for social change around this country, and helping those genuinely dedicated to this movement find their non-profit niche.

PART SIX

Reflections

Chapter 1

REFLECTORS ANONYMOUS
Six Recovering Service-Learners Share Their Experience, Strength and Hope

My visit to site this week was a horse of a different color. The site visit was for the purpose of obtaining my Western Wayne Correctional Facility volunteer identification card. Because I was about twenty minutes late, I had to wait in the lobby for Chaplain Daily for a while. As I waited, several officers were trying to figure out who I was. I just pretended that I didn't know what was going on. They kept asking me if they knew me from somewhere. You know most corrections officers pride themselves on remembering faces. And I wanted to see just how long it would take them to figure out who I as.

Finally, I couldn't take it any more, and I admitted to having been locked there some three years ago. Everyone was glad to see that I had made it. They all said they never doubted my intentions of making it when I left Western Wayne Correctional Facility in 1989. When asked why I came back there, I responded by saying, what better place to do my practicum than the place that had entirely changed the course of my life? I feel like I owe this organization something for setting me straight. I went on to say that I appreciated the decent officers who opened up to me and treated me with respect. I think that I could have become much more frustrated and aggressive had the staff been rude and inconsiderate. I even confronted Assistant Deputy Warden Sherman, who told me from the start to pursue a degree in social work. He was the most shocked to see me back and in the capacity that I had promised I would be in. You see, Sherman has only seen so many inmates leave that he knew wouldn't be returning to prison. Coming back he had little faith in a brother's ability to beat the system. They are talking about doing a newspaper article on me, for all to gaze upon my newfound success. If I can do it, anybody can. All you have to do is live your life right.

—Rick D.

Which one am I? For Christ's sake. I'm from West Bloomfield, and although I went to some boarding school with an ivy-covered campus situated on forty acres of lakefront, I still managed to wind up in rehab. I believe out of my graduation class of thirty-one, eight of us went to rehab, ten from the class before me, and seven in the one behind me.

We didn't go to some local hospital. We flew on airplanes to the rehab capital: Minneapolis. It was supposedly the finest adolescent rehab in the world. It had a 25% success rate. There were two bills, one from the shrink for twenty thousand, and one from the hospital for about that same amount. A friend of mine, Peter, actually had his fines waived because the rehab was so costly. Peter was convicted of ten counts of breaking and entering. The judge, believing Peter was a well-mannered and proper boy, let him slide with rehab and one year of probation, completely letting the fines go. It didn't really matter much since Peter's dad was the president of an insurance firm. Pete was fully covered, besides I think his father still managed to write it off.

It all sounds so silly; the silly rich kids from West Bloomfield fucking themselves up and then getting a slap on the wrist. It is ridiculous, I don't deny it. I'm damn fortunate. I don't feel guilty, lucky, but not guilty. I think we should all be treated the same, meaning the poor should be treated like us, not us like them. Peter is touring the world, but will go to law school next year. I am here. I should think judges could see rehab did us well and send more people there.

I feel more in touch with the prisoners as a result of my experience in rehab. I know why their poems are inspirational. I know why they seem so interested and cooperative. They are. I know what it's like to wake up after a couple weeks, after hitting a dark bottom, and find out you're doing just a little better. You know you've got nowhere to go but up. It's a serene feeling. You start to look forward to each day.

Josh talks about the fellow who said he writes because he can't control himself physically. I guess it is something that I might be concerned about. But I'm not. Somebody in there told him to do that, and it works. He is just telling us. I don't think I've ever met more honest people than in rehab. The prisoners are the same way. That is why the guy writes, because he's honest. Honesty can be scary. People would be afraid of me if I was honest about why I do things.

—Mack M.[1]

...Project Community has greatly affected my life, especially my relationship with my mother. I now feel that I have a better understanding for what she is going through, and I can begin to sort out my feelings. I now feel an empathy for her situation I have never experienced before. I know that I told you that my mother has decided to go to AA., and I am very happy to report that things are going very well for her. She now realizes what she has been putting us through (although I don't think she knows to what extent). She told my sister that our talk with her over Christmas Break really helped her to change her mind about getting help. I guess it would be pretty hard not to get help if your kids told you flat out that they thought you were an alcoholic.

I have to commend myself for a moment. I feel that I spoke intelligently to her about her problem, the effects it has had on my life, the ways she could get help and things she should do for herself. I attribute my ability to do this directly to my Project Community experience. The articles I have read, the discussions with other people in similar situations as my own and going through the Growing Tree Program myself, I am now beginning to better understand myself. I went through a terrible time during which I just completely hated my mother. I felt terrible about it all the time, because she knew how I felt about her and accused me of it. Now, I no longer feel that hatred; I feel love. I really do love my mother, even though I still dread to see her sometimes. I think that now it will be better, because she will have gotten help, and it won't be the constant worry about whether she is going to be drinking the whole time and picking fights with me. I am really proud of her, because it is a big step in the right direction. It seems to me that a big weight has been lifted off my shoulders. I used to be ashamed of my mother and not want people to know what was going on in my house, because I was embarrassed of her, and she would always try and embarrass me in front of my friends. I can now see the light at the end of the tunnel, and I am so excited about what is to come! I really don't know how to express my gratitude for the program and all of the help it has given me in my own life.

—Whitney M.

The articles in Wiz, especially "Doctors In Denial" sum up my experience with doctors, psychiatrists, and the whole medical profession in the long road I encountered before finally being diagnosed, (largely self-diagnosed, in a way) an alcoholic. Many of the symptoms described in the article, physical, mental and emotional, were present in my life but the blame was placed on everything other than alcoholism. I lacked motivation, I was too concerned with politics, I was too emotionally involved with all issues of the world, I was paranoid, I was the youngest of four children. After being hospitalized for the first time for the delirium tremens, which I was told was an anxiety attack, I was placed on tranquilizers (Xanax, if I remember correctly). I was taken to psychiatrists, by whom I was told not to read the news, eat more healthily, and get more exercise.

It's a long story, but in short, alcoholism was the last thing to blame. It was such a significant cause of my symptoms that it's amazing to me how much effort was taken to avoid recognizing it as such. This is not only a fault of the doctors and my parents, who played a small part, but also my own minimization and efforts to try and find another reason for my problems. To blame them on alcohol would have meant denying myself what was my only true love in life. I guess the important thing is that one has to come to the realization for oneself. I know that even if I had been told straight out that I was an alcoholic at an early stage, I probably would have taken it, as the coursepack states, as an accusation rather than a diagnosis. I am sure I would have put up some amazing defense mechanisms against such an accusation. From my experience, the readings were right on target.

—Tom A.[2]

I stumbled upon Project Community entirely by accident. I was all set to register into Anthropology 201 when it closed and I was reduced to frantically flipping through the course guide trying to find anything to take its place. My eye was struck by a section entitled "Alano Club[3]." I had been very wrapped up in recovery literature during the last few months, reading AA schedules, meditation books, and so forth. I wondered how some of it had crept into my course guide! I thought it was almost too good to be true when I saw the opportunity to gain university credit through community work, especially working with the AA program. I found out more about Project Community and became really interested in working as an academic tutor at Alpha House, a long-term treatment center for adolescents.

At first I was sure that it was probably full or too late to register. My excitement went beyond just taking a class which I felt I would really enjoy but affected my entire life. I myself had just gone through a stay at a treatment center for alcoholism which had taken my life through an incredible turn. Without going into a complete "drunkalogue," suffice to say that at 23, I had been diagnosed as a late-stage chronic alcoholic, had alcoholic hepatitis of the liver (stage two), had been kicked out of the University for terrible grades. Prior to treatment, I was a paranoid addict with no self confidence, zero self-esteem, and an all around dismal future. The only question was whether I would go completely crazy or die first.

The other alternative was recovery. Through extensive therapy, AA meetings, and a deep, honest, and uncompromising search of myself, I came to an understanding of my problems. The change which took place I can only call a spiritual and mental revelation. Things became so much simpler to me as my mind and my soul began to clear. Self-confidence naturally came back as my fears went away. The promises which a sober life offered to me in treatment and by AA had begun to come true. Problems themselves didn't disappear, but the need to drink over them had. The changes which took place in me are difficult to describe and probably sound sappy, but perhaps they have to be experienced to be appreciated.

Needless to say, with all this came an intense gratitude which was hard to hide, but which I hoped I could express by volunteering at Alpha House. The changes in myself didn't occur overnight and were dependent upon a continual honest and uncompromising inventory of myself. My newly discovered serenity would only remain as long as I made a day-to-day commitment to my recovery. I knew that with just one drink, I would once again become a slave to my addiction. I've read "that nothing will so much to insure immunity from drinking as intensive work with other alcoholics: and I hoped tutoring at Alpha House would offer this opportunity.

Added to my enthusiasm was my hopes for getting my teaching certificate along with my English degree. I had earlier found out that to be accepted into the School of Education, I would probably need some type of experience in working with students, of which I had none. Since I would have to apply by January and it was already September, I didn't see how this would be possible and had written off this option as a lost opportunity due to past mistakes. Well, Project Community offered the solution.

This is just one example of how solutions to problems just seem to take care of themselves in recovery whereas during my drinking years they would be so difficult or impossible to solve. After treatment, I was accepted back into the University, gained my job back, and my health continually improved. It's amazing the rewards received when surrendering to addiction, and it is this seemingly "outside" help, which has allowed me to gain faith in a higher power.

In order to register for Project Community, I first had to have an interview with the Project Coordinator[4]. I was afraid that my short time in recovery would work against me being admitted to work in a Project Community site. I've heard of the dangers of "two-stepping"—trying to carry the message to other alcoholics of revelations gained (Step 12) after taking only the first step towards ones own recovery. I was sure the coordinator would be aware of this problem as would the staff at Alpha House.

This was a question I put to myself before I decided to go to the interview. Was I putting myself at risk by doing this too soon? I asked for advice at AA meetings and from my therapist, who gave me suggestions, but I knew the final decision would have to be my own. The fact that my real purpose to volunteer would be academic help and not to teach the program was probably what led me to my final decision. I decided that it was okay for me to go ahead with it as long as I didn't let it interfere with my personal recovery. Provided that I was actively taking careof myself, I felt it could be a helpful learning experience which couldn't be gained inside a traditional university classroom.

I was a little nervous at the interview but felt that I was going in with the right mindset. At the interview, I expressed my gratitude for my recovery, my hope that I could express this by helping others who were in treatment, as well as my realization of my true purpose in volunteering. I felt that my admittance into the section depended on how much I could convince him—the Project Coordinator—of my sincerity and commitment to remain sober as well as diminishing his fears that I would relapse. The interview turned out to just be more of a matter of becoming acquainted with my interest in the project than being interrogated by the coordinator. He helped me to relax by saying it wasn't for him to decide how strong my sobriety was. When he finally wrote out the override for me to register into the class, something concrete seemed to sink in as to the changes recovery brought. Just a year ago I was a Jim Morrison wannabe, with visions of myself as this nihilistic, drunken poet who was "expanding" his mind and breaking on through to the other side. Now, here I was, trying to help others who had made the same mistake, and pursuing it with the same zeal with which I had formerly pursued the bottle.

The next step was for me and other students volunteering from the University to meet with the director of Alpha House. Walking into the center I saw some of the residents and actually recognized a couple from Alcoholics Anonymous meetings. One of the residents sat on a chair with her head in her hands, obviously crying, and my thoughts went back to my first days of treatment, where I also cried periodically and was in a deep depression. This outbreak of emotion from the students, usually tears, was something which would become quite common. It seemed that at least one resident a week missed class as they discussed their problems, through tears, with a therapist. So many feelings come out in treatment that it's impossible, if one is being honest with themselves, not to break down. Indeed, this is almost necessary before any rebuilding can be done.

The director described the philosophy of the treatment center, its policies, and asked us why we were interested in volunteering. I was happy for the opportunity to quickly get off my chest that I had also been in treatment, how I hoped to help others, and of my plans on a possible career in education. I assured him that I realized I wasn't there to give therapy, nor was I qualified, and this turned out to be one of the main points he wanted to speak to us about. He stated that the students would often bring up personal problems in the class room and that we should direct them to their therapists without getting too involved. He even said I shouldn't tell them that I myself was in treatment except to answer a direct question. We weren't to be stone cold, of course. The teacher, Rose, also stated how she was glad to hear I would stick to the academic side of the program.

Yet I didn't feel that just being involved in the academic side of the treatment center meant I was exempt from playing any other role in their program. Recovery, at least for me, was involved in every single aspect of life. You can't be in recovery during an AA meeting and then out of it at work or playing basketball, it stuck with you like a birthmark. For example, to be academically successful would likely be very helpful in finding one's sense of worth, while only being unsuccessful could be a detriment to one's self-esteem. All of this is related to recovery, and I saw how I could be of aid in this aspect.

I went to the first day of tutoring with many apprehensions, which I knew were ridiculous, but nevertheless were there. I had one vision of myself under a constant threat in the classroom by a hostile gang armed with guns and knives. I had still another foolish vision of myself connecting immediately with the students, turning them all into geniuses and discovering their hidden talents. I knew the importance of keeping an open mind, and after being introduced to the students, what I found was a group who would be indistinguishable from any other their age. The classroom itself was no different from others, barring the flag with AA's 12 steps on it.

Most of my tutoring involved correcting papers and providing help when needed, although Rose, the teacher, explained how this was to be done on a success-orientated method. Most of the students had only been told what they could not do and therefore dwelled on their past failures. I thought of the old saying that if you tell someone they're stupid enough times, they'll believe it. In grading their papers, I was not to mark anything wrong, but rather, to circle errors, have them corrected, and the student could only continue when they left the assignment with zero mistakes. The idea behind this approach is that if there weren't any negatives to be dwelt upon or punished for, the student maintained a healthier attitude. I often tried to offer encouragement, but in an effective way. I realized a smiley face on their paper wasn't going to do the trick.

Since the residents were all of different ages and in different levels of education, there wasn't much conventional classroom teaching but rather it was done on a more individual and personal level. One thing Rose told us to watch out for was encouraging "learned helplessness". When a student had problems and asked for help, they were often just trying to get someone to do for them what they could do themselves if they tried. If things were continually done for them, they would learn that they were helpless to do them by themselves. As the tutoring went on I found out how much help to give and how to simply steer them on the right track.

Just as in any classroom, the students' study habits varied. Some worked the whole time while others would consistently fool around. Rose handled them very effectively, I thought, and generally the behavior of the students was better than I expected. I was glad that I didn't have to become a disciplinarian toward the students.

During the school day, the students were allowed two breaks which gave me a chance to mingle with them on an informal basis. I made a conscious attempt to be loose with them and offer them an alternative to being taught by an authority figure. It was during this period which I was able to gain their trust so they would listen to me in the classroom and not be afraid to ask for my help.

One of the first questions a resident asked me was if I was a member of the AA program. I told him I had also been in a treatment center and was glad he asked, remembering the directors' comments. I felt that for the group to know this would allow for a strong and more immediate mode of connection between us and was relieved the next day when it had already gotten around to the other residents. It's an interesting phenomenon how strangers in AA can quickly relate to one another by their common bond of alcoholism. A room full of unknown faces becomes almost like family when they all have the same problem.

I remembered my days in treatment and how important it was for me that my therapists were also in recovery. It opened me up to them considerably more than if I thought they were just telling me what they had read in a book somewhere. They could draw on their own experiences and you could hear it in their voices as opposed to others who taught the program secondhand. Knowing that they had once been in your shoes was a tremendous asset in developing trust and communication. I hoped this would help me in my experiences at Alpha House as well. Perhaps the fact that I was an alcoholic, had experienced extreme academic difficulties, but through recovery was able to be once again enrolled in the University, would help them to think again about their own capabilities.

The last period of the school day gave me the best opportunity for some insight into their lives as well as the possibility for giving my own input. The students spent this time writing creatively or reflecting on current events in the news. One assignment was to write a story about the best day of their lives. I mentioned to Rose how this was especially relevant to the saying in AA, "My worst day sober is better than my best day drunk." The students all wrote about days spent clean and sober, but I wondered how much this was done to please the therapist and to avoid writing something "inappropriate".

Some of the stories and other assignments seemed to be incredibly revealing. One student wrote a story about three blind mice who went on a violent killing spree with machetes and machine guns. The blind mice eventually killed themselves by accident since they were blind and couldn't see who they were killing. Being an English major and constantly being faced with analyzing literature through a psychological scope, I couldn't resist seeing the twisting of a nursery rhyme as reflective of the student's own present situation. The mice kill the authority figure from the nursery rhyme, resist authority, but are then victims of their own revolution in that they end up killing themselves. This was a possible reflection of his own rebellion though drug abuse which turned on him and placed him here. They were both "blind" rebellions that had self-destructive results. I didn't know his personal background, so I could only speculate, but I must admit it was fun. I asked him about this twist on the nursery rhyme hoping to find out more. All he replied was that he always felt sorry for the mice and I didn't bother him with my interpretation.

Another story, which I thought was told in remarkable detail, especially coming from one of the youngest residents of the group, was about an old man who was interested in black magic. The old man is in a home for senior citizens and is very lonely there. He uses his witchcraft to bring about the end of the world. The story ends with the old man extremely pleased with what he did.

Once again there is a violent revenge story but with a happy ending. Also, the old man is in an institution, like the student, and feels very lonely, which I also assumed the student felt. I mentioned to the resident that the old man survived this apocalypse and asked him how it would be possible. He didn't know, of course, but I just wanted to point out that he couldn't be immune.

This violence is something which was a common factor in many of the stories. Another title of a story was "Fifty Ways to Torture a Monkey". I was sure some of it was just for the effect—when they read the story to their classmates, everyone would laugh and 'ooh' and 'ahh'—but I was also sure it was indicative of their of their own lives. I could only guess the extent to which this was true, but they definitely did not seem to be at peace with the universe. Rose explained how this was healthy therapy and a way to explain hidden feelings, and I agreed whole-heartedly. It was a great way for them to take their aggression out and not to keep it locked up until it built resentments.

The day was set up on a consistent schedule. Rose explained how the students needed the safety and security of a set schedule, and she, in turn tried to keep her actions consistent. This was also done through the weekly schedule of the residents so they could learn to live by a schedule and get used to routine. I remembered the strict routines I experienced in treatment and how this loss of freedom felt like a boot camp.

Connecting with the students didn't come quickly, nor did it build steadily, but rather, it seemed to develop in leaps and bounds one day while on another there wasn't any development. However, as the relationships progressed, the residents developed an almost childlike need for attention. These types of feelings were actually encouraged by the staff since many of the residents had missed much of their childhood. For instance, upon entering the center, they were each given a teddy bear, which some would bring to class. Just as in AA meetings, students would often hug each other in class, something which those Project Community volunteers who were not in recovery did not understand.

I began to see my sincerity in volunteering reflected in the students reactions to me. Things such as attending a group recreation session and staying past my scheduled time when needed helped them to become more receptive to me. They asked when I was returning and seemed to look forward to seeing me again. This dependence was something I was sure I would have to be wary of, but it seemed to be unfolding in a healthy way for myself and for the students.

I was concerned about establishing and maintaining healthy boundaries with the kids, and this did present itself as an issue. For instance, each resident has the option of calling an impromptu "concerns group" in which they get together to discuss any concerns over how the group is interacting. One day, during break, I walked out of the bathroom and into the room when they were having a concerns group. I excused myself and began to leave when they said I was free to stay. I didn't because I felt it would be violating my boundaries to do so. For one, it was a student who asked me to stay and not one of the staff. Also, I remembered how a seemingly peaceful or mellow group could explode in an outbreak of emotion and vehement feelings and I didn't want to get involved in that.

One day Rose brought in a tape of one of the presidential debates to watch during third period. There was only one registered voter among the group, but they were all told to pick a candidate who they thought had won the debate. Their insight was amazing, even the staff watched as the residents analyzed and could see right through many of the candidates' responses. This is probably a reflection of their insight, or maybe these candidates are just becoming too easy too figure out. They commented on Perot's common sense, straight forward approach, but realized that he was not presidential enough, and said all that

Bush and Clinton were doing was fighting amongst themselves, and they didn't know if they could believe a word they said. I was disappointed, however, that they did not mention the drug war, prevention, or treatment in this debate as they had in the first debate. I mentioned to Rose she might have the students examine the candidates various policies. When Clinton ended his concluding comments with the words, "the courage to change"[5] the students right away noticed this as also a part of their recovery literature. Most of it was in a joking manner, but it was definitely noticed, and I was sure it was inevitable given its daily onslaught. It didn't seem to effect their view on the candidate, however.

I couldn't really adapt this idea of the courage to change in recovery to Clinton's platform myself, not because I didn't see that it was necessary politically, but because somehow to make it a political issue seemed to taint it. Even though he will probably get my vote, I didn't want to see myself as "pulling a Clinton" by having the courage to change, which I felt was something that went much deeper than the world of politics.

This "recovery humor" happened often, and I would have been left in the dark if I had never heard the sayings before, but as it was I could understand the jokes. The students would say, "That's a half-measure,[6] Miss Silver!" Or if someone got a problem wrong, "There are such unfortunates." They had the promises completely memorized, and someone would often mockingly bring one up when the room got too quiet. I think that this is probably a healthy way of taking off the life and death seriousness of recovery and the humor using the sayings is not detrimental if it is not meant derogatorily towards the program. The fact that it is used also seems to be proof that it is sinking in that the language becoming a part of ones vocabulary shows it is often thought of. I'm sure there is something subliminal about humor, and if it is a recovery saying which comes up during a joke, then the program must be sinking in to the sublime. I often find myself resorting to a language which I had learned through the program, and find that I have to switch gears depending on who I am talking to. This is all a part of the usefulness of those being in recovery helping those in treatment, and was another channel I used to connect with the residents.

"Getting Off Task"

I never tried to discipline the students when they were fooling around, or "getting off task," as the teacher put it. I was grateful that I wasn't expected to because I didn't think I could bring myself to be stern, and also, I didn't want to cause any resentment towards me in the students. I remembered the way I thought of authority figures at that age and hoped they didn't see me in this manner. The result was, as the teacher put it, I acted like their grandmother. The most I would do when they got off task is warn them they were going to get in trouble and lose their break if Rose caught them.

Many of the incidents of disobedience that occurred in the classroom paralleled the social situations of drinking and drugging, which the students themselves seemed to be aware of. In one case, a student, who was getting restless, got up out of his chair with a sly look on his face and changed his seat saying, "I'm going to go get Robyn off task." This was out of earshot of the teacher but I heard and walked over to them to try and head off the situation. It was only a matter of minutes before the student who was working was distracted by the other, they engaged in their typical tomfoolery, and Rose gave them their first warning. Rose wrote this status on the board when the student whispered "See, I could have just gotten you drunk, Robyn."

The student was aware of the influence of peer pressure and how, if you push the right buttons, you can get others to do things that they wouldn't do otherwise. This was dependent, however, upon the other student not being conscious of giving up his/her personal control and not putting a stop to it. I thought of all the times I drank because of the actions of others who had pissed me off and how I had similarly allowed them to get me off task. The idea of being on task, it seems, can be applied to larger contexts than the classroom.

This idea of control and how it related to their recovery was something which was often misinterpreted. It seems that a parallel can be drawn with how people often misinterpret the idea of being powerless over alcohol. In one case, a student was doing an assignment in his workbook while the answer key lay at the end of his desk facing the opposite direction. I noticed him glancing at the answer keys and, once again to avoid any real discipline, I said, "you wouldn't do that," jokingly ignoring the fact that he already was.

"Of course I would, I'm an addict," he said, just before Rose came by and scooped up the answer keys.

I saw an opportunity to offer myself as an example and said, "That's no excuse, so am I," probably sounding self-righteous.

I saw how he was letting the idea of being powerless over the drug and alcohol addiction leak into other aspects of his personality where it had no business being. This was definitely something he could have power over. I thought of all the times I drank thinking, "of course I'm going to drink, I'm an alcoholic, and that's what alcoholics do." I saw how this rationale was flawed. For me I dealt with the disease concept of alcoholism as a partial explanation of why I kept drinking to excess after the first drink. As for the students, being a genetic alcoholic did not mean you were genetically predisposed to cheating or getting off task.

There was one student in particular whose academic habits reminded me of myself. He was very intelligent but an underachiever, which he himself admitted. He only pushed himself in order to stay ahead of others thereby remaining on top. This, in turn, seemed to give him some kind of grant to disobey the teacher. I did notice that his actions seemed to be punished less severely than identical actions of others less gifted, and remembered how this was true for myself during my high school days.

The student's lack of applying himself was not entirely his fault, however, since he didn't have anything to challenge him. He had finished the highest levels of textbooks Alpha House had to offer so instead he spent his time working on the same material in different texts but of the same level. "I'm going to finish all the books in here before I leave," he said. In one sense, this really made me feel lucky for my opportunities, and also sad that his very real potential was being denied. I guess it was "first things first" and that he had more serious and threatening issues to take care of, so school was not his top priority. I asked him once if he wanted me to bring in a calculus book—Alpha House had none—to which he replied "wouldn't be prudent at this juncture," doing his best George Bush.

He didn't lack ambition entirely, however, and he did hope to go to college. I couldn't deny the sad truth, however, that in applying to colleges, he would only be able to use the fact that he passed the GED rather than a grade point average from an established high school. Additionally, I assumed that AA meetings as extra-curricular activities would hardly be looked on favorably by a major university. He asked me numerous questions about me and the University, how much homework they give you and such, and he decided, "If you can do it I can do it." This gave me the opportunity to tell him that he wasn't any different than I was at his age, and that he would be able to handle it.

His situation made me think about the age at which I entered treatment and how my life would be different if I had gone to treatment at their age. At their age, I was sure my problems were just as severe, and I looked at the Alpha House residents as images of my own background. I drank heavily every weekend in high school, and towards my later years, was sneaking vodka from my parents' liquor cabinet on a fairly regular basis. It escalated every year until it became daily by the time I was ready for college. There was always a way I could think of to get something to drink, and I am still amazed at the lengths I would go to. At that point, I had no idea I had a problem, and would therefore have never done anything to change what I didn't think was wrong in the first place.

Perhaps things would have been different if I had done something at that age, but probably not. I think I needed the hard lessons that could only be learned as the disease progressed: delirium tremors, paranoia, physical deterioration, etc. My bottom was a bit lower than those of the Alpha House residents but it needed to be reached before I could convince myself to get sober. I looked at it in a spiritual manner. Some people face the inevitability of death saying "the Lord takes us when he wants us," I had the same view at the time when I entered treatment.

There was one occasion in my high school years when my parents threatened to place me in treatment after I was caught with a quarter ounce of dope. My parents went through the typical freak out, wondered where they had gone wrong, and saying "how could a smart kid like you do something like this?" To my relief, they eventually forgot about it, but I'm not sure what I would have done had they gone through with it. My view of treatment at that time was a place they put you in a straight jacket in a padded room and hid any suicide-aiding objects (for example, Alpha House residents do have to check out their shaving razors). I also thought of the two residents from my high school who had gone through treatment. One returned to school and was successful in recovery but was avoided by virtually everyone, in part because he always seemed to be preaching. The other came back to school, shortly returned to drugs and eventually stuck his head in a noose and jumped off a chair. This confirmed my earlier belief that I wasn't like those "nutsos."

There was, in fact, one resident, (at least only one that I knew of) who had committed suicide after leaving Alpha House, and there was also one presently in treatment who had been dangerously suicidal and had to be taken to the hospital one time. She seemed to be manic-depressive, laughing at anything and nothing in class on one day, and the next day, spending the entire period just laying under the serenity bench or sitting on the floor in the corner, mentally and physically off in some other world. It didn't seem to matter where she was at, if a mood swing hit, she would just lay down and not talk to anyone, often crying softly. When she was active, she was the most self-expressive of the group, and in my conversations with her, was very pleasant. While in class, she would spend most of the time writing letters to friends from home, writing in her journal, or just doodling, meaning that Rose would have to tell her to do her work or she couldn't stay in class. Rose was careful not to push her, realizing she was very unstable, but had to make sure she was doing something academic. It was something about the board of education and how much state aid Alpha House would get towards numbers of students who participated in the class based upon applicable tax percentage per capita. In other words, some kind of bureaucratic bullshit which was so often necessary in Alpha House (and I felt detrimental) but where there was no individual to blame. Consequently, she was hardly in class, hated it when she was, and this added to her precarious existence. I realized she was probably in the right place and was where she needed to be, but she didn't show any signs of improvement and I could often sense the frustration of the staff about this situation. The promises of AA were definitely something which had not yet come true for this resident.

"The Pink Cloud"

It has been said that being in treatment is like being on a pink cloud. You are in a safe environment, surrounded by people who understand addictive behavior, and you are removed from the real world. This makes it a safe place to practice a life of sobriety but it is once removed from the sobriety-threatening world. As soon as you leave, you are bombarded with beer commercials and glamorized abuse, and once again have to deal with peers and family who earlier played a part in your abuse. You realize that even though you may have changed through treatment, the world has not. As simple as it sounds, its' effects are weighty for the newly-recovering person.

Re-entry into the outside world is a delicate process. Alpha House residents first spend six weeks just going home on weekends, plus there is an elaborate after-care program, but it only takes a moment alone to pick up a drink or a pipe. One person I was in treatment with, I found out, didn't last one hour. I talked with a resident from Alpha House who had previously been in treatment, and he told the same story of being drunk hours after going home. The day I got out of treatment the thought of heading directly to the usual party store crossed my mind. It was the natural thing to do since I had done it for so many years. No matter how long you remain on the pink cloud, you have to come down to Earth where there's a party store and an opportunity to get drunk waiting on every corner.

This is one of the reasons why Alpha House doesn't release residents until after the holiday season. One resident was due to leave in December, but was staying until mid-January. The holiday season is a time with much more substance abuse and this creates more threats for the newly-sober person than are usually present. What might be deemed to be addictive behavior during the holiday was attributed to seasonal cheer and this was potentially dangerous to a person in recovery. The problem was something I was very aware of, but my experience of it proved to be even rougher than I had expected.

It all started on the Wednesday before Thanksgiving when my family and some friends all planned on going down to the Red Wings game, hockey being another one of the events which I found I could still enjoy without being wasted. The game started at seven-thirty and my parents said they were leaving at six.

I asked them why so early, being suspicious, and they replied that they would probably stop for a drink on the way, meaning that they definitely would. I had been well-trained for such a situation, asked them to leave me two tickets, and told them that me and a friend would meet them at the game. Part of me thought they were being very insensitive, but I realized they were just doing what they always did and that I couldn't change that. After the game we went to dinner and I had the option of leaving before the post-dinner drinks, but this wasn't a problem since I didn't feel the need to leave.

The next day was Thanksgiving, which was being celebrated at our house, and which would therefore pose a much different scenario. I didn't have the option of leaving early—no escape route. Holidays in my family meant fifths of Vodka and cases of beer as much as turkey and presents. With my new sober outlook I could see clearly the abuse of alcohol that went on in my family and remembered what a convenient purpose it had served to hide my own problems. I could compare, minimize, and rationalize so easily amongst this crowd. I sadly remembered my grandfather who used to come to these family gatherings with the shakes until he had his first drink. He would continue to drink until he stumbled around the room, slurring and forgetting my name. Finally, at my aunt's birthday party, he fell, hit his head, went into the hospital, and never recovered. I wondered what the coroner listed as the cause of his death.

But it was business as usual at my house, and when the party got rolling, I spent most of the time playing with my younger cousins. I offered to give one a piggy-back ride down the stairs, but he seemed reluctant, saying "I don't trust you." He eventually got on my back, we rambled down the stairs, and I let him down saying, "See, you can trust me." "Only when you don't drink too much," he replied, and I wondered how many more times it would take until he trusted me completely.

As the party went late into the day, I felt a sense of powerlessness[7] which was very distressing. Powerlessness over alcohol was one thing, but not being able to control it being poured right under my nose was another. It wasn't like I hadn't been around drunks before, but it was never in a situation where I was expected to be present and where I couldn't leave if it became intolerable. This was probably one reason being in treatment was so safe because this control was never taken away. I talked to one of the Alpha House residents about this problem, specifically about my sister's upcoming wedding where I was sure I would be uncomfortable at the reception. I told him I thought I might leave early, and the resident said, "Then they'll be like, *'But she's you sister'*", and I knew that he understood completely.

Another one of the problems with holiday drinking is that it was "happy" drinking. Alcoholic repercussions give way to the spirit of the season. There was my uncle, who had lost his job, whose wife had left him, whose house was falling apart, who looked twenty years older than his age, but he was all smiles. The last thing I needed to do was associate these happy images of holiday cheer with what my abuse was like. I couldn't afford to distort the truth about what had happened to me and which was still waiting for me if I chose to pick up. The situation left me feeling frustrated, erratic, and like what people in AA refer to as a "dry drunk."[8]

I eventually left the house to go to a midnight meeting. It wasn't so much that I was afraid I would take a drink—I am on Antabuse, for one thing—but I didn't want to spend a day with my serenity so out of whack. One day of bad sobriety could spoil the many months of inner peace which I had been striving to maintain. The meeting was crowded, full of people with similar problems, and seemed to hit the spot. Having such a place to go made me feel extremely grateful. I realized my first mistake of not planning a definite meeting to attend that day beforehand, and made sure not to make the same mistake on similar days to come.

The next day I woke up with a sigh of relief—"made it," I thought. I called a friend who was home from school and he said him and a few friends were planning on going to see "Malcolm X". I got ready to go, called him back, and learned that their plans had changed. They were now going to the pub in the mall before the movie. I canceled and started to think the whole world around me, everything and everyone it, was on a bad drunk. It wasn't unusual for us to gather at a bar while being home from school during the holiday season, it was just that my outlook had changed and it would have been foolish for me to expect anything different. Alcohol makes the world go around for many people, especially during the holidays, and this wasn't going to change even if it almost killed me. I reminded myself that the disease is insatiable, never satisfied when it claimed a life and eternally patient to claim another.

I went to an afternoon meeting and was able to talk more about my problem as I started to understand more about what I was going through. I had to work the next two days and was actually thankful since this provided a sanctuary from what I felt was a very unpeaceful holiday. Recovery related decisions were still present, however. The date for the work Christmas party was set and I had one week to RSVP. I hoped these decisions would get easier the more time I had in sobriety.

I went back to Alpha House the Monday after Thanksgiving half-surprised to find it still standing. I was comforted by the environment, the 12 step flags, the serenity bench, and could feel something different in the air. Even Sherlock, the loyal Alpha House dog, somehow seemed more sober than my own dog. It was a fresh breathe of sanity, and it felt good to be back among the pink cloud, if only for a few hours. I began to fully realize the idea of helping others in order to help yourself.

I jumped right back into tutoring, helping a student who was taking the math GED in a few days. I was working out a problem for him when I messed up a simple multiplication problem. "I think I lost my mind over the weekend," I mumbled. "You didn't go out and use did you?" he asked. "No," I reassured him, but at break I got a chance to tell him a little of my ordeal and my feelings of frustration. He said he felt lucky that none of his family used and that one family member was even in the program.

As I got to know the students, they would tell me about their lives in greater detail. They also asked me more questions about my own use and abuse of drugs. In one of these confiding moments, one said, 'I don't want you to use this as an excuse to think you don't have a problem or nothing, but you don't look like you could have been much of a drunk. You just look like a studious college boy." I laughed, understanding what he meant by not wanting me to use his statement to minimize my problem, and told him a couple of stories to let him think otherwise. I hoped I could offer myself as an example of the disease's policy of not discriminating against any class, race, or religion, and how it disregarded IQ as a prerequisite. It was truly an equal opportunity destroyer.

I was able to use the philosophy behind "one day at a time"[9] in tutoring. One student had just finished a workbook in science and had to take a test to measure his degree of mastery. The test was seven pages long, and the student felt he had no chance of passing since he had never taken a test that long. I held the test in front of him and covered up all the questions except number one. He got it right, and I uncovered the second question which he also got right. "Maybe it is possible," he concluded. He took the test and got 81%. The same step by step, day by day, small victories seem to be necessary for sobriety. I've never been sober this long before either, and if I look at the big picture I am overwhelmed just as the student was, but I can handle it for today.

"Politics, Serenity Benches, Derelicts, and Deadheads"

During the campaign, the students spent much of their time during third hour looking through the newspapers in order to find out where the candidates stood on a list of issues. I brought up Clinton's stance of treatment on demand for substance abusers. It was something that the students were directly affected by and something I felt strongly about. During my own stay at a treatment center, I had seen many patients enter the hospital who were only allowed to stay through a three day detox before their insurance ran out. They left the center with a slightly clearer head but with no attitude change and with no chance opportunity to learn how to stay sober. I remember talking to one guy who was there for his eleventh time. As soon as he was medically stabilized, he had to leave the hospital. His insurance wouldn't pay for what was really needed, that being the therapy available in the treatment program. It was a vicious merry-go-round which kept turning due to lack of funds. I saw at least six people during my short stay who had to leave, and even though they were pointed in the right direction and given steps to take such as going to meetings, I've got to believe that this wouldn't be enough and that they would go right back out again. I know I would have. As much gratitude as I have, I also realize that recovery is not only life and death, but big business.

I asked one student if they'd seen or knew anyone who wanted and needed treatment but was denied because they couldn't pay. The one I talked to about this said he had but he didn't seem too affected by Clinton's proposal. The fact that Clinton mentioned this issue in light of his brother's problems seemed to make the cause self-serving. This exemplifies the extreme cynicism which became increasingly noticeable in the residents as they read the candidates various promises and proposals and categorically called them lies. I wasn't sure onwhat basis their judgments were founded. It couldn't have just been one misreading of the presidents lips. Perhaps it was just the given thing for them to do, distrust anyone in authority and thereby they were always safe from being lied to. I really couldn't decide how much to read into their cynicism as to how it related to their lives. I was glad that they didn't blindly believe what they read, but I thought they were out of balance.

Politics was something I was learning not to get too worked up about. It falls into that shady region where one can never tell what s/he actually can change—how powerful is one vote or act of political activism?—And that which one cannot change—how impenetrable is the established system to any individual protests?. The wisdom to know the difference is especially hard to come by dealing with this issue. In my heavy drinking and drugging days, I really thought I was making a political statement through massive drinking. I wanted to see myself as some oppressed artist who the "system" drove to drugs as an outlet. It was all a part of the way in which I blamed everything and everyone except myself. To become clean and sober was to sell out, I thought, and in turning to alcohol, I effectively made myself incapable of any influence whatsoever. This is the irony of it all. If you do truly feel that you are entirely powerless to change anything in the world, once you turn to drugs, you have successfully turned this feeling into fact.

The students' processing of the campaign issues culminated when they had a debate the day before the election. I was happy to find out that one of the other students who had been there longest did have strong feelings towards the issue of drug treatment. She emphasized this issue when debating for Clinton's platform and criticized Bush for his lack of funding. I hoped it would convince the others to feel the same.

In the spirit of the campaign, the students found that their arguments were more weighty if they focused on the other candidates' negatives qualities. When Clinton's marijuana use came up, the fact that he didn't inhale was met with the saying "minimize and rationalize." Other hot topics were, no new taxes, draft-dodging, and marital fidelity, although they were also able to discuss more relevant issues. The students asked a thousand questions of me and who I was voting for. I told them I wasn't sure so that they would make their own decision without my influence. The one resident who was going to actually vote was pondering if he should vote for Perot or if this would merely result in a vote for Bush. The fact that he even thought about this revealed he had an understanding of the process. When I said that I had never voted before even though I was eligible (which was true) the residents thought I had broken some kind of law and asked if I got into any trouble.

Alpha House was full of recovery-related external stimuli to try to encourage the internalization of the program. There were two hamsters named Dr. Bob and Bill Wilson,[10] art therapy designed to learn patience, and group recreation designed to learn to trust others, but one which I found especially useful and creative was the serenity bench. I found out about this one day when I arrived a few minutes early. One of the residents was doing laundry and spilled detergent all over. I guess this was one in a long line of mishaps she had that morning because she spouted off about how she was having a terrible day and was fuming with anger. Instead of going to class she sat on the bench while the rest of the students went to the classroom and took their seats. The teacher took role, called for this student, and one responded, "She's on the Serenity Bench" and the teacher seemed immediately understood. I began to think of all the other times I'd seen residents sitting there, crying with their head in their hands or talking to the therapists. I guess this explained it. The student was in class in a few short minutes with her composure back.

It was an idea that would sound corny if it wasn't so effective. Actually, I think everyone needs their own "serenity bench"—a place to sit and regain their perspective and perhaps repeat the serenity prayer until it started to help. Mine would have to be my bedroom, where I would retreat to whenever I lost my balance, and would put on music to fit my mood until I could find an inner peace again. Listening to Sinead O'Connor's "I Do Not Want What I Haven't Got" always did the trick for me. I talked to other residents about it, and they compared it to the pity-pot where people go when they feel sorry for themselves. They can sulk until they're ready to join the group again. I remembered the expression that being depressed is a sign that you're thinking about yourself too much. The serenity bench seemed to have a dual purpose. I could never look at it the same way again, and the students probably experienced a certain feeling when they thought of this designated area as well.

As I began to enjoy the tutoring at Alpha House and was really able to turn it into a learning experience, I was taken back one day when my sister visited my house and asked, "So, I hear you're teaching a bunch of derelicts?" At first I took it as a personal attack and wanted to defend them. Here I was, watching them struggle with their emotions, seeing what it is like to deal with both becoming an adult and freeing themselves from addiction, seeing them work the program, and in one passing sentence they had been reduced to "derelicts". My next emotion was one of sad admittance of what they had to look forward to when they joined society again, for in the eyes of larger society they would always be derelicts. This was the type of attitude they had waiting for them when they got out of treatment and I knew they would need to learn to rise above it.

I thought of my first apprehensions as to checking into a treatment center. I had firstopted for outpatient treatment mainly because I didn't want to be associated with those who had been in rehab. Somehow outpatient was more "normal." It was partly due to my own prejudices, but also because I knew the way society viewed these people.

Although there does seem to be a widely growing acceptance towards people in recovery, there will always be a prejudice as long as it is misunderstood. I suppose in a perfect world, AA would no longer have to be anonymous, but as it is, it seems to be necessary. One starts to forget the attitude of the real world after spending so much time in circles of recovering people, and this must have been especially true for the Alpha House residents who spent six to nine months in this recovering atmosphere. This is also one reason why it is easier to relate to others in recovery while in treatment, for one is virtually assured that they do not carry any negative prejudice towards addicts.

The changes one has to make in recovery affects many aspects of their life-style. This means what type of people you hang out with, where you socialize, and even what hours you sleep. This change of life-styles came up when I was talking to a student from Alpha House who asked what kind of music I liked. I told him of my wide range of interests along with my experiences travelling to see Grateful Dead shows. I came to find out that we had attended some of the same shows and we talked about different experiences. I wanted to avoid glamorizing this life-style, seeing what it had done to me, and told how I didn't plan on attending any shows in the near future and might not ever be able to go again. It wouldn't be worth the risk. The parking lot of a Dead show is like Dante's Inferno for someone in recovery.

This issue is extremely difficult, for I am not ready to make any type of moral judgement as to the quality of this life-style. I still enjoy the music and have some of the same beliefs, yet in the long run it was killing me, and I have found a much greater peace and freedom without the drugs.I couldn't renounce what had been some of the happiest days of my life. I suppose I had entered the "Be kind to your mind" camp.

I relayed to the student some sayings as to the effects one's surroundings have on their recovery, like, "If you sit around the barber shop long enough, you're gonna get a haircut" and "You don't go the to the whorehouse to buy a loaf of bread." As it was, the students weren't even allowed to wear any of the clothes that might be associated with the "drug culture," which went so far as to include ripped jeans or bandanas. I wore my black leather jacket to the treatment center until I found out that the residents weren't allowed to wear them, so I stopped doing so out of courtesy. I suppose this policy of Alpha House was a way of going to one extreme until a happy medium can be found by the individual, but sometimes it seemed to border on sick thought control rather than healthy reasoning.

Towards the end of the year the students worked on a newspaper with articles both about Alpha House as well as outside issues. One of the editorials I helped a student write concerned Dr. Kervorkian and the right of the terminally ill person to choose their own death with medical aid. This led to an interesting although hypothetical question concerning recovery. The student asked, "If you had a disease and were given two years to live, would you go back out (go back to using drugs and alcohol)?" This was a difficult question regarding the preference of a sober life, since, if you genuinely preferred being sober, you'd want to live out your remaining time drug-free. Right? I thought about telling him what I thought he should hear, that I would stick to the program and live happily ever after. Instead, I answered with a straightforward reply, saying that I couldn't honestly say what I would choose to do, but that I was enjoying my life as a sober person. I felt this was an honest expression of some doubts I had, yet at the same time was optimistic. The student asked if that wouldn't just be an excuse to go and use again. Sure it would, but what an excuse! Furthermore, to imagine future difficulties in recovery seems to go against the "one day at a time" philosophy which is so central to the AA program. Especially such incomprehensible and strange circumstances. It could keep an addict up nights wondering "What if you were stranded on a deserted island and a bottle of vodka fell from an airplane?" I realize that he was being hypothetical and even joking, but thinking back, I should have probably advised him to stay in the day. Once again, I didn't know how far to go in offering advice since the border between giving therapy and just offering support was shady.

This led to a more relevant conversation, and one in which we both agreed on, and that is any type of drug or alcohol use could never be the same. We talked about the program being so ingrained in the back of our mind and how it would now always be there (unless they found some way to have it surgically removed). Any kind of future use has fortunately been ruined. He told a story of someone who was in the program for a lengthy period and went back out and took some acid. They had a bad trip, and were mentally tortured by all the AA slogans which kept flying at them in their mind. I was sure that any of my own use would also be undermined by my knowledge of a better life and hopefully this would deter any sustained using. This would probably even apply to a drink taken alone on a deserted island, miles from a meeting and out of view of anyone.

The end of the term offered a breaking point to measure the progression of the course, both for the residents and for myself. Alpha House was a very dynamic place in which to work. Changes were taking place constantly, but it seems that they are only noticeable when looking at a sustained period rather than day to day. The resident who had threatened suicide and was in mental shambles, who had the habit of lying under tables or the serenity bench, was now attending class regularly and was able to concentrate on her school work. All of the residents who had taken their GED's had passed and were getting jobs. Many were starting their weekend trips to home and beginning their reinstatement into society. At least three clients were being released in January. The newer residents were slowly being "broken," which is the only way I could describe the way they have to grudgingly give into their circumstances. Things were not perfect, but I began to see Alpha House as a largely effective institution which I had not felt towards many others.

As for myself, I was feeling an extreme sense of purpose, especially in comparison to the uselessness I had felt a year earlier. I had grown very comfortable dealing with the residents. I realized that I realized that I did have something useful to give and with this feeling came a new confidence which I had not known before. This was not derived solely from Alpha House, of course, but it was where the changes were most evident. I had tried to find self-esteem and confidence in a bottle, but had not found it there. Now I was finding it within myself in all aspects of life. I still had pangs of irrational fear, feelings of despair, and slightly nihilistic tendencies, but these were fewer and, most importantly, I knew how to deal with them.

I also had different feelings towards volunteering itself. In the past I had thought of volunteer work as somehow pretentious but now I realize it can be done out of genuine sincerity. My feelings towards the education system had changed as well. My past courses at the University had been so far removed from my personal life that it lacked any relevance to my well-being as a person. Here I found something I could grasp and integrate into my own situation. If that isn't important enough for the University to consider for all students then something much bigger is wrong. I still felt the University had its problems, but I had found proof that there was alternatives to its present situation.

I also realize, however, that at times I probably have substituted success in Project Community for success in recovery instead of treating them as supplements to each other. It was something I would be wary of. I could usually tell when this was happening during the course when I would treat the seminar with the other tutors almost as if it were an AA meeting instead of as an academic situation. It wasn't so bad that I tried to read "How it Works" to start the seminar or lead them in the Lord's prayer at the end as is traditionally done in AA meetings, but I sometimes forgot the others were not in the program and expected them to have the same viewpoint as my own.

At the end of the term I was asked to be co-coordinator of the section. I was reluctant to change the situation which I had become so comfortable in. I thought of the saying, "If it isn't broken, don't try to fix it," and I didn't want to mess with something that was working so well. I decided to accept the new challenge and not to just rest on my laurels. For one, I was sure it would accentuate the academic aspect of the course where I had focused on the recovery side, and that it would also force me not to become complacent. I compared it to an experience I had at an AA meeting which I had attended for a few weeks. I had always sat at the first step table and said the same type of things when it was my turn to speak. A person who had been in AA for a long time got to know me, and advised that I should try not to be stagnant but to keep moving in the program. The next meeting, I led a table for the first time.

—*Matt M.*

I discovered Project Community through a very good friend of mine. Although she had not actually taken a class through Project Community herself at that time, and therefore wasn't able to fill me in on many of the specifics, she did at least know where to send me, and I went to the office as soon as I could get there. The thought of doing something other than sitting in a classroom three or four hours a week for credit sounded just too good to be true. I never expected to become as attached or involved as I did.

As a young, single mother of two very young children pursuing my undergraduate degree at the University of Michigan, I often felt like I stuck out like a sore thumb Add to that the fact that I am a recovering alcoholic and it becomes easy to see why I almost always felt like an outsider. My life-style was very different from that of the "average" undergraduate student. There were many times when I felt as though I didn't really belong there. My sobriety and sanity depended on balance—something I found to be largely lacking in the UM experience as a whole. For most UM students it appeared that there was no balance of work and stress with anything other than drinking, and there certainly was no contact with, or discussion of "reality" in the day-to-day classroom life.

I had learned by that time in my sobriety that I needed to be able to be who I really was, to the best of my ability, at all times in order to stay sober and sane. This is large part of what I mean when I say "reality." In the day to day classroom life at the U M there was never the time or the opportunity to share one's feelings, or to hear what really goes on in peoples' lives, and how, if at all, that related to the material at hand, or the overall college experience. I am perfectly willing to admit that this may simply never work in your typical classroom setting at a college like the University of Michigan—or any other college for that matter. It may simply not be conducive to the type of teaching and learning that is expected to go on at an institution such as this one. And I did, of course, fill the void, and was able to be my "real self" at other times, and in other places. I have a very strong, close-knit group of AA friends on whom I rely and can be my "real self." And of course I always had my meetings.

It was just that I got very tired sometimes of putting on my school face and attitude in the mornings, and wearing this mask all day. I felt like we all had to be little school robots, and it simply exacerbated my feeling out of place, distanced from everyone around me, and sometimes from the experience itself. I made it through my undergraduate career without a drink, however, and with my sanity (largely) intact. I even enjoyed the experience (occasionally) along the way. It was just difficult, and frustrating even, because I felt like school was my non-reality, and the rest of life (both mine, and life as a whole) was my reality, and never the twain shall meet.

This, of course, is where Project Community comes into the picture. I don't remember why, as a recovering alcoholic, I did not choose a Chemical

Dependency project as my first stab at community service work through Project Community. Perhaps all those sections were closed, or perhaps they didn't fit into my schedule, but for some reason, I didn't choose one. Instead, I chose an education section—high school tutoring—as my first go-around with Project Community. Many of the other classes that I have taken at the university have faded into the oblivion of my transcript, but not this one. I know I will never forget it, nor will I forget any of the other PC sections I took after this first one. Since then it has seemed unfortunate to me that everything I have to share about my PC experience sounds corny—unfortunate, because they are all so true. Taking this class changed my life.

Initially, I thought that the community service component would be the best, and most interesting part of this class. As students, we had to choose one of the three local high schools that participated in the PC project and establish a connection with that school. It was largely up to students to determine how we would be involved as tutors; it was up to us to set the time, get involved with a student or a class, and simply tutor. None of us had any formal training in tutoring, and it was largely up to us to figure out how to do it. This was very scary for me at first, because I am a very literal person. I like to be told exactly what to do, so that I can then do it, and know whether I did it well or not. It was very foreign to me to do this fly- by-the-seat-of-your pants stuff. I soon figured out, however, that this was part of the learning process. I found that I experienced a much greater sense of accomplishment through establishing my own connections with the teachers, classrooms, and students. And when I got one of my students to write a paper for the first time, I knew that I alone had come up with the idea of how to motivate him, and not some lesson plan that I was forced to follow.

This, of course, was a real self-esteem booster, and of itself, would have made the PC experience worthwhile. What I came to enjoy and anticipate even more than this, however, was our weekly seminar/discussion group. The seminar was comprised of approximately 15 students, all of whom were tutoring at one of the 3 high schools, at different times. Our seminar time, then, was the only time that we got to see each other, and we spent a large portion of it talking about our experiences. We also spent some time talking about our weekly readings, because inherently the two were connected. Furthermore, because how we felt about our practical experience was often a central part of that experience, I finally got the integration I so desperately craved. Finally I felt as though the whole of me was wanted, appreciated, and needed for a complete learning experience. Practical experience, helping others in the community, feelings, and "book knowledge" all worked together, and as a result, I didn't need to wear my school face to this class.

Although I've often been hesitant to say it, because I've been worried that I will scare people away from PC, the principles are very similar to the AA program. I, and many of the people that I know in AA try to go to meetings and concentrate on sharing our experience, strength and hope. I try very hard, although I'm not perfect, not to give advice, or tell people what I think they should do. What I try to do instead is to share how I may have made it through a situation similar to one that somebody else shared about, or how maybe I experienced a completely unrelated set of circumstances that brought out the same sorts of feelings that are being discussed, and how I was able to work through them or not. In this way, with everybody sharing about their own experiences, or fairly openly giving their own thoughts about a certain subject, I have learned a great deal. Sometimes I will walk away from a meeting with a new tool for handling a specific problem, sometimes I will be reminded of something I already knew but hadn't used or thought of in a while, and sometimes I will simply feel validated.

Very early into this first PC seminar I began to feel this same way when I would leave class. Just hearing that my classmates often had the same worries and problems that I did with their students was very reassuring. Sometimes we came up with some answers and suggestions among ourselves, and sometimes our project coordinator would have some ideas for us. Often, however, we weren't able to come up with a specific way to solve a particular problem. I soon realized, however, that was part of the point. It's just like my recovery from alcoholism, and my struggle to live a more sane and sincere life. Often, there are no perfect answers. The experience of trying, sharing that with other people is often the end in itself. Therein is the learning, and therein was my reality.

I clearly liked PC so much, that I registered for a brand new project for the next term, which happened to be spring-summer session. Although the project was new, and we often felt like we were floundering, by now I was a little more used to the "self-starting" atmosphere, and felt a little more comfortable flying by the seat of my pants. I have since discovered that this is an optimal learning environment for me, because I just seem to absorb more when the responsibility is on me, and when I am forced to take risks. The project I was a part of during my second term as a PC volunteer involved visiting a migrant worker camp about an hour away from campus, in mid-Michigan. Because no PC class had ever been there before, we had even less of an idea about what we "should" be doing than we had during the high school tutoring class. We had complete freedom to decide what activities, if any, we wanted to do when we visited.

Again, forced to think for myself and work within a group at the same time, I felt my self-confidence grow just a little bit more. It's not as though I was certain at all times that I was working miracles in these peoples' lives. In fact, there were plenty times in this project, as in all the others I worked on, that I really didn't know if I was doing any good whatsoever. This became a very important thing for me to learn to deal with and is where I used the principles of the AA program the most. Being in a position where I was trying to help other people and trying to balance that with principles from my program such as: don't try to "control" situations, don't try to control or change the behavior of other people, the best "help" you can be to other people is sharing your experience, strength, and hope, etc., was a very difficult dichotomy for me to deal with on occasion.

As trying as it was on occasion to balance these two positions, I think it really helped me to enjoy the experience more. I think it helped me approach situations with realistic expectations about what I would and would not be able to accomplish, because I was not looking for the earth to move every time I tried to "help" somebody. Many of our activities at the migrant worker camp inevitably centered around crafts and games. And on the surface at least, this is certainly not the most empowering, "helpful" thing that we could have done for a group of people like that. When I slowed myself down and tried to approach the situation from a less grandiose and controlling perspective, however, I began to see the opportunities to "help" that I might not otherwise have seen.

Once again, at the risk of sounding like a broken record, it came down to sharing my experience, strength, and hope with these people. Once I had established a better relationship with some of the children and their mothers, I began to feel more comfortable asking questions about their schooling for instance. Occasionally I would get several questions of my own in return, like was I a college student, what was I studying, how does one go to college, etc. Then I got to share with them what I had been dying to share with them all along, but hadn't known how to approach the subject. I happily shared with those who asked the fact that I was a high-school drop-out. It was very exciting to see their reactions when I dropped that bomb, and I knew that I needed to brace myself for the round of questions that invariably followed. I will never know if I influenced the future of any of those children, but, ever the optimist, I would like to think that I did. To be honest, though, I try not to delude myself with the fantasy that I somehow single-handedly influenced any of these children to pursue a college education. More than anything, I am proud of the exposure I both gave and gained through the experience.

For some reason that I am unable to recall, I didn't register for another project the following semester. What soon became clear, however, was that if I didn't pursue Project Community, it would thankfully pursue me. I knew that I had been gaining confidence in my ability to reach out and connect with people, and it was really nice to look objectively at what had been happening in my own life and realize that I was now freely sharing, and almost feeling some pride in some of the things of which I had been ashamed for so long. I was, however, completely unprepared emotionally for my next level of involvement in Project Community.

One night early in that next semester (the fall of my junior year), I got a call from the woman who coordinated all of the education projects at PC. I was familiar with her name, and may even have briefly met her before then, but certainly had not dealt with her on a regular basis. My instinctive reaction then, on hearing her name on the other end of the phone was fear. This probably stems from being an alcoholic, and wondering what I had screwed up to deserve this call from the coordinator. I have sat at many a "fear" table during my years at AA, and can now, thankfully, laugh at my fear of people, places, and things every now and again. It has been a long, slow process, however, to learn that I am not a screw-up, and that I no longer have to back track, and constantly look over my shoulder like I used to when I was drinking.

At any rate, my fear soon subsided when it became clear that the purpose of her call was not to reprimand me for something I had done wrong. We chit-chatted for a little while, and then she dropped the bomb: she wanted me to be a facilitator for one of her projects that semester. All of a sudden the fear was back, and stronger than ever! Oh my God!! I knew I wasn't worthy of this, or capable of this, I knew I was going to fail, etc., etc. This was like being a teacher!! There was no way I could handle doing that, because I still wasn't sure that I was worthy of being a student at this University! There were times when I was still convinced that the Admissions Office had made a mistake when they accepted me, and now I was being asked to be a facilitator?! This could not be happening.

Through the fear, though, was a great deal of excitement. Despite myself,

I began to feel genuinely proud of the time and effort that I had put into Project Community, which was now being recognized and rewarded. I accepted her offer before I could talk myself out of it, hung up the phone, and reveled in the moment. I'm glad I did, because it didn't take very long before the old self-doubts began to creep in. As a matter of fact, I spent the majority of the semester vacillating between being very proud of what I had accomplished and was capable of doing, and feeling as though I was a complete joke and had fooled everyone into thinking that I was capable of doing this, when I really was not.

Part of being a project facilitator entails attending weekly staff meetings. Because I came on board a little late that semester, I had already registered for a class that was held during the same time as the staff meetings. Consequently, I met with the coordinator by myself on a weekly basis to discuss how seminar was going. These meetings were very helpful, and I was able to get some feedback in terms of suggested ideas of how to generate discussion on certain topics that we covered in seminar. Because it was just myself and the coordinator, however, I sort of felt like I had to share what was going on in a way that suggested that I had all of the answers to my questions, instead of simply feeling free to share some of the frustrations I ran into, and my feelings about what I was doing. Although I was trying to conduct my seminar from the "experience, strength and hope" perspective that I have mentioned previously, I was not really approaching my meetings with the coordinator in the same fashion. In this sense, I think I missed at least some of the learning experience that is involved with being a facilitator—sort of what it would have been like to be student in PC, and only do the community service work, and not go to seminar. How much of this was due to the simple fact that I was not able to meet with her and the other facilitators I do not know. But, if nothing else, it did highlight for me the importance of the group process in PC's learning experience.

And again, I come to a parallel to AA. Of course, as a recovering alcoholic, it is very important for me to "work my own program" as we call it. I must be responsible for my own actions; I am responsible for my own learning and growing, getting myself to meetings, and doing my own soul-searching. Nobody else can do any of those thins for me. But the beauty of it is that I could not do any of those things if it were not for the other people in AA. I would not go to meetings if I knew I was going to be the only one there. I wouldn't stick it out and trust that growth is either at hand, or around the corner, if I didn't see and hear about the growth of others around me. And although it sounds strange, I take pleasure in other people's problems. It is always comforting for me to know and remember that I am not the only person in the world with problems. We alcoholics joke that we all think we are terminally unique, and none of us could be any further from the truth.

Although I didn't realize it at the time, it was the group process that I missed during my first term as a facilitator. I did get to see and be a part of my own group of students, but it wasn't quite the same. I couldn't share with them the frustration I felt when they were frustrated, and didn't feel like they were accomplishing anything. I couldn't share with them the frustration that I felt when I couldn't generate any discussion with them in seminar. I couldn't share with them the frustration that I felt when I wasn't able to make them see that they were responsible for their own learning and experiences in PC—that PC was different from any other class on campus, and that they weren't going to be spoon-fed facts and formulas that they would be responsible for regurgitating on a test at the end of the semester. I wasn't always able to make them realize that each of them were teachers to both themselves and the other students, and that my role was not to have all the answers. Of course this last one was doubly hard for me, because I always feel like I have to have all the answers. I, myself, was still in the process of learning this new way to learn through PC.

None of this is to say, however, that I did not enjoy and learn from the experience. I took a great deal with me from my first term as a facilitator. I was simply emotionally exhausted by the time I was done, because I had no one with whom to "share" these emotions. I didn't yet know if other facilitators felt the same way, and wondered if they were approaching the task similarly. I still had a fair number of doubts about my "effectiveness" as a facilitator, although I had survived the experience, which is always a self-esteem boost. Apparently I was able to express all of these issues quite well in the paper I had to write in order to get credit for my work. I got my first and only A+ at the University of Michigan for the combination of this paper and being a facilitator. My paper was also submitted to the Dean of LS&A at the University, so I not only was satisfied with my academic performance as a facilitator, but I also got a nifty honor to make a notation of on my resume and law school applications![12]

I still had some concerns, though, about how effective I had been with my students. Because I was so crazy about PC and felt it had done so much for me, I wanted all my students to be as crazy about it as I was, and to get as much out of it as I had. I felt responsible for making them enjoy the experience, and be as committed to it as I was. Short of that, it was still very difficult for me not to feel as though I had failed them. I had to turn again to the principles I had learned in both PC and AA to help myself work through this issue. I had to remember that I could no more make somebody thrive on and learn from service work the way I had, than I could make somebody stay sober. The most that I could be responsible for was my own performance and learning, and helping to create a safe and stimulating environment in which the students could learn.

The way I write about it, it sounds as though I had it all figured out, when in truth it took me a while to come to that understanding of my role. In fact, even today I sometimes feel like that's a cop-out way to look at it, and that I really should have been able to fire up my students a little more than I did. At any rate, having plenty to digest after my first shot at being a facilitator, I took a break from PC for while. I felt like I just needed to focus on my "real" classes a little bit more, and not "give" so much. I felt like I had put in my time, and done my good deeds for the community, and now I deserved a rest. This probably sounds strange coming on the heels of all the cheerleading I've done for PC in the previous pages, but facilitating had taken a lot out of me emotionally.

At any rate, I took the break I thought I needed to focus and concentrate on my classes, and surprise, surprise! I was less committed to school than ever! I can laugh about it now, thankfully, but I truly was on the verge of not finishing college for a while there. Certainly, not all of it had to do with the fact that I was not involved with PC for the first semester in a long time. I was exhausted, having attended school non-stop since my first semester (summers included), and I was also afraid.

I was afraid of graduating, because that would mean that I had been successful at something, and God knows I hadn't had much of that in my life. I was afraid because I didn't have any idea what to do after college. I knew that I wanted to go to law school, but I was afraid I was going to be rejected, or that I was going to flunk out. So, clearly I had other things going on in my life other than my lack of PC, but I know it played a part in my lack of involvement with school.

And again we return to AA There is another principle in AA that I don't think I completely understood until my semester away from PC. This principle states that you have to give it away to keep it. This, of course pertaining to sobriety, is meant as I understand it to encourage recovering alcoholics to "become involved" with the program and other alcoholics. One can set up for a meeting, make coffee, open a meeting, or help clean up. One can also become involved more directly with other people by supporting patients in local treatment centers—visiting with them, or taking them to meetings, for example. There is also direct involvement with other members of AA through sponsorship of newcomers, or just helping a friend go through a rough spot. All of these things, and many others, fit the label of "giving it away," a lot like community service work. For me, it's about realizing that I have been given a gift—sobriety and a college education—and it is beholden to me to share it with others who may be less fortunate, and possibly could benefit from my help.

The other half of the principle, of course, is that this is the best way to "keep" what you have. This in no way means, I don't believe, that you can't stay sober (or keep your college education) without sharing the wealth. What I do think it means is that we're all dependent upon each other to a certain extent —which one of us can honestly say that we would be where we are today without a little bit of help? I also think it means that a commitment to other people is the best way to stay involved and invested in what you're doing— be that school, sobriety, work, or whatever. I also think that it is the best way to bring meaning to these things—because what good is keeping what you have if it doesn't mean anything?

This is what brought me back to PC. No, I didn't have all of this clearly formulated in my head when I came back, and no, it didn't hit me like a ton of bricks. I did, however, know that I felt more committed to and involved in my education, and simple time spent on campus, when part of that time was spent at PC. So, I spent my last two semesters of undergrad as a facilitator in a Chemical Dependency project, where I enjoyed myself immensely, and finally felt like all of the fragmented areas of my life were integrated.

Along with the head of the chemical dependency/criminal justice section of PC, I got to develop a brand new project. This project came to be something very near and dear to my heart. One morning and one evening a week my students and I provided child care for AA meetings at the Washtenaw Alano Club. As a recovering alcoholic and a single mother, there were many times that I myself had needed such a service. Having attended some of these meetings in the past, I also happened to know some of the people for whom we provided child care. This project turned out to be a unique opportunity for me to "give it away" to both my AA program, and my education. Some of my students were also recovering, and occasionally we would talk about the pressures of being a recovering person, and also a student. I finally got to pass along the enthusiasm for PC that I had wanted to for so long. We all got to openly integrate the AA part of our lives with the student part of our lives, and learned a great deal, I think, about how to fit one in with the other—that it's okay to learn with an "AA attitude." In fact, I think I learn better with an AA attitude.

What is an AA attitude? After having read back through what I've written so far, I think an AA attitude is a lot like a PC attitude. I think it has a lot to do with learning from yourself and learning from others at the same time. I think it has a lot to with teaching yourself, sharing what you've learned, and thus teaching others at the same time. I think it has a lot to do with realizing that how you feel is not totally separate from what you learn. I think it has a lot to do with being responsible for you own experience, and being responsible to the rest of your community, too.

The final piece of my life that was integrated into my last project at PC was my children. Because my son was in kindergarten during my last year of college, his mornings were still spent at home. Consequently, he did what I did the first part of every day, which included going to the Alano Club once a week and helping take care of the children. Shannon, my daughter, came with us for the evening meetings. My children had been to the Alano Club with me many times before, but usually for me to go to a meeting where they were either cared for by somebody else, or thoroughly bored while they waited for me to get through with my meeting. On these occasions, instead, they got to "give it away" too. I think it also did a little bit of integrating for them, too. It took them a little while to fully grasp (if they ever did) that the reason we were baby-sitting was because of a class I was taking. I remember talking to them about how learning can come in many different forms, and doesn't always have to come from a book. I don't know how much of it they grasped, but I do know that they were very proud that they were a part of Mom's college class. I also know that they are always interested in my AA meetings, and what people do there, etc. I think they have felt a little more involved in that part of my life since then.

All in all, it was a wonderful way to help wrap up my college career. No, it was not perfect, and I did have some of the same frustrations these last two semesters that I had experienced during my first semester as a faciliator. This time, however, having been through it once, I was more certain that it was just part of what it is to be a facilitator-teacher-type-person, and that it was part of my learning experience. I also had the benefit of staff meetings with other facilitators during my last year, which completed the picture quite well. Everything that I had loved about my first seminar as a student in PC was there, and then some. I learned a great deal from these meetings, and had a really nice time doing it.

In the end, PC meant more to me, and played a larger role in my life than is even possible to express in words.

NOTES

1. Mack M.'s entry is a response to the Ron and Chris activity in Off to See the Wizard, Chapter Six.
2. Tom A.'s journal is a reflection on "Doctors in Denial," originally printed in the Spring '90 Washtenaw Alano Club Newsletter. My thanks to the Club Board for permission to reprint.

3. AA's Sixth Tradition reads, "An AA group ought never endorse, finance, or lend the AA name to any related facility or outside enterprise, lest problems of money, property, and prestige divert us from our primary purpose." Howevr, as private citizens, individual members of vaious recovery groups can create "Alano Clubs"—non-profit organizations who actually own the meeting houses which rent space to 12 Step groups such as AA, NA, and Alanon.
4. Clarification: at the beginning of Matt M.'s extended journal, he is referring to me when he writes about "interviewing with the project coordinator.
5. The Serenity Prayer, "God, grant me the serentity to accept the things I cannot change, the courage to change the things I can and the widom to know the difference," is recited by AA members at the start of their meetings.
6. "How it Works" is an excerpt from Chapter Five of the AA "Big Book" (1976). This excerpt is usually read aloud after the Serenity Prayer at the beginning of a meeting, includes the 12 Steps and the phrases, "There are such unfortunates" and "Half measures availed us nothing."
7. AA's First Step reads, "We admitted we were powerless over alcohol—that our lives had become unmanageble."
8. "Dry Drunk"—refers to an alcoholic who has stopped drinking but who is not using the 12 Steps to change any aspects of her or his life.
9. "One Day at a Time"—To a practicing alcoholic, the prospect of having to quit drinking forever may appear overwhelming: a more concrete perspective is "can you make it through today without drinking?"
10. Bill Wilson and Dr. Bob Smith founded AA in the 1930's.
11. Since Mark Chesler became Project Community's faculty advisor in 1975, he has honored six papers by submitting them to the Dean's Office "as examples of the outstanding intellectual work that our students do."

Appendix

Doctors In Denial

Recently, Board Member Joe Galura interviewed Lyn Hadley, an Ann Arbor area Physician's Assistant regarding chemical dependency and the medical profession. Last summer, Lyn and Joe presented an inservice to the U of M Health Service Staff entitled "The (Chemically) Impaired Health Care Profession". Following is a summary of the interview.

Lyn listed nine reason why chemical dependency is not diagnosed by medical professionals.

The first is poor training. When Lyn became a Physician's Assistant in the late seventies, she received only four hours of training on alcoholism. She states that things are better now, noting that a a recent professional meeting featured seven lectures on chemical dependency during a four-day conference. Still, Lyn told me, the bottom line is that chemical dependency involves AT LEAST 10 percent of the health care provider's caseload, but professionals do not receive 10 percent of their training in this area.

Second, patients with a drinking or drug problem often give misleading or inaccurate information regarding their chemical use.

Third, Lyn noted that there are no diagnostic lab tests for chemical dependency. Positive lab signs such as cirrhosis of the liver come fairly late in the progression of the disease.

Fourth, as we know, there is no "magic cure" for chemical dependency. Pills or surgery, effective medical interventions for other conditions, cannot "fix" the alcoholic.

Fifth, alcoholics and drug addicts may try to avoid and delay their regular physical examinations. Lyn told me that often the first clue in the diagnosis of alcoholism comes through the family members: her experience is that when she sees a patient with unexplained symptoms of depression, that person is almost always living with someone who is abusing chemicals.

Sixth, medical professionals do not know how to react if they do diagnose chemical dependency. Treatment centers may have long waiting lists. Physicians may be reluctant to prescribe antabuse because the Physician's Desk Reference cites a long list of complications (including death, in some instances) that arise from alcohol antabuse interactions. Finally, Lyn says, that to many health care professionals, "AA sounds like witchcraft."

Seventh, and related to the last point, many health care providers have their own issues around chemical dependency. In the case of doctors, Lyn stated that 10 to 15 percent are chemically dependent themselves, and that between 20 and 40 percent have at least one chemically dependent parent. "Being a doctor is the perfect job for all those family heroes," Lyn said.

Eighth, often, the only contact some professionals have with alcoholics and drug addicts is the "OD" or the "ER drunk", brought to emergency after a street fight or a major accident and still out of control. Lyn concluded that "if this were my ONLY experience with drunks, I wouldn't want to have to deal with them one second longer than I absolutely had to."

Last month AA sponsored a symposium to educate physicians about denial. Invitations were mailed to 1200 area doctors.

The agenda was five AA's who were also professionals.

A hotel convention room was rented. Coffee was provided, as well as vegetable snacks.

TWO DOCTORS SHOWED UP!

Ninth, health care professionals may have "bad experiences when they do confront chemical dependency." As we know, denial is part of the disease, and when that is confronted, it often leads to anger.

Overall, there is a tendency to diagnose the presenting symptoms rather than the underlying cause of chemical dependency. After all, doctors can cure gastritis, bad nerves, and fractures, but there is no "cure" for alcoholism. Part of the reason for this tendency, Lyn posits, may be that the medical professionals do not like to diagnose what they cannot cure.

In sum, Lyn concluded that the medical profession's denial surrounding chemical dependency really has three root causes. First, health care professionals may have their own issues around chemical dependency. Second, medical service providers may have received inadequate training. Third, the patient's denial may complicate diagnosis.

A final note: Lyn instructed me to cite Dr. Gerry Vandervordt, of the Michigan State Medical Society (listed Lansing phone number) as a resource person for impaired health care professionals. Dr. Vandervordt heads up a group of recovering doctors that will make "12 Step Calls" (my words, not Lyn's). Other professional groups have similar services. Lyn wanted to emphasize that the medical profession is "getting better and doing more regarding the disease of chemical dependency, "but it still isn't nearly enough."

(Editor's Note: Lyn Hadley died 12/20/91.)

Chapter 2

OZ PLUS FIVE

Reflections on the Longitudinal Effects of Service-Learning

By Michelle Blankenship, Kathleen Doherty, Joe Galura and Trish Marsik

My first term as program director was Fall '88. Three coordinators attended my Tuesday staff meeting that term: Michelle Blankenship, Kathleen Doherty and Trish Marsik. We have maintained our correspondence with each other over the past five years. Michelle was presented with a Senior Leadership Award when she graduated in May '89 and received her Juris Doctor from the University of Detroit in May. She hopes to practice Criminal Law in Kentucky. Trish also graduated in May '89 with a Senior Leadership Award, and received her Master of Social Work from Columbia University in May '91 where she served as President of the Student Union. Trish works for the Legal Aid Society in the Bronx. Kathleen graduated in May '90. She taught middle school social studies for two years at Our Lady of LaSallette in Berkely, Michigan, and was the recipient of the Charles S. Kern Award from the School of Education in 1991. Kathleen completed her Masters Degree in Educational Administration at the University of Wisconsin at Madison in August.

I asked each former coordinator to re-visit our work together five years ago, reflecting on what it meant to us then and what it means to us today. The following is a transcript of our conversations.

—Joe

What Did Project Community Mean To Us Five Years Ago?

I got involved with Project Community after a bad semester as a business school student. My biggest problem in the business school was that I felt like what I was learning didn't matter. I was learning how to maximize profits when people were struggling every day to live on meager salaries. After becoming involved with Project Community, I finally felt like I was doing something important. Sure, I had the idea that I could single-handedly change the world but one thing Project Community taught me was that I have to understand what needs to be changed before I can change it. Books make change look so easy, but sometimes they can make you forget the human side of problems. Project Community also helped me learn that not all change is on a large scale. By going to the prison[1] once a week, I wasn't really changing the prison system, but in a small way I was. Even if our group was only a diversion from the dullness of prison life, I felt that was important and this feeling was good.

—Michelle

Five years ago (!) Project Community meant that I was out in the field in which I wanted to work. I was working with people, sharing what I believed, with those in whom I believed. It was a place to develop and evolve a philosophy about our society, and my responsibility and place within it. It was a place to receive feedback on my development as an educator, as a facilitator of learning on many levels, and on myself. It was a door that had not been open in my life, given the family and neighborhood where I grew up. It meant having a support network where I was encouraged to do what was best for me, and how that "best" could help others.

—Kathleen

Five years ago, Project Community was a safe place for me to really test some of the theoretical stuff I was constantly spouting—to place it in a context. Not only was I struggling with my own ideas of how the world should be but I was helping others to struggle with their's—an awesome responsibility. It's amazing that I was able to handle it. And the safety was very important because I wasn't just exploring theoretical issues vis a vis practical issues in youthful offenders' lives, I was exploring my own personal issues relative to how I behaved in groups and to the inequalities I was learning about.

—Trish

Project Community reminded me that there was a "community" that I had forgotten about in the business school. I wasn't alone with my ideas or problems. I realized that there were other people who had similar ideas and who were willing to help me out. For the first time, I didn't feel alone at a big university, I felt like part of a group.

This sense of community was immediate within my seminar group. Going to a prison seems to really bring people together. I remember my first seminar group. Not everyone was taking the class because of social consciousness. People needed a class, or social science credits. We were people who wouldn't otherwise know each other, but the common experience of Project Community brought us all together. On the way home from the prison, we had long conversations about what we had learned, what bothered us, or what our lives were like in general. I think we all left the group with our same basic "liberal" or "conservative" politics, but I think we had a better understanding of the other side's perspective. I think I found out that all "conservatives" are not bad people and you really can't judge people by what they appear to be. It sounds like a lesson that you teach children but I think we (especially "liberals") are all guilty of this. I realize now that I can work with anyone (I may not like it, but...). There is some common ground if you take the time to find it.

One of my most vivid memories about earlier staff meetings was this woman with big bangle bracelets who waved her arms around a lot when she talked. I remember, once, after a staff meeting, she stopped me and said that she had seen a Saturday Night Live episode about the presidential debates and they were mimicking Bush and Dukakis. I thought, "How would she know that

I liked this? Was I that transparent at staff meetings?" Well, she was right. That person was Trish and that comment started a friendship that has lasted through the present time.

—*Michelle*

Staff meetings also meant consistency in feedback from you, Joe—a peaceful continuity in a world of craziness. You helped me to grow intellectually too, challenging me to think about myself, my work with children, my mentees, my students, my seminar members.

—*Kathleen*

My relationships with Michelle, Kathleen and Trish were important as I worked through how I would define my role as program director. Previously, I had run therapy groups, supervised graduate and undergraduate field placements, and taught secondary students using both affective and traditional methodologies, still, none of these experiences corresponded precisely with my new job. To paraphrase Freire (1970), this definition emerged for me in dialogue, as a teacher/student in solidarity with student/teachers.

—*Joe*

My final reflection question had to do with our relationship and whether I was concerned about it being a mixed role—boss, facilitator, therapist. I cherish the relationship we have for several reasons. The most important is that it is free from the traditional teacher/student roles. I benefit greatly from knowing you on different levels and in different settings. We can interact as people rather than as roles. I respect what you say because you know me and can talk to me knowing there is more to me than just Project Community. This enhances what we try to accomplish within Project Community. I can bring all of me to PC, not just my PC side because I know that it will all be accepted. I can't go in to see most of my professors with anything other than questions on the topic. I come to them in a vacuum and that restricts and takes away from what I am trying to learn in their class. (I suppose that I could go in and share other parts of my life with them, but they don't really offer that as a desirable option.) I feel very comfortable with our relationship and am thus willing to ask more questions, try more things and become more involved. I feel as though I have a stake in what is happening with my life and that makes me work harder. I am sure that is an individual thing, though, in terms of me giving you suggestions for particular benefits that you could give to students in future terms. I thrive on "whole relationships" and imagine there are other students who could benefit from the same type of relationship.

—*Kathleen*[2]

Joe was the most support I had ever had from someone in a position of authority. He never told me what to do, he just made suggestions and listened to my ideas. I took Project Community for an extra credit which meant that to earn this, I had to meet with Joe once a week and discuss potential course pack articles. We discussed articles but I think that's when I really got to know Joe. He not only knew me as a staff member, but as a person. When I graduated, I wanted to do social work. No one would hire me because my degree was in economics. I finally got a job in a lock up facility for teenage girls. I felt like I got the job because Joe had spoken with the people and gave me such a good recommendation. The job turned out to be a very bad experience. One thing that kept me at the job was that I didn't want to let Joe down. I finally quit and when I told Joe, he supported my decision. He made me feel like I had done the right thing. Like always, he understood and accepted me.

—Michelle

On an extremely personal level, Joe, you made that interaction between the personal and the political (to borrow a phrase from the sisterhood) possible. I was able to lay my vulnerabilities on the table—and Michelle and Kathleen were integral in that as well. I felt very complete even as I was struggling with a million things in terms of my own development. I think Project Community was an incredibly holistic learning experience. And it allowed me to do all the process and theoretical work that I so loved.

I've read over my old journals and I'm amazed at the level of analysis which I was exercising as well as the level of disclosure. I could have never (and I never did) done that in graduate school. Your questions, Joe, were what led into those disclosures and analyses along with the support I got in the coordinator group.

I also do remember being stressed out, and struggling SO much with issues of power and authority and structure. But I had a place to try on different roles, whether verbally or physically. And I was very energized and fulfilled, particularly during the Chesler saga.[3] I think it was Alinsky who said life is conflict and only in conflict are we truly alive. While I don't see this as my life's motto, I do think it was very relevant at that time in my life.

—Trish

What Does Project Community Mean To Us Today?

Project Community instilled many values into my philosophy about learning, life and relationships. It means that I place much importance on community building and group cohesion, that I value input from all who are involved in a community, that engagement in learning is an essential element to reaching someone, that we have a responsibility to those in our community and they have a responsibility to us, that experiential learning is an effective way to create an atmosphere of shared responsibility.

—Kathleen

In the last six weeks I have to say I've thought about Project Community a tremendous amount. I'm supervising twelve people including two social workers just out of graduate school. My image of what, or rather who, I should be as a supervisor is grounded in what I learned in Project Community. Anecdotally, there is another social worker at Legal Aid who went to UM and then Columbia's MSW program and spent a term at Maxey Boys Training School. She's a 1986 alum, however. Anyway, the same issues that came up for me as a coordinator are now arising for me as a supervisor—and I now have no Joe to turn to.

As I stated earlier, even in graduate school I was not forced to integrate so much of myself with my learning process. I think that some people would talk about boundaries at this point but I'm not quite sure that that's what this is about. I think that there needs to be a negotiated point—a safe point—where people can struggle with their growth and their learning process on an interpersonal level which somehow remains at a professional level as well.

I can't believe that I thought UM was so brainwashing and Project Community such an oasis of free thought. Compared to the rest of the world, UM was an oasis of critical thinking and Project Community a utopia of tolerance.

—Trish

In law school, I had a criminal sentencing class. On the first day, we saw a video about the Michigan prison system and a former inmate spoke with us about his experiences in prison. All that I could think about while I watched the video was, "I've been there." I know I haven't been in prison, but I think I understand it a little better than a lot of law students. I don't think the solution to crime is to "lock them up because they deserve punishment."

While the former inmate lectured, people were asking him questions. One guy asked him about solitary confinement. He said, "Do you think things like solitary confinement should be used more often as an effective means of punishment?" I couldn't believe it! All I could think of was Rico, who I had met at Cassidy Lake. He has spent a lot of time in solitary. He felt like they only wanted to break his spirit. He fooled the system, though, because, as he explained to me, you can only be incarcerated in your mind and he wasn't.

The former inmate responded to my classmate that he thought that solitary confinement was a good example of inhumanity. That's just what I had wanted to say.

—Michelle

Project Community helped develop my attitudes regarding crime. Probably this occured most in the sense of understanding its reason for being. Although I don't think the ends justify the means, I think it's important in looking at solutions that you address some root causes. The deterrent theory is not applicable in the arena in many ways because people still have the motive to commit crimes even if prison may take away the mechanism.

Project Community has also affected how I view different elements of our society. Education doesn't just mean giving students a book to read and testing them on it in one week. It means issue raising, feeling, sharing and dialogue. It means experimenting, validating feelings and beliefs. It also means looking at a child as more than just the physical child sitting there, rather that he or she is coming from a greater myriad of society, which needs to be addressed in conjunction with the child's educational learning. It means that "fault" ought not to be so readily judged. It means one instructional program isn't going to work for every child. And Project Community has instilled in me the need to be a reflective practitioner—that I, along with the feedback of my students and colleagues, form the best sense of professional development that I could probably receive. And that it is important to receive feedback from members to ensure that their needs are being met. In the same vein, I think it is important to include learning community members in the development of the course of study. For example, when I teach social studies, I don't teach it in a vacuum.

I look at the students' needs, and along with them, develop a curriculum that is appropriate for them.

—Kathleen

I carry less of what Project Community taught me about looking at others who were different with different life experiences (mostly because I got that in a lot of places my senior year) than I do carry interpersonal growth resources about the learning process. I know what building community looks like and I know how it feels when it exists. The extent to which I learned about working with people and tolerating other viewpoints I gained from Project Community and it amazes me. Quite frankly, graduate school attempted to undo all the connections I made by depersonalizing both the educational and therapeutic process. I have really had to wrestle my own beliefs out from under the "shoulds" of the service community.

Part of this, I think, has to do with working in the correctional/legal community. The rigidity is astounding and one is forced to deal continually with a conflict/adversarial model of attaining a goal. Happily for me, I am a part of the growing field of alternative sentencing advocacy which enables the court to consider "a compromise." A radical notion for an archaic system.

—Trish

How can you listen and not care? How can you sit and not feel sad that a fellow human being was put through this or that and wonder how strong you, yourself, would be? I wanted to hug him. His mom, (Terrence's) had been addicted to cocaine. As a child, he saw a box fall from the top of the refrigerator. My mom hid the cookies, his hid the cocaine. He hated her. Even the day she died, he hated her. I was crying. Harry was introduced to cocaine at age 13 by the guy his mother was "messing around with." I really felt that he knew no other way. These are the "dealers who are killing our children." No they aren't, we are! They are only doing what someone else did to them. They're left no other choice. All I could think about was slavery and how blacks have never been given a chance and know their chance for the almighty money and power comes from drugs. I don't think any one of us here can say we would not do the same thing to survive. I really care and tonight it was really real. I felt sorry for them and I wanted to say it will be all right and that I'm sorry. I NEVER want to lose this feeling! I NEED to do something. This isn't a problem in the newspaper; tonight it was real. And to think some of us missed Valentine's Day with a significant other for this! How sad.

This is what I want to remember, Joe. I want to remember all that I've learned in the past one and a half years and do something about it."

—Michelle[2]

I view drug addiction as one of many addictions with which a person can become involved. It is a dis-ease that can manifest itself into personalities, families, significant relationships. Everyone involved with an addicted person has a role to play in the person's addiction. Given this, although they can't force the person to stop taking drugs, they can certainly stop enabling them to do so. And that approach crosses over into other addictions as well, be they self-defeating/sacrificing behaviors in relationships or martyr behaviors. It also taught me that "you can't save anyone in a sinking ship." On an airplane they tell you to secure your own oxygen mask before helping others, and I think that illustrates my point.

—Kathleen

Looking back at My Valentine's Day journal, I think I knew even then that I would forget how I felt. Everyone told me that I would change when I got older. I didn't want to change. That journal entry was my reminder to myself so that I could never let myself forget how I was feeling at that moment.

Well, I have forgotten some things, some people and some experiences, but I can remember the intensity of how I felt that night. I'm not as idealistic as I once was, but my "realism" has only helped me explore other means of change.

During law school I volunteered with a group that did prison visitation. It was a good experience, but I was looking for something like Project Community. I really missed the way it made me feel. I haven't had any experiences since that have come close.

I am dedicated to prison reform and am currently interviewing with several public defenders' offices in Kentucky. The people I met at Cassidy Lake made me see the other side of crime stories I read in the newspaper. No matter how "realistic" I get or how my life changes, I won't ever let myself forget the need to change that I felt when I wrote that journal Project Community didn't give me the need to change, it just gave me a way to do it.

—Michelle

I also think about Project Community in the context of direct practice because much of my work consists of drawing correlations between criminal situations and a person's life experiences. And I think because I've done this every day since I began at Legal Aid, I sometimes lose sight that Project Community taught me to do this. Additionally, having learned how to draw these connections in Project Community, I forget that it isn't always so clear for others, particularly those whom I am now supervising.

Project Community continues to have meaning for me because it allowed me to forge relationships with people who continue to serve as role models and sounding boards for me and for most of the ideas that I developed and discussed with them to begin with.

Project Community served to clarify my thinking about working with offenders, both in terms of broader political issues and as individuals. I think that it continues to provide me with a sense of direction and a framework with which to process new issues. Yes, I've forgotten some of the names and some of the experiences but they continue to inform my work even now.

—Trish

As I sat through my classes in graduate school, surrounded by people who have many more years of administrative and teaching experience than I do, I am comforted by the thorough foundation I built during my time in Project Community. I feel as though I have already been trained in many facets of administration.

For example, I have worked through the stages of groups, community building, experiential learning and the inclusion of people in an organization. I have already been instructed that affective teaching needs to accompany intellectual teaching. I already know that lecturing to people eight hours a day is not an effective learning strategy for most. I also have felt more capable of identifying and dismissing stereotypes, which came not only from UM's commitment to diversity, but directly from exposure to different groups of people at my sites. Through Joe's modeling, I have also been taught the value of active listening. I know the importance of not just listening to what people say but listening to how they feel. And in the process of organization and culture building, that's important.

Project Community also helped me to shape my beliefs about the purpose of education, which is to develop and meet the needs of students. Equally important though, is the goal of making students aware of the society in which they live, helping them to find their place in it, and how they can best contribute to it.

My interest in curriculum development also stemmed from the freedom I was given in Project Community to develop activities for site. We were given ideas for activities to carry out in seminar, but we were also given the encouragement and the philosophy with which to develop our own. As I design curriculum, I know the importance of inclusion, the importance of receiving feedback from students, and the importance of knowledge and having somewhere to hang it. When information is given to someone, they need to be able to process it at their own speed, and be able to decide where they want to hang it. Joe always gave us "information" at the beginning of staffings, then through the process of reflection and dialogue, allowed us to take what we needed and leave the rest. That sense of empowerment is the key to any successful organization, but more importantly, I believe, the key to real learning.

As an administrator, you are also an instructional leader, which hopefully means that you can guide teachers to become the best teachers they can be. Or as Joe puts it so much better, the idea is that "counseling is the idea/process of leading people gently back to themselves." That philosophy guides me as a teacher with my students and will guide me as an administrator with the teachers.

—Kathleen

NOTES

1. Michelle's placement for three terms was at Cassidy Lake, before it was converted to a Boot Camp in 1990.
2. Trish organized a coordinator protest over how Sociology 395/695 grades were assigned during Winter '89.
3. Excerpts from '88/'89 journals are italicized in the text.

Chapter 3

AN INSIDER'S ROUND TABLE

By Anita Bohn, Margaret Elias, Joe Galura, Jeff Howard, Rachel Meiland, Randy Ross, Claudette Rowley and Rick Smith
(This final chapter was originally recorded on July 15, 1993.)

Joe: This is today's opening Jeopardy! clue—Freire might use this three word phrase to describe today's meeting. Anyone? (Silence.) The three word phrase is "talking a book." It's because Freire describes his dialogues with Ira Shor (1987) and with Miles Horton (1990) as "talking a book." In both cases, Freire talked with people about applying his pedagogy: these conversations were taped, transcribed, edited and then published as books. This methodology has been used by writers and editors several times in Praxis II. Today, we've gathered several service-learning insiders to have a round table discussion of some key ideas. I anticipate that our conversation will have three overlapping points:

1) As a service-learning insider, what advice would I give to another campus interested in either starting up a new program or strengthening an existing one?
2) Related to #1, how is this advice connected to the dilemma of implementing a Freire-influenced pedagogy within our institutional constraints?
3) Since Freire's goal is social change, does service-learning really accomplish social change?

This will be the last chapter in the Praxis series. Are there any questions about this before I have everybody introduce themselves? The next trivia question is about introductions—my name is Dr. Bob and I'm an alcoholic.

Rick: What is the way you introduce yourself in Alcoholics Anonymous?

Joe: Yes. Dr. Bob was one of the co-founders and this is an example of what you do, traditionally, before you speak at an AA meeting. Let me start by introducing myself: let's each give our name and our insider's connection to service-learning. I'm Joe Galura, OCSL program director for Chemical Dependency and Criminal Justice. I'm also the originator of the Praxis grant.

Margaret: My name is Margaret Elias. I am the OCSL program director for the TVC programs which are homelessness, youth at risk, adult literacy and the elderly.

Randy: My name is Randy Ross. I guess now I'm a Praxis II editor. I've been involved in PC on several different levels as student, coordinator and at staff level.

Rick: My name is Rick Smith. I've been a two term coordinator of the Cotton Correctional Facility PC section. I wrote a chapter in Praxis II about my experience. I'm also on the editorial board.

Rachel: My name is Rachel Meiland. My one semester with PC was at the Alano Club's Women's Meeting. And I've been working with Praxis II, as an editor.

Claudette: I'm Claudette Rowley. I work at Project SERVE as a graduate intern. I'm in the School of Social Work.

Jeff: I'm Jeff Howard director of OCSL and editor of volume I of Praxis.

Anita: I'm Anita Bohn, director of Project SERVE. Claudette and I co-wrote the SERVE chapter.

Rick: What advice would I give another campus interested in starting or strengthening a service-learning program?

Randy: Read the Praxis volumes!

Joe: Also available on audio cassette.

Margaret: Well, a practical piece of advice based on starting the TVC is start small. Pick a very small, manageable population or area you want to work with, start with that and build on it.

Randy: I wanted to just get back to the history of PC It started out as one particular project and it's grown over the years. Basically, where have we picked up the numbers and when did we officially become PC and grow like we have grown? I don't know if that's more for clarification on my part or if it would help other campuses to see what we've done and how we've grown—like Margaret said, "start out small."

Margaret: Jeff probably knows that the best. I think it's interesting that it has lasted for something like thirty years through times when service-learning was popular and times when it has not been popular.

Jeff: The very beginning is kind of fuzzy. One thing is to make sure that there is a faculty member who is very committed because that would add credibility and increase the chances of insuring that there is academic rigor.

Joe: One of the things I've been noticing as I've been reading some of the Praxis II chapters is it's really important to work for institutional change: not only having a faculty member involved but also having a course structure so that as the initial students who are committed to a particular cause or site or section graduate, there is something in place so that it continues after those folk are gone. Then, whether or not these students have intentionally recruited people to be their successors, what they started will be continued. That's really important. I think another thing, as I, too, have kind of glossed the history in looking for introductory material for this volume, is that it does seem you're right Jeff. Everything is real fuzzy in the beginning as a bunch of students started a breakfast program in elementary schools and it didn't really take off until faculty started to get involved. Exactly when that was I'm not sure.

Jeff: I think in addition there has to be, to increase the chances that there will be progress towards institutionalization, an accent on the learning side of the service-learning equation and that gets back to the faculty involvement and the rigor that leads to credibility. That credibility can then increase the chances that there will be other faculty who are interested in following suit and therefore make progress toward an institution-wide commitment.

Joe: Rick and I have talked at length about the status around volunteering. Once you attach it to a course it becomes an academic process. It's seen and valued in a whole different way.

Margaret: I think that that's true. But I think it's important that we not overlook the fact that this project was started by students who just really wanted to do something in the community and were passionate about it. Through their efforts and their passion it eventually became a legitimized course. It really starts with people wanting to do something.

Jeff: That's how things unfolded with PC but there are examples in which faculty started courses and recruited students often times by word of mouth because the way it was captured in the class listing did not make it apparent that the course involved work in the community. So, there are many examples where faculty have initiated the service-learning course, but without the commitment of some students who are really prepared to make an investment in the community, it's not going to work.

Rick: I'm thinking about the audience of these volumes and if I understand correctly the audience is going to be primarily faculty and administrators, not necessarily students, unless a student randomly picks one up in a library somewhere or an office. I would hope that if it is indeed faculty who are reading this that they would lend support .

Jeff: The other piece of advice that comes to mind is not to develop a service-learning course or program in isolation. To find some students who want to be involved, to seek faculty collaborators or at the very least get feedback from faculty who might be able to make a contribution toward refining the program. Then beyond your own campus and network of colleagues, seek out other service-learning courses, whether it's through the Praxis volumes or making contact with some of the national organizations that are familiar with service-learning courses around the country and could refer folks who are new to the field to some of the veterans who could help work up a service-learning course. So, don't work in isolation.

Joe: A related point to that is that it's real important for the members administering this to be connected to community agencies and actually know what's going on with whatever the population is that you're attempting to serve. Jeff hired me and knew that I had experience in certain areas and new projects evolved from me working here because of professional connections.

Anita: I think that there's a fine line when you try to define your primary audience in a course like this or any service-learning program. You have to consider whether your primary audience is students and your primary goal is their learning or if your primary audience is the community and your primary goal is social change. I think there's a very fine line and it's hard to balance those two so that you're being respectful to both. I think it's very easy to do one or the other and not balance. It's hard to find projects that not only are very learning-rich, but also do meet needs of the community. It's important that we be respectful of those community people that we work with and not just use them as a learning vehicle but make sure that their needs are being met as part of these programs.

Randy: During my two terms as an administrator, I really noticed that, in dealing with community service agencies, people don't always realize that it takes a lot of effort to train volunteers and have people come in. You're not just going in there and helping them and being free of any bureaucratic constraints or guidance or anything like that. It's a lot of effort at any type of agency to oversee volunteers.

Anita: And the reason that most of these people and most of the organizations that we work with need volunteers is because they are ridiculously understaffed and under-funded. Those things which make them need volunteers also make it very difficult for them to work with volunteers because they don't have the kind of staff that they need or the money they need to train them adequately, supervise people and make sure that they're doing meaningful work. It's important to help the agency make it a good experience for the students as well, but a lot of times they just don't have the resources to make that happen.

Jeff: What you just said, Anita, makes me think about the importance of nomenclature and with regard to that, we ought to stay away from using the word "volunteer" and stay toward using the word "service-learner." I think about this from both the campus audience and the community audience. On campus, using the word volunteer can conjure up an image that downplays the potential learning opportunity of working out in community service and I wouldn't want faculty to have that kind of image because that will then speak against the credibility factor. In the community, calling the students service-learners instead of volunteers immediately puts the community on notice that there's a learning aspect that's part of the campus agenda for the students and that they're there to learn, not just to serve. This, in turn, will precipitate conversations between the campus and community about how the community can facilitate learning almost as if those people in the community are adjunct instructors.

Anita: A couple things about that: One, is I think that's ideally a great idea, but I also think that because of the constraints that are on the community agencies, we need to realize that their first priority is going to be the issue or the clients that they're dealing with. The other thing is that I think that whole nomenclature issue is important for other reasons as well. The word volunteer calls things up in your head about the seventies idea of volunteerism which was rich white women who didn't have anything better to do with their time. They felt sorry for those pathetic poor people and out of the goodness of their hearts, thought they would go give them a couple hours a week. That's something we're trying very hard to fight against because it puts such a hierarchy in volunteerism. We don't use that word either, for that reason. It connotes charity, the privileged, the under privileged, handouts and helping the needy and all those really condescending things that we think of when we think of volunteerism. We really try to promote something that looks like community responsibility or community work. With your membership in this community comes your responsibility for dealing with the problems no matter how directly they affect you or your family. "Volunteerism" also connotes to the students that the work is passive and something that's very non-change oriented. If you're talking to a bunch of activists and you're telling them that "well, we're going to do some volunteer work," they think it connotes very trivial, non-important work that doesn't bring about change. I think that a lot of the work that we're doing, hopefully all of the work that we're doing at least in some small way is working toward change as opposed to easing our guilty consciences.

Randy: It would also appear to students as a lack of responsibility, "Oh, I can just do this whenever I feel like it." We really can't do that.

Rick: Some students in my section exhibited a lack of commitment towards it. The felt that if they had a free absence they could ditch site when a paper or exam comes up. Some felt like it was sufficient to show up at site each week and resented having to do papers, readings and journal entries. It's a shock to many students who sign up for PC to find that it has an academic component. That's something that should not be ignored when initiating a service-learning program on campus.

Rachel: I think of other connotations when I think of volunteerism. I think of rich white women, but I also think of the work as being under-valued. A lot of the things that women do are under-valued anyway and a lot of the social service work, regardless of who it's done by, isn't seen as work and isn't valued very highly. I think that people who are volunteering don't necessarily see themselves as doing work either. That's a problem and something that ought to be changed but I don't know if it will be changed. I hear what you said about people who do social service work being seen by people who think that doing social change work is serving the system. In Women's Studies we fight about that a lot and it makes me mad because I think in a real broad sense, doing social service work is a form of social change because it gets people to take social responsibility. And even if that's all we're doing, attempting to teach younger people to think of themselves as being alive in the social world and to take responsibility for that is social change in itself. That's really theoretical but I think that it's important to underscore that point.

Margaret: I'm going to take a risk here and say something that may be obvious to everyone. I have some concerns about being so hard on those rich white women who we think of as having been doing volunteer work. I think it's real easy for us to make judgements about what is acceptable service and about the people who have been doing whatever type of service they've been doing. It seems like it is not okay to judge them anymore than it is okay to judge the homeless people we work with, or others.

Anita: I probably mispoke myself, but my point was more that we have to broaden the definition.

Margaret: I hear your point. I think you have a pretty deep understanding of the issue and were just using that to illustrate a point. But I think some of the students we work with may tend to categorize the rich white women and see them as bad and not look further than that. I guess its just another stereotype and we have to be careful of that.

Anita: I think one thing that's really important as sort of facilitator of this whole process is to draw connections between our own sections or our own individual work that we do or individual students' work to a larger movement that's happening in the country, on campus, or even in the state or country. But I think one thing that's real powerful is knowing different people feel comfortable with different pieces of this work that we do. I don't mean to belittle the kind of work that's been going on for years like staffing homeless shelters or serving soup at a soup kitchen because those things need to be done. We can't let people starve in the fight against hunger, but there are people that are comfortable in that piece of it. There are people that are comfortable trying to figure out what world hunger is and the economic distribution and all these other issues that affect world hunger. There are some people who feel comfortable in the homeless situation working at a shelter, there are some who lobby legislature and there are some that chain themselves to buildings that should be used as low-income housing in their opinion. But I think it's important to be aware of the connections between those different efforts towards the same thing and to be respectful about where each person is and where they're comfortable with and what piece of it they want to take as their own. Because they are all necessary in order to move forward.

Margaret: I like that idea of everyone sort of taking their piece. So that, somebody might be handing out magazines in a hospital, and it sounds small but that person might be bringing a great deal to one individual patient. So that, you're seeing the forest and the trees and you're not forgetting the individual who might be getting a little bit of something that day.

Anita: I think there's much more of a likelihood that that person feels like they're doing something very valuable if they see the connections between their individual work and the larger picture either around health care or around youth activism etc. I think a lot of people get frustrated when they go out for the first time to do service work and they aren't horribly well-received by the agency: the agency's just too busy, they don't have anything to do, so they just sort of wander around the halls of the hospital. There's a tendency sometimes when you're doing one little piece to get frustrated and feel like you're not really doing anything worthwhile. The connections with people that are doing the same kinds of work and working toward the same goals are important. I think it's important to do that across the lines too, we can't just do that with other young people, we have to seek out the people and other organizations, whether it's traditional kinds of volunteer groups or whether it's churches or synagogues, etc. It's important to connect with those people too.

Rick: If we're going to value both service and social change, I think it would be important to develop site placements not only in more established social service agencies, but also social change organizations so that students have the opportunity to have a first hand experience with lobbying, activism or canvassing. Most students only think community work as community service—just show up at a shelter or soup kitchen for a few hours, or play with some youth-at-risk—that's it. Getting involved in a social change organization would broaden the educational experience of the students.

Rachel: I wanted to make a general comment about the educational question and about the academic rigor of PC courses. And this is a criticism. I understand how people have the stereotype that they have and the idea of being able to come and go out to a site once a week and get two academic credits. If we're going to talk about wanting this to be seen as having a serious academic component, it also has to have that, because I don't think that things stand as, at least in the group that I was involved in, it didn't have the sense that it was all that academically difficult. I think that there are easy ways to make it more so, and I don't know about a lot of the other areas.

Margaret: What would have made it more rigorous?

Rachel: I think maybe doing more writing. I didn't have to do much writing, and it wasn't like I was saying to somebody, "Hey, make me do more writing." I took a course in Women's Studies that was "Women in the Community" then I took a second related one and those both felt very academic in a way that my PC experience didn't. So I think that there are easy ways to make PC classes more "academically rigorous."

Anita: Do you think that has anything to do with having the course TA or faculty led as opposed to student led?

Rachel: I think I had the sense in that course that I had to be there and I had to participate and I had to do the reading in a way that I didn't in PC. That may have been who it was coming from.

Claudette: I also wonder if it depends on the students in the section. I coordinated an adult literacy section last year both terms. My first semester the students were very committed and always came. If they didn't they called and left a message on my answering machine saying why they weren't coming and they always went to site. I told my second semester students all the same things that I told the first semester people and they didn't call me and they sometimes wouldn't show up and I did all of the same things. So, I wonder if it's the students. They definitely took it less seriously and they thought, "What do you mean we have to write this paper, this is just a two credit course?"

Anita: I think one thing that's really important about the whole learning aspect of it, too, is that we need to really pay attention to invaluable learning that happens outside the seminar or in other service-learning experiences that happen without a faculty person or facilitator person. The kind of learning that happens on site where you're working with people and you're reflecting with agency staff or the clients or the van rides back and forth to site. Those kinds of things are really powerful, and I think it's important that we give some value to those kinds of things too.

Rachel: I think we do that really well. I think that's mostly what happens. I don't think larger society does that necessarily; values those experiences. At least within the Office that does get valued a lot and within those courses that's what gets underscored the most.

Anita: My inclination is, if our goal is really to develop civic responsibility or social responsibility, that doesn't happen for the students because all of a sudden they get the whole sociology of it and then they think "Maybe I should be socially responsible." It's from those kinds of discussions and seeing those kinds of things on site. I think that's where the profound learning happens. That's just my gut feeling. Not to take away from importance of the academic component of it because those connections need to be made as well, but I think both those parts are equally important.

Margaret: I think sometimes some of that learning happens on another level entirely and one is never conscious of it, it just happens. You're changed.

Anita: That's the kind of learning that you don't forget after a term when you sell your books back.

Margaret: And it makes you more civically responsible.

Jeff: So, if a student goes out in the community and does some community service, we're saying that those folks are learning in a way that contributes to a greater chance that they'll be more socially responsible, lifelong socially responsible. But in addition, I think an important ingredient in helping all the different kinds of leanings that can occur is to have the opportunity to be engaged with other people. What really brings to mind this point is when Anita mentioned riding home in the van. Now, what happens riding home in a van from a prison or a homeless shelter can be all kinds of things but if there's an intentional effort to have the students both en route and returning to talk about the community service work that they're about to go to or they've just come from. I think having the opportunity to talk with other people about it will multiply the leanings in contrast to an individual student going out and doing some work in a prison and individually coming back in their private car and not talking about the experiences with other people. The chances are greater that the students who are involved in a group are going to have greater learning outcomes, all kinds of outcomes, than the student who does community service privately.

Randy: That's where the seminar aspect comes into play. I had the County Jail group where the people did go out individually and we did spend a lot of time in our seminar focusing on what we had done. We shared common experiences much like people do when they're in the car riding to and from a site. Not to discount sites that have individual placements.

Jeff: The message is to find avenues for students to interact with other service-learners.

Anita: Or with other people. The challenge for us is to broaden our definition of who you can learn from. We used to think traditionally that you had to talk to, or be talked at, by a faculty member if you wanted to learn anything. Then we thought maybe we could learn from TA's because they're grad students and they're almost there, then maybe some student coordinators who are trained in this process and maybe if they talk to these students maybe they'll learn something. So as our ideas continue to evolve about who you can learn from, I think eventually we will try to work with community agencies and get their volunteers together to get some reflection about what they're doing. So whether it's with the other students on the van ride home or with community agency people, the critical point is, when you engage with somebody about an issue it forces you to be critical and think about what you're saying, and define things more than if you're just thinking about it in your head. And that could be your roommate when you get home at night. The more opportunities we give people to engage about what they're doing in their service experience, the more likely they are to get real valuable meaning out of it.

Rick: One of the things those in my section learned about our clients is that some are well educated men. They have different levels of education, but often times we discussed seminar issues, for example, the effectiveness of prison and drug rehabilitation, or racism and prisons. We might have had an extremely dry seminar at UM, but in Cotton these discussions took on a sense of immediacy because of the experience of the men in Cotton. We needed those forty minutes in the van to debrief the intense site experiences.

Margaret: I think one of the concerns that has been expressed before about people just going out and doing service work on their own without a chance for reflection with others is that their stereotypes can be just reinforced. Talking to other people, on the other hand, like in a seminar situation where those stereotypes are being challenged and peoples ideas are being presented makes it less likely that any stereotypes will be reinforced. I can see someone going to a homeless shelter with preconceptions about the people there and in some cases, if those preconceptions are not challenged, that person might come away still believing them.

Jeff: So, if a student goes and becomes involved in community service, say in a prison, and there's an accompanying academic program back on campus, and there's even discussion in the van, a question is, "can we say that we know for sure that by being involved in the community that a student's stereotypes will be successfully challenged?"

Anita: I don't think that's necessarily true. I think if you do a good job they will be challenged. That needs to be part of your goals, but you need to be intentional about that.

Jeff: Being intentional increases the chances that it will happen.

Margaret: But there are no guarantees.

Randy: You can't force somebody to change their stereotypes. You can give them an opportunity to see that maybe they need to be challenged. If you could, I don't think we'd live in the society that we do.

Anita: I think that the reason service-learning is more effective in doing that though, is because people are more likely to believe it if they see it. Unfortunately, what happens in this world is that many people come to be this old and they haven't seen a lot of what goes on. The fact that prejudice and racism and sexism and everything else comes out of ignorance is well known. There are a lot of people who know differently but are still racist or sexist. The thing that is powerful about service-learning is that you can show people the difference. They can meet people and work with people who are different than the stereotypical images. And that's a lot easier to believe than somebody lecturing you and telling you that you're not right.

Rachel: When I think about challenging stereotypes, most of the learning I've done about that in terms of my personal life and in terms of my racism or classism is working in large group of diverse women. I work at SAPAC on the counseling line and I think that's where a lot of that has happened. That's the group I can talk to about what goes on when I answer the phone because I can't talk to anybody else about that. That's where I've learned the most, from other people that I work with. I think one of the things I would like to see happen here is to try to attract a diverse group of people. I think it's a real good opportunity to learn.

Anita: I think if we don't do that, what happens is we help perpetuate the stereotype by making a statement about who are service providers and who are service recipients, if we don't make an intentional effort to have a diverse group of people on this end of it.

Rachel: And to have a diverse group of people running it, too.

Anita: The whole thing is about power relationships. Everything that we do, on every level we're about transforming power relationships whether it's between faculty and students, the University and the community, rich and poor, the individuals from the university who provide service and those people who are using agency services. We're trying to make them more equal relationships.

Rick: When I walked into my first workshop at site, one of the men asked, "How come there aren't any Black people doing this? Why are only white people coming here to teach us creative writing?" We looked at each other and bumbled around for an answer. I think it's an important challenge for service-learning groups to recruit from all facets of the community. Systemic racism is very visible to the clients you serve. They know what's up. You can't hide it.

Jeff: In order to ensure that all viewpoints are represented in the seminar that accompanies the community service experience, why not have the seminar at the community service site, and not only involve the university students but also the prisoners or patients if it's a health care facility, or the elderly if it's a gerontological placement.

Margaret: Or the preschoolers.

Anita: That would definitely make a fun seminar.

Rachel: Then they would ask "How come everybody's so old?"

Jeff: Of course when they start quoting Piaget, we're really in trouble.

Anita: We're conditioned from childhood to believe that if learning is taking place, then it has to be difficult and rigorous and you have to stay up all night doing papers and reading enormous amounts to take very difficult tests that you're set up to fail. And it isn't a good course unless you're struggling to get a "C" in it. When you ask people to take responsibility for their own learning, it's like an open school. We don't care if you come to class or not. If you want to learn you're going to have to come to class and read and engage with these people and be involved in the discussions at seminar and be involved at site. But that's not going to be my responsibility, it's yours. The bigger question is, if students are interested or willing to take that responsibility. That's part of our work too, is to empower students to take responsibility for their education and to find those students who are really invested in learning or to spark something in them that makes them interested in learning as opposed to just being here because it's expected of them or because they need a job or want a job that requires a masters level degree etc. I really think that's a secondary motivation for most people in a university setting, the actual learning. I know people that work in the office now and they'll go to class and come back really excited because of what they've learned and I don't remember ever feeling like that. They're really engaged and I can't really identify with that and I think it's true for a lot of people, unfortunately.

Rick: Although our culture seems to have a strong value on a rigorous education, in my experience as a recent graduate, I've had many people say things to me like, "Now you're entering the real world, you'll see what it's really like." This suggests a stronger underlying value on life experience beneath the glossy veneer of academic learning. I think many people think academic learning is fluffy no matter how hard paper assignments get. To me, service learning brings academia out of the clouds and into the streets where first hand learning about "the real world" can take place. I like to compare service learning to lab courses in the natural science. A good chemistry course comes with a good lab where a student can do quality research. It only makes sense that we demand this for the social sciences and humanities.

Jeff: That's a pretty scary thought for those of us in community service learning because you're saying students come to our program with enormous baggage about how the teaching/learning process should proceed and you combine that with their lacking the kinds of skills and competencies that are needed to fully learn from community service learning experiences, and we have a very scary situation—people under-prepared to adequately learn from a community service learning course. A discussion around student (and instructor) baggage can be found in Mark Chesler's chapter in Volume I and some of the skills and competencies that would be useful for students to have to maximize their learning in community service learning are discussed in Al Menlo's chapter, also in Volume I.

Margaret: That makes me think of the first question about what advice we would give. I think we're always looking for some kind of balance, the balance that Anita mentioned in the beginning about a quality site experience for students while keeping in mind that the agency has it's clients as it's first priority. And the balance between offering challenging reading and academic work while recognizing that students also learn from the experience of site. You're always working toward some kind of balance and having to reexamine things. I think the coordinators in our program are the most frontline in facing those dilemmas because they work with the students in the course every week. They really always have to be aware of this role.

Anita: I think it's also true for us as educators, or whatever we consider ourselves. It's sometimes a case of delayed gratification in that I think because of the way students are conditioned to think of education, during their time in our course or seminar or even as they're exiting the experience, they may not think of it as some incredibly powerful educational experience. It might be something in retrospect to think that that was really powerful for me and that's when I figured this out. But it might not be recognizable in the context of what education is supposed to be in their heads. The other thing is important to add on to Rick's point about the real world v. the academic world is that the rigors of academic life discourage you from being involved in larger things, larger issues that affect places beyond the campus. After being involved in service-learning or activism or whatever you've been involved in around the community during college, people come out with a vision that they have developed or some sort idealism or focus on change in the society and often are put off if you say, "You haven't been in the real world." All the time, people say to me, "When you start paying taxes, you'll change your mind about all these issues." That whole kind of thought that you've been sheltered on a campus and you're being idealistic and you're not being logical or realistic and that once you get into the real world you'll figure that all out and change your mind.

Margaret: I think though, that there are changes that people go through in their natural life cycle and that those include changes in perceptions of the world. We have to accommodate all of those people. For example now that I am a parent and have a child in public school and pay property taxes my perceptions of some things are different from what they were 10 years ago. I'm aware of many more questions and seeing issues as more complicated. I'm not saying we should accept the idea that once you have your piece of territory you can just sit out and hold on to it or that someone who is 20 and not paying property taxes is any less in the real world than someone who is older and is. I guess I'm arguing again for some kind of view that includes people at many levels, coming from many directions and doesn't discount them at either end.

Anita: I think it's just another demonstration of how there's such a distinction between your academic life, the rest of the world and the rest of your life. This is a way to bring those two things together and hopefully help, at least define what those questions are. And it's really frustrating to be put off, based on the fact that you haven't experienced "real life" yet.

Rick: We could also talk about how service-learning can be a good PR plug for your institution. I remember watching the ABC News plug about OCSL that UM used for it's five billion dollar kickoff campaign. I thought, wow, I'm into something big.

Anita: I know we talked about how universities, in general will use service-learning as a PR tool. This sprung the point about how smart the community is and how they understand that it's a PR thing. Hopefully in our actions we can build a real commitment and real relationship with community that's based on trust and actual commitment to each other as opposed to being based on PR. Service-learning and service in general is a perfect ground for coalition building on campus between groups because there's not a cultural group on campus that's not involved in community. Unfortunately they're involved very separately in most cases. There are all kinds of culturally based organizations. For example, the Black Greek system is probably more involved than any other group in this community. Their defining mission is service to the community and part of our task is to build those coalitions and then build coalitions among diverse groups of people up with diverse groups of people for the community so this becomes a real community building thing on all levels in the campus community and in the larger community.

Jeff: Another piece of advice is to be mindful of the kind of learning process that goes on in the community for students in contrast to the kind of learning process that traditionally goes on in the classroom, and how very inconsistent the principles that underlie those two are and that a piece of advice would be to try to seek to be as consistent as possible between the principles underlying learning in the community and the practices that are utilized in the classroom.

Joe: Let's talk about social change

Margaret: The question was, "Does service-learning really accomplish social change?" and I wonder if first we have to ask, "Does it have to?"

Anita: I think it goes back to the point I made much earlier in that we need to define who our primary audience is. If our primary audience is our students, then maybe it doesn't have to. Maybe we don't even have to work toward social change, with their primary goal being their learning, around issues or around civic responsibility or around alternative educational models. If our primary audience is the community, then there's probably more of a push towards change work. I think the interesting thing is that within a campus, change can happen on different levels for different programs. I think some programs on a campus can be very focused on a student whereas others are very focused on the community and much less focused on intentional learning, especially student run programs. There's diversity depending on who your target audience is. My point before that I would hope that these programs are at least aiming towards social change whether it be through actual change as a part of that program or whether it be through affecting student attitudes so that they will be involved and work toward change throughout their lives, or whether it's through educating a student about an issue so that they become involved in different levels throughout their lives. If they're working at a soup kitchen now, and the soup kitchen doesn't have any intentional efforts towards ending hunger, but it's just feeding the people who come through every night, which is totally necessary; a potential outcome of that could be that the student gets really turned on toward the whole issue of hunger, starts taking other courses related to that and gets involved after the section is over with a national hunger organization that's working on world hunger issues or redistribution of food.

Margaret: I think Randy made an excellent point too, that we have to define social change as well. I think that's true. But I also have something of a dilemma here. I personally have certain political beliefs and advocate for major social change in the way I see things. But in the three years I've been here I've met students with certain very powerful religious beliefs or liberal or conservative political beliefs and beyond challenging those or asking them to try looking at things in other ways, I'm not sure it's my role as program director to promote social change. So sometimes I feel a dilemma when I try to present a balanced coursepack or a balanced seminar topic syllabus to students because I'm aware of my own values and beliefs and I'm also aware that we have, for example, some very conservative students who take the course. We're working with a lot of different people with different beliefs. This seems to have been especially true in an election year. I'm not sure where to go with that.

Jeff: What you're saying sounds like you're making a distinction between your personal level role and your professional level role. For me, I try to blur the distinction there, and it relates to this question about social change. What I try to do is to combine my personal and professional ways of behaving with regard to community service learning. And so I am intentional about trying to have students understand the perspective of social change. I don't believe in objectivity. I believe everything is value-laden. And students have been exposed to the status quo value throughout most of their formal educational experiences, and when they come to our service-learning programs, I'm interested in exposing them to a different set of values. Now, I know that there's going to be varying degrees of success in moving people from where they were to where I'd like them to be, but I actually believe that one of the promises of community service learning is that, though we may not change them at the end of the term, that over time there may be change. Will it be social change? Probably not because in this society much is in place that makes it near impossible to change at a systemic level. Though community service tends to be very individual rather than social change or systemic level, the promise of service-learning is that over time, they'll be active at a level that's in between individual and systemic, the "meso" level. As an example of a meso-level outcome, a student might graduate and become a business person and she might own a company and that company might have as one of its employee principles that you have to spend three hours of your forty working on behalf of the community. That would be a meso level outcome that I think community service learning can move people toward.

Margaret: I think what you've done is give us a kind of definition of social change and that is the idea of the meso level. That may be acceptable to a broader range of people. I guess I try to resolve my dilemma by trying to find the commonality. For example we all agree that there should not be homelessness. But how different people look at how to make sure there is not homelessness—and that's largely what the course is about - is where it becomes something of a dilemma. I may see it one way while others see it in a very different way. As a social worker I believe you have to try for some objectivity when you are working with other people, at the very least you have to be aware of how your values and beliefs are influencing your own behavior. One thing I try to do in the course, and maybe this is a kind of social change, is to minimize the polarities that seem to occur. We get very polarized—conservative, liberal, democrat, republican—and then it is harder to work together. Maybe some of what's happening more among young people today is that they are bypassing that. They're just going out there and doing what they see as needed and that makes social change happen. Another point in response to what Jeff said is that a lot of students that come into my program tend to be not so much the status quo but tend to hold a lot of liberal beliefs. I sometimes feel like I want to have some protection built in for those students who hold very conservative beliefs so that they don't get further polarized from the process in our seminars. I want to make it so that we can all share ideas and realize that there are ideas from all different realms that are useful. I think that we have to be careful again with social change language because to some people that means one thing and to others it may mean something else.

Anita: I think it's also very good and fine to be straight with students that this is your opinion. I can't really compromise my opinion. I'm no good at that. So try to make people understand that it's one individual opinion out of this group of ten people and that because I happen to be a facilitator or a staff person or a TA or a faculty person, that it speaks again to this whole traditional view of education that since I'm the leader, you need to agree with me. So if you can give your opinion as strongly as you want to give it in a context that makes it your opinion and only that, it's another way to resolve the dilemma.

Randy: Because if you make that the official line and the desired outcome of the course, you threaten a lot of people and scare them away.

Margaret: Perhaps the very people who should be taking it.

Rick: I noticed that the conversation moved from the topic of social change to the process of teaching social change. This gets back to the goals of PC as a social change vehicle or as an educational vehicle. Perhaps both efforts can reach the same goal. Also, I think Freire would have something to say about Young Republicans who might feel threatened in a PC seminar that explicitly held social change as a norm. He would think that the would feel threatened because they're the ones who have the most to lose if their class privilege is shared through democratic and economic reform. Of course, people who benefit from the status quo will feel threatened by change. Since PC is an educational venture, I think a lot of social change achieved through the program will come through the education of college students in the course. Students might become committed to social change in their life's work, like some of the students highlighted in "Oz Plus Five." It doesn't hurt to develop sites devoted exclusively to social change. I would hope many organizations in college areas would be excellent candidates for a potential social change site.

Anita: Along with the whole issue of social change, there's the question of "Is that our goal?" There's the question of "How do we do it?" The other question we can really address is the whole empowerment question. Do young people feel like they're capable of that? Do young people feel like they have the power or resources or whatever that they need to create change or work with people to create change? I think that that's a whole other piece of it that we can be very helpful with: building those connections between people and trying to build the confidence and the vision. Those things make change feel possible.

Jeff: Empowerment is such a hot word these days. Recently I heard someone say that empowering others is an oxymoron. The question that gets raised out of that for me is how can people help other people to feel empowered? How do we move people from feeling dis-empowered to feeling empowered so that they can accomplish more good in whatever tasks they undertake? We hear a lot that one of our goals in community service learning ought to be to empower communities. By doing that we may in fact be dis-empowering them. But how do we help them to feel empowered?

Anita: There's two parts to answering that question. One of them is that empowerment comes through experiences and relationships; basically for us to provide the kinds of experiences where people feel like they are doing something important, necessary and valued. If we have sites where people are licking envelopes for an organization, (which the organization totally needs, I realize), but if that were the only thing they were doing for the organization, that's not helpful in empowering students. The other thing is that we need to help them connect with either people in the community or people on campus, on other campuses or people around the country who care about and want to make change around the same issues that they do. I think a lot of empowerment comes in knowing that you're part of something much larger. If it's one person working on one issue in one town, it's very different than one person working on one issues in one town and being connected with all these other towns that have all these people working on them.. There's a very strong sense of empowerment that comes with knowing other people care about this too and that their efforts combined wit yours are what's going to make the change. The other thing we try very hard to do, but don't often do is realize that we need to empower students around our programs. On a lot of campuses what happens is that a lot of faculty and staff design these programs. We end up doing exactly what we say we don't want to do. We design these programs and give students token jobs that make them feel like they're having some sort of leadership, but they're not involved in setting up sites, decision-making around what's going to happen and decision making around what direction the office is going to take. That would be a big piece of advice for me for coordinators: don't be so afraid of losing control of your program that you don't give it to students. That's empowering and they can take it to other pieces of their life to know that they were part of a program for other students. That they put it together, they ran it and they were powerful in an organization, not in a derogatory way but in a real sense.

Rick: I once heard a satirical definition of empowerment: "We don't have the time or money to take care of your needs so why don't you do it yourself." Empowerment can become another way of denying the connection with the clients one works with. For example, coming into the prison, the residents were often seen as the radical other. After a few months, some of my fellow students said things like, "You know, some of these men could have been in a class at UM and I wouldn't have known the difference." The wall is dissolved. Empowerment for me is including yourself in the community you work with and including your clients in your community. Another part of empowerment is combating the "things don't change" myth. That is an educational challenge. The universe is not static, never was, and won't be in the future. Change should not be seen as an impossible goal. Change, in fact, happens all the time. That doesn't mean social change or empowerment are easy dilemmas to solve, but it does mean that they are appropriate and reasonable challenges.

Anita: I heard a great analogy about empowerment from a student who works with the children's theater program here. It's one step further in an old proverb: Give a man a fish, he eats for a day. Teach a man to fish, he eats for a lifetime. The student put another step on it and he asked, "What would be ideal?" To teach a man to fish would mean that you know how and he doesn't and he needs you to teach him. He takes it one step further and says get to know this person, figure out what it is that they know. Help him to connect with others around him who know other things who will help him get this fish. It's like that other proverb that says when the greatest leaders leave the people think they did it themselves. The ideal is not to teach the person to fish but to work with them to figure out where their resources are, to figure out what they already know to build on: to empower them. To figure out how to get the fish on their own. It takes all the helplessness out of it. It takes all the condescension out of it. It takes all the hierarchy out of it.

Margaret: The implication otherwise is that you have the power and you are choosing to give it to someone else.

Randy: That's not empowerment.

Margaret: Right. That's how we use the word. We say "I'm going to empower this person. I've got the power and I'm choosing to give it to you." As opposed to enabling someone to be empowered.

Randy: It's not always just empowering. It's like opening their eyes to see that they do have power, they just need to realize how to use it.

Anita: Oppression does that to people. When you're pushed down for so long you forget what resources you have. Sometimes that's all you need to do is help people re-recognize the strength that they have or the resources that they have within themselves or around them that can allow them to make change for themselves.

Jeff: Sounds like an important tenet of empowerment—helping others to re-recognize the strengths within.

Margaret: I was going to say that along with people re-recognizing their strengths is not overlooking the reality of the obstacles they face. This has been really interesting. I've learned a lot.

Randy: I was thinking that we form a small network within this office and as a group we don't always get to sit around and talk like this. One of the great things is that we've been able to have this discussion. I hope that other people are able to do this.

Rick: I feel like this was a very fruitful conversation.

Anita: I think one thing that is sort of an overriding point for me is that the two primary groups of people that are involved in this relationship that we're trying to build here are students and community. Often those are the only people who are not a part of the decision making when it comes to these programs and I think it's essential in every piece of it that those voices are heard. I think it's more important than faculty and staff being heard. And not in a token politically correct sort of way. Not because you're supposed to listen to those people and therefore put one person on a committee and say that you have student or community representation, but really letting them be an integral part of the decision making is the fastest way to a successful program.

Joe: My hope is that we put these principle we're talking and writing about into action because what we do together because it is important stuff. Yes, there is Final Jeopardy! Today's Final Jeopardy! category is...Project Community Historicity. I wanted to conclude by acknowledging that our discussion has roughly followed the first and second term papers, which coordinators write for Mark Chesler, our faculty advisor. Name the year in which Mark Chesler first became the Project Community faculty advisor. (Various responses) The official year is 1975.

BIBLIOGRAPHY

Bibliography

Ansley, L. (1993, January). How to kill crime. USA Weekend, pp. 8-10.

Banaszynski, J. (1992, March). The ties that blind. Modern Maturity, pp. 32-36.

Barton, W., Schwartz, I.M., & Streit, S. (1991). A blueprint for youth corrections. Youth corrections in the 1990's: A blueprint for policymakers.

Bayse, D.J. (1993). Helping hands. Arlington, Va: Kirby Lithographic Company.

Beale, L. (1989). The latest word on drugs: Legalization. (1989). Detroit Free Press. pp. 1B-2B.

Beattie, M. (1987). Codependent no more. (pp. 1-47). Harper & Row.

Belenky, M.F., Clinchy, B.M., Goldberger, N.R. & Tarule, J.M. (1986). Women's ways of knowing. Basic Books, Inc.

Berenson, D. (1988, Nov./Dec.). Alcoholics Anonymous: From surrender to transformation. Utne Reader, pp. 70-71.

Black, I. (1982). It will never happen to me . MAC Printing and Publications Division.

Borba, M. (1989). Esteem builders: A K-8 self-esteem curriculum for improving student achievement, behavior and school climate. Rolling Hills Estates, California: P Jalmar Press.

Buell, B., Clarke,V. & Leone, S. Alternatives to the Peace Corps, Institute for Food and Development Policy. San Francisco, California.

Bufe,C. (1988, Nov./Dec.). AA: Guilt and god for the gullible. Utne Reader, pp. 54-55.

Bush, G. (1989, October). Drugs and the college student. The Michigan Review, p. 5.

California Task Force to Promote Self-Esteem and Personal and Social Responsibility. (1990). Towards a state of esteem: The final report of the

California task force to promote self-esteem and personal and social responsibility.

Channing, L.Bete Co. (1983). What you should know about self-esteem. South Deerfield, MA: What You Should Know Video.

Chesler, M.A. & Crowfoot, J. (1989, November). Racism in higher education I : An organizational analysis. Center for Research on Social Organization.

Clemes, Harris, Bean, Reynold, and Clark, Aminah. (1990). How to raise teenagers' self-esteem. Los Angeles: Price Stern Sloan.

Collett, L. (1988, Nov./Dec.). Step by step: A skeptic's encounter with the Twelve-Step program. Utne Reader, pp. 69-76.

Collins, W. (1983). Black men fighting for their manhood. Jericho: Newsletter of the National Moratorium on Prison Construction, pp. 5,8. Washington D.C.

Cowan, J. (1991). Good works: A guide to careers in social change. New York: Barricade Books.

Davis, S. (1988). Volunteer Training Manual. Unpublished manuscript.

Deparle, J. (1990, August). Use of term "underclass" is under fire. Detroit Free Press, pp. 1C-3C.

DeShaw, D. (1992, December). On good and evil: Why prison visitors sometimes get a distorted view of inmates. Corrections Today, pp. 22-24.

Dewey, J. (1963). Experience and Education. New York: Collier Books.

Epstein, M.K. & Epstein, E.K. (1990, September). Codependence as social narrative. Journal of Reviews and Commentary in Mental Health, 4-7.

Flynn, M.L. (1991, January). Black juvenile offenders. University of Michigan News and Information Services.

Forsgren, A. (1989, October). A cold, logical stare at legalized cocaine. The Michigan Review, p.5.

Freiberg, P. (1990). Rehabilitation is effective if done well. The Monitor, American Psychological Association.

Freire, P. (1973). Education for critical consciousness. New York: Continuum.

Freire, P. (1970). Pedagogy of the oppressed. New York: Continuum.

Friel, J. & Friel, L. (1988). Adult children: The secrets of dysfunctional families. Deerfield Beach, FL: Health Communications, Inc.

Gerne, T.A. & Gerne, P.J. (1986). Substance abuse prevention activities for elementary children. New Jersey: Prentice-Hall.

Gilbert, D. (1993, March). Personality type determines response to peer pressure. University Record, p.10 University of Michigan.

Gillard, J. (1993, March 29). The 'if Ann Arbor were' game. The Ann Arbor News.

Gilligan, C. (1990) Making connections: The relational worlds of adolescent girls at Emma Willard School. Cambridge, Mass.: Harvard University Press.

Goldstein, A.P., Reagles, K.W. & Amann, L.L. (1990). Refusal skills: Preventing drug use in adolescents. Champaign, IL: Research Press.

Greve, F. (1989, October). Sex and Cocaine Addiction. Detroit Free Press, 1A and 7A.

Haaken, J. (1993). From Al-Anon to ACOA. Signs, pp.321-345

Hadley, L. (1990). Early detection and treatment of alcoholism. Journal of American Academy of Physicians Assistants, 3, 253-60.

Haney, C. & Zimbardo, P.G. (1973). Social roles and role playing. Behavioral and Social Science Teacher. Behavioral Publications, 1, 25-45.

Hengesh, D.J. (1991, October). Think of boot camps as a foundation for change, not an instant cure. Corrections Today, p. 108.

Herman, E. (1988, Nov./Dec.) The 12 step program: Cure or cover? Utne Reader, pp. 52-63.

Herrnstein, R.J. & Wilson, J.Q. (1985, August). Criminals: Made or born? New York Times Magazine.

Horton, M., and Freire, P. (1990). We make the road by walking: conversations on education and social change. Philadelphia, PA: Temple University Press.

Howard, J. On Experiential Learning. Unpublished Manuscript.

Howard, J. (1990, Jan./Feb.). Using experiential learning in the classroom. National Society for Internships and Experiential Education, pp. 3,9.

Kahn, M. Some Thoughts About Seminars. Unpublished Manuscript.

Kime, W. & Wanger, E. (1993). The penalty of death—what it does to the living. Detroit Free Press Fax: Document # 2410.

Kipps, H.C., (1991). Volunteerism: The directory of organizations, training, programs, and publications. R.R. Bowker.

Kirschenbaum, H. & Glaser, B. (1978). Skills for living. Quest National Center.

Kozol, J. (1991). Savage inequalities: Children in America's schools. New York: Crown Publishers.

Krajik, K. & Gettinger, S. (1982). Do prisons accomplish...? Overcrowded time: Why prisons are so crowded and what can be done, pp. 13-18. Edna McConnell Clark Foundation.

Kubler-Ross, E. (1970). On death and dying. New York: Macmillan.

Lamb, L. (1990, May/June).Is everyone co-dependent? Utne Reader, pp. 26-28.

Larsen, E. (1985). Stage II recovery: life beyond addiction. San Francisco, CA: Harper and Row.

Lewis, W. & Milano, C. (1987). Profitable careers in non-profit. John Wiley and Sons, Inc.

Luft, J. (1984). Group processes: An introduction to group dynamics. Palo Alto, CA: Mayfield Pub. Co.

Mauer, M. (1992, February). Americans behind bars: One year later. Washington D.C.: The Sentencing Project.

Martin, A. (1982). A different kind of justice. Victimology: An International Journal, 237-241.

Martin, D.M. (1993, November). Committing journalism: The prison writings of Red Hog. New York: W.W. Norton Co.

McIntosh, P. (1989, July/August). White privilege: Unpacking the invisible knapsack. Peace and Freedom, 10-12.

Meadors, B. (1989, October). A student rebuttal. Legalize Drugs. The Michigan Review.

Mills, C.W. (1959). The Promise. The sociological imagination. Oxford University Press.

Muldoon, J.A. & Crowley, J.F. (1986). A flexible model. One step ahead, pp. 49-60. Community Intervention Inc.

Napier, A.Y., & Whitaker, C. (1988). Family crucible. Harper & Row Publishers.

Nindorf, B. (1989, October). Community corrections: Turning the crowding. Corrections Today, pp. 82-88.

Olhms, (1981). The Disease Concept Of Alcoholism. CMHC volunteer handout based on The Disease of Alcoholism videorecording. Belleville, Ill.: Gary Whiteaker Corp.

Palmer, P. (1987). Community, conflict and ways of knowing. Change, 19, no. 5, 20-25.

Peck, M.S. (1978). The road less traveled, pp. 46-50. Touchstone.

Peck, M.S. (1987). The different drum. New York: Simon and Schuster.

Peele, S. (1988, Nov./Dec.) On the diseasing of America. Utne Reader, p. 67.

Perrin, P. & Coleman W. (1988, Nov./Dec.) Is addiction actually a misguided move toward wholeness? Utne Reader, pp. 58-59.

Perry, W. (1970). Intellectual and ethical development in the college years. New

York: Holt, Rhinehart, and Winston.

Reiman, J. (1984). Ideology, class and criminal justice. And the poor get prison, pp. 77-110. John Wiley & Sons.

Rohnke, K. (1984). Silver bullets. Dubuque, Iowa: Kendall/Hunt Publishing Co.

Rosenblatt, R. (1982, September). Portrait of a prisoner. Time Magazine, pp. 57-58.

Roush, D., (1990, December). The crisis for juvenile care workers: Sorry, I can't make a living at this wage. Corrections Today, pp. 20-26.

Salamon, L.M. (1992). America's non-profit sector. Foundation Center: John Hopkin's University.

Salerno, A. (1991, October). A dissenting view: Let's give shock incarceration the boot. Corrections Today, p. 28.

Schaef, A.W. (1986). Co-dependence: Misunderstood-mistreated. San Francisco: Harper & Row.

Schaef, A.W. (1990). Meditations for women who do too much. San Francisco, CA: Harper.

Schaef, A.W. (1988). Recovery as process. Utne Reader, p.73.

Schaef, A.W. (1987). When society becomes an addict. San Francisco: Harper & Row.

Schoem, D., Frankel, L., Zuniga, X. & Lewis, E.A. (1993). Multicultural teaching in the university. Westport CT: Praeger.

Schorr, L. (1988, August). Let's stop recycling poverty. The Washington Post, p.B2.

Serju, T. (1993, July 5). Never too late: center helps older adults deal with substance abuse. The Ann Arbor News, pp. D1 and D2.

Shine, C., Mauer, M. (1993). Does the punishment fit the crime? Drug users and drunk drivers, questions of race and class. The Sentencing Project, Washington D.C.

Shor, I. & Freire, P. (1987). A pedagogy for liberation: Dialogues on transforming education. South Hadley, Mass.: Bergin & Garvey Publishers.

Smith, A. (1988). Grandchildren of alcoholics. Deerfield FL.: Health Communications, Inc.

Smith, D.C. (1990). Great careers: Fourth of July guide. Garrett Park Press.

Stauffer, G.A. & Alvarez, T. (1992). Personalized Preventioin Training.

Stonewater, B.B & Stonewater, J.K. (1980). Developmental clues: An aid for the practitioner. National Association of Student Personnel Administrators

Journal.

Trends in the Michigan Criminal Justice System: From Crisis to Chaos (1993, March). Research and Evaluation Division of Michigan Council on Crime and Delinquency.

Walker, S. (1985). Both liberals and conservatives are guilty. Sense and nonsense about crime, pp. 6-11. Brooks/Cole Publishing Co.

Williams, P.J. (1991). "Teleology on the Rocks", The alchemy of race and rights. Harvard University Press.

ABOUT THE CONTRIBUTORS

About the Contributors

(All degrees are UM unless otherwise noted)

Michelle Blankenship (BA '89) was the Project Community coordinator in Fall '88 and Winter '89 at Cassidy Lake Prison. She received her Juris Doctor from the University of Detroit (May '93), hopes to work in the Public Defender's Office and is currently preparing for the Kentucky Bar Exam. Although Michelle does not enjoy studying for the Bar, taking practice tests or being stuck in her apartment all day, she did recently buy a black pick-up truck.

Anita Bohn (BA '86, MSW '88) has been the director of Project Serve since its founding in 1988. She also sits on the Board of the Interfaith Council for Peace and Justice. She is committed to student and community empowerment and believes strongly in the power of young people to confront social problems and create change.

Esmeralda Cadena coordinated the SALSA project during the Winter '93 term.

Mary Jo Callan recently graduated with a BGS and secondary teaching certificate. Her experience with Project Community may only be described as monumentally life altering, as it taught her that it's not what you know, but rather how you know it that really matters. She plans to pursue an MSW, an Ed.D, and continue her commitment to help children grow into healthy, productive adults. Mary Jo would also like to continue coaching middle school basketball. Please feel free to forward job offers to the Project Community office.

Areli Cavazos-Kottke is the co-initiator of the SALSA project and the SALSA grant's project director.

Mark Chesler is Professor of Sociology, and Core Faculty member of the Program on Conflict Management Alternatives, University of Michigan. He has been involved with Project Community for 18 years. He is an activist scholar, whose field-based and experiential approach to research mirrors the approach to pedagogy discussed in this series.

Scott Dent is entering his senior year and is studying Sociology. During '93/'94, he will be the Project SERVE children/youth issue coordinator and organize a debate club at Western Wayne Correctional Facility. After he graduates, Scott would like to work in elementary education.

Kathleen Doherty graduated in 1990 with a degree in Sociology and Secondary Social Studies Teaching. After teaching middle school social studies for two years, she returned to school, completing her Masters Degree in Educational Administration at the University of Wisconsin at Madison in August, 1993. Kathleen is interested using Hyper and Multi Media to integrate math and social studies curricula—and listening to the greatest hits of the 1970's. Kathleen is also Project Community's all-time record holder, participating in the course for eight terms as an undergraduate.

Margaret Elias (BA '76, MSW '82) has been the program director of the Trained Volunteer Corps since it was founded in 1990. Her professional work has included early childhood education and clinical social work with youths and their families. She is the mother of two wonderful boys, Nicholas and Jonathan.

Chellie Ferczok is the coordinator of Bursley Community Volunteers. She is currently pursuing her MPH in Hospital and Molecular Epidemiology. As an undergraduate, she lived at

Bursley Hall, which she selected as a top choice after hearing about Bursley Community Volunteers. Chellie can be caught moonlighting as The Invincible Tofu Queen across computer networks everywhere.

Joe Galura (BA '80, MSW '83) has been the OCSL's Chemical Dependency and Criminal Justice program director since 1988. For eleven years, Joe was a member of the Growth Works staff as a graduate student intern, therapist and director of an alternative secondary school. He lives in Ann Arbor with his wife Cathy and their two cats. Joe and Cathy's first child, David Alexander, was born January 14, 1993.

Jeanne Gray graduated in 1990 with a dual degree in Psychology and Sociology, then went on to get her MSW in 1992. She currently is in a job transition, moving from work in juvenile justice to the Michigan Campus Compact. She strongly believes in a commitment to the community in which you live and plans to make this an integral part of her teaching and work.

Amy Holmes is currently pursuing her MPH. She graduated from a program in Sociology in 1992, concentrating in social change. After participating in Project Community, Amy has continued her interest in participatory education and education for social change as a teaching assistant/instructor in the Pilot Program. Amy has also continued to work with migrant farmworkers as a rural health educator on the DELMARVA peninsula in Virginia.

Jeffrey P.F. Howard is the director of OCSL. He has been a service-learning educator with this office for 16 years, and is Editor of <u>Praxis I: A Faculty Casebook on Community Service Learning</u>. His research interests include the academic and social responsibility outcomes for service-learners. He presently chairs the Curriculum Development Committee of Michigan Campus Compact.

Jenny Kellman (BA '92) coordinated PC's Maxey Boys Training School, Court Watching and County Jail service-learning projects. Jenny is currently a graduate student in Social Work.

Tracy Kollin (BA '93) coordinated PC service-learning projects at the County Juvenile Detention Center and Maxey Boys Training School and is presently living in New Jersey.

Trish Marsik graduated from UM (and PC) in 1989 and attended Columbia University's School of Social Work where she served as Student Union President. She is currently the Social Work Supervisor for the Bronx Criminal Defense Division of the Legal Aid Society. Trish and her neuroses have adapted well to New York City and she plans to remain there until she sees Woody Allen (the penultimate New York experience) or re-integrates all her clients into a non-incarceratory setting—whichever comes first.

Rachel Meiland (May '93) holds a dual degree in Psychology and Women's Studies. She is employed as a chemical dependency counselor-technician at an inpatient hospital program for adolescents. She also works as a counselor on a phone line for survivors of sexual assault and their friends and families. She plans to pursue a Ph.D in clinical psychology if she does well enough on her GRE. On the lighter side, Rachel enjoys watching pro and college basketball, reading detective novels and hiking. If you're rich, she is single!

Christiana Ochoa recently received her BA in History and American Culture. She is very dedicated to creating and participating in programs that promote social justice and community empowerment. Her future plans include working in Latin America as an ESL volunteer and returning to school for graduate work. Her interests include cultural research, hiking and gardening.

Craig Regester recently graduated from the Residential College with a BA in Social Science. Through his extensive involvement with Project SERVE, which included the creation and establishment of SERVEwork, and his work as a site leader for a Detroit Alternative Spring Break, Craig was very active in encouraging fellow students to incorporate community service into their academic experiences. Craig has plans to continue volunteering for the Detroit anti-violence organization, Save Our Sons And Daughters (SOSAD), and hopes eventually to become a staff member. He is presently a senior Direct Care Worker at a residential group home for chronic mentally-ill adults in Ann Arbor.

Randy Ross (BA '92) has, at various times, been a member of OCSL's student, professional and editorial staff. He is Assistant Commissioner of the Coast to Coast Rotisserie League and team owner of Mr. Mojo Risin'. In the Fall, Randy plans to be busy, either as a graduate student in Social Work or as the new owner of a Stucchi's franchise.

Amy Rotberg is a senior majoring in Psychology. She has been very involved with youth through her work in numerous settings, including housing projects, halfway houses, training schools, drug treatment facilities and summer camps. Amy is a firm believer in experiential learning and in prevention oriented youth programming. After graduation, Amy plans to attend graduate school to study either criminal justice or child psychology.

Claudette Rowley (BA '91) is a graduate student intern at Project Serve. She will receive her MSW in December, 1993. Her interests include community organizing and women's issues.

Joan Scott has been an OCSL program director since September, 1984. She oversees project sections in Education and tutoring settings, as well as Health and a number of "Special Populations" settings. Joan has a background in Secondary Education and an MSW. She has been professionally and personally involved in experiential education and in the variety of ways people learn ever since she began her own education. She says she learns most from her student coordinators and from her own involvement with social justice issues and service in the community. Joan defines "fun" as getting away from the "ivory tower"—to the garden, the hiking trails, camping.

Rick Smith is from urban St. Johns, Michigan's Mint Festival City, and received a BA in English Language and Literature with an emphasis in Creative Writing in May '93. His interests include skiing, pagan rituals, theatre, philosophy and vegetarian cooking. He hopes to pursue an MFA in Creative Writing, an MSW and a just way of distributing economic goods in this country and the world—but not necessarily in that order.

Carmen Wells is a senior, double majoring in African-American Studies and Communications. Throughout her college career, she has volunteered and worked with a number of programs focusing on the education of young people, including the King/Chavez/Parks Program, Each One/Reach One and Project Community. Carmen has also participated in the Black Student Union as Secretary and the University Activities Center as Vice-President of Promotions. Upon graduation she expects to further her studies by earning a master's degree in education and to locate a position in a school district which can best utilize her skills, energy, talents and devotion to the education of children.

Janet Wylie recently completed her BSNR degree, and currently works as Program Supervisor for the UM Challenge Program. She helped develop and now facilitates the Project Community course, "Environmental Education for Preschoolers." Based on her adventure education background, Janet uses initiative activities with her Project Community students to help build a sense of community within the class, and to encourage students to employ experiential approaches to learning throughout all aspects of the course. Janet enjoys adventures of her own as well, including rock climbing, backpacking and mountain biking. She is also interested in developing a therapeutic outdoor adventure program for women.

I need a photo opportunity
I want a shot at redemption
Don't want to be a cartoon
In a cartoon graveyard . . .

The Praxis II staff: (standing, l to r) Mary Jo Callan, Joe Galura, Tammy Agnew; (seated, l to r) Rick Smith and Randy Ross. Not pictured: Rachel Meiland.

DATE DUE

DEC 1 2 2000

12/8/2000

MAY 0 2 2002